D1147330

Martin Johnson was born in Solihull, West Midlands, in 1970. He joined Leicester Tigers' senior squad in 1989 and has since gone on to lead the side to four successive Premiership titles (1999–2002) and two European cups (2001 and 2002). He is the club's longest serving captain of all time and his international career has been equally distinguished. Martin Johnson made his England debut in 1993 and first captained the team in 1998. He has also, uniquely, captained the British Lions on two separate tours, to South Africa in 1997 and Australia in 2001. His third successive World Cup and second as captain, in Australia in autumn 2003, took him to a total of more than 80 caps and culminated in an historic victory for England.

MARTIN JOHNSON

The Autobiography

headline

First published in 2003
by HEADLINE BOOK PUBLISHING

First published in paperback in 2004
by HEADLINE BOOK PUBLISHING

10 9 8 7 6 5 4 3 2 1

ISBN 0 7553 1187 6

Headline's policy is to use papers that are natural, renewable
and recyclable products and made from wood grown in sustainable forests.
The logging and manufacturing processes are expected to conform to the
environmental regulations of the country of origin.

Typeset in Centaur by Palimpsest Book Production Limited
Polmont, Stirlingshire

Printed and bound in Great Britain by
Mackays of Chatham plc, Chatham, Kent

HEADLINE BOOK PUBLISHING
A division of Hodder Headline
338 Euston Road
London NW1 3BH

www.headline.co.uk
www.hodderheadline.com

To Mum, Dad, Kay and Molly

CONTENTS

FOREWORD

My career has contained lots of highs and lows. I've been fortunate enough to lead successful Lions, England and Leicester sides to play on the highest stage and enjoy the rewards that offers. But fantastic as some of those public moments have been, the memories you hope always to keep are the hidden ones you share with your team-mates. Sitting together in the changing room – whether with my mates at Wigston RFC as a teenager or with the victorious Lions in South Africa – just enjoying the feeling of having played and won together . . . you can't beat that. Rugby is a team game and whatever I have achieved, it has been down to fourteen other guys as much as me.

Much of what happens in a fifteen-year rugby career, and the life before it, vanishes before you notice. One minute you're a seven-year-old kid riding his bike around in the summer sun, the next you're being asked to write your autobiography. I hope this book gives you an insight into how I've tried to play the game. I've made mistakes, and plenty of them, but I've always tried to be honest. I've enjoyed my time in rugby. I hope you enjoy reading about it.

CHAPTER ONE

UGLY MUG

If you think I'm ugly now, you should have seen me when I was born. Let's just say I was not the best-looking baby in town. Fortunately, no proof of this exists because my mum, slightly unnerved at what she had produced, banned anyone from taking photographs of me in the early weeks of my life. The first pictures were snapped when I was a few months old – they show a rather chubby Johnno. I liked my food, apparently, and my mum encouraged me. She believed in getting children on to solids early and started cramming bowls of Weetabix into me from about six weeks.

So, ugly and big – I was obviously made for rugby. It helped that my parents were sports mad. My dad, David, is from Orrell, on the outskirts of Wigan, and has always been an avid follower of the famous rugby leaguers. His father had briefly played lock for Orrell's union side, giving up because, as a strict Methodist, he did not like the game's drinking culture. Dad met my mum, Hilary, at university in Liverpool in the sixties, falling in love with her and Bill Shankly's great Reds side at the same time. Later, when they married and moved south, he took to the fifteen-man game and is knowledgeable on most sports, watching just about anything on the box. Some of my earliest memories are of lying in bed and hearing the *Match of the Day* music start downstairs; to this day, the sound of those trumpets is very evocative for me.

My mum didn't watch much. She was far more interested in competing. I have vivid recollections of her on school sports days. She would arrive on a bike, wearing shorts and a vest, and would go through a little light stretching and warming up ahead of the mums' race. Then she would scorch home 60m clear of the field, breasting the tape like Allan Wells as a gaggle of puffing, panting ladies with hitched-up skirts and bare feet trundled along in her wake. It was vaguely embarrassing, actually.

I used to wonder why she was so different to the rest of the mums. She was a PE teacher, a physically strong woman – she always did the DIY in our house – and a tremendous athlete, with a very competitive nature. In her teens and early twenties, she had run the 440yds and 880yds for Durham before settling down to family life. Later on, after my younger brother, Will, was born, she joined the local athletics club. At first, she was a jack of all trades, attending meets and taking part in various disciplines, ranging from the shot putt to the hurdles to middle distance. She took up serious running in the mid-seventies, entering marathons before they became fashionable and, eventually, graduating to 100km 'ultra-distance' races for Great Britain. On one occasion, she took part in a mad, twenty-four-hour race staged on a tight, 200m track indoors somewhere. The winner was whoever covered the greatest distance in the given period. You can imagine the state she was in after running thousands of bends on that little oval; she couldn't walk straight for a week.

She had fantastic endurance and, while I have never been

blessed with tremendous pace, I think I inherited some of her stamina. I probably got some of her competitiveness, too. As a youngster, though, I was no sportier than the next kid. We played football in the back garden, but that was about it. At five or six, I was given a full England soccer strip for Christmas, the old Umbro version with the round-neck shirt, and I remember being rather bemused by it. Today, I guess most young boys dream of being David Beckham or Michael Owen, but at that age I doubt I could even have named any England footballers, let alone rugby players. I was more concerned with getting out and about on my bike or playing soldiers.

My friends and I were armed to the teeth, which was good because our main occupation was killing Germans. I had an impressive gun collection – a realistic-looking SLR rifle, of the type used by the British army in those days, and various pistols – plus camouflage uniforms, a plastic helmet and assorted bandoliers and grenades. I was an avid reader of *Warlord*, one of the superior war/secret agent-type publications of the day and, for indoor action, had a small regiment of Action Men, with the full range of military paraphernalia and hardware. Looking back, it was all a bit strange, particularly to modern thinking, but that was what you did in those days.

My memories of early childhood are all happy ones. I remember long, hazy summers; winding bike rides; family outings to obscure athletics meets in places like Cwmbran (Mum haring round the track like a nutter, Dad dutifully watching, me and my brothers amusing ourselves in the background); or hours spent crashing through the undergrowth on orienteering afternoons. This odd pastime became a bit of a passion for Mum, because it allowed her to exercise her competitive nature, keep fit and spend time with her family. Well, at least in theory she spent time with us.

For the uninitiated, orienteering involves navigating your way around a forest with a compass and a map. You call in at various waypoints, stamping your competition card with a clicker you find there to prove you have covered the route, until you reach the finish line. I would really enjoy it now but as a young lad it is not your idea of a great day out. We would all drive out to Cannock Chase and Mum and Dad and Andrew, my older brother, would spend the next few hours tearing around the woods, leaving me in the car to look after Will. Sometimes there would be a play area nearby where we could mess around until they came back. At one place there was an old crane and some abandoned cars and we spent the afternoon clambering all over them. As I got older I was press-ganged into taking part myself. Mum, fantastically enthusiastic and gung-ho as always, would race on ahead and I would wander around on the kids' course without a clue where I was or what I should be doing, dragging a somewhat bewildered three-year-old with me. If we were lucky, a kindly, passing family might take pity on us and let us walk round with them. More often, we ended up getting lost or stuck in bushes.

Eventually, I found a solution. Will and I were stumbling around in the undergrowth about 200m from the start. We had not even found the first waypoint marker, we were utterly lost and Will had understandably started bawling his eyes out again. Various wild-eyed lunatics were racing around the place with compasses in hand and I overheard one of them saying he had lost his competition card and had had to retire. Bingo!

The cunning Johnson brain sprang into action. A shifty look round to make sure no one was looking and my own card was suddenly lying at the bottom of a ditch. Tragically, we, too, now had to retire.

It was an unusual way to spend your weekends, but then my folks, and my mum in particular, were slightly eccentric. Back at school on Monday morning we had to write a piece about what we had done the previous weekend. After about fifteen consecutive weeks talking about how I had got lost in some woods, I started making it up. After a few years, I finally put my foot down and refused to go any more, demanding I be allowed to stay and play with my mates.

My parents were very loving, very straightforward and fair. Andrew, older than me by a couple of years, Will and I were the apples of their eyes, but they were not afraid to dish out a smacking if our behaviour really warranted it, though more often than not we would end up being sent to our room. We lived in a semi-detached house in Solihull Road, Shirley, a solid, middle-class area on the outskirts of Birmingham. My dad, who had read chemistry at Liverpool University, worked at Lucas Industries. In the mid-seventies, the motor industry was far larger than it is today and the Midlands was full of car factories. Lucas was a major parts manufacturer, making electrical components, and Dad worked in the battery division's laboratory, helping to develop the technology and improve battery performance and life.

As a youngster, I thought Solihull Road was an incredibly wide street – the houses opposite seemed miles away. Years later, I happened to be in the area and drove by just to see the old place. Of course, it was just a very nondescript, sloping suburban road. As a kid, I attended Blossomfield Infants School a mile or so away. My mum must have taken me there the first few times but, from as early as I can remember, I would ride my bike to school by myself, keeping to the pavements all the way. When I was three, I had wandered away and got lost as my mum shopped in the local Woolworth's. Somehow I got out of the shop, got across the road and was on my way home when a neighbour spotted me. Mum, who had called the police, was obviously beside herself with worry and afterwards she made it very clear that I was not allowed to cross roads by myself. I can remember coming home on snowy January afternoons and standing opposite our house, shivering in my school uniform shorts, waiting for Mum to spot me and come out to wave me over. I was regularly ambushed and snowballed by older kids, but I never ventured off that kerb.

Having an older brother, I rode hand-me-down bikes until we were of a similar size. There were three basic models back then: the Raleigh Chopper, the Raleigh Grifter or a racer, with dropped handlebars. The Chopper was trendy. It was great for pulling wheelies, with a seat you could lean back on, and had a fancy, three-speed gear lever on the crossbar. It was the preferred mode of transport for the neighbourhood bad lads – the kids' equivalent of the Hell's Angels' low-rider. My mum thought they were dangerous, though, so a Chopper was out of the question for the young Johnson. The bike I really coveted was the Raleigh Grifter. This was an early mountain bike, with a twist-grip gear change and big, knobbly tyres. It was the absolute governor, but the closest I ever got to a Grifter was borrowing my brother Andrew's.

When I finally got my own brand-new bike, aged seven, it was a racer – brilliant on paths, where you could get up plenty of speed, but next to useless on rough terrain. On summer evenings, I would ride all around the neighbourhood, with my 'territory' defined by roads. If I went up Solihull Road I would hit the Stratford Road, a busy dual carriageway. But if I went down the gentle hill there was no main road and I could wind my way round the streets for hours, only stopping when I got to somewhere I didn't recognise or when the sun started dipping behind the roofs. It's hard for parents to give their children that sort of freedom today. Although I was only young, I don't remember the same scares about paedophiles and abductions that we have today. The main danger was being knocked off your bike – and with less traffic about, the risk of that was lower, too.

When I was four, my brother Will was born. My mum was always up for a challenge and she decided that three kids, including a baby, weren't enough, so she fostered two young black lads. They were half-brothers, around my age, from a difficult background in Birmingham, and they lived with us for three years, effectively being brought up as my brothers. It meant Andrew and I had a couple of instant playmates, but their tough background – in and out of social services' care, education and family life totally disrupted – meant they had difficulty fitting in.

Away from home, they were always getting into trouble of one sort or another. At school, they would steal other pupils' lunches and generally cause mayhem, and one or the other was always standing outside the headmistress's office, waiting to be dealt with. There were various visits to hospitals, too.

I remember how one of them walked into a wall and split his head open really badly – after fifteen years of serious rugby it is still the worst head injury I have ever seen. On a visit to see some friends in Coventry, the other brother fell from the top of a slide on to tarmac. He knocked himself out cold and had to stay overnight in hospital.

I realise now that they must have led pretty tough lives. Because of their background, they were always going to find it very hard to adjust to a new family, get on with other children or do well at school. When I was seven, Mum told us they were leaving and shortly afterwards they were gone. I was sad for a while – we had become pretty close – but it soon passed. A month is a long time at that age, but I have often wondered what happened to them. I hope they made something of their lives, but the odds were stacked against them.

That summer of 1977, my dad left Lucas and took a job in the lab at Tungstone Batteries, the largest employer in Market Harborough, Leicestershire, 50 or so miles away. It was a nine-to-five job and, nowadays, you would commute that sort of distance without batting an eyelid. In the seventies, though, it was quite unusual for people to live so far from work and we moved over to Harborough. Dad went first on his own. He would stay there during the week and on Saturday he would come home to fetch us and we would all head back down the M6 and spend hours driving around looking at houses.

My mum was a hopeless romantic and almost persuaded him to buy a run-down country mansion on the Corby Road, just out of town. It was uninhabitable and would have needed a huge amount of work. Mum, totally enthusiastic about everything, would have thrown herself into the DIY and eventually it would have been worth a million quid, but Dad obviously saw it for the ten-year nightmare it was going to be and talked her out of it. In the end they settled on a more realistic place, in Burnmill Road on the north side of the town, bordering the village of Great Bowden, and we all moved in. It was like a whole new world – a much bigger house than we had been used to, with four bedrooms and a huge garden full of apple trees.

We didn't like Harborough at first. In contrast with the modern-seeming Shirley, it was made up of Victorian and Edwardian red-brick terracing and, until the nineties, was a fairly smoggy town. It was on the old main drag between Leicester and Northampton, with lorries and other vehicles going through the centre all day long. Since then, the new A14 and the bypass have taken away all the heavy traffic and it has reverted to what it must have been like in the fifties – a pretty, well-to-do market town. As a teenager it was the sort of place we were desperate to get away from. Nowadays, it's booming, with lots of the people who left returning and vying with commuters to buy property, as prices escalate.

Andrew and I were both sent to Ridgeway School, not far from our new home. This was something of a culture shock. In Solihull, I had been at a traditional infants school. At Ridgeway, we did not wear uniforms and some of our lessons were in mobile classrooms. There were also older kids – it went up to age eleven – and some of them were fairly rough. The school had a wide catchment area, including the local council estate, and the intake went right across the range. Knowing that there was no uniform, but determined not to let the side down, my mum kitted Andrew and me out in clothes that would perhaps best be termed 'smart casual' – neat slacks, nicely pressed shirts, that sort of thing. We must have stood out a bit, next to the local hard lads in their jeans and trainers.

I can't remember being picked on or getting into any fights, but I do recall the massive shock of seeing seven-year-olds casually smoking, and clearly enjoying, fags. One day, a boy who was in my year brought into school a bottle of brown ale that his uncle had given him. The teacher confiscated the booze, but bizarrely gave it back to him after school, and this lad and his mates supped it outside the gates at going-home time. A few of these lads spent time in borstal, periodically returning to school after serving their 'time'.

It all felt strange and new and I kept my head down for a while until I had settled in and made a few friends. Of course, you don't always choose the friends your parents might want you to have and, while plenty of my mates went on to university and now run businesses or work abroad, a few were from the wrong side of the tracks. Years later, one of them famously made ITN's *News at Ten*. Drunk, and either bored or in a bungling attempt at video game theft, he kicked through the window of a computer shop in Church Street. Unfortunately, he left a piece of his calf on the glass; the police were able to match the lump of flesh to the gaping hole when they visited him in hospital. Another kid, my best friend from those days, went on to serve time for drug dealing. He was a bright lad, but he had a very difficult upbringing; given a better start in life I am sure things would have turned out differently for him. My mum must have worried about us being friends, but she and my dad had instilled in me a basic sense of right and wrong and ultimately that kept me on the straight and narrow.

It may surprise some readers, but I was a reasonably intelligent child and I enjoyed schoolwork, particularly maths – I would skip art lessons to go off and do algebra. My favourite subject, though, was PE. If two or three years earlier I had known little about sport, that was all changing now. I had finally bowed to the inevitable and joined my dad in his obsession with Liverpool FC. That year saw one of the worst days of my young life when Kevin Keegan left Anfield to go to Hamburg for £500,000. He was my idol and I just could not understand why he would leave us – to go to Germany, of all places (remember, I was still fighting WWII, like some lone Japanese soldier left behind on a Pacific island). It made no sense to me at all. Then we heard they were bringing in some guy called Kenny Dalglish to replace him. I remember wondering who the hell he was and knowing, just *knowing*, that he would be useless. Luckily, I was wrong on that one.

I grew up with that great team of the late seventies and early eighties – led from the front by King Kenny. Ray Kennedy, Terry McDermott and Graeme Souness were my heroes. Sadly, I never made it up to Anfield to watch the boys. In fact, the only time I've been there was with England for a game in our 1999 Rugby World Cup build-up – and, on the odd occasion I saw them live, playing away at grounds closer to my home, I was something of a jinx. We went to see them against Villa in the 1978–79 season. Liverpool were all-conquering at that point; it was the year they won the league and broke the record for conceding fewest goals while doing so – from memory, they only let in sixteen all season. It was all set up for a great win but, unfortunately, Jonah Johnson was there. I managed to see three of those sixteen goals on one day, as Villa trounced us 3–1.

It was a bad day, made worse because we had walked straight into a violent confrontation between home and away fans beforehand. We came round a corner, heading for the Liverpool end, and suddenly we were in the middle of a riot; police with truncheons drawn, glass flying everywhere, lots of shouting and screaming. Dad grabbed me and my brother and we legged it as quick as we could. I found the whole thing frightening and, more than that, bizarre: I did not understand why they were fighting.

I also saw Liverpool lose 1–0 at Leicester City, the home goal a brilliant strike by Andy Peake from Market Harborough. That was obviously just great for me, back at school the following Monday, surrounded, as I was, by Leicester fans. I had no love for the Foxes; around that time, they also beat us at Anfield to take away our long unbeaten home record. And we went to watch Liverpool play Nottingham Forest at the City Ground one Boxing Day, but could not get in. We had just bowled up, as you do, without tickets and found it was a sell-out. That was a pretty miserable experience and the journey back felt like the longest drive of my life. Liverpool probably won that one.

I loved playing soccer, too. I used to get to school early in the morning so I could join in a kickabout before assembly. We would play on the netball pitch, a tarmac square with a lot of loose pea gravel over the top: it was absolute murder if you fell over, taking the skin off your knees and embedding itself in your flesh. We would play football at break, play more football at lunchtime and stay at school afterwards to play a bit more football. Right from the start, I was desperate to get into the school team, made up of the ten- and eleven-year-olds in the third and fourth years. We had a good side and the school provided cracking shirts, claret and blue like Aston Villa's or West Ham's.

The big local competition was the Golden Wonder Cup, a knockout for all the school teams, sponsored by the well-known local crisp makers. The final was played at the Symington's Recreation Ground in Harborough. This was the classic Victorian company rec, a huge area in the middle of the town originally owned by a local corsetry manufacturer and the site for the annual travelling funfair. By this time it was falling into rack and ruin, but was still used for football and cricket and it felt like the big time. I had watched Ridgeway win the Golden Wonder as a seven-year-old and my dream was to play in a final.

As a first or second year, though, there was no chance of being selected. As a third year, you might get a look-in and I managed to get myself chosen for a trial game. I played in goal and had one shot to stop, which I virtually threw into my own net. My opposite number had two shots, stopped them both, and my goalkeeping dreams were dashed. Shortly afterwards, though, I finally made it into the side as a centre-back, and there I stayed until my last few months at the school, when I had a falling out with Mr Richards, the teacher in charge. The problem was that I took the whole thing very seriously and Mr Richards didn't.

By now captain of the school side, I was also turning out

for Harborough Town Juniors, where my dad was involved with the coaching. Every weekend, I played alongside boys from other schools in the area and that made the rivalry between us when our school teams met even stronger. I was desperately keen to stuff it up the likes of Fairfield Road, Farndon Fields, Little Bowden and Welford. Under the Richards regime at Ridgeway, however, pretty much anyone who turned up and trained got a game – usually at full-back. Those of us who put in the hard yards, day in, day out, on that gravelly netball pitch knew who could play footy and who couldn't. Mr Richards, on the other hand, didn't have a Scooby Doo. Some of the guys he picked didn't even have two left feet. It was a mad selection policy that threatened to undermine everything we were working for and I, for one, was not going to stand for it. I made my feelings known and relations started to deteriorate.

Breaking point was reached one afternoon in an after-school training game. Mr Richards was refereeing and trying desperately to make the game a draw, so that everyone went home happy. I was trying just as desperately to win the game, tearing around, playing like an absolute lunatic. We were a goal in front with a minute or two to go when Mr Richards intercepted the ball at the halfway line on our little forty-yard pitch, looked up and hoofed it over our keeper's head into the back of our net. I couldn't believe what I'd seen. He had got his draw, but this was horrendous. Half-player, half-referee? It was all wrong.

With our relationship already fraught, I made a fatal error; he arranged a meeting to pick the team for our next game and I forgot about it. When I didn't turn up he must have assumed it was a deliberate snub and he dropped me. We went on to lose 4–0 or 5–0 to Kibworth in the Golden Wonder Cup semi-final, with a pair of no-hopers at full-back, and that was the end of Johnson of the Rovers at Ridgeway. (For the record, Mr Richards, I honestly forgot about that meeting, and I *am* prepared to accept that your 'give-everyone-a-game' policy might have been reasonable at under-eleven level, but I still say tense cup semi-finals are no place for inexperienced defenders.)

I was a competitive youngster, though no more so than many of my friends. It was not as though I would have cheated at snakes and ladders to win. I just took my footy seriously. I wanted to win and I did have a natural – or perhaps unnatural – understanding of the tactics and mechanics of a soccer match, gleaned from following games on the telly very closely. While most of the other kids were sprinting about wherever the ball went, I would be trying to play the offside trap and telling the full-backs to push up, push up. I was probably an obnoxious little brat, to be honest. Years later I found out that, after I was dropped from the side, my dad had rung Mr Richards to find out what had happened. I imagine he was told that his middle son was a cocky little git who needed to learn some patience. Dad's response was no doubt along the lines of, 'Yes, you're right, he probably does.'

Apart from soccer, we played cricket, netball, rounders and British Bulldog. This is basically an excuse for a riot between ten-year-olds, but it's tremendous fun. Every year we started playing it in September and every year it was banned by October because kids were being killed and maimed all over the place. I had no real interest in rugby at that point, though

I might have been able to name a few of the great Welsh names of that era. Everyone knew of JPR Williams, JJ Williams, Gareth Edwards and Phil Bennett. Dad had taken us to see Solihull RUFC play one Saturday afternoon, just for something to do, and I recall being distinctly unimpressed: no stands or terracing, just a load of fat blokes rolling around in the mud, all wearing tatty kit with a few of their mates watching from the touchline. I remember thinking to myself, 'Football's not like this ... they've all got the same colour socks at Liverpool.'

When I was around ten, we also went to see Orrell play at Coventry. Given the family history, we were rooting for the northerners, but Cov, a strong side in those days with guys like Geoff Evans, Peter Rossborough and Fran Cotton in their team, were too good. This was a bit better, but top-flight English rugby at that time was on the slow side, so the jury was still out. In 1980 I made my first visit to Twickenham. Mum got hold of some tickets through contacts at the school where she worked and Dad and a couple of teachers took Andrew and me down in the car. We saw England beat Wales 9–8 on their way to the Grand Slam, with the Welsh flanker Paul Ringer sent off early on for a late tackle and a certain Clive Woodward playing in the centre. I remember leafing through the match programme and spotting his name. I hadn't the faintest idea who he was but I noted it because – along with other guys like Paul Dodge, Peter Wheeler and Dusty Hare – his club side was Leicester. It is weird, now, to think of the impact Clive would have on my life as England coach fifteen years later. Within a decade, too, I would be playing at the Tigers alongside Dusty and Dodgy, which also feels a bit spooky.

It was a big game, but I don't recall that much of the day: the long walk to the stadium from where we had parked our car, the old Twickenham itself, the huge crowd, snatches of the play . . . a jumble of mental pictures and half-recollections. Possibly the clearest memory is of my dad telling me he had just stood next to the Labour leader, Michael Foot, in the loos. He's always been one for spotting celebs, my dad. I enjoyed the day enormously and, for the first time, rugby was seriously on my radar.

If you had pulled me to one side in the shadow of the stadium and asked whether I would rather run out there or at Anfield there would have been only one answer, but a seed had been sown. I began to take an interest in the game on TV, chatted with school friends who regularly went with their families to watch Leicester Tigers and started to glean the basic rules. At eleven, I would be leaving Ridgeway for Welland Park, a high school which serves Market Harborough, where they fielded a strong school XV, and I began to look forward to getting my hands on an oval ball. I knew I would be quite good at it, because I was big for my age and, while I wasn't lightning quick, I wasn't slow either.

Welland Park was a great experience for me. Academically it was, obviously, more serious than junior school. I was in the A stream for maths and doing pretty well in most other subjects. PE was still, by far, my favourite, though. If you were any good and you wanted to play, there were school teams throughout the age groups, with matches on Wednesday afternoons and Saturday mornings, and pretty soon I was in the football and rugby sides. I wore No. 8 in our rugby team, having rapidly learned that playing in the back row meant I got my hands on the ball and the opportunity to use my size. I stayed at the back of the pack right the way through school.

A tremendously committed bunch of teachers – guys like Andy Turner, Ian Anholm and Phil Spittle – gave up hours of their own time to coach us and we developed into a reasonable team. Spittle was the biggest influence on me back then. He basically taught me how to play rugby, which is a difficult thing to do with youngsters. I remember the first proper game we played, against Spencefield School. Phil and their teacher treated it as an extended training session. We would play for five minutes and then they would stop the game, tell us what we were doing wrong or right, and start it again. We won 4–0 and I came away buzzing.

We had a full fixture list, with football one week, rugby the next. On Saturday mornings we would travel on the bus with the older teams to play away at schools in Hinckley, Kettering and Leicester. Our football side was poor but at rugby we won more often than we lost. We were pretty unsophisticated – tackling as hard as we could, running around a bit and booting the ball back over the opposition's heads when it seemed like the right thing to do – but we enjoyed it immensely and made occasional forays into the latter stages of the Leicestershire Schools Cup. We had a big, strong pack and our speciality was the pushover try. As often as not I was the one who dotted the ball down. I had been made skipper of the side. I was also captain of the school football team, but our relative failure with the round ball started to turn me more towards rugby.

Welland Park had access to free schoolboy season tickets for Leicester Tigers so Andrew and I badgered my dad to take us down to Welford Road. The first game I saw was against London Welsh in 1981. Paul Dodge scored a great try and Leicester won in front of a big crowd. I loved every minute. This was a million miles from the Solihull match I had seen a few years earlier and, for the first time, club rugby could almost compare with club football. There were several thousand people watching; the players were fit and skilful; and there were no odd socks in sight. After that we started going fairly regularly, watching around ten games that year.

Leicester were domestic top dogs then, with England players like Dodge, Woodward and Hare in their setup. They had won the cup for three years running, with Bath yet to emerge as the dominant force in English rugby. While Dad and Andrew watched from somewhere else in the ground, I would meet up with friends from school by the clubhouse, watching the players run out and then finding a vantage point of our own. If it was dry, we might watch the first half perched up on the big bank at the end of the ground where the Alliance and Leicester stand was later built. At half-time we would buy ourselves a hotdog and switch to a seat somewhere else, before racing round to see the players as they left the field, running on to pat one or two of them on the back if they had done well. Somewhere along the way, my interest in football was diminishing. I kept an eye out for Liverpool's results and wanted them to win, but it no longer ruined my weekend if they lost.

At fourteen, we all left to go to Robert Smyth, the senior school in Harborough. It was huge, with well over a thousand pupils. It was less fun, too, because suddenly we were choosing our 'O' level options and being asked to think about

'A's and even university. Careers teachers were lecturing me about my future and missing a lesson was serious. My best mate was Julian Murray, a big lad with a crap mohican and a rebellious attitude. We knocked around together for a few years until he left at sixteen and we lost touch. Years later, after the 1997 Lions tour, I was asked on to a late-night phone-in show with Danny Kelly. One element of the show involved Danny inviting people who had been at school with his 'celebrity' guest to call up with their memories. Sure enough, a call comes through. It's Julian from London on line one.

'All right Johnno, remember me?'

It's Murray.

'Yes, mate. How are you?'

'Fine, thanks. Do you remember punching me in that match we played in?'

I had to admit I did remember it. He had been lying across me so I had whacked him and been sent off for violent conduct. Not that I started early or anything.

There's a bit more chat and then another caller – Etienne du Toit – comes through on line two.

'All right Johnno, remember me?'

If you've been at school with someone called Etienne du Toit, you remember him.

'Yes, mate. How are you?'

'Fine, thanks. Do you remember punching me and split-ting my lip open in the dinner queue?'

Oh God. Etienne had been messing around and I had half-heartedly cuffed him. There had been blood everywhere. Anyone watching the show would have formed the impres-sion that Johnson was the school bully, but these were just about the only incidents I was involved in and they were, honestly, not as bad as they sound. Later, Julian and I met up again and we have stayed friends ever since. He now designs clothes, but has not changed a bit, and he says the same of me, which I take as a compliment.

While we played rugby in PE and between houses, there wasn't much of a school team at Robert Smyth, but luckily that didn't matter too much, because by now I had been selected for Leicestershire Under-14s. This was a fantastic thrill and had introduced me to a lot of boys from other schools in the area who were as keen on their rugby as I was. The following season, many of them were planning to play at Wigston RUFC, a busy junior club on the outskirts of Leicester, and I was invited to go along. It was tempting, but left me with a dilemma. Training and games were on Sundays. If I joined Wigston I would have to stop playing soccer for Harborough Town. Ultimately, it wasn't a hard decision. Playing footy for the Town, you just met at the ground and you played. My dad coached us and, with all due respect to him, he was just my dad. We did not win many matches. It felt like we were turning up to lose and I was not enjoying it any more. By contrast, Wigston felt like the real thing. It had a clubhouse with a bar, changing rooms, several pitches and coaches who seemed to know what they were talking about.

Dad would drive me the twelve or thirteen miles up to the club two or three times a week. It was fantastic: we trained alongside the older guys, listening to their banter, trying to impress them and learning from the coaches. I had my first pint at Wigston, a lanky fifteen-year-old thinking I was a real jack-the-lad rugby player. We went on tour to Wales that

Easter, leaving on the bus early on Saturday morning, fitting in a game against a side on the outskirts in the afternoon and then desperately trying to large it around Cardiff at night, with a couple of quid each in our pockets. Obviously, we were immediately kicked out of anywhere decent and ended up in some grotty, side-street pub drinking Gold Label barley wine and trying to look like we knew what we were doing. Next morning, we travelled up to the Valleys to play Blanau, the coach stopping repeatedly for vomit breaks, and were hammered by a stone-faced bunch of Welsh lads on a horrible, wet, foggy Easter day. There was more of the same that evening and another defeat on Easter Monday before the long journey home. It was the stuff of legend.

Our coaches were Graham 'Tufty' Taylor and Rich Yeomans, a couple of ex-players prepared to give up their time. I used to love hearing Rich's stories about beer drinking and rugby tour exploits. He and Tufty must have been decent coaches, too. We travelled around the Midlands and won the vast majority of our matches, including, for two years running, the Leicestershire County Championships.

I held my own when I moved up to the Colts – the Under-19s – at fifteen and kept my place in the county side. England Schools, though, was my main objective. Leicestershire played all the other East Midlands counties and then the East Midlands Select XV would play the West Midlands to find the Midlands team. I managed to get through and was invited up to Catterick in Yorkshire for a game against the North. I remember feeling fantastic about this – travelling up there on the train, all expenses paid, like you were *somebody*. Unfortunately, we were pretty poor and the North beat us, so the trip back home was a little less enjoyable. We had been told that those selected to go forward for the full trial would receive a letter, so when nothing had arrived by Wednesday I knew I was not in. I was very disappointed.

This was my first real sporting setback and it knocked my confidence. Obviously, I was not good enough and it was not going to happen for me. I was at that stage, starting to grow up and entering the sixth form at school, where other distractions were around and, as the following season started, I was far less motivated than I had been before. Over the summer I had started playing American football with the Leicester Panthers and was enjoying that a great deal, and I could very easily have stopped playing rugby altogether. In the end, though, I drifted back to Wigston and to the Leicestershire Colts once again.

However, the coaches rated a lad called Craig Barrow very highly and wanted him to play No. 8, suggesting that I play second row instead. I was not too enamoured of this because, with all that ball-in-hand running, the back row was a much more glamorous and sexy option than the tight five. I went along with it, though, and in hindsight it was obviously a good decision. Being tall and not as fast as some of the other guys, I was more naturally suited to being a lock. I made it to the Midlands side in my new position and, eventually, all wide-eyed and naive, into the England Under-18 setup. My selection, a year young and very raw, was a fantastic honour and made me realise that I must be a half-decent player. At Wigston Colts, we trained once a week and looked forward to a beer afterwards, whereas most of the other England lads were drawn from the public school circuit, where they had great coaching and excellent facilities.

My first season, playing France, Scotland, Wales and Ireland, was pretty mixed – we lost two and drew two. The most memorable thing that happened was the dropping of Neil Back. Backy was by far and away the best player in our team, but he was left out for some public school kid rumoured to have a connection to the coaching setup. We played the Scots lads midweek and then the Welsh in Ebbw Vale. Then we had a few days off before we met up again for the games against Ireland and France. No Backy – dropped not just from the team, but from the whole squad. It was scandalous, really, and a lot of the other boys were in tears at the injustice of it all. It was my first taste of the garbage that surrounded English rugby for far too many years.

I played again the following year, joining the Tigers at the beginning of that season. Amazingly, they had never approached me, despite the fact that I was playing for England Colts and lived just down the road. Nowadays, in the professional era, young lads in my position are snapped up by Premiership academies at fourteen. It was different back then – a bit more shambolic. A mate of mine from Wigston, Jason Aldwinckle, had started training at Leicester the year before and I bumped into him near Welford Road one day. He said I ought to give Leicester a go. I was quite shy about just turning up without a formal invitation – it felt like walking into Manchester United and asking for a game – but I eventually made my way down there. I didn't know anyone and I felt nervous as anything. My heroes played here. Dean Richards was sitting in the sponsor's hut having a pint, fresh from the 1987 World Cup, for heaven's sake. This really was the big time! Wide-eyed, I went out and trained with the other youngsters and, much to my surprise, found I could live with the standard, winning selection for the Tigers Youth team at the start of the season. Unbeknown to me, the pattern of my life had been set.

CHAPTER TWO

JUNIOR ALL BLACK

At nineteen, I was the typical teenager. No real direction, just drifting along, odd-jobbing on a building site and going with the flow. I had made it out of Leicester Youth into the lower reaches of the senior sides, playing a handful of times for Leicester's second and third teams and just a couple of low-grade games for the firsts. But while rugby was great, it was hardly a career, was it? The closest I had come to a big plan for my future was a half-thought-out idea of following my mum into PE teaching. Then, out of the blue in the spring of 1989, a bizarre letter plopped on to our doormat.

A guy called John Albert had written to me from New Zealand. Amazingly, he wanted me to fly down there and play for his team. Albert had seen me in action for England Schools that summer. We had toured Australia with a good side featuring a number of lads who eventually went on to international honours, including myself, Ade Adebayo, Steve Ojomoh and Damian Hopley. The Australian Rugby Union had arranged a three-way tournament, with New Zealand Schools also coming over. The fixtures had been drawn up so that the final game was Australia against New Zealand, with England cast in the role of whipping boys along the way. We had spoiled their party by first beating the Kiwis 15–8 at the famous Concord Oval in Sydney and then going on to beat the young Wallabies 13–0 in Canberra. We were long gone by the time they played the planned 'decider'.

Albert was involved with a little junior club called Tihoi in the King Country province. If I was interested, they would pay for my flight out, find me a job and somewhere to stay, and give me a few games. I had no ties. Ahead of me was, probably, a season with the Tigers seconds. I could always put off going to PE college. I didn't have a clue where King Country was. I didn't even know much about New Zealand, other than what I had gleaned from my dad's Max Boyce records, with their songs of huge, sheep-farming rugby men striding up and down hills with a ram under each arm. But what did I have to lose? I would be going in April, so if things didn't work out I could still come home in time for the next English season, having seen a bit of the world. I called him to accept, little suspecting that it was a decision that would change my life, opening my eyes to a different sporting culture, helping me to develop into the player I would become and, along the way, introducing me to the woman who would become my wife.

Interviewers often ask me if it was all part of some Johnson masterplan: get selected for England Schools, head over to the other side of the world for a spot of fine-tuning with the Kiwis and then come back ready to step straight into the full England side. Er, no. It was more like, 'Want to come out to New Zealand and play for us, mate?' 'Er, yeah. Why not?'

A few weeks later, I found myself on a Continental Airlines 747, breaking the world record for sleeping *en route* with a monster kip across the centre seats all the way from L.A. to

Auckland. John picked me up at the airport. He was a Maori guy in his mid-thirties, all smiles and very friendly and enthusiastic about my arrival. It was a three-and-a-half-hour car journey along what was then a winding, single-lane road from Auckland to his home at Taupo, in the middle of the North Island. John was full of chat as he drove, telling me about the club and the area and saying I was going to be great for the team. Watching the green New Zealand countryside whiz by, I wondered whether he had the right Martin Johnson.

Taupo is a beautiful place; a picturesque, tourist town of about 20,000 people, set on a huge freshwater lake in the middle of the country. In the winter, skiers travel to the mountains at the far end of the lake and a cold wind blows off the peaks on to the town below. The summer brings weeks of temperate, blue-sky days and holidaymakers from all over the country. The nearest big town, Rotorua, is an hour away and Tihoi, which was playing its rugby in the lowest division of the King Country league, was thirty minutes' drive, a hamlet stuck out in the middle of nowhere. I had arrived on a Friday. There was a game the following day and I agreed to play.

It was quite a surreal experience. Jetlagged, knackered and disorientated, I just pitched up in John's car. We changed in a shed and then had to walk over a little hillock before straddling a barbed-wire fence covered in tufts of wool to get to the pitch. One, undulating pitch, covered in sheep – and sheep muck. I lasted for about an hour until I got jelly-legs from the flight and had to come off. I think we won, though the result was the last thing on my mind. My head was spinning from the whole, weird afternoon as I was introduced to my new club-mates and shared a few post-match beers with them. Before arriving, I had worried about the playing standard and whether I would be able to cope with the renowned physicality of the New Zealand game. After all, this was not England Schools. As it turned out, I had coped pretty well.

I was staying with John Albert and his wife and kids and the next priority was a job. I was on a six-month tourist visa with no work permit, so the idea was to get me a little cash-in-hander. Most of the work was in agriculture, the central pillar of New Zealand's economy, either labouring on farms or logging in the huge forestry plantations which stretched for miles around. Logging was out, though, because the nineteen-year-old Johnson was far too callow to get involved in that game. Those forestry workers were amazing blokes. A van would come through and pick them up at 5a.m. for a two-hour drive out into the bush. They would spend most of the day felling trees and sawing off the branches before the long drive back to town in the evening. Many of them were Maoris, who are naturally big, and the work put a lot of muscle on them, so they were pretty scary characters.

I eventually got a job in a bank, which was more my scene. However, I did work for a few months on the farms in the area and I remember these guys coming in to cash their cheques at the weekend, stinking of cigarettes and petrol from their chainsaws. Evenings they would hit the bars in town, drinking crates of DB Draft, smoking a few joints and having the occasional brawl. There is this theory that New Zealand is like Britain supposedly was in the fifties; full of polite, quiet people drinking lots of tea and going to bed by 10p.m. There are certainly parts of the country that are like that, but there are parts, too, which are a good deal more rough and ready.

After just a couple of games with Tihoi, more serious rugby beckoned when, to my surprise, I was invited to a training session with the King Country provincial side. I made my way down to the session at Taumarunui, two hours and 150km away along another typically long and winding New Zealand road. I was further surprised to find myself selected for a game ten days later. I was very flattered, though I think it was more to do with a shortage of second rows than any obvious brilliance on my part. Despite having the legendary former All Black lock Colin Meads as its president, King Country languished somewhere near the bottom of the second division of the national championships. It was not a fashionable province, like Auckland, Canterbury or Wellington, and players were not beating down the door to get a game. Additionally, New Zealand as a whole had experienced problems producing good, tall forwards. King Country, clearly, was no exception to this rule and I guess they thought they would give me a go.

Early in the season, provincial rugby consisted of 'friendlies' – though there was absolutely nothing friendly about them – played midweek, with guys continuing to turn out for their club sides on Saturdays. After the club season was over around the end of August, the provincial championships proper kicked in. My first game was one of those friendlies, against Auckland B. Glynn Meads, a top guy and Colin's son, skippered us and gave us an aggressive pre-match talk. He had no love for these Auckland 'city slickers' and was desperate for us to beat them.

At that time, the full Auckland side was without doubt the best team in the world outside the All Blacks, with legends like Sean Fitzpatrick, Michael Jones, Grant Fox, John Kirwan, the Brooke brothers and more among their ranks. Many rural New Zealanders saw them as flashy and cocky – the fact that some of these guys owned car phones irked the country-dwellers, for instance – and they resented their success and the way they featured so heavily in the national side. After a period of absolute domination of world rugby by the Blacks, the touring French had recently given them a good run for their money. Some of those supporters out in the sticks had been very quick to blame the All Blacks' 'slicker' element for this perceived drop in the national side's performance. In tune with this mood, Glynn badly wanted us to beat Auckland's second string.

It all added to the nervousness I felt about how I would cope with the pace, physicality and skill levels of the match. All I really had under my belt was that handful of second- and third-team games for Leicester and a couple of first-team matches, against the RAF and against Bath on the weekend before my flight to New Zealand. The RAF had been a low-key game and in the Bath fixture, with a Cup final beckoning, both sides had rested their big guns. I had no clue as to how I would handle provincial rugby in New Zealand.

Despite Glynn Meads' pep talk, the Auckland boys were way too good for us and we were well beaten, 20–0. I had a reasonable game, not man-of-the-match, but not an embarrassment to England, Leicester or myself either. One of their centres absolutely ripped us to shreds, playing like a man from a different planet. Afterwards I asked the other players who he was. Frank Bunce was his name, they said, but he was in his late twenties and past it. I was staggered. He had not looked past it to me. If he had been in England he would have been a rugby superstar, the best player in the country by far, and here he was playing for Auckland's B team. It was my first taste of the gulf in class between the hemispheres and the awesome strength in depth of Kiwi rugby. Bunce, of course, would rise to prominence with Western Samoa in the 1991 World Cup and later went on to enjoy a glittering career with the All Blacks, so don't say I can't spot talent!

I held my place for the second warm-up game against Counties – later Jonah Lomu's province – at Otorohanga, one of a number of towns where we played 'home' fixtures. They were a mid-table first division side and we beat them for the first time in years, which was a major result for King Country. Again, I played reasonably well until I was whacked from behind in the closing minutes. I was knocked out and had to be helped to the changing room, where I eventually came round. Later, a reporter from the *New Zealand Herald* came over to talk to me. It was one of the odder interviews in which I have been involved, as I struggled, groggily, to cope with some not-too-complex questions:

'So, whereabouts in England are you from?'

'Er, dunno . . . sorry.'

'So, how long have you been in New Zealand?'

'Erm, not sure, to be honest.'

'What did you think of the match?'

'Um . . . sorry, I can't really remember it.'

After a while he gave up and wandered away, shaking his

head and presumably wondering if this pale English youth would survive the hard school of New Zealand rugby.

The win over Counties gave us a real buzz and we all went out for a few beers that night. It was back down to earth for our next fixture, though, when we were soundly beaten by Wayne Shelford's senior North Harbour side. I had actually met Shelford before the game, when he pulled up alongside me in a beat-up old car to ask directions to the ground. There was nothing beat-up about his team's performance, though. I remember feeling during that match that I was up against guys who were on another level to anything I had faced before. They oozed professionalism and organisation and would have slaughtered the Tigers' first XV of that era. I could not believe I was sharing a pitch with Shelford. A couple of years before he had been an untouchable, iconic god of the game: a star of the fantastically talented and glamorous 1987 Rugby World Cup-winning All Black side. Here was I, not long left Wigston and fresh from a Harborough building site, trying to tackle him. He was not as big and imposing as I had thought he would be, but he was, undoubtedly, a brilliant player.

Facing guys like Shelford and Bunce was the start of my rugby education and, subconsciously, perhaps I was beginning to understand a little more about the sport at the very highest level, even if it usually involved dusting myself off or watching conversions sail through the posts above my head. We managed to beat Taranaki in our next match – another first division side and an even better result than the Counties game because it was away from home. This was a major achievement. The big provincial sides were well drilled, very skilled and extremely fit. King Country was more old school. We would meet up on Sunday, most of us nursing hangovers, and train for a couple of hours before sinking a couple of beers together afterwards.

Back at Tihoi, the regular club season was drawing to an end. It had gone reasonably well and we had a good team spirit and a decent side. Even at that lowly level, you were never short of good players. If the full-back had to pull out, they would ring someone up on the Friday and he would pitch up next afternoon. He might not have played for six months and his boots could be a couple of sizes too small, but you always knew whoever stepped in would know the rules, would be half fit and could play – they were all physical guys, aggressive tacklers, with a few ball skills, too. And we were well supported. There was nothing much to do locally without driving the half hour into Taupo, so on Saturdays people would come from the surrounding farms down to the ground to watch the game. We would often get crowds of 150 there and afterwards the teams and the spectators would go back to our shed and socialise. Crates of beer would be opened – DB Draft, Lion Red and Waikato – and we would eat a traditional Maori hangi. To make this you dig a pit in the ground in the morning and line the bottom with hot rocks. You pour water on to them and then you place wire baskets of lamb and vegetables on top. These are covered with thick cloths and the pit is then filled over with mud. It cooks slowly all day and is ready in the evening, producing food with a pleasant, if earthy, taste.

At one of these post-match barbecues I met a pretty girl called Kay Gredig. Her dad, Malcolm, was chairman of the club and he and his family were regular attendees at Tihoi.

Kay and I got chatting and shared a drink. A few days later, Malcolm invited me round to his farm to watch some rugby videos and I bumped into Kay again. Her end-of-term school ball was coming up and she asked me to go with her. After that we started to see each other fairly regularly. Her dad had plenty of jobs which needed doing on his land – fencing, rounding up livestock, digging – so I was often over there working for him and eventually moved out of John Albert's house and into their spare room. A few quid in the pocket, a place in the King Country side and a new girlfriend – what more could I want?

The provincial season proper started at the end of the club season and went pretty well. I played in all but one of the provincial games, getting sin-binned for fighting by the referee, Mr Hilditch, in a game against Bay of Plenty, and we finished near the top of our division, losing just two or three matches all season and beating eventual champions, Southland, along the way. My performances must have been reasonable because I was invited to the All Black Under-21 trial at the Police College in Wellington ahead of their annual game against Australia. I was delighted, obviously, if a little bemused. After all, I was English.

Colin Meads was obviously keen to get one of his players down there, even if it was some random Pom, and must have pulled a few strings, but I felt rather strange and awkward as a Brit walking into the junior All Black camp. The first guy I saw was Matt Sexton, who had played hooker for the New Zealand Schoolboys against us the year before, and although friendly enough, he was, to say the least, taken aback to see me there. We played a match on the Friday – I was OK – and then trained the next day, ahead of the final trial game on the Sunday. My Saturday group contained people like Walter Little, Craig Dowd, Pat Lam, Va'aiga 'Inga' Tuigamala and Norm Hewitt, who were obviously very talented young guys. At this point, I started to get my hopes up and imagined myself in a black shirt – with these names in the Sunday team there was no way we would lose and I therefore stood a better chance of shining and making the final XV myself. Of course, when Sunday came around Little, Lam and co. did not play at all, because they were already selected, so I ended up in a side that had never trained together before. We were soundly beaten, my services were not required any further and my brief All Black experience appeared to be over.

At this point, as we headed into the Kiwi spring, I should have been booked on a flight home. I had originally planned to spend just six months down there, playing one season. However, I had injured my right shoulder before I flew out from the UK. It felt a little loose and would often 'clunk' out while I was playing. Although it was not properly diagnosed at the time, I later found out it was regularly 'sub-luxing' or semi-dislocating. The injury had not cleared up during my time with Tihoi and King Country and the last thing my body needed, I reasoned, was to be plunged straight back into an English season with Leicester seconds. Better, surely, to spend a relaxing Kiwi summer in Taupo, working on my fitness and letting the shoulder heal?

King Country had had a good season, I was enjoying the rugby and I fancied another crack at promotion to the provincial first division. Kay and I were getting more serious, too, which probably clinched the whole deal. Her mum sweet-talked someone in the immigration department to get me a work permit and one of the King Country coaches, Phil Taylor, found me a job in the National Bank of New Zealand branch in Taupo, so I had a little more security, with regular money coming in. The decision, in the end, was a fairly easy one.

That summer was spent working, training and barbecuing. Kay's younger brother, Pete, and I also spent a lot of time together. Like many Kiwis, Pete loved – and loves – hunting. He would trap and shoot rabbits and possums, practices which were officially encouraged and which, in those days, could earn you NZ$5 for the skins from local furriers. Both are non-indigenous pests – the only native mammal to the country being the bat, apparently – and the possum, in partic-ular, is hated by Kiwi farmers. Far from being the cuddly, big-eyed creatures of British imagination, they are aggressive, cat-sized animals which cause a lot of damage to trees and fencing and are believed to carry bovine tuberculosis.

On one occasion, doing my rounds of Pete's gin-traps, I came across a snared possum. I didn't want to let it go – it was injured and would have crawled away somewhere to die a long, agonising death – so, with nothing else to hand, I grabbed a fence post to put it out of its misery. Despite the seemingly unequal contest – Johnson, 6ft 6in, 17 stone and armed with log; possum, 2ft, two stone and unable to move – it didn't die immediately. Finally, though, it gave up the ghost.

If we were not trapping them, we were shooting them. Next door to Kay's parents lived a man employed by the New Zealand Rabbit Board, who was paid by the government to trap and kill rabbits. Pete would nip over and scrounge bullets from the guy, usually coming back with a couple of boxes of rifle ammunition. Once it was dark, we would head off into the country with a powerful searchlight and a gun. One of us would shine the torch on the rabbits and possums and the other would pick them off with the rifle as they stood there, mesmerised by the beam. Sometimes they would just keel over and you could collect the corpse for the skin and maybe for meat for your dogs. Often, though, you would see or hear the impact of the bullet and they would just scamper off, presumably dying somewhere later.

Pete also introduced me to pig hunting. The bush is home to groups of feral pigs and tracking and killing them is a very popular sport among the men of rural New Zealand, with several magazines devoted to it. Pete would ask his dad for any spare sheep guts, spreading them in the dirt in the fields around the house. Then we would sit and wait for the pigs, attracted by the smell of the offal, to come rooting around.

The older guys actually went out looking for them, which is a pretty hazardous pastime. The general idea is to strike out into the woods with dogs until you come across a pig's scent. The dogs catch the smell and race off into the under-growth and a few minutes later you hear the raucous squealing of a cornered hog. The dogs' job is to hold on until you can get there and your job is to leap on to the animal and stab it in the heart with a hunting knife. It's perfect training for back-row forwards. The boars, particularly, can be huge crea-tures, hundreds of pounds of solid muscle, with razor-sharp tusks and powerful jaws. Often, they will kill the dogs – Pete had many pictures of the carnage – and they can certainly do a lot of damage to a careless man.

Occasionally, we would tag along on these hunts. The first time I went out for an afternoon's hunting with Pete and a few of his friends we drew a blank and were heading back to the farm in a pick-up when suddenly a herd of pigs came racing across a wide-open paddock. The driver screeched round and set off after them across this hilly field, with one of the guys in the front leaning out the window, trying to get a clean shot as the truck bounced up and down, and me in the back hanging on desperately. We managed to separate one of the pigs from the herd and watched as it got to the bottom of the paddock and across a narrow river. As it pinned its ears back and ran off the guy with the rifle aimed and fired. There was an enormous 'boom' – it was a big, old gun – and the pig cartwheeled over, stone dead. The guys gutted the carcass and sewed it back up before lighting a fire and holding it over the flames, using a knife to scrape off all the singed hair. Later that night, I had my first taste of wild pork, a delicious meat with a strong, gamey flavour.

Kay's dad was also a keen hunter, with deer his main target. I remember him waking me up early one Sunday morning. He had shot a stag in a ravine near the farm and wanted me to carry it back. As with the pigs, you threaded the forelegs through the hind ones to create a sort of rucksack and hoisted it on to your back. It was a heavy beast and took some hauling out, but I was paid NZ$50 for my trouble, a share of the fee from the meat plant it was sold to.

It all felt even further from Market Harborough than it was. The rural Kiwi is connected to the land in a much more real way than his English counterpart, even in a farming county like Leicestershire. I live in a small village surrounded by farmland but neither I nor, I would guess, many of my neighbours have much idea of what goes on out in the fields. We are a fairly squeamish nation. In New Zealand, almost everyone is linked to agriculture and they live a harder, less sentimental life than the average Briton. It is a rawer existence than ours, but, ultimately, perhaps more honest.

The following season, I changed clubs, leaving Tihoi and joining College Old Boys Marist, one of several big clubs in Taupo. They were in the first division of the local competition and I needed to be playing a higher standard of rugby than Tihoi offered. John Albert was a little upset at my decision to move on, but his was a transitional club, with players coming and going regularly, so I didn't feel obliged to stay. I chose College Old Boys because a couple of my King Country team-mates, a fly-half called Nigel Swain and my second-row partner Russell Alve, were there. We played at the Owen Delaney Park stadium in town. This was a fantastic, municipal rugby facility, better than many modern English Premiership clubs have. It had a main pitch, with seating for a large crowd on one side, and five or six others surrounding it, and was built on highly porous, volcanic pumice stone which drained brilliantly and meant the surfaces were always firm. We shared it with the other teams in the town – Taupo, Taupo Athletic and Taupo United – alternating home games on the big pitch. We would get crowds of six or seven hundred to watch us; it might not have been the major leagues but it was bigger and better than Wigston, which was a comparable English club.

I enjoyed my time there and had some memorable games, including a feisty local derby against Taupo United which ended in me being sent off for a high tackle on Dale McIntosh, later the Pontypridd and Wales No. 8. I played only around seven games for the club, suffering a lot of niggly injuries. I sprained my wrist, missed a game. I got a dead leg, missed a game. I was now suffering with my left shoulder, too. It was the same problem, sub-luxing, though it felt more serious than the previous injury, which had all but cleared up. That ruled me out of a few other matches. Overall, the locals probably viewed me as a bit soft, but I made some good friends who I have stayed in touch with.

Halfway through the season I received a second invitation to Wellington for that year's New Zealand Under-21 trials, ahead of the annual tour to Australia. Again, I suspect Colin Meads wanted someone from King Country to be there and, again, I was the one they sent. It was the same format: two games between four teams, on Friday and Sunday, with sides made up of probables, possibles and the rest – the weaker players and younger guys who might get a chance the following year.

I was with the 'rest', along with a young Todd Blackadder. As a fan of the Rowan Atkinson TV series, his name made me chuckle, though no one else seemed to find it funny. Having watched *Blackadder Goes Forth* on Kiwi TV, I could see why. To fit the episodes into the slots on their commercial station they had to chop huge sections out with the result that, when you watched it, it didn't make any sense at all, let alone make you laugh. Blackadder's name was about the only amusing thing about the selection, though. Once more I was stuck in what I perceived to be the weak side, which irritated me. I knew I was very lucky to be there at all, but I didn't want to waste my time again. It was not that I felt I was the best player there – there were some excellent young New Zealanders knocking around. I have just never been interested in turning out to make up the numbers.

We played early on the Sunday. I am never at my best on a Sunday morning and I remember thinking just before kick-off that I couldn't really be bothered with this. But then we were out on the pitch, the whistle went and straightaway I made a good tackle. That woke me up a little, so I decided to make the best of things and went on to have a reasonable match, all the while assuming it was in vain. As soon as we had showered and changed we were all called into a conference room where they read out the squad. And there I was – 'Second row, Martin Johnson.'

John Hart, a national selector and one of the best coaches in world rugby, had been named to lead our party, they told us. We would play three matches, including a Test against our Wallaby counterparts. I didn't take in much more. In rugby terms, it was, and remains, the biggest shock I have had. Along with the shock, I immediately felt an enormous sense of responsibility. This was not quite the same as being selected for the England Under-21 side. For starters, they announced the squad on the national news that evening. Back home, they did not even give the full Test team on the TV; you had to search for it on Ceefax. I felt the weight of public expectation, the fact that I was walking where absolute legends of the game had trodden before. Back in my hotel room – I was staying in Wellington overnight so I could obtain an Australian visa for the tour the following day – I phoned Kay, who was delighted. Then I called home to tell my mum and dad what had happened, before lying back on my bed and trying to think. My head was spinning. I did not sleep too well that night.

I flew home to Taupo on the Monday evening. Kay collected me at the tiny local airport to drive me home, pulling into the College Old Boys on the way 'to pick something up'. We wandered into the clubhouse and I was confronted by a room full of streamers, balloons and everyone going crazy. They had thrown a surprise party for me, with all the lads and the club officials there. They were delighted for me and for the club – they had never had a player selected for the All Black Under-21s before. Later, I spoke to Colin Meads. A typical, dour Kiwi, he is not an effusive kind of guy; he just congratulated me, shook my hand and impressed on me the importance of representing myself, the club, the province and the Junior All Blacks to the best of my ability.

We warmed up for the tour by beating a strong and aggressive NZ Barbarians side in Auckland. Mark Cooksley and Blair Larsen were the second row and I was on the bench, but Cooksley was injured halfway through the game and I came on. His injury was enough to keep him out of the trip so I boarded the plane with high hopes of making the starting XV. First up, we faced New South Wales Country Under-21s. I did start and we won fairly comfortably. Midweek we played Western Australia, who were touring the east coast, at Eastwood Rugby Club in Sydney. This was the senior Western Australia team and, with rugby union not being so popular in Perth, the state side is traditionally full of expat Kiwis.

This line-up was no exception and they were obviously pumped up for a game against their Under-21 compatriots.

They were determined to show us who were the bosses and the game was very physical, with a couple of big brawls. Fists were flying throughout the match – I remember Blair, who was already a policeman at that point, rolling around in the dirt scrapping with one of their players with the match going on around them – and I just tried to keep my chin out of the firing line. We won and I got through OK, though we were quite battered and bruised coming up to the Test against the Wallaby Under-21s. John Hart was livid. He is a very strict man with a firm belief in fair play and he was very severe on us, saying we could easily have had a man sent off for fighting.

He was obviously pleased with our performance, though. Western Australia were no mugs and we gave away plenty to them in strength and experience. Our forwards had stood up to the challenge and come through, which was important. Pre-tour, everyone had talked about our back line, which contained guys like Craig Innes, a full All Black, full-back Jasin Goldsmith, who, in 1988, at eighteen, had toured Australia with the Blacks, and Inga Tuigamala, who was obviously devastating. Our forwards had been thought the weak link, with very few guys playing first-team provincial rugby. However, players like Craig Dowd, Apollo Perelini and Larsen had now proved themselves the excellent prospects they were.

On the Saturday, we played the junior Test match at the Sydney Football Stadium as a curtain-raiser to Australia's Test match against France. This was a huge game, by far the biggest I had played in. It was an annual fixture, always broadcast live on New Zealand TV, and the Wallaby team featured one John Eales. We took an early lead and, although they came back with a couple of late tries, we managed to hang on. As we sat in the changing room afterwards, John Hart came over to me. 'Well done Martin, you really competed,' he said. I thought that was a bit odd: they had thrown line-out ball to me only once in the game and I hadn't won it! I had been jumping against Eales and I guess they thought he would have the beating of me. To be fair, he was obviously already a tremendous player and he would go on to win the World Cup final with the full Aussie Test team just fourteen months later. Whatever, I did not care. I had played and we had won. We trooped back into the stadium to watch France beat the Wallabies and then headed for the Randwick Rugby Club for some food and a few beers with the Australian lads. I was just wide-eyed, trying to take it all in. A year or so before I had been finishing my 'A' levels at the Robert Smyth School in Market Harborough and turning out for Wigston and then Leicester seconds and thirds at weekends. Now here I was, supping beer in one of Australia's oldest clubs after beating the Wallabies in Sydney.

I went back to Taupo for the rest of the domestic season and was embarrassed to be greeted like some sort of returning hero. The other guys were mobbing me for bits of stash – free All Black Under-21s gear – and asking me for chapter and verse on how it had been.

The rest of the season passed with me on a high. College Old Boys Marist had a great season, winning the King Country equivalent of New Zealand's Ranfurly Shield – a challenge trophy won by beating the holders on their home ground –

when we defeated Waitete in a match which also saw us win the King Country Championship. We had another good season with King Country itself, too, just missing out on promotion to the first division of the national championships when we lost to Hawkes Bay near the end of the season.

And suddenly, October arrived and it was all over. I could have stayed on for another New Zealand summer, resting my shoulder again, looking to retain my place in the All Black Under-21s and, one day, hoping to progress through the New Zealand system. How close did I come to taking that route? John Hart certainly expected me to do so – it had been a condition of my selection that I was not just some kid over in New Zealand for a holiday. I felt more of a King Country player than a Leicester one. I had a Kiwi girlfriend, a decent job, lots of mates and, now, a foot on the All Black ladder. The sun was shining and Taupo looked great. Back in England, it was the Tigers second team and the wind and the rain at a muddy Welford Road. On the other hand, I had been away for eighteen months and I wanted to get home. Like a lot of Kiwis, Kay wanted to travel so – not without sadness – I booked two flights to Heathrow.

How much did I learn in New Zealand? A huge amount. The whole experience broadened me as a person and helped me grow up. I had barely left school and suddenly I was living as an independent adult on the other side of the world. It was in terms of my rugby education, though, that the real changes came. I might have ended up the same player I am now – though that is not a foregone conclusion – but it would have taken a lot longer. Everyone recognised that the All

Blacks were the kings of the world game, but I had never really considered how they had achieved this. Now I at least had some idea.

It started with the letter from John Albert. Here was a guy trying to poach people from 12,000 miles away in the hope of making his tiny, sheep-field club that little bit more competitive. Meanwhile, Leicester, at the top of the English game and roughly ten miles down the road from my home, had never approached me directly, despite the fact that I was an England regular in my age group. There were none of today's academies and scouting systems. In New Zealand, Todd Blackadder – to take just one contemporary example – had been identified at a very young age as a lad with a great deal of potential and was being looked after accordingly.

Then there was the physicality of Kiwi rugby. A nation that works predominantly outdoors and breeds blokes like the Taupo loggers, or guys who carry 250lb wild boars for miles out of the bush, has to have a head start over a country of office workers, Nintendo addicts and travelling salesmen. In recent times, professionalism has enabled English players to work on their fitness and strength to the point where we can compete and even, say some, overtake our southern hemisphere colleagues. Back in the early nineties, however, Leicester Tigers' matches were really no rougher and tougher than low-grade club rugby with Tihoi.

Additionally, professionalism, by any other name, had already come to New Zealand when I was there. I do not mean simply in cash terms, although the very top players in the big provincial outfits were being paid serious match fees and boot money and found 'jobs' which allowed them to train almost full-time. I am talking about a culture of professionalism that pervaded the major provinces and the national sides.

With the All Black Under-21s, everything we did was serious. Imagine a coach instructs his players to run two laps of a pitch. In England, guys would cut corners on the first lap and cut even more off the second. Those young All Blacks *never* cut the corner; they never even thought of touching the playing surface. The players set themselves weights targets and increased them every day of the tour. They understood about nutrition and the requirement to take care of themselves – and if they did not they were rapidly reminded. There was very little boozing on that tour to Australia. The players were tremendously disciplined and they felt a very personal sense of pride in training as hard as possible and playing well. The expectation of a country, the history of the All Blacks – it all filtered down to us and made the hairs on the back of your neck stand up. I am sure the England boys would have felt a patriotic desire to win, but in New Zealand it was much more than just a game. Losing was not even considered.

Finally, they were helped by excellent coaching. John Hart was years ahead of his English counterparts. He would talk about back-row and back-line moves, running angles and set-piece plays. It was like a foreign language to me. It was much more scientific, more thought out, more professional than anything I had come across before and, I believe, anything in the English game at that time. Analysis of opponents was thorough and taken seriously. Before we faced Western Australia, for instance, Hart watched them play and identified flaws in their No. 8 and moves we could employ to expose him. Leicester did not even employ a full-time director of rugby in 1991.

Interviewers usually say to me, 'You must have learned this move or those tactics in New Zealand.' I definitely benefited from the experience and it shaped the player I became. But it was not a case of ticking off the various skills as I acquired them. It was about exposure to a higher standard of rugby and an insight into what had made New Zealand such a formidable rugby nation.

I am also repeatedly asked, 'Could you have been an All Black?' There is no guarantee I would ever have been selected. They have had some fantastic players down the years and I might well never have made it. I would certainly have been honoured and proud to play for New Zealand had things worked out differently. Representing the All Blacks is massive, bigger than playing for any other country, because of the tradition and the history that goes with it. Ultimately, though, I am glad it never happened. If I was ever going to make it as a full international, I wanted it to be in white, not black.

I was tremendously lucky in my time there, not least because I got the approach from John Albert in the first place. I managed to pack a lot of fairly high-quality rugby into an eighteen-month period. I played twenty-five games for King Country and others with Marist and Tihoi – when, back home, I might have had a couple of runs in the Leicester firsts and a lot of slogging around in the mud with the second and third teams. I could easily have drifted out of rugby, particularly given the few games of any intensity or impor-tance in what was, at that time, a generally meaningless English season. I was lucky, too, that John wrote to me from King

Country, a relative backwater. In Auckland, say, I would probably have sunk without trace. Out in the sticks, I got a shot at provincial competition in the second division – about my level at that time – and, from that, a chance with the All Black Under-21s. I was returning home a lot harder, mentally and physically, and a lot more experienced. The question in my mind, though, as we landed in London, was, 'What happens next?'

CHAPTER THREE

BREAKDOWN AND BREAKTHROUGH

It was late in October 1990 when I arrived back, with a wet English winter – just the sort of thing to make you wish for Taupo's warm spring sun – around the corner. I must have been in people's thoughts at the Tigers because all sorts of wild rumours were circulating about me – I was going to stay in New Zealand and try to play for the All Blacks, I had got married out there and gone native, that sort of thing. For some reason, no one had bothered to call me to find out what was actually going on. It would have been fairly simple. My mum and dad had my number, after all. Instead, I just bowled up at training one Thursday night and got back into it. The season had been underway for six weeks, with a new, paid director of rugby, Tony Russ, in charge, and, unsurprisingly, the reaction to my return was fairly muted: 'Oh, you're back ... Fancy a game Saturday?'

So a few days later I was away with the thirds, thrashing around in the mud against our Saracens counterparts and feeling almost as if my matches against Auckland and the young Wallabies had been a dream. I played a couple of games for the second team, at Moseley and Bath, but I wasn't setting the world on fire with my play – certainly nothing that would have made you think I was a junior All Black. If I am honest, I felt a little unmotivated, wondering what the hell I was doing back in England in the cold and the rain when I could have been enjoying that Kiwi sunshine and looking forward to the next season at King Country. Although Leicester was a big club, in those days things were still fairly amateurish in comparison to what I had experienced in New Zealand. It was clear, too, that people there were in awe of New Zealand rugby.

That first training session was a classic case in point, with the third team coach almost deferring to me. 'You've played for King Country, haven't you?' he said. 'Is Mr Meads still there?'

'Colin?' I said. 'Yeah, he's still there.'

'Colin?' he said, recoiling in horror. 'I wouldn't call him Colin. I'd call him Sir or Mr Meads.'

As we went through a few drills, he would stop and turn to me. 'Is this how they do it over there?' he would say. I felt a bit bemused and embarrassed by his questions, but the answer was, 'No, it wasn't.'

The Kiwis practised playing. They kept running until they were tackled. Then they rucked the ball back and started again. It was not brain surgery, but it was well executed and well thought-out. A lot of what we did in English rugby at that point was shambolic and consisted of running through training-ground drills which bore little or no relation to what goes on in games. Coaches did things because they had been told to do them themselves as youngsters, or because they thought they looked or sounded right. They never seemed to stop to think whether these were actually the right things to do. For instance, there was the famous 'arrowhead drill'. You ran up the field together with a guy in the middle holding the ball and everyone else strung out in two lines on either side of him. He would pass the ball either left or right, the receiver would move to the front and the whole process would continue until someone died of boredom. When do you ever see this happen in a game? And when do you ever see players running up the field bent double? That was something else we did in training, but it was absolutely pointless and the schoolmaster mentality of many of the coaches meant they would rarely listen to opinions or suggestions.

We won that second-team match at Bath, but the firsts had lost their corresponding fixture at Welford Road and Alex Gissing, one of the starting second rows, had hurt his ankle in the game. That ruled him out of the following week's game, a cup match, again at Bath. The choice was between me and an older player called Malcolm Foulkes-Arnold, a guy I had watched in action for Leicester ten years before. They bravely went for youth over experience. However, a number of first-choice players, including Rory Underwood and Neil Back, who, despite being very young, was firmly established as a highly talented flanker, had pulled out through injury. This meant we weren't given much of a chance against a Bath side that was packed with internationals and the top team in the country at that point. The Rec, particularly in those days, was about as far removed from the dry, fast, pumice-based pitch at Taupo as you could get. Lying close to the level of the nearby River Avon as it does, it can get very wet and that Saturday it was an absolute bog. By today's standards, very little rugby was played in the game, but we did manage to beat them.

I must have done reasonably well. There was a little tea room at the ground, where the players congregated post-match, and I was standing there chatting to my dad when their coach, Jack Rowell, came through. I didn't really know who he was at that point, but I remember him saying, out of the side of his mouth, in his 'Jack' sort of way, 'I'm glad you didn't play last week.' Because our result was an upset, the papers made quite a lot of it and a few of them gave me good reviews, though probably only because the New Zealand angle and the fact that I was the new guy in the team gave them something to write about.

So, fairly rapidly, I had gone from pitching up at training and playing for the thirds to being written about in the national press. If ever a player had had a breakthrough game, then that Bath encounter was it. I had put myself in the senior rugby picture and showed I could handle myself at that level. Maybe things were looking up. However, there was a substantial cloud on the horizon.

My sub-luxing left shoulder had still not been diagnosed and by the time that Bath game came around it was dislocating three or four times a match. Not really knowing what was happening, I would just stop, pop it back in, and carry on playing. Over a period, this obviously does serious damage. In the short term, it leaves your shoulder, and therefore your arm, weak, and as it drags on, a residual soreness develops, too. With hindsight, I should have stopped playing immediately and worked on rehabilitating the muscles of the rotator cuff – the subscapularis, the supraspinatus, the infraspinatus and the teres minor – which give the shoulder its stability. Then it would either have held up for eighty minutes or I could have made the decision to have an operation. Unfortunately, at that stage I didn't know a teres minor from a Morris Minor. The club physiotherapist was no authority on shoulders either, diagnosing the injury as a tendon problem. All it needed was taping up, he said. I was dubious – it didn't feel like the tendon trouble I had had before and I told him so – but he was the expert, and whenever I went back to him the response was always the same: tendon and tape. Ultimately, I bowed to his greater knowledge, but it was a frustrating and confusing time for me: they would tape me up, the shoulder would come out, I would miss the next week's game with sore-ness, and so it went on.

The week after the Bath game, I was selected for the Midlands in the old Divisional Championships. I think my Kiwi experiences had helped to open the door. I was known in the England 'system', having played as a youngster, but had obviously disappeared for a couple of seasons. Now I was back and people seemed to assume that the fact that I had played in New Zealand meant I must be good. The divisional setup was supposed to be a stepping stone between first-team club rugby and the international game, and these were poten-tially competitive games, featuring the cream of the country's players in action.

The shoulder was sore, though, so I sat out the first match, against the South West at Moseley, with Tim Rodber taking my place in the second row. I did play the following week against London, who were the strongest of the divisions, with lots of England players in their ranks. Their first-choice pack was international quality, featuring guys such as Jason Leonard, Brian Moore, Jeff Probyn, Paul Ackford, Mickey Skinner, Peter

Winterbottom and Dean Ryan. Their backs were fairly useful too, with Will Carling, Rob Andrew and Simon Halliday among them. Though the Midlands XV was not quite that strong, we still had some good performers in our team. Rupert Moon was at No. 9, Bayfield and Richards were in the pack, with Gary Rees and John Wells alongside them and some good, younger and lesser-known players, like Stuart Potter, made up the side. We went down there and gave London a real fright, getting ahead early on. Moon, who would later play for Wales and was, in my opinion, perhaps the best all-round scrum-half in the country at the time, played brilliantly; Deano was his usual excellent self; and Potts made some good breaks. Despite my injury, I performed pretty well, managing to steal a line-out ball or two off Paul Ackford, but the Londoners were bigger, stronger and more skilful than us and eventually ground us down to win the game.

I was knackered the following week as the whole infuriating process repeated itself – play a game, miss a game, play, miss – and the physio still refused to accept I had a serious problem. Towards Christmas, Leicester played Coventry and my shoulder was really bad. I lasted about twenty-five minutes and it must have sub-luxed six times. From then on, I missed most of the rest of the season. I appeared a couple of times for the club, but was injured for the big Leicester versus Barbarians game at Christmas, for the match where Wasps knocked us out of the cup and for other big Tigers fixtures. This was deeply annoying. I had just about established myself as the leading front-jumping, line-out player at the club, but I was unable to capitalise on the fact.

My lucky break was to be selected for the Midlands Under-

2Is side for a game in the south, right near the end of the season. After a series of sub-luxes, I had to come off, and I was sitting miserably in the changing room thinking about putting the shoulder back in when the host club's physio walked in. He took one look at me and told me what was going on. 'No, mate,' I said. 'It's just this tendon problem I've got. It'll be fine – it will clunk back in a minute.'

'No, it's not,' he said. 'It's a dislocation. I'm a lecturer in this sort of injury. Do you mind taking your shirt off so I can take a photo of that for my course?'

'No,' I said. 'Do whatever you want.'

Then I looked down at my chest and noticed this strange bulge below my collar bone, where the shoulder had shot forwards. It was the first time I had seen it like that – previously I had popped it back while I had my shirt on. 'Oh,' I thought. 'Maybe that *is* a problem!'

I was driven down to the Accident and Emergency unit at the local hospital where they X-rayed me and then sat me in a cubicle. Apparently, the doctor had to get on the phone to a colleague asking how to put a shoulder back in. By this time, having been dislocated for so long, it had become seriously painful, but fortunately it shot back in by itself as I lay down on the bed. A few days later I was in Nottingham showing my X-rays to a specialist called Angus Wallace. I explained the 'tendon theory' as it had been told to me. Angus, looking at the X-ray up on his screen, said, 'No, we'll get you in on Tuesday and operate.'

I felt a mixture of apprehension and relief. No one likes surgery, but at least I had finally found a guy who seemed to know what he was talking about. Within a few days I found myself in a ward in an NHS orthopaedic hospital. That was quite an experience. Most of the other patients were getting their hips and knees replaced, so there were five pensioners, me and another young lad.

'Hello, mate,' he said, as I walked in, presumably pleased to see someone else on the right side of eighty in there. I introduced myself, he did the same and then he ran through the names of the old blokes. 'That's Frank,' he said. 'And that's Frank over there. He's Frank, as well, and so's he. And him over there, he's Frank.' It's the honest truth. There was me, this lad — whose name I have forgotten — and five Franks.

The op was pretty unpleasant. I was in theatre for about two hours and when I came round I felt awful. I must have looked a right state. Kay came up to visit me the next day and was genuinely upset to see me. I was in a lot of pain from where they had sliced a six-inch incision to get at the joint and my mouth was horribly dry. I remember lying there, half-unconscious from the anaesthetic, groaning and vomiting as they tried to get me to take some water. I had a tube in the joint to drain away the pus and blood into a little bottle, though it was nothing to what some of the Franks had — they looked like they had homebrew kits stuck to them. One of them had dreadful wind. He used to burp all day and actually woke me up one night with his backside going. It was an incredible noise that sounded like the roof was coming down.

In a funny way, the saga of my shoulder had quite a major impact on my career. Because the surgeon didn't get his hands on me until April, I had to spend the summer recuperating. Had the operation been carried out the previous December, when one might reasonably expect the correct diagnosis to have been made, I would have missed the rest of our season and almost certainly have gone back out to New Zealand to try to play some part with King Country. That had certainly been my intention and, who knows, I might have ended up staying out there for good. As it was, I was out of action until August so I stayed put in England.

In 1991–92, the Tigers were a bit of a mixed bag. Our back row – Dean Richards, John Wells and Neil Back – was the strongest in the country, but elsewhere guys who had been part of Leicester's 1987 league-winning side were coming to the end of their careers and we finished mid-table as Bath claimed the title. Meanwhile, Backy and I both made it to England B and I played against the French and the Italian second strings, having missed the first couple of games because of concussion. I was then due to tour New Zealand with the B team over the summer, but, unbelievably, damaged my shoulder again in training at the end of the season. Obviously, I was upset and annoyed, but I'm not one to mope and I had the club refer me to Angus Wallace again. He was a renowned surgeon and he had done a good job on me first time around. However, he could have been the best in Europe, or the universe, and it would have made no difference, because I had undergone next to no rehabilitation after he had sewn me back up.

The operation had involved a major cut through the muscles of my shoulder. Then I had spent six weeks with my arm in a sling. When I finally came out of the sling, my shoulder and arm were obviously very weak. It was important for me to get working on it immediately, and in the right way, to build up the strength of the area that protects the joint. It's actually a fairly simple process and a routine part of any player's workload now, whether injured or fit. What you do is use heavy rubber bands attached to wall bars, pulling against them in various constant movements to work on the muscles of the rotator cuff. No one really explained that to me, though. To be fair to the club physio, he did draw me a diagram of some self-build, Heath Robinson contraption with paint tins and pulleys in various positions. It would have worked, I think, but who on earth is going to go home and set that up in their garage? I can't imagine why he didn't direct me to one of the gyms in Leicester. All I really needed was a little cable cross machine, but I was pretty much left to my own devices. Now I had to undergo the surgery all over again; this time, with a proper rehabilitation programme mapped out for me afterwards.

Looking back, I'm pretty angry about what happened. I had two operations and lost a season's rugby through being messed around by people who failed to diagnose me. I had suspected early on it was something serious, but no one would listen and I spent weeks being taped up to no effect. Had it been left to fester, it would have got even worse the following year and who knows how I would have finished up? It could have ended my career. It would certainly have slowed it down. This was all typical of the amateur nature of English club rugby, even at the highest level, back then. One lesson I learned from this whole episode, which I always pass on to younger players, is that if you have a persistent injury you need to seek specialist help. Speak to your club physio or doctor and if you aren't happy with their response, go and see a consultant like Angus Wallace, who knows exactly what he is talking about.

It can be hard to track them down. The medical world, I have found over the years, is full of people with big egos. They are always right, the other bloke is always wrong. Talk to nine different people and you can get nine different opinions. To an extent, that goes with the territory. Sports-injury medicine isn't necessarily an exact science and different people respond differently to treatments and heal at different rates. But what you rarely get is a guy admitting he doesn't really know what's wrong with you. They don't want to be seen not to know and they don't want to refer you to anyone else. Doctors don't like physiotherapists, physios don't like doctors, no one likes chiropractors – and you get caught in the middle of it. Thankfully, modern standards of physiotherapy and medical care are very high, particularly with England. All injuries are treated thoroughly, with a lot of time and care spent on injury prevention, so it's not just about reacting to problems once they have occurred.

As the 1992–93 season got underway, Leicester started to develop a pack which would go on to dominate English club rugby for almost a decade. Richard Cockerill, an abrasive, aggressive twenty-one-year-old hooker, joined us from Coventry. Graham Rowntree, also twenty-one, came in on the loose-head and Darren Garforth, a scaffolder from Nuneaton in his mid-twenties, established himself as one of the best tight-heads around. I was twenty-two, my second-row partner Matt Poole and Neil Back were twenty-three. Dean and John were the only guys pushing thirty. Suddenly, we had a young, exciting group of forwards, and with guys such as Rory and

Tony Underwood, Stuart Potter and John Liley in our back line we began to look as though we might at last challenge Bath for the league title.

We played England in a celebration game for the centenary of the Welford Road ground at the start of the season. I was still recovering from my second lot of surgery, so I missed the match. However, it made for good viewing, with Leicester getting a push on against the England pack at one point and Cocker alternating between getting all feisty with Brian Moore one minute and sticking his tongue out at him the next. It was all good stuff. We were cocky and, within reason, that's a good thing in a rugby team. As the season unfolded we put together some good results and myself and Neil Back were again called up to England B.

The B team and England used to meet up at the Stoop to train on Wednesday nights. We had a fairly young bunch of forwards – myself, Backy and Ben Clarke were in our early twenties, for instance – with a couple of older heads like Graham Dawe, the Cornish hooker who had played ahead of Brian Moore on occasion, adding experience. It was around the end of that great England pack – Probyn, Skinner, Teague, Winterbottom, Dooley, Moore – but lots of the great names were still there. The game was changing and more athletic packs were starting to spring up, but in the tight these guys were among the best there have been. They had taken England to the brink of a World Cup victory a couple of years earlier, dominating the Wallaby eight, and they were determined not to yield to us. The first time we went down to train with them they intimidated us a little and a few of the younger guys took a bit of a step back. As the season wore on, though, we started to give it back to them a bit, building a real rivalry. Dawe and Moore had to be separated at one stage and there was plenty of niggle as we ran through live line-outs and scrummages against them. I thought it was brilliant, almost better than the actual England B games, because we were taking on a far better set of forwards and really testing ourselves.

That autumn, South Africa had toured. I had no expectations of being selected, so I was not disappointed, and Wade Dooley and Martin Bayfield played in the second row. Nothing changed for the Six Nations. France were first up, trying to stop a third consecutive English Grand Slam. The day before that game, I was up in Leicester with the B team, preparing to play France B that night at Welford Road. We had trained in the morning and were just about to have a pre-lunch meeting in John Hall's room (he was captain) when Peter Rossborough, the B-team manager, pulled me to one side. He said he had just had word from London that Wade Dooley was a slight injury doubt with a thigh strain. They wanted me to head down there to cover for him. I thought that was a bit strange. It was less than twenty-four hours to kick-off. By then, normally, you're either fit or you're not. I headed off to the team meeting, John Hall scowling at me because I was late, and, feeling self-conscious with all the guys' eyes on me, stammered out the immortally dull words: 'Er, lads ... I've got to go to Twickenham.'

I think Rossborough must have known I was going to play, but I guess he wanted me to get down there and hear it officially. It certainly hadn't dawned on me at that stage. At that age, I was quite young in some ways, perhaps a bit naïve and not particularly self-confident, so it was daunting enough just to be asked to travel down. I didn't know the senior England team very well. I had been to Lanzarote with the squad in 1992, along with a few other younger players, more for them to train against than anything. Nowadays, guys of twenty-two and younger, well-prepared by professionalism, come into the England setup with all the poise and assurance of veterans. The more experienced members take care to break them into the squad and are, basically, nice to them. Back then the capped players took the opposite view: he's a young lad – let's get stuck into him. The mickey-taking was lethal if you said the wrong thing, so you tended to shut up, keep your head down and try not to be noticed. We were always very aware of the pecking order.

In a bit of a daze, I nipped home to get my car and then started driving down. I had often been to the Petersham Hotel, Richmond, where the England team were based, so I knew where I was going and was able to spend time turning things over in my head. I slowly started to twig that maybe I would be playing. There was the outside possibility that they were planning a late fitness test on Wade, but if so, they were pushing it. He was either fit or he wasn't and it seemed pretty likely that he wasn't. I started trying to prepare myself mentally for the match. I was obviously nervous. Apart from anything, I had never really trained with the senior side, only against them. More importantly, we were playing France in the opening game of the Five Nations. It was a big, big game, against a very tough side with one of the best packs in the world.

As soon as I arrived I bumped into Kevin Murphy, the physiotherapist. He was quick to stick out his hand. I asked him what was going on and he realised I had heard nothing official. He knew it was not really up to him to break the news to me. Instead, he gave me a bit of a nod — you're playing, mate, but I haven't told you — and then Geoff Cooke, the England manager, came over and told me what I already knew. In a *Boy's Own* story, I would have felt immensely proud, thrilled and exhilarated, and those feelings were definitely in there somewhere. The main thing running through my head, though, was what the hell the line-out calls were. The first thing on everyone else's mind, however, seemed to be whether I had a DJ for the following night's post-match dinner. I didn't even own one at the time, so without further ado we headed off to a hire shop in Sunbury, so I could rent an outfit. Friday afternoon was free time and the players had all gone out on various jaunts. They started straggling back in the early evening. One or two of the guys had been planning to go to the cinema in Richmond, but Moore insisted on the forwards heading off to a local sports hall to do a little line-out work. It didn't take long. The line-out was much less complicated in those days. There was no lifting, you marked man-for-man, but you might experiment with a different number in the line. There were only two or three different combinations and calls to remember, as opposed to maybe ten now. Along with the line-outs, we ran through some penalty moves that I never, ever saw them use and then trooped back to the hotel.

I had been put in a tiny room right at the top of the building. I thought I might have trouble sleeping, but I went out like a light. Wade had stayed down — it was his last season so he would have wanted to stick around — and he came up to see me in the morning to calm me down and pass on a few tips about the French. As he sat there, saying so-and-so was prone to this and such-and-such was known for that, it all went a bit over my head as the nerves started to build. There was a meeting for the forwards in Brian Moore's room a little later. I made sure I was there early, which Mooreo liked, and while we waited for the other guys to show up, he started chatting with me about his own debut, just trying to put me at ease. Playing for England then was an even bigger step up than it is today. Say you were used to playing at the old Sale, in front of a couple of hundred people, and then suddenly you're playing for England and there are 60,000 watching you. It's a massive difference, although at least Leicester were regularly attracting crowds over 10,000 and I had played in front of some big houses in Australia and New Zealand. Nevertheless, I understood where Brian was coming from. 'You're going to be terrified out there for the first five or ten minutes,' he said. 'But then you'll realise it's just another game of rugby, you'll find you are doing OK and you'll realise you can handle it.' That was an excellent confidence booster for me.

I remember getting to the game outside the old West Stand at Twickenham and climbing off the team bus alongside Will Carling, Rory Underwood and Rob Andrew, with hundreds of England fans milling around, slapping their backs as they walked by. My back went pretty much unslapped though – I was just some bloke they didn't really know and I was feeling a bit out of place and overawed. That was the right way for me to feel, though, rather than, 'Yes, this is me, I belong here.' It would probably have been worse if I had been selected to play in my own right. I would have had two weeks of media pressure, of thinking about it, and I would certainly have been more nervous. In fact, apart from the complete lack of training or preparation with the team, it was not a bad way to make your debut. Being a late replacement meant there really wasn't any pressure on me. In the early nineties, forwards didn't have to think too hard about the game. You weren't going to find yourself out on the wing and you didn't have to worry about defensive patterns, so no one really expected me to do anything more than a holding job. If I worked hard, caught a bit of line-out ball and got to the rucks and mauls, I would have done well. If I smashed a few people along the way, that would have constituted really putting myself about and eyebrows would have been raised approvingly. Again, that is in stark contrast to England 2003, because new players have to be able to do their job to international standard wherever they play. There are no hiding places now.

As the game approached, the changing room was a businesslike place with little banter or joking and sitting there felt a bit weird. I was used to being a part of the B team and we drew much of our spirit from our rivalry with, and dislike of, the senior team. Of course, we all wanted to play for them and if anyone was called up, as the likes of Ben Clarke, Ian Hunter, Tony Underwood and Stuart Barnes had been, we would congratulate them. It was just slightly strange when it happened to you. Their last home game had been against South Africa and, for some reason, they were handing out brand-new Springbok shirts – they must have swapped a load with them. 'Get Johnno one,' said Will, which I thought was nice of him.

My dad probably has the match tape at home somewhere,

but I have never watched it. I must ask him to dig it out, because I reckon it would make amusing viewing, looking at how we used to play and looking, too, at my hairstyle. I had some kind of big, bouffant mop stuck on my head, and had been planning a haircut in Leicester the afternoon before, but events had overtaken me. I remember running out on to the pitch feeling anxious, just wanting the kick-off. I stood there for the anthem – odd, I was used to watching this on TV and now I was actually in the line-up – and then we were off.

France got ahead early, attacking us from the off and scoring two tries through Philippe Saint-André. This was quite shocking, given that England had not lost since 1990 in a championship game. There was no panic in the team, though. We just met under the posts and Will calmly talked about what we needed to do. I was impressed with the senior guys' level of discipline and organisation. We got back into the match after Ian Hunter followed up a kick which rebounded off the upright to score but, unfortunately, the whole of the middle of the match is a blur. I suffered a concussion early on, clashing heads with the prop, Laurent Seigne, in a ruck. You stayed on the pitch in those days and I remember groggily coming round, believing I was watching the match on TV. Of course, the trouble was that with concussion you lose your short-term memory, so I kept thinking the same thing over and over again: 'Good game ... Oh no, I'm actually in it ... Good game ... Oh no ...' You manage to get by on auto-pilot, not realising you are concussed until you clear your head, but with twenty minutes to go, I finally came to.

I was jumping against Abdelatif Benazzi, normally a back rower, a No. 8 or a blind-side flanker. He was a very athletic guy, they had been throwing quite a few short line-outs and he won quite a bit of ball against me. His partner, Olivier Roumat, was having a good game against Martin Bayfield, too. In fact, so much so that, on our own throw, they eventually had to turn to me. Benazzi was good at jumping for his own ball, but was not so used to competing for the opposition's, so I started to win a few. We ended up taking the match by just a point, but everyone was disappointed with the way we had played. It had not been a vintage performance – it was one of those horrible, grey, late January/early February Twickenham days where the game never really gets going – but England had won. I was presented with my cap at the dinner that night. Although we were the victors the atmosphere was subdued. The team set itself high standards and they felt they had fallen short.

Back at home on the Sunday, I read through the papers. A few of the journos seemed to think I had played OK and, once again, there was that sense of breakthrough. In the space of three days, I had gone from being a club player, who had some potential, to playing for England. I remember driving to work on Monday, going up quite a narrow street with cars parked on either side. It was the kind of irritating road where you have to pull in to let people through, just hoping others will do the same for you, and as I squeezed past a van, the driver stared at me and started winding his window down. 'Here we go,' I thought. I wound my window down and waited for a load of abuse. 'Well played on Saturday, mate,' he said.

'Oh, thank you very much,' I replied, the wind completely taken out of my sails.

In some ways, England rugby was a bigger thing then than

it is now. The national team was going for a third Grand Slam in a row, matches were live on terrestrial TV on Saturday afternoons and, with less televised football and no club rugby on the box, everyone seemed to watch it. When I got to work, one of the bank's directors called to congratulate me, other people wanted to talk about the match and the enormity of it began to hit me. A decade on, it is difficult to remember exactly how I felt, but I think the whole thing was a bit of a haze. It happened so quickly, and I was so conscious of trying to do the best I could, that I never really got the chance to sit back and take it all in. I was pleased and proud, obviously, but careful not to get too far ahead of myself. I knew Wade Dooley would return for the next match, against Wales in Cardiff.

Back at Leicester, our season finished well, with a cup final against Quins fair reward for our hard work. It was a Tigers cup tradition that the side would leave on the morning of the match, rather than travelling down the night before. I arrived at the ground at 9.10a.m. – for a 9.15a.m. departure – to find the bus going the other way. By the time I had nego-tiated Leicester's one-way system and stopped at a few sets of traffic lights, they had gone. I headed for the Post House Hotel, where all the supporters were, thinking maybe they would head there to pick me up. Unfortunately, at this point no one had actually noticed I was not on the bus.

I was told they were heading down the M40, though in fact they used the MI, so I shot down there in my Sierra, driving like a nutter with one eye on my petrol gauge, which was getting a bit low. There were no services on the M40, so I had to pull off the motorway and trawl through rural

Oxfordshire looking for a petrol station. Once I had filled up, I found I couldn't get back on to the M40 southbound. Into Oxford I headed, trying to read a map and drive through a city centre crowded with shoppers at the same time, with the biggest game of the club season just a few hours away. It was the stuff of nightmares. Eventually, I found my way on to an A road which joined the motorway further south and finally met up with the boys at the team hotel. They were certainly happy to see me, but mainly so they could take the mickey.

It wasn't a great way to prepare for a cup final, but we beat a good Quins side – it was Peter Winterbottom's last game for them and Will Carling and Jason Leonard also played – and I scored the winning try from a tap penalty move that had been handed down through the generations at Leicester and which I have never seen work before or since. This was a major victory for us, our first silverware since the league title five years before.

That summer, I would achieve the ultimate in British rugby when I flew down to New Zealand to join the touring Lions as a replacement for Wade Dooley. It was a fantastic honour, if an ultimately disappointing trip, and gave me the feeling, finally, that I had arrived.

The next season, home and away fixtures were introduced in the league for the first time. For the first time, too, we offered Bath a serious challenge for the title. We beat them at home in a mud bath, one of those old-fashioned games which would send you to sleep in two minutes if you watched it now, where we mauled them to pieces – and not even dynamic mauling – all afternoon. It was the kind of match which led to all those complaints about Leicester being a boring side, who could only play through their forwards. Apart from the fact that this was not true – we had some good three-quarters who scored some great tries in the early to mid-nineties – we were just playing to our strengths. Bath had the country's top backs so they tried to play through the back line, but a few years earlier, when they had had one of English rugby's more dominant packs, they, too, had been a forward-orientated team. We lost in the return match, in another mud bath, and Bath went on to win the championship and also to beat us in the cup final.

Internationally, the England team changed a fair bit. Winterbottom and Dooley had both retired after the 1993 Lions tour, Jeff Probyn had also called it quits and Jonathan Webb was gone, while Kyran Bracken and Jon Callard made their debuts against New Zealand in the autumn of 1993, the match in which I won my second cap. I had suddenly gone from being the new kid on the block to having played three Test matches, two of them for the Lions against New Zealand. While I was relatively inexperienced, I guess my selection wasn't that unexpected. I played alongside Ollie Redman, with Bayfield injured, and we beat the Blacks 15–9. It was a typical England win of that period: a strong forward performance based on aggression and attrition, but no tries.

There were rumblings about the non-selection of Neil Back at open-side flanker. Backy was, by a distance, the best pure open-side in the country, but Geoff Cooke had gone for the first of those big, powerful back-row combinations, with Ben Clarke at 7, Dean Richards at 8 and Tim Rodber at 6. The choice reflected our fairly limited game plan. We didn't really look to move the ball wider than Jerry Guscott, so continuity of the sort that a player like Back could offer was not such an issue. Ben and Tim probably had more sheer speed over the ground than Backy, but they didn't have his guile, his ability to get down, snaffle ball and get up quickly, or his phenomenal ability to operate at a high work-rate all game. Instead, they were used as big ball-carriers, bashing through the New Zealand defence to make yards for us. Alongside them, Dean did the dirty work in the rucks and mauls, securing and winning ball and slowing the opposition ball down. You couldn't play that combination now, where attacking teams need quick turnover ball to enable them to get around well-marshalled defences, but it worked for that time, with all three guys playing very well.

Tony Underwood had had our best chance of a score, but just couldn't get home. However, we didn't care. Wins against the All Blacks are rare and, while this was a transitional Kiwi side, it still featured some very good players and we were delighted. They had thrashed Scotland the week before, putting a hell of a lot of points on them. Jeff Wilson had made his debut then, kicking lots of points, but he had a bad day with the boot against us and, in the end, that probably made the difference. The Blacks, I think, thought we were a bit cocky in victory, a feeling probably exacerbated by some personal antipathies left hanging over from the Lions tour. They didn't like losing, particularly to us, and said we were gloaters when we won. In fact, that continues to this day, with Andrew Mehrtens claiming in 2003 that we were 'pr**ks to lose to', although I don't know how he knew, because he'd never lost to us!

The 1994 Five Nations championship came off the back of that All Black win and I think we were a little over-confident. We almost paid the price in our first game, with Scotland coming close to beating us after we had made a great start. In the end, it was down to Jon Callard to put us clear with a late penalty. Dean Richards was out with a dislocated elbow and Backy made his long-awaited debut in a re-jigged back row. I felt sorry for him. His arrival on the international scene was almost the exact opposite to mine. There had been a long and heated debate around the country about his non-selection and the pressure on him was huge. It would have been almost impossible for anyone to live up to the expectations, but he played well and was picked again in the following match, against Ireland at Twickenham. However, instead of using his continuity skills to keep us going forward, we relied on Rob Andrew's boot to gain territory. The Irish were not great, but we were worse. We never really got going and lost at home in the championship for the first time in years – my first defeat in an England shirt. I think we missed Dean, one of the great talismans of the team. When we were on the back foot, he would perhaps have been able to rally us and change the course of the match. For the following game, away at the Parc des Princes in France, Backy, along with Bracken, was dropped, without having done anything wrong.

For many of us, it was our first senior trip to Paris and the French were very pumped up. Despite this we won, playing doggedly without ever coming close to dominating them and having to hang on towards the end. Again, we failed to score a try – three games, two wins and a loss and all our points from the boot. This was disappointing, and it was something we were all conscious of, but the days of us scoring 40 or more points in internationals were still a few years off. Wales were going for the Grand Slam when they came to Twickenham. Dean came back into the team and we had the Clarke, Rodber, Deano back row together for the first time since the New Zealand victory. We played well, finally scoring a couple of tries, and, although they came back at the end to score one of their own, we were worthy winners. It gave everyone a buzz – the Welsh were champions, but we had kept them from winning a Grand Slam at Twickenham, which would have been horrible.

At that stage, Jack Rowell took over from Geoff Cooke. Geoff had turned England from an under-performing nation into World Cup finalists and Grand Slam winners, and he needs to take some of the credit for laying the foundations of the successful, modern England side. Where Geoff had been a fairly straight-talker, Jack was a little more acerbic, but the changeover was fairly seamless and in the summer of 1994, he took us on tour to South Africa.

It was an eye-opening trip. England had not been there for a decade and we knew very little about their top players. We went out there as perhaps the northern hemisphere's strongest side, a team which could have won the Grand Slam that year. Despite the historical superiority of Springbok sides, we were fairly confident, but we came up against a bunch of guys who were playing rugby at a level above anything in Europe. We lost our first three games, against the provincial sides from Free State, Natal and Transvaal, and we were also beaten by South Africa A. We managed to defeat Western Transvaal, our only victory in the pre-international games. That match saw another of my concussions, when I was knocked out by Johan le Roux. He later went on to infamy and a nineteen-month ban for biting Sean Fitzpatrick's ear, but no one seemed to give a monkey's when he nearly took my head off.

The concussion ruled me out of the Test, and the rest of the tour, so I watched from the stands at Loftus Versfeld in the Afrikaners' rugby heartland. The Springboks were a genuinely great side – they were headed towards a World Cup victory the next year – and we feared a hiding, but they must have looked at our performances in the earlier games and become over-confident. Our guys, with their backs against the wall, played brilliantly. Deano really taught the Boks a lesson in the arts of tight loose play, Rob Andrew controlled things well from stand-off and Tim Rodber had a stormer. It was almost over by half-time. The home crowd, normally very boisterous and vociferous, was in shock and went very quiet, even as South Africa came back at us in the second half. It was a fantastic win for the squad, but sitting in the stands was no substitute for playing. The Boks came back to win the second Test, though I had flown home soon after the first. I had the option to stay and watch, but I didn't want to feel like a tourist, just hanging around or going boozing. I was also conscious that I ought to get back to work. The bank was fantastic in giving me the time off that I needed and I was keen not to abuse that trust.

As I say, the South Africa tour had been a revelation: it was like our soccer Premiership out there, a massive game played on great pitches, in fantastic stadiums in front of huge, wildly enthusiastic crowds. It was almost a different sport – more speed, more excitement and more tries – and it was also professional in all but name. We watched that year's Super Ten final at Durban, when Natal played Queensland the week before they played us. I realised, for the first time, what an international provincial championship could be like. It just couldn't be compared to our Courage League back home. When we played Transvaal, they showed phenomenal pace, precision and physicality and it was clear these guys didn't work behind desks during the week. It was no big secret that by this stage they were being paid, albeit in breach of international rules, and a number of our guys were talking about getting contracts to play out there. I could see that English rugby had to change – and sooner rather than later. We needed to get as big and fit and well drilled as they were or the gap between us was going to get ever wider. To do that, we needed a professional game. The crowds and the razzamatazz in South Africa had convinced me that it was possible, though I had no idea it was so close. Almost as soon as we arrived home, you could sense things were starting to change. There was more sponsorship money around and it was starting to trickle down to guys like myself, not just staying with the superstars.

The 1994–95 season was a big one for Leicester and for England. Domestically, the championship was once again really down to us or Bath. We managed to get a draw at their place just after Christmas. Tony Underwood, who was living in London, had been caught in horrendous traffic on the M4 and didn't get there until half-time. In his absence, we had played the young scrum-half Jamie Hamilton on the wing. We thought about bringing Tony on for the second half, but Dean, angry at Tony's late arrival, would have none of it. His decision was vindicated when 'The Baby' – Jamie, still very fresh-faced, looked about twelve at the time – scored the equalising try. It was the first time in some years that we had come away from the Rec with any points at all, and when we beat them in April at home the title was almost in the bag. In World Cup year, though, there was an agreement that international players could appear in only a couple of matches in the last month of the league, so I sat out the clincher, our defeat of Bristol at Welford Road. Watching from the stands upset me a bit: I had started almost every game that season and to miss the one in which we were actually crowned champions was annoying. It was the first time the Tigers had won the league for seven years, finally breaking Bath's dominance as we had threatened to do for a couple of seasons. Things were looking good and we had plenty of youth in the team, whereas Bath's squad was slightly older.

Internationally, we had a busy calendar, starting with a strange autumn build-up, which involved matches against Romania and Canada. Not surprisingly, we scored a lot of points against both of them, but the matches didn't really compare with the annual November clashes with Australia and South Africa we have now. However, we had targeted a Five Nations Grand Slam to send ourselves off to the World Cup in the best possible way. Our win in South Africa, and the way we had beaten Wales in the crunch game at the end of the previous campaign, had given us a lot of confidence, so we thought we could achieve it. Additionally, in the autumn Mike Catt had come into the side at full-back and was giving us a lot of attacking options that had been missing with previous 15s, like Jon Callard.

Our first game, in Dublin, was the windiest I have ever

known. We could barely stand up straight during the anthems. We played into it in the first half and had no choice but to play quick and direct; there was no point kicking for territory. We won well, tearing into the Irish from the start. Deano mauled them to death and Will Carling, Tony Underwood and Ben Clarke all scored tries. Will had been under a bit of pressure ahead of that game, but he had responded with one of his best games in an England shirt. I had tweaked my hamstring ahead of the game, but came through OK, hobbling a bit towards the end, with Steve Ojomoh about to replace me when the whistle went.

Next, we faced a French side which had recently beaten New Zealand in Auckland and South Africa in Johannesburg – two tough and very rare feats. However, they had not beaten England anywhere since Will Carling's first cap in 1988 at the Parc, and we were determined to keep our run going. Mooreo had stirred things up nicely ahead of the match, giving the press that infamous line: 'Playing the French is like playing fifteen Eric Cantonas – brilliant but brutal.' All good wind-up stuff, with the papers immediately nick-naming the match *Le Crunch*. Again, we mauled them all over the pitch, but it was by no means a forwards-led victory. Our backs played very well, with a try by Guscott and a brace from Tony Underwood in the final five minutes – one a move straight off the training ground which I thought would never work – giving us a 31–10 win. It was our eighth successive victory over them and the biggest against France since 1914.

Then to Cardiff and the old Arms Park – a stadium with great atmosphere and tremendous singing from the fans when the Welsh got on top, as they had tended to do over the years.

England had won there only once since 1963, but the great days of Welsh rugby were coming to an end and we turned them over, winning 23–9. The match was distinguished by being the first international in which a player received a red card. With the game already won and lost, the Welsh tight-head prop, John Davies, was given his marching orders for stamping on Ben Clarke. The Welsh could not scrummage without a tight-head, but straight substitutions were not allowed. Ieuan Evans asked the ref, Didier Méné, what to do. Méné shrugged his shoulders. Ieuan Evans asked Will Carling whether he had a problem with a prop coming on. Carling said he hadn't. Hemi Taylor, the flanker, then developed a mysterious hamstring injury while standing still. Hugh Williams-Jones was able to come on for Taylor, who jogged off. The International Board were forced to introduce new laws to cope with the situation afterwards. Rory Underwood scored the forty-first and forty-second tries of his England career and Victor Ubogu got the other.

With the odd exception, we have beaten Wales fairly consistently since that point. I feel for their fans. They love their rugby, but they have never quite got over the seventies, when geniuses such as JPR Williams and Gareth Edwards were around and were thrilling the world. The players are under massive pressure to perform to that level and when they do it is never recognised. Rob Howley, for instance, is an all-time great scrum-half, who has scored some cracking tries. He deserves to be mentioned in the same breath as their legends, but he rarely is. Their new provincial system, introduced in 2003, aims to increase the competition and improve the national side that way, but we will have to wait and see.

As we were celebrating our win, we heard the news that Scotland had won in Paris, which meant they would be coming to Twickenham for the Grand Slam. There was plenty of build-up to the match in the press – lots of talk about the 1990 Scottish Grand Slam win – and I felt pretty nervous ahead of it. But it was something of an anti-climactic game – the high point was probably the unpleasant sight of a half-naked Victor Ubogu standing in his jockstrap holding his tattered shorts and waiting for someone to bring on a new pair – which we never looked like losing. We failed to score any tries, but beat them 24–12, with Rob Andrew kicking seven penalties and a drop goal on his way to reaching 317 international points, breaking Jon Webb's England record in the process. Still, a win is a win and when it brings you a Grand Slam you don't care too much about style. I had had something of a dream start to my England Test career, playing in just one losing match to Ireland. The World Cup beckoned.

CHAPTER FOUR

WINDS OF CHANGE

The 1995 Rugby World Cup was a massive turning point in rugby. It was the third World Cup and it took off in a really big way, increasing the sport's global profile hugely as a result. South Africa was a great place to hold the tournament – an exciting, exotic, rugby-mad country with impressive stadiums packed with fans from around the world. The political upheaval created by the end of apartheid gave the whole event added significance. The fact that the host nation went on to win the competition made for a bit of a fairytale ending, too, and those pictures of Nelson Mandela – a black guy in a Springbok shirt – holding the cup with François Pienaar, appeared on TV and in newspapers everywhere. Jonah Lomu burst on to the scene in a big way – unfortunately, mostly at England's expense – and became rugby's first global icon in the process. Live TV coverage, beamed back home at realistic hours, meant millions of Brits tuned in.

The most important thing, though, was the way in which it made everyone realise that rugby could no longer stay amateur. The change had been coming for some time – I had seen the beginnings of it in New Zealand and it had been more explicit still in South Africa the previous year. After the World Cup, though, with all the glitz and glamour, all the

TV exposure and the worldwide interest it had generated, you knew it wasn't just on the way, it was happening in front of you.

We had flown there with reasonable hopes. England had been beaten finalists in 1991 and a number of players were left from that team – Leonard, Moore, Carling, Guscott, Andrew and Rory Underwood – with some good younger guys in there, too. However, we didn't start too well. In fact, we could have lost to Argentina in our opener and weren't that impressive against Italy. We only really seemed to get going when we picked a young side with some second-string guys to play Samoa in our last pool game. They are always a wild-card outfit, hard-tackling and pacey and full of guys who play their rugby in New Zealand, and there was potential for an upset. There were four Tigers in the pack: Dean Richards, back after being out with injury, Neil Back, Graham Rowntree and myself. I remember Backy saying before kick-off, 'Come on lads, let's show everybody what Leicester forwards can do!'

Basically, the answer seemed to be, er, limp off. By the final whistle of a fast and loose game, I was the only one of us left on the pitch, as we suffered a bizarre number of injuries. Brian Moore and Kyran Bracken ended the match playing as flankers, but we had won.

Our spirits were high. Our weakest team had secured our best win and we were off to the quarter-final as pool winners, where we would face the world champion Wallabies, who had finished second in their group after losing to the Boks. We stayed in Johannesburg, at altitude, only flying down to Cape Town for the game, which was ridiculous. We should have been based near the ground to minimise the hassle and time-wasting involved in travelling, but, like everyone else, we were stuck in the hotel the tournament organisers had booked for us.

Australia had been the leading team of the early nineties. Their defeat by the Boks was no disgrace, but they didn't seem to be clicking. Their team was slightly ageing, with many of the same guys who had won in 1991, and that enabled us to compete, fielding a side that possibly had more talent, man for man. It was a fast-paced game from the start. We edged ahead through a 60yd Tony Underwood try and at half-time Jack Rowell came on to the pitch to speak to us. 'Don't you lose this game now, don't you lose this bloody game,' he kept saying. This was sound advice from the big man, but straight after the restart they scored when Damian Smith rose above Tony Underwood to grab a cross-field bomb put up by Michael Lynagh. The game went backwards and forwards from there until it was tied right at the death. As extra-time beckoned, we had a line-out on the left-hand side of the field. Martin Bayfield had played very well that day against John Eales, who was then one of the world's premier middle-jumping line-out forwards. Martin got the ball, we made some yards and Dewi Morris got it out to Rob, who smashed over a monster drop-goal and ran round the pitch with a silly grin on his face.

And we were through to the semi-final. Fair play to the Aussies, they were great guys and very gracious in defeat. On the way into town that night our team bus broke down outside the Aussie hotel, so we all piled into their bar and had a few drinks and a laugh with them. I sat chatting to George Gregan, Rod McCall, Phil Kearns and David Wilson. I remember McCall, my opposite number, laughing as he told how, with the scores tied, he had turned round to his fellow forwards and said, 'Look guys, they're all knackered over there!' before realising that, actually, so were he and his mates.

The World Cup had now come alive. Back home, people were apparently getting very excited and we felt pretty confident. We were one game away from the final and anything could happen. Off we flew back to Jo'burg to train again before heading back down once more to play in Cape Town. You could feel the hype from the press, who were getting ahead of themselves and talking about finals, but I am something of a pessimist and I had my doubts about whether we could triumph over the All Blacks. They had beaten Scotland the week before pretty comfortably, with a guy called Jonah Lomu doing a fair bit of damage. They were certainly a very good side, but I felt we would give them a good game and it would be close. The New Zealanders, though, were very, very keen to beat us. It was more than just another World Cup semi-final to them. I think they felt that we'd got above ourselves after beating them in 1993 and they wanted to take us down a peg or two. I recently saw a documentary about the Rugby World Cup on TV and they showed Will Carling's team talk ahead of the match. It was a typical Will speech, along the lines of, 'Let's get the ball out to Jerry and the wingers and we'll rip these boys to pieces.' I had to smile to myself – we all know how things turned out.

The game kicked off and everything was fairly normal for about sixty seconds. Then the ball was pinged out to Lomu on the left wing and he bust through three or four tackles to score. From the kick-off, Walter Little smashed through Jerry Guscott and Josh Kronfeld touched down, after a move which travelled almost the length of the field, for their second try. Lomu broke through the middle to touch down again minutes later and inside the first quarter the game was already virtually lost. I have never felt so powerless, so impotent, on a rugby field. It was humiliating. One moment encapsulated the whole thing. From the off, the game had been so fast and unstructured that we were knackered, but we were a good mauling team and we managed to get our hands on the ball and started rolling forwards. We made about five or six yards and then Rob Andrew tried a drop-goal. He missed – and it was not a particularly close miss, either. The New Zealand supporters in the crowd just laughed at us and Zinzan Brooke, a No. 8 forward, rubbed our noses in it by knocking a drop-goal of his own over from 45m. It was a horrible feeling, knowing that we had lost a World Cup semi-final even before half-time. We managed to come back into it a bit, with both Will and Rory scoring a pair of tries, but the final score, 45–29, flattered us. I guess they had relaxed with the result in the bag.

Looking at the tape of that game now, we were defensively very naïve and New Zealand, starting to play to a plan which involved getting the ball wide very quickly, were able to expose us. Lomu, who scored four tries, was genuinely awesome, though. Will called him a 'freak' afterwards and that wasn't too wide of the mark. With his combination of pace, power and size he was very hard to stop and if you gave him five yards of space he could score tries that no one else would have been able to. If he had been English he would be a legend for life but, strangely, the Kiwis have never rated him as highly as we do. They are very hard judges, less likely to

Me aged six months with random pink elephant (right).

My mum (left) with my dad just behind her, and the judo star Brian Jacks sometime around 1980. We entered a competition, fronted by Jacks, to find Britain's fittest family. I am front right, Andrew is centre and Will is on the left.

A chubby Johnno, aged seven months, with my brother Andrew and Nog the dog.

Great jumper. Me aged seven with Andrew (left) and Will (right).

Wishing I was King Kev. Turning out for Harborough Town Under-13s in the early 1980s. My dad, David, is at the right of the picture.

Wigston Under-15s. I am in the centre trying to look hard. There were around ten county players in this side; one week we beat Coventry's Barkers' Butts by a cricket score, with a young Neil Back in the losing side.

If the blazer fits ... almost! Selected for Leicestershire Under-14s. Look at the creases on those trousers!

D. HITCHCOCK/FOTOPRESS

When John Albert contacted me to go and play for Tihoi in the King Country province in spring 1989 he was to transform my expectations as to what rugby could offer me. I was soon turning out for the province, as here where we take on the much more fashionable Auckland in 1990.

In at the deep end. Taking on John Eales in the Under-21 clash between the All Blacks and Australia. We won, but this was one of the few occasions when the ball was thrown to me at the line-out.

ROSS SETFORD/FOTOPRESS

Still looking relatively fresh-faced on my return from New Zealand. Not only was I bringing back a lot of experience gained in the tough world of Kiwi rugby but also Kay, my girlfriend.

Graham Rowntree gives me a helping hand in the line-out as Leicester close in on the Courage League title in April 1995.

Kay, Mum and Dad join me as I pick up my OBE at Buckingham Palace in 1998.

Kay and me on our wedding day in 2000.

Catching a rare moment of rest with baby Molly who was born on 9 March 2003. My only regret is that my mum didn't live long enough to see her granddaughter.

Celebrating at Welford Road in May 1999 after we'd won the Allied Dunbar Premiership title. In the professional era the Tigers have become one of the most dominant forces in English rugby.

Leaving the RFU disciplinary hearing in Bristol with my solicitor Caroline Healey after receiving a three-week ban for punching Saracens hooker Robbie Russell. I felt I'd been very badly treated over this incident.

Same pose, different reaction

The celebrations begin after we win the European Cup for the first time in 2001.

One year on and I seem not to have moved, but in this case I'm less than pleased that my try against Munster has been disallowed.

Celebrating back-to-back European titles in May 2002.

go over the top than we are, and they've probably seen some of his less impressive provincial performances, so they put people like Tana Umaga ahead of him. It's true that Jonah has saved his most devastating feats for games against us, but I still say he is a phenomenal player. There's been no one like him before or since and the kidney illness which seems to have cut short his career is a tragedy for him and for rugby. Having said that, I've always felt the subsequent focus on Lomu was a little unfair to the rest of that All Black team. They all played very well, with quick hands and feet, great vision and strength, and even without him I'm sure they would have beaten us. It's just that the shock factor he brought to the match made it certain. They took the game to another level and should really have won the World Cup.

After we lost, I remember sitting in a spa bath with Dean and feeling very, very low. We had gone from beating the Australians and feeling on top of the world to – bang! – you're out of here. We all had to fly back to Jo'burg again, with the All Blacks up front in business class and us with cheap tickets at the back of the plane, sharing a few beers. We were flying second class and we felt second class. Our World Cup dream was over. The third-place play-off against France, who had lost their semi to South Africa, was a bit flat. Who cares about third and fourth places, really? Jack has since said he was planning to play the young guys, but that some of the more experienced players convinced him to change his team, saying that, as Grand Slam winners, they knew how to beat the French. Whatever, we let ourselves down, losing 19–9, with guys like Brian Moore, Dewi Morris and Rob Andrew pretty much at the end of their international careers.

We enjoyed a few nights out on the town with the French boys as we stayed on in South Africa for the end-of-tournament dinner. Sean Fitzpatrick, the losing finalists' captain, with only a couple of years to go to the end of his career, made the usual speech, with all the normal pleasantries and thank yous. Then, as a throwaway line, he added, 'It looks like Kerry Packer's money has come too late for me.' At the time, I wasn't exactly sure what he meant, and after we had been so comprehensively stuffed by the Blacks, I couldn't see anyone offering to pay us to play. Of course in retrospect I realised that the English TV market was potentially more valuable than the three southern-hemisphere territories put together. I also found out that Packer, an Australian sports and media mogul, was just one of a number of very rich businessmen who had started looking at rugby with a view to buying up players and creating their own rugby circuit. They had tried this in cricket in the late 70s and we were next on the list.

As soon as we got back to England, clandestine meetings started to be held with representatives of various organisations. We were all apprehensive. Remember, people who had crossed over and taken rugby league's money had been banned from the game for life, technically not even allowed in their old club houses. No one wanted that and we were keen to act together so we couldn't be isolated and picked off. As various propositions were put forward by this consortium or that financier, I would go round to Deano's house to chat them through with him and other players. Guys would throw the names of the southern hemisphere superstars around like confetti: 'Yeah, I spoke to Sean and he said this . . .' or 'I was on the phone to Zinzan and he reckons that . . .'. Clearly, all the serious wheeler-dealing was being done by guys down there. It was exciting, but I was still sceptical.

We definitely wanted it to happen. Playing at the level we were at was already close to impossible and if we were ever to get to where the All Blacks and Springboks were, something had to change. At that point, I was training every Tuesday and Thursday at the club, and every Monday and Wednesday at the gym. I didn't get home until 10.15p.m. on any of those nights. Friday night I would chill out, but on Saturday morning I would be heading down to the club to play or catch a bus, as early as around 9.30a.m. if we were travelling to somewhere like Orrell or Bath. Often, post-match, I would jump in a cab straight to the nearest airport and fly down to London for England training on the Sunday, finally getting home around 3p.m. on the Sunday afternoon. You had no real time or life outside rugby. I didn't complain, and I actually quite enjoyed it, but there was a limit to how much of this you could take and for guys with families it was getting very tough.

Of course, you also needed a very understanding employer, because we all had day jobs. I remember once two RFU committee men came in to speak to us and the conversation turned to how much work we had to do outside rugby. Dean, a policeman back then, told them about how he worked night-shifts before games. They didn't realise we were ordinary working guys and they couldn't believe their ears. Midland Bank, now HSBC, were brilliant to me. Every year, I was away three days in the week ahead of each of the four Five Nations games and for the two or three autumn internationals. In

MARTIN JOHNSON

1993, I went with England to Canada for three weeks. I came back into work and said, 'I've been called up to join the Lions tour. Could I have another five weeks off?' In 1995, I had cheekily asked for six weeks off before the World Cup, so I could train properly. They agreed, even though the tournament itself was going to take five weeks. When I came home I was knackered and asked for holiday. Once again, it was approved and I was off for another fortnight – a thirteen-week stretch.

Each time, I felt very sheepish, conscious that I was taking the mickey a bit, but I was lucky in that HSBC were very sympathetic and most of my colleagues were fine about it. I would get the odd remark like, 'Wish I played rugby,' to which I used to reply, 'Yes, I think you should,' but I think people understood. Eventually, they moved me to a 'promotions' role, which gave me a lot more flexibility and enabled me to work round my training and matches. I am extremely grateful to HSBC for all of this, but others had a harder time. Darren Garforth, who worked with a scaffolding firm, would come straight from the building site, racing to crucial league matches in his works truck and arriving forty-five minutes before kick-off. One time, Dean Richards, a Leicester policeman, got home off his nightshift, had an hour's sleep, drove a few of us up to Manchester to do some commercial work for Cellnet (now O_2), drove us back to Leicester for 5p.m., had another hour in bed, came down to training at 7p.m. and then went back to his next nightshift afterwards.

There had always been cash in the game, even though it was in breach of the strict code of amateurism. I knew from my own experience that it had long been common practice

90

in New Zealand for clubs to pay players. When an invitation team from Waikato came to play us down in Taupo, for instance, we imported some guys from North Harbour to bolster our side. Afterwards, they were given 'generous expenses' in the changing room. In England, clubs used the same scheme to keep their top players. Some clubs paid a little more to lure others across from a rival team. The only genuine reasons for moving club in those days were because of a work relocation or to further your international ambitions. Yet there were players who moved to weaker clubs – why would they do that unless they were being paid to do so? I was approached myself by a guy called John Fowler, whom I had played alongside in New Zealand. He had come over to join Richmond. There was a place in the side for me, he said, and those 'generous expenses' would be on offer. I declined, but didn't blame those guys who accepted. Many had families and mortgages and were sacrificing a significant part of their off-field lives and careers to play top-level rugby.

Clubs were taking gate money – in considerable amounts at grounds like Leicester and Bath – from paying spectators. Why shouldn't the players see a little of that? This was a view I developed early in my amateur career. Shortly after I had returned from New Zealand, I was named in the Leicester side to play the Barbarians in our traditional Christmas game. Many people bought season tickets just to be sure of obtaining a ticket for that fixture and a full-house was guaranteed. My boots were falling to pieces and I asked Tony Russ, our director of rugby, to get me some new ones. They duly arrived from adidas, but were handed over only after I had written out a cheque for £45 in the changing room pre-match. I was labouring on a building site at that time and didn't have tuppence to my name, but everyone else paid for theirs, so I just accepted it. Underneath, however, I was irritated, annoyed even. There were 14,000 or 15,000 people out there to see us play. Surely the club could buy me a pair of boots?

At international level, the contrast was greater still. The money was flowing in, but the tap was tightly turned off as far as the players were concerned. After my 'breakthrough' game for Leicester, our cup victory over Bath, I remember listening to Dean Richards and the Bath and England scrum-half Richard Hill talking about plans to bring commercial money into the national squad. The 1991 World Cup was not far off. It would create huge revenues and had massive implications for the profile of both individual players and rugby as a whole. They felt, quite rightly in my view, that the players should get a slice of that action. By the time I emerged on to the international scene, things had advanced slightly. There was still no chance of any direct earnings from the RFU, of course. The best we could hope for there was the time-honoured expenses fiddle. We were paid 20p per mile to attend England sessions and matches, so we would pack five into a car but all claim the mileage, also trying to argue that Leicester was 130 miles from London to squeeze an extra couple of quid out of the Twickenham coffers. On a more serious and organised level, though, Brian Moore and Rob Andrew had started seeking sponsors for the England team. They did a deal with the cider brand, Scrumpy Jack, which saw all England training shirts plastered with their logo. They brokered a deal with Cellnet, which involved all the players receiving free phones and the squad getting some money. This was pooled and paid out between the players as dividends.

Meanwhile, bigger and bigger personal sponsorship deals were flying around. Boot money – guys being paid to wear boots – had been the big scandal of the seventies, but by the mid-nineties it was commonplace. The likes of Jerry Guscott and Rob Andrew were being handed decent four- or five-figure sums to wear certain 'shoes' and one of the younger players had even been offered two or three grand. That was my idea of heaven. At that point, I would have been happy just to get some free kit. Actually getting paid to wear it was like some sort of crazy dream, but there weren't too many offers coming my way.

The Johnson boot deal saga is a bit embarrassing, really. In 1994, Reebok pitched up at Leicester and started dishing out boots and kit. They offered me clothing worth a thousand pounds a year, saying I was in the same bracket as Richard Hill (the flanker, not the scrum-half) and Tony Diprose. Surprising myself, I decided to argue the toss, pointing out that I had played in two Lions Tests and was also a capped international. Hilly and Tony were great young prospects at that point, but they were England B. I said I thought I should be on a better deal than that, one comparable to that which other England players were on. 'Oh well,' said the guy from Reebok. 'That's the way it is. Take it or leave it.' I left it, immediately wondering whether I had done the right thing.

However, Tony Underwood was with Mizuno and he introduced me to them. We agreed a fee and I started wearing their kit, feeling a bit like I had arrived. This felt like the big time. A year later, things had changed. Both players and clothing companies were operating on a more professional basis and I had an agent, Darren Grewcock, who had good connections with adidas. From a playing point of view, adidas boots had always been my favourite and I was a fan of their clothes, too. I grew up in the 'casual' era, when all the kids strutted around in expensive sports gear by brands like Nike, Kappa and Lacoste, and I had spent any spare cash I had on adi tops. Darren persuaded me to drive up to Cheshire with him, where we met the adidas crew. They offered me a significant deal and, feeling guilty, I agreed to sign for them. Mizuno had been very good to me and they weren't happy when I told them I was switching to adi, but we agreed a compromise for a year, where I continued with Miz boots but wore adi kit. I still feel pretty bad about the way it all happened.

As we held those shady post-World Cup meetings at Deano's place, the rugby authorities obviously knew that something was afoot. Peter Wheeler called all the players to a meeting at Leicester. Peter is a good guy, he was understanding and would probably have been keen to go professional himself as a player. His basic message was that, whatever happened, Leicester FC would continue, amateur or pro. One suggestion that had been tabled was for a system of franchises throughout the UK with Leicester forming the basis for the East Midlands one. We would be offered something like £120,000 a year – fantastic money in those days and still good today. We would basically have been the Tigers, but with money, and we were all keen to sign up. We all put our signatures on some papers and they were promptly whisked away to be held in a solicitor's safe until everything was finalised. It went quiet for a while and then the organisation – I never got to the bottom of exactly who they were – came back with more money. Now they wanted to pay us £150k each. I thought this was a bit strange. It smacked of desperation and at that point I suspected that particular scheme wasn't going to come to fruition. Later, it emerged that the South African players weren't signing up because they were talking to their union, SARFU, which was the first to bite the bullet and sign professional deals with its players.

The summer after the World Cup, some guys made moves that were clearly for money before the IRB and the RFU officially declared the game 'open'. Newcastle were being funded by the multi-millionaire, Sir John Hall, and were being very aggressive in trying to recruit players and Rob Andrew went up there, along with Dean Ryan from Wasps and our own Tony Underwood. There was no bitterness about Tony's departure – none of the guys blamed him for going at all – but there would have been some alarm at the top of the club. The picture was all very confused and unclear. No one knew how things were going to pan out, but, clearly, losing your best players wasn't going to be a good thing whatever happened. Along with Quins and Bath, Leicester had the best squad of players, including some excellent young guys who were expected to form the backbone of the team for the next five years or more. But none of us were contracted to the club and, although I think a combination of our local roots, team spirit and love for the Tigers meant it wouldn't have happened, in theory we could have walked out on five minutes' notice. If that had been the case, the club would have been in serious trouble.

England had similar worries. If players were to be paid, the RFU didn't want it to be by Aussie media moguls. We played Western Samoa and South Africa in the autumn of

1995 and suddenly, out of the blue, a big cheque from England turned up. It was for around £20,000 and came with a note saying, effectively, 'Sign this agreement to play for England for a year and don't worry about the tax – we'll sort that later.' They were clearly desperate. It wasn't a massive amount compared to the £120,000 and £150,000 that had been talked about in Dean's living room, but it was official, it was legit and it was there in front of us. We all took it. Around the same time, the club paid us another £20,000 for 'image rights'. I guess they still weren't sure of the ethics of the situation and chucked this our way to keep us sweet until the new order could be finalised. A year before it would have been unthinkable. I have often wondered what would have happened if we had signed up for a Kerry Packer circus, but now we would never find out.

Many of the clubs were now recruiting feverishly. I was still working at the bank when Rob Andrew rang me one day. He wanted to know if I was interested in coming north. I was non-committal. Another guy called me up out of the blue. 'Hello, Martin,' he said. 'I am So-and-so. I can't tell you which club I'm from, but we're in the First Division and I would like to talk to you.' I saw no harm in talking and we chatted for two or three minutes. He was very cagey and wouldn't talk specifics, either about money or the club he was from. Eventually, it became clear he was going to have to go back to someone above him and get permission to reveal their hand. 'Look,' he said. 'I'll call you back.' I put the phone down and dialled in 1471. It came back with a code I didn't recognise, so I flicked through the phone book until I came across it. Alderley Edge – that will be Sale, then. A couple of days later there was a message on my phone. 'Er, hello Martin, it's So-and-so from Sale Rugby Club . . .' – long pause – '. . . Ah! I wasn't supposed to say that, was I?' Then there was another long pause and the phone went down.

The England back rower, Ben Clarke, was another one who approached me. Some bloke wanted to talk to me and would give me anything I wanted, apparently, if I would join his club. I assumed he was talking about Bath, his own club. A short while later I was interviewed ahead of a game. 'I hear Richmond are after signing you,' said the interviewer. 'Er . . . no,' I said. 'What you on about?' I thought Richmond were a little Third Division outfit and, typically, I didn't have a clue what was going on down there. I wouldn't have gone to Sale at that point, and I never heard from Clarke again, but I didn't want to go to Richmond. I had played there and seen their crowds and I knew that the only way they could afford to pay a team was via a sugar daddy. Who knew how long that would last?

The potential approach from Newcastle was interesting. I have a lot of family in the Northeast, it was a big setup, they had recruited some good guys and John Hall had serious cash and a genuine interest in sport in his region. It was the only move I would have taken without a silly offer, so in the end I stayed put. I was never formally approached, anyway. Someone leaked to a paper that Newcastle were sniffing around, Rob was forced to deny it and it all got a bit daft. Not long afterwards, rugby officially went professional.

It was an exciting time and it showed how wrong I had been in thinking the southern hemisphere would necessarily lead the way. Within eighteen months of winning the Rugby

World Cup, François Pienaar and Joel Stransky were playing in England (Joel with us) and other great players, such as Michael Lynagh, David Wilson, Tim Horan, Jason Little and Josh Kronfeld came too in the years that followed.

Initially, there were lots of stupid ideas being bandied about, along with crazy money. Some clubs, or their backers, seemed to be hoping that the good times would roll and roll. People who wouldn't make the Leicester team, and who would barely make our first-team squad, were on massive contracts elsewhere as everyone fought to increase their squads, over-paying players just to try to compete and stay in the First Division. I was lucky with the timing. I had just come through as an established, even sought-after, player, so I was offered a club contract that was good, though not unbelievable. With basic pay and appearance money I would be earning six figures and I signed a five-year deal. A number of other players advised me against agreeing such a long-term contract, saying two years was a better term, because you could then renego-tiate when rugby exploded, as they obviously thought it would. I wasn't so sure and preferred to do a deal which I felt I justi-fied and which was responsible; one the club could afford in terms of what it was generating through the turnstiles and its other activities. Although Leicester was the biggest club in the country, we didn't have millions of pounds to splash out on wages. It was obviously going to be hard for a business like ours to change overnight and go from paying relatively small salaries to a small number of backroom staff to supporting a full playing staff and the necessary professional infrastructure.

A number of players left us to join Moseley on big deals,

but by the time they had sat down in the changing room the place had gone into administration and the contracts were worthless. Richmond and London Scottish were others that were finished as pro rugby clubs before too long. Coventry sold their ground to pay off debts. Rosslyn Park, a top club of yesteryear, decided to stay amateur and just faded gracefully from the scene. Since those slightly mad early days there has been some belt-tightening. A salary cap was introduced and things were rationalised a little, and there was a period when many guys, including myself, took pay cuts. I was fortunate to be one of the better-paid players, though, with other income from commercial sources and from playing for England, so it didn't hit me as hard as it did others.

In many ways, professionalism has been a tremendous thing for the English game. In a few short years we have created a competitive league system that has produced clubs that can beat the best in Europe. The ceiling on what you can earn has helped level the playing field so that anyone can win the league – we were four times champions when Leeds beat us on the opening day of the 2002–03 season. Players have more time to train, though in the early days an awful lot of them talked a good game. 'I want to go pro because I want to be able to train full time and do it properly,' they all said, but many of them didn't do that. Instead, they took the money and settled for an easy life, professionals in name only. It has taken a good few years for those people to be weeded out of the game, but now they've gone, the guys left behind are bigger, stronger, fitter, faster and more skilful than they were. In a dramatic, collision sport like rugby that means the game is more exciting to watch.

An exciting game attracts more fans and we have been seeing record crowds pretty much every year.

The clubs have invested in improved facilities – better drained, quicker pitches, better stadiums. Northampton's new Franklin's Gardens would now rival a lot of soccer stadiums and is better than some First Division football grounds. Saracens used to get decent crowds in the mid-nineties, but the facilities were shocking and not a great advert for the game. Now they're at Vicarage Road, the home of Watford FC, and have played in front of 19,000 people. Not everyone likes Vicarage Road, but I think it's a great place to play rugby: it is certainly a big stage for the game. Newcastle have a great setup, Leeds Tykes are at Headingley and Quins attract good crowds with their new stand, where the atmosphere is always good.

Additionally, the national team is benefiting from the strength of the Premiership. Purse-strings are held tight, so there is a bigger emphasis on playing your young English guys and developing them through the academies. Many of the clubs are involved in a strong national Under-21s competition as a result.

There are some drawbacks, though. The pro game has also created a new class of men who are going to be out of work by the time they hit thirty or thirty-two. Household names will have earned more and should have saved wisely, plus they should always be able to find work, in the media maybe, or speaking engagements. For the slightly less well-known players, who will not have made serious money through rugby, times could be tough. Gone are the days when you came into the game with a trade to fall back on. For instance, Darren Garforth recently retired and has rejoined his family scaffolding firm. For many modern players, professionalism is all they have known. In our job, although it's hard work and we talk about the length of our season, you get a lot of time off each day. It's very easy to fritter that time away with your Playstation or just hanging out. You need to put your feet up – in fact, we are instructed to – but every player needs to think about their retirement. In the first flush of professionalism, a lot of guys were spending money on flash cars and so on, but that has mostly gone now. At Leicester, certainly, there is realism and a lot of people plan for their futures. A few of them spend time learning a new trade, either at college or with our sponsors, so they have something to go on to. It is not a total sob story, though. They might start work on the bottom rung, but they will still be a lot better off than youngsters doing the same thing.

Another unfortunate spin-off of professionalism is the amount of rugby we now play. Some of the purely money-making elements of the game need to be reined in. I am thinking, for instance, of the end-of-season Barbarians games against England or the league champions. These are just a revenue-earner for someone; they certainly aren't for the benefit of the players and they dilute the quality of the game overall. People say, 'Ah, the Baabaas, the running game, the spirit of rugby,' and seem to assume it is some sort of exhibition match. Rugby is either full on or you don't play at all, and those games are a contest too far. It's the end of the season and the lads are knackered. You've gone through the emotional highs of winning the league and to get dragged back out on to the field one more time can be a nightmare. And that's even more the case when many of the people you're playing against are from the southern hemisphere, at the peak of their season and raring to go. In fact, Leicester's game against the Baabaas a couple of seasons back is one of the very few times in my life I've run on to the pitch thinking that I really didn't want to be there. OK, there are some arguments for the England matches, because at least a few young lads get to play for England and people who would otherwise struggle to get tickets go along to Twickenham. However, with little at stake they can be slightly irrelevant to play in and watch.

The wider game seems in good shape. So far, thankfully, there are few signs of rugby going the same way as football. A few benefactors have walked away. John Hall has gone and Malcolm Pearce has ceded control of Bristol, but there seems to be enough money in the game to keep it going, as long as we are careful. People want success and they need to be wary of paying silly money to players to get that success. Professional rugby is an expensive business. If you want to be a competitive team you need a playing squad of at least thirty. Rugby isn't like football, where clubs can survive on fifteen- or sixteen-man squads. In soccer, guys can slot in at different positions and in an emergency a midfielder can play as a striker. You can't slot in at tight-head, though, so you need at least two, and preferably three, plus cover in the other really specialist positions as well. Leicester had a thirty-plus squad when we won the European Cup – that was thirty guys who could all play Premiership rugby and needed to be paid accordingly. If we assume the average salary at a Premiership club is, say, £50,000 per year, that's a wage bill of £1.5 million on players alone. If you factor in a couple of England stars on maybe two or three times that, it becomes tougher still to balance the books. Currently, the clubs receive an annual injection of cash from the RFU, a fair repayment for the clubs supplying their players to England, and that helps enormously, because without it, few clubs could survive.

I think Leicester is a good model for any senior rugby club. We were fortunate in that we had built the big Alliance and Leicester stand before professionalism. That gave us a good capacity – maybe there wouldn't have been the cash to afford that project once players needed paying. The club was already well supported, and the backroom guys have worked hard to improve that and also to bring in sponsorship. Our executive boxes and hospitality suites generate important extra income, as does the club shop. We are profitable and we don't need to rely on a sugar daddy. We had a shaky start to professionalism, but we had a share issue, which helped raise some much-needed capital. I bought a few of the shares, as did most of the boys.

I worry that some junior clubs are getting too serious, though, paying players increasingly large sums of money, desperately trying for promotion to the national leagues and, presumably, one day to the Premiership. Is that what rugby at that level is about? I'm not sure and I think those clubs need to ask themselves what they are there for. I think they exist so that local people can go and play rugby. If you produce a good team and go up a division or two, then that's great. If, as that team ages, you come down a division or two, it's not the end of the world, is it? Once you play national league rugby, guys have to travel around the country – more than we have to in the Premiership. A side such as Nuneaton will have to go and play in places like Kendal in the Lakes – they travel further than we do. I have friends who play junior club rugby in Leicestershire who will travel to north Lincolnshire for a game, but that's mad, because there are loads of local clubs to play locally, in Leicestershire, Warwickshire and Northamptonshire. Surely three hours' travelling takes the fun out of it if you're working all week? A serious punt at the big time will cost millions of pounds and masses of pressure and I wonder whether it is worth it.

Maybe we should look at a ring-fencing system. In an ideal world, rugby would be a truly national game and the rugby league clubs would either never have broken away in the first place or would come back to the fold now. In the real world, we ought to be looking to bring in a club in the West Midlands and maybe one in Cornwall, a real rugby heartland. The Bristol story is a sad one, really. Historically, they were bigger than Bath, rivalling Gloucester in the Southwest, but I've always felt they weren't very well run in the pro era. Somehow, they couldn't retain good players – guys like Martin Corry, Josh Lewsey, Mark Regan, Garath Archer, Simon Shaw and Julian White have all come and gone – and because they didn't do so well on the pitch they didn't get great crowds. If you look at it coldly, you could say that two teams in the Southwest is enough, so let's allow Bristol to fade away and bring up Worcester, so we have a team in the West Midlands.

Once you settle on what your Premiership should be, it is important to recognise the important part that benefactors have played in the sport since it went pro. Malcolm Pearce pumped a lot of his own money into Bristol until, eventually, he had had enough. Let's face it: guys like Pearce are net contributors to rugby. It's not as though they make their millions out of rugby clubs. They lose them there, and if we want to keep them involved – and until gates and commercial revenues are big enough they have to be – we have to remove some of the disincentives for them. Rotherham and Worcester have been the cream of the first division. As I write, Rotherham are back in the Premiership, but are struggling. To survive they will have to spend a lot of money on players; money they don't have. Sadly, it looks probable that they will be relegated again, and the same would apply to any team without a sugar daddy. Naturally, not everyone will want to invest millions of pounds of his own money in a club that has a pretty fair chance of being immediately relegated, so one answer is to settle on a Premiership and close it off.

Plenty of people will hate this idea. Famous old clubs such as Moseley and Coventry, for instance, would probably feel they ought to have the chance to make it to the top. I just think that ignores the realities of modern sport, where the gaps between those at the top and those below them are wide and widening. This is even more marked in rugby than in any other sport, where the physicality of players who have trained full-time for years will be too much for guys who have only just been able to start doing that. People point to Leeds as the counterpoint to this argument, and it's true that they have done fantastically well, staying up and consolidating their position. True, they have done a very astute job of building their squad, getting older guys like Mark Regan, not wanted by Bath but a British Lion and England international, on board. It has certainly revitalised Ronnie's career and he has been great for them, too. They obviously have a good team spirit and coaching setup, with some excellent young players coming through. But don't forget that they were relegated without actually going down in the shambles over Rotherham's non-promotion. Would Tom Palmer and Dan Scarbrough, both guys with serious international ambitions, have stayed if they had gone into Division One? Would Mark Regan have gone there? Who knows, but I suspect their squad would have been weaker. That problem will be faced by any team coming up. They are likely to go straight back down and players will leave – they may even have their contracts terminated to save money. Coaches and office staff, too, will be cut to save costs.

If needs be, keep Rotherham up and bring Worcester up, too. Create a fourteen-team Premiership, ring-fenced and split into two pools of seven with end-of-season play-offs. What benefit is there to rugby as a whole if any of the existing Premiership teams go down? After all, we are starting to get a good geographical spread and some stability with the youth academies, new stadiums and so on. I know there are no right answers. If you pull up the trap door, will everyone else below give up? Maybe. There is certainly no need to act in panic. Overall, for a young professional sport, we are actually doing a remarkable job of getting things about right.

CHAPTER FIVE

BARBED WIRE

As the professional era began, Leicester made some good signings, bringing in Will Greenwood, Austin Healey and the Scottish back, Craig Joiner. While Will and Austin, in particular, turned out to be excellent buys, they were not big names. The same could not be said, however, of our new director of rugby. Bob Dwyer, who joined in May that year, was perhaps the most famous coach in the world at that time. He had guided the Wallabies to their 1991 World Cup win and the move to Leicester was a major statement about the future of the club.

His predecessor, Tony Russ, had been appointed the club's first full-time coach in 1990. His role had been increasingly difficult to justify in the amateur days. More squad sessions, an expanding league rugby system, more sponsorship money coming in and games live on Sky TV all added up to make the game much more serious than it had been and the burdens on players grew. As a paid employee, Tony's livelihood depended on how well the team performed. The players, though, were theoretically still playing for fun. Resentment grew as we were asked to use more of our free time to train harder and pressured to make fewer mistakes and win more games. You would play a cup final and most of the squad would have been working until 6p.m. the night before. At times, guys would arrive late for training and Russy would raise his eyebrows, but their sentiment would be, 'I don't get paid £35,000 a year to sit here all day, Tony.'

Once the game turned pro, the general feeling was that we needed some fresh impetus. We had won the Courage League the year before, beating Bristol 17–3 at Welford Road, but we lost out to Bath on the final day of the 1995–96 season and suffered a dreadful and infamous defeat, also to the West Country outfit, in the Cup final. It's worth looking at that match. In many ways, it's still the worst and most painful setback I've ever experienced in rugby. We were hugely motivated to stop their double. Although their backs were still very good, we were becoming a stronger team than them in terms of our forwards. Chilcott and Hall had gone, Ollie Redman and Graham Dawe were coming to the end of their careers. Smarting at losing our title, we wanted to show them who were the bosses in that Twickenham final. Darren Garforth personified our attitude. Early on, he took the ball at the back of a line-out and went on a barnstorming run up the centre of the field, smashing Bath players out of his way and creating a big hole for Niall Malone to romp in to score a try. Matt Poole scored from a line-out in the second half and we should have been well clear, but our back line had failed to spark and we hadn't done much with the ball. Additionally, John Liley, looking nervous, had missed a few kicks. So, time was ticking away, but they were still in the game. They had nothing to lose and, as we became a little protective of our lead, they started to come back at us strongly. They were attacking and put us under some pressure in our 22. We gave away a penalty or two but suddenly the referee, Steve Lander, peeled away and ran under the posts, signalling a penalty try. In doing so, he effectively handed Bath the game, as Jon Callard converted to make it 16–15 to them. There were still a few minutes on the clock, but we were so shocked that we were unable to come back.

Nowadays, penalty tries are far more common, but back then they were very rare. They should only be awarded when the attacking side is definitely going to score and is prevented illegally from doing so. We used to win them occasionally because our forwards were strong enough to dominate teams and put them under pressure to the point where, sometimes, they would illegally collapse a scrummage or pull down a maul. Even then, it was never instant, though. The opposition's scrum would be going backwards on their line and would collapse. It would be re-set and the same thing would happen. This time the referee might warn them. If it happened again you were in penalty try territory.

In that final I didn't even see a penalty offence, but irrespective of that, a penalty try was certainly not appropriate. We were ten or more yards from our line, our defence was solid and a try was not imminent. I've since heard it said that Lander had warned the teams before the match that he might use the penalty try option, and also that he warned us it was on the cards just before he gave it. All I can say is that I certainly don't remember this. As it was, he took away the possibility of Bath scoring through their own efforts and robbed the game of a dramatic natural finish. Normally, rugby is a pretty fair game and teams get what they deserve. I have played in and lost cup finals, Grand Slam deciders, Lions

Tests. We have been outplayed and, while I have been disappointed, that is part of life. But I never been in a team that felt as robbed as we did that day and it is still the most painful defeat I have suffered.

As the final whistle went, I turned on my heel and walked off the field, disgusted. Behind me, all hell was about to break loose as Neil Back, equally angry and upset, pushed Lander to the floor. I can't excuse what Neil did – players can't be allowed to manhandle officials, no matter what the perceived provocation – but, hand on heart, I can't say I wouldn't have done exactly the same thing myself if Lander had crossed my path after blowing the whistle. And I would have had to take my punishment the same way Backy took his eventual six-month ban. In the changing room, quite a number of the guys, John Wells and Dean Richards included, were either in tears or very close to it. Others sat in silence, visibly stunned. I was just very, very angry. We were supposed to troop back up the stand and receive our loser's medals and a glass tankard each, but I was in no mood for that. I pulled on my track-suit and said, 'Come on lads, let's go home, now. I don't want to be any part of this.' Plenty of the other players felt the same way, but eventually Dean Richards and, strangely, Richard Cockerill – not normally someone associated with the calm voice of reason – persuaded us that we had to do the decent thing. The changing-room floor was carpeted with smashed glass as soon as we returned, though.

Some unbelievable garbage was written in the next few days. What Backy had done was wrong, certainly, and he was rightly suspended, but the press attacked us all – we and our fans were a disgrace. Stuart Barnes seemingly spoke for quite a few people when he argued in an article he wrote that the result was 'morally correct', given that Bath had played the most rugby against our boring, negative, forward-oriented game. We have heard this thousands of times down the years, though less so since the arrival of guys like Austin Healey, Will Greenwood and Paddy Howard. The ludicrous conclusion of Barnes' argument was that points should be awarded for style, rather than tries and goal-kicking. There are plenty of ways of winning a game and doing it through the forwards is one of them. It may be limited in scope, but it just so happened that this was our strength at that time and you play to your strength. I remember a game against Bath sometime around then in which our centre combination had played fewer club games than Guscott and de Glanville had international caps. Were we supposed to take them on in the middle of the park? And Barnes was conveniently forgetting the eighties, when Leicester had a great back line, but no forwards, and Bath had beaten everyone up front with their massive pack.

The upshot of all this was that, having deserved to come out of the season with at least one trophy, we ended up with nothing. Although I was sorry to see Tony Russ sacked, I felt strongly that we needed a new approach and was surprised and delighted when his replacement, Bob Dwyer, was announced. We first met Bob when he called a pre-season meeting in the Crooked Feed restaurant at the club. We were all crammed in together, craning our necks to see Bob and his assistant, the former Wallaby prop, Duncan Hall, and hanging on his every word. His message was simple and to-the-point: 'Being professional is not about being paid to play rugby. It's about the way you behave, the way you train and the way you play. I'll see you all at the gym for weight training at 7a.m. on Monday.' There was a sharp intake of breath and a few people exchanged glances, but we all turned up as commanded the following Monday.

Up until then, our weights work had been fairly haphazard. A few players, like Neil Back, took it seriously. Some hardly bothered. Most of us, like me, did what we could in the time available. I had always worked hard on my fitness, but my strength work was limited to two nights a week in the gym. Bob introduced training programmes tailored to each of us, spelling out the importance of weight training for strength and injury prevention. We spent time at Loughborough University, where the gym was much better equipped than ours, learning how to lift free weights properly – much better for power training than lifting on machines.

On the training ground, Bob worked with the backs or on team tactics and motivation. He could be blunt and sarcastic – not for nothing was he known as Barbed Wire – but I found him amusing and inspiring, too. 'Imagine if each one of you can dive on one loose ball in the match,' he would say. 'That's fifteen loose balls a match. Dive on it – dive on that loose ball! Think of it like a hand grenade you've got to dive on to save your family. It's that important . . . Well, maybe it's not quite *that* important, but it *is* important.' You had to listen to him. He demanded attention, because of his record and because of the way he was. 'Carrumba . . . you beauty!' he would shout, if something good caught his eye. It was all pretty exotic compared to what we were used to.

Duncan Hall, his assistant, was our forwards coach. Unlike Bob, he was a quiet, reserved guy with a laid-back Aussie drawl. I would ask him what he thought of something I was doing and he'd reply 'Yeah, well, Rome wasn't built in a day, mate.' A former Wallaby lock and No. 8 with fifteen caps, who had played Down Under for Bob, Duncan was brilliant, with a tremendous gift for analysis and a scientific understanding of the game. He had the ability to break down the various disciplines involved in sport into their component parts and understand them. Previously, we had practised line-outs simply by lining up, jumping and catching, as if in a match. Now Duncan had us working on the individual actions. First, we got down on our knees and worked on catching, leaning to the left and right, back and forward. Bad balls would be deliberately thrown so we could work on hooking them in. Then we would work on jumping, catching and offloading in the air or landing in the right position to give the ball for a drive, or for the scrum-half to get it away to the backs as quickly as possible.

He also completely changed the way we scrummaged. Instead of just packing down in an eight and pushing against a machine or another eight, as we had, he made us think about our body positions and where our feet should be. We would form up three against four: the tight-head prop, a second row and a flanker against the loose head, his second row and flanker and the No. 8. That enabled him, and us, to look more closely at what we were doing – impossible in a mêleé of sixteen guys. He introduced individual tackling practice, too, concentrating again on each player's body position, on what his legs and arms should be doing.

It all sounds blindingly obvious now, but it was a whole new way of working for us, and the first time I had come into contact with this style of coaching. Previously, there had been almost an anti-coaching attitude, particularly with senior players. 'You play for England, you know what you're doing, you don't need any coaching . . . It will take the flair out of you,' was the attitude in British rugby at that point. After Duncan, I would go home in the evening feeling fantastic: I had actually learned something that could measurably improve my game that day. As a pack, we were stronger, more cohesive and better, and that was exciting.

We trained our backsides off in that first year. From meeting up two or three evenings a week and playing on the Saturday, suddenly we were all at the club twice a day. Some guys found the new regime a little tough, but I loved it. I could jog down to the gym at Oval Park from where I lived, train and then walk home for breakfast and a sit on the lawn in the sun before heading back for the afternoon session. I was earning a lot more money and I had a life. In the amateur era, I had never been at home before 9p.m. on a week night. Now I was finished and back at home by 6p.m. After two or three months, I couldn't imagine how we had ever managed before.

If training was hard work, playing was getting tougher too. In the old days, the bottom side would hardly ever beat the top team and, a few hard games apart, the standard of rugby was pretty low. The league had been about Bath, Leicester, Harlequins and, maybe, Wasps. These clubs had most of the quality players, while the others would struggle to hold on to talented guys. People would flock to a place like Bath, knowing that if they were in the first team at the Rec they stood a good chance of getting into their national side. Saracens, on the other hand, lost great assets like Ben Clarke,

Jason Leonard and Dean Ryan in a relatively short space of time. With money men coming into the game, clubs like Sarries could now compete. Suddenly, they were hiring Philippe Sella and Michael Lynagh and beating us for the first time. We had our own big-name signings – Joel Stransky, for instance, joined in December 1996 – and some great wins, too. The atmosphere at the club was really positive and, best of all, there was Europe.

We went over to Ireland and beat Leinster in the European Cup, the sort of fixture that would have been a dream only months before. Then we travelled to Pau, in France, a lovely southern town with a nice stadium. It was the first time we had ever faced a French club side in a serious match. It was a roughhouse of a game, with biting, gouging and fighting going on all over the pitch and almost spilling on to the side-lines. Leon Lloyd injured his shoulder and needed to come off – this was before tactical substitutions were introduced to the sport – but the French doctor insisted Leon was fit to continue, coming very close to blows with a furious Bob. The crowd was as hostile and aggressive as any I have ever known. At one point, a woman sitting two or three rows in beckoned Richard Cockerill over, shouting 'Monsieur, monsieur' at him. As Cockers wandered over to see what she wanted, she spat at him, to cheers from all around her. Impeccable taste, the French. All around the stadium they were spitting at us, hurling objects on to the pitch and screaming abuse. Periodically, Bob would turn round from his seat on the bench and shout back, which probably didn't help matters. Pau had the best of the first half, but we came back to take the lead and were clinging on towards the end. Right at the death they scored a try, but the crucial pass was forward and the ref, to his credit, disallowed the score. The crowd were howling with rage as we walked off through a barrage of phlegm and insults.

Back in the changing room, Bob strode in, pleased but businesslike. 'Right guys, great win,' he said. 'We need to go back out there now and warm down, but please don't antag- onise the crowd.' Out we trooped, running the gauntlet again, to find Bob standing in the middle of the pitch goading their supporters. Post-match there was a buffet in a marquee with hundreds of the fans, but all their hostility had drained away and we had a great night together. The floor was covered in beer and guys were taking running starts and sliding across the floor, smashing into the bar and catapulting over to the other side. Later, we went into town and found a pub. After a few beers, Daz Garforth got up and started dancing on the bar. Inevitably, he slipped and fell straight off on to the floor behind the taps. The whole bar seemed to freeze for a second, everyone thinking he was either dead or at least unconscious and bleeding. Then he popped back up with a silly grin on his face and the whole place went mental.

I loved every minute of it. Sure, the rugby had been hard, aggressive and, at times, dirty, and the crowd had been loud and partisan. But that was how I felt rugby crowds should be – without the spittle – and we had stuck together and come through to win. If this was the new era, I couldn't get enough of it.

Those kind of victories, and the evenings that follow them, are fantastic for bonding a team, and spirit was high in the camp for most of that first season. Bob's abrasive management style had not gone down well with everyone, though. Some of the senior players – Rory Underwood, John Wells and Dean Richards, in particular – had not warmed to him. The first cracks started to appear when we got to the European Cup final in the early spring. We had demolished Toulouse in the semi-final on a freezing January day with a just-about-thawed pitch. The groundsmen had worked like crazy with hot-air blowers and blankets to get it more or less playable. However, we knew that the French guys, used to having the sun on their backs at home, wouldn't want to play in those conditions. European rugby was great, wasn't it? We were winning everything and we were in the final against some little-known French club called Brive.

They had very few star names in their ranks – although a lot, like Lamaison, Vendetti, Carbonneau and Penaud went on to achieve much greater recognition – and we went into the match in the wrong frame of mind. I remember we travelled down to Cardiff, the venue for the final, on the Friday night and were doing live links from the hotel with our local Central TV. In retrospect, perhaps this was a bit cavalier. On the other hand, Brive had really done their homework on us. We had stuffed Toulouse in the line-out, but Brive got into us there, a lot of it bordering on illegal, and closed us down. Their backs played very well and we were well beaten 28–9 in the end. That was the last of Dean Richards as first-choice No. 8. He had been exposed for pace a little, though that alone certainly didn't cost us the game, and Bob brought the young Irish back rower Eric Miller in from then on.

The end of that season was very disappointing. We did manage to win the domestic knockout competition, beating

Sale narrowly in one of the worst finals ever, and that piece of silverware meant we ended with smiles on our faces. But it could – and should – have been better. Our cup runs were great, but we ended up being victims of our own success, playing more games than we would have liked to get there. With league games being rescheduled midweek to help the backlog, we ran out of steam, and a number of players suffered injuries – towards the end of the season I felt like I was running through treacle on the pitch. Everything had gone. We had beaten Bath heavily away in the Cup early in the New Year. Towards the end of the league season, we went back to the Rec and fell apart, conceding plenty of points. That showed how far things had swung.

We had to play Sale in our last league game of the season. They got a big points score up on us in a violent encounter marked by two mass brawls. We came back to sneak a draw at the end, with the ref blowing up right on time. This incensed the home crowd, who thought they had been done out of injury time and the chance to win the match. They ran on to the pitch and scuffles developed as a few of them started pushing Leicester players around and shouting abuse. I was a target – their No. 8, Charlie Vyvyan, had broken his ankle as I had tackled him and the Sale fans thought I had done it deliberately. Actually, he had just caught his foot in the ground and fallen awkwardly, but passions were obviously running high. We made it off the pitch in one piece, leaving Bob out on the grass waiting to give a live interview to Sky. Just as the studio cut to him, a Sale fan ran up and started ranting about the missing injury time. Bob pushed the guy away, saying, 'Mate, f*** off!' The anchor interjected, but when they went back to Bob, he said, 'Yeah, I actually agreed with the fella. They should have had four or five minutes more.' He came into the changing room five minutes later. 'Well played, fellas,' he said, in his deadpan Aussie voice. We had ended fourth in the league in 1997, with only the Cup to show for our efforts. In one season, we had played more games, and trained longer and harder, than we ever would again.

For those of us who were part of the international setup, it had been an even more tiring season. With England, too, we had enjoyed the novelty that professionalism offered. Gone were the days of the seventy-two-hour build-up to Test matches. Now we were together all week, staying in Marlow and training at Bisham Abbey, where the England soccer side trained. In retrospect, we worked too hard in those early days. Because we had a week together I think the coaches felt they had to use it, so every spare minute seemed to be taken up with training. It was a time of personnel changes. Brian Moore, Dewi Morris and Rob Andrew went, to be replaced by the likes of Matt Dawson, Paul Grayson and Mark Regan. We had a good Five Nations in 1996, losing just one game – a tryless 15–12 match away in Paris – but we were a team in transition. That summer, there was no tour and we had a fairly weak autumn series. We overwhelmed Italy 54–21, a game in which I managed to get the first of my two tries in England colours. We struggled to beat Argentina 20–18, with Jason Leonard scoring his only international try, and lost a tough match against the New Zealand Barbarians side, Carlos Spencer scoring the killer try towards the end.

In the Five Nations in 1997 we played some very good

rugby. First up we beat Scotland 41–13 at Twickenham, not a great match but one in which we sprinted away towards the end. At Lansdowne Road we won 46–6. Jon Sleightholme scored in the first half and Austin Healey came off the bench, his freshness and pace helping us, again, to pull away in the final quarter. That set up a big game with France. We dominated the first half, Lawrence Dallaglio sprinting in from 30yds off an inside pass to send us in ahead. We really should have killed it off after the break, but the French changed their tactics in the second half, starting to drive at us and take us on more. A lot of the guys from Brive's European Cup-winning team were in that side – the likes of Alain Penaud, Christophe Lamaison and Philippe Carbonneau – and they battled very hard. The key moment came when they scored with a kick to Tony Underwood's wing and it ended 23–20.

That was a massive blow to us. We had played really well and should have been on for a Grand Slam. Now we had to go to Cardiff and, while we won 34–13, it all felt slightly flat. It was Will Carling's last game for England. He had earlier given up the captaincy to concentrate on playing, with Phil de Glanville taking over, and he would obviously have wanted to go out with another Slam behind him. Jonathan Davies was another who hung up his boots that day, making his last appearance for Wales, and the match was also notable for Jack Rowell's decision to bring Rob Andrew out of virtual international retirement to sit on the bench for one last game. That didn't go down too well with the guys, who felt that Alex King should have been given a shot, but Jack was obviously taking a more conservative line, going for experience and trying to ensure we at least came away with the Triple Crown.

Our performances for club and country had been noted by the British and Irish Lions selectors. Indeed, they named a number of Leicester's England players – myself, Neil Back, Austin Healey and Graham Rowntree – in the Lions party to tour South Africa, along with the uncapped Will Greenwood and Ireland's Eric Miller. I thought the club was in pretty good shape as I left it that summer. Certainly, we seemed poised for better things and a championship seemed attainable the following season. However, there were problems behind the scenes that were just about to surface. As Dean Richards reached the end of a magnificent career, his demotion to the bench in favour of Eric Miller might have been the right decision in rugby terms, but Bob could have handled it better. He was very blunt about it: Dean was out of the picture. Deano had been the mainstay of the Tigers for the previous decade and was hugely popular, both with the fans and those who worked at the club. Coming as an outsider to a place like Leicester, Bob would have been well advised to ensure someone of Dean's stature was onside with him. It was typical of Bob. He came across as someone who always wanted to do things his way. Dean was not the only club stalwart to feel hard done by. Shortly after he had joined, a reporter had asked him about Dosser Smith's situation. Dosser, one of our coaches, was a well-liked, respected servant of the club who had been around for years. It was obvious he was on his way out, but there are ways of softening that sort of blow. Dwyer was not into soft. He replied, bluntly: 'He wants to coach. He can't. I'm doing it.'

Rory Underwood was another who also quickly found himself on Bob's wrong side. Underwood's commitments as an RAF pilot meant he had been given exemption from some training — something the coach hated. Bob lost no opportunity openly to run Rory down and made it pretty plain he rated the young three-quarter Leon Lloyd ahead of him. 'I've got an eighteen-year-old lad, Leon, alongside me in the stands,' he would say. 'He can see the opposition are going to kick and he can see Underwood is out of position. He's shouting "Rory, drop back, drop back!" Meanwhile, I've got a guy with eighty caps on the pitch who can't see it.' Eventually, Rory was dropped for Leon. One guy was just starting out, the other was coming to the end of his career, so maybe it was a fair decision. However, Bob was certainly capable of acting out of spite and, as with his demotion of Deano, I am sure it was partly to stamp his authority on the team and show everyone who was boss.

His man-management was not the only issue. There were elements of the way he wanted the backs to play which some of the guys didn't agree with and, as we entered the new season, this started to cause problems, too. Austin Healey and Will Greenwood were exciting young runners who had been part of a Lions squad which had ripped South African sides to shreds with fast, dynamic rugby. They wanted more of the same when they got back home, as did other guys like Eric Miller and Neil Back. Bob, though, wanted our back line to be a lot more physical and confrontational. He wanted Greenwood to take the ball up, smashing into contact and trying to bash holes. Will didn't share this vision of his game, rightly judging that his forté lay, instead, in running clever lines and finding gaps, beating guys with guile rather than power. A division started to open between the player and the coach. By now I was club captain and Bob confided in me that he wanted to get rid of Greenwood. This was not something I could understand or agree with.

With all the behind-the-scenes discontent beginning to bubble up, our play started to suffer. We should have been set up for a great nine months, after our great cup runs of the previous season. Joel Stransky was available for Europe, having previously not been registered and, while we had lost a few guys, Bob had recruited, too. Martin Corry had joined from Bristol, the Springbok lock Fritz van Heerden was on his way and the little Fijian sevens genius Waisale Serevi was also now a Leicester player. This was, on the face of it, an incredible signing – he was almost rugby's Pele, and we were all excited to have Wiz playing for us. I remember his first training session, where we warmed up with a little game of touch rugby. We were standing there like school kids, eyes wide, waiting to see what tricks he would pull out of his bag. Wiz was a top guy and all the boys loved him.

He was obviously a phenomenon one-on-one – similar to Jason Robinson, for those who never saw him play at his best. However, he had trouble with our weather and, on cold days, he would wear rubber thimbles, like the ones bank tellers use to count notes, to try to keep his fingers warm. However, when the sun was on his back and the force was with him he could be incredible. Some of the things he did are still talked about in our changing room to this day. Against Toulouse, he chipped over the top and raced through to catch his own kick before putting Will Greenwood away to score. Playing Milan, he intercepted the ball five metres out from our line and was clear. He kept slowing down to let the Italians catch him, then giving his little hitch-kick to get clear again. It was joie de vivre, though, not arrogance – he was a very unassuming guy. The trouble was that he didn't have too many 'hot' days. It wasn't really Wiz's fault. Bob seemed to have brought him into the setup without giving any thought to where he would play. In the fifteen-man game, Serevi can only really play fly-half. With Joel Stransky ahead of him, though, he was never going to make the No. 10 jersey his own. Having spent so much on his salary, Bob now had to fit him into the side somewhere. He experimented with him at scrum-half, on the wing and at full-back, but none of these positions worked. He lacked the authority for scrum-half and was ruled out of the back three because he was neither a powerful enough finisher of tries nor the keenest defender on the park – at tackling practice, he would come out to train wearing two scrum caps. Bob's attempts to shoehorn Wiz into the side caused unrest because, lovely guy that he was, it meant he was usually playing at the expense of someone else who was actually a better bet in that position.

Bob made some other strange recruitment decisions. Michael Horak was playing full-back for us and struggling a little, so Bob brought in a bloke called Andrew Leeds. He was an Aussie rugby league player who was coming to the end of his career and was only with us for a few months between seasons back home. I felt it was strange that Bob wanted to bring him into the side just for a short period like that. Worse still, the Fijian winger Marika Vunibaka was brought over, but failed to get a work permit first. Vunibaka just hung around for a few weeks without playing and eventually had to return to Fiji.

Bob wasn't helped by the fact that, while Corry and Fritz would turn out to be excellent buys, they didn't have their best seasons first up. Those who had travelled with the Lions were also experiencing something of a come-down – Eric Miller was one who wasn't playing as well as he could and, given that Bob had chosen him over Deano at No. 8, this didn't help matters, either. It was a strange time – unsettled, with no harmony in the squad, no fun around the place and lots of bitching and backbiting going on. We lost our way and, with it, more games than we were used to, going out of the European Cup at the quarter-final stage as Pau avenged their defeat of the previous year, which was very disappointing.

Guys with an obvious problem were openly whingeing about things and those who didn't have a problem were affected by it. Austin Healey and Will Greenwood were house-mates and Will's unhappiness had spread to Austin, with arguments that I felt were unnecessary on both sides starting to erupt between him and Dwyer. I was getting in the way of petty rows between the two and often had to phone each of them, acting as a go-between to try to make the peace. Things came to something of a head after one bust-up on the training ground. Bob had told Austin he needed to run a tighter line in a particular move. Oz said he couldn't possibly do that, Bob said he could run it himself, and it just to'd and fro'd like that. Dwyer took it all personally and dropped Healey from the squad. It was becoming a them-and-us situation between the coaches and the players and that isn't a good thing. At a professional rugby club it is vital that you pull together. Days like Pau, winning away from home in a hostile environment and then having a great night together afterwards, bond a team together. Training-ground rows have the opposite effect.

It was getting to the point where Healey, Greenwood, Richards and Wells were all thinking of leaving. Fatally, for Bob, he also started to have difficulties in his relationship with the board. He wanted to be involved in everything, including back-room stuff, and that didn't go down well. Some of them felt his decision to drop Austin, clearly a very talented player, was the last straw. In the February, a board meeting was called to discuss Dwyer's future. Bob had got wind of the meeting and had asked me what I thought about it. He ran through the names of the board, ticking off those people who would support him. I had to tell him that I knew for a fact that some of those he named were against him. This upset him, obviously. I was down with the England squad when Peter Wheeler, our chief executive, called me with the meeting's results. He told me the board had decided to release Bob and Duncan.

I felt bad – guilty, even – about it. It was as though I had let them down – especially Duncan, a guy whose coaching I really respected and whom I liked as a bloke. I felt we should have been pulling out the results that would have kept them in their jobs and I felt also that, as captain, I could and should have done something about it. I also didn't like the sense of instability that it brought. Was this what professionalism meant? People getting fired after a bad run of a few months? The first year of being paid to play had been great. This was very sobering, particularly when taken with what was happening elsewhere and the experience of the guys who had left to join Moseley, only to see that club go out of business. At Leicester, the press were all over us. It was like a football situation and I found the whole thing very disturbing. I'm a pretty loyal person and I was more pro than anti Bob. I had known things weren't right, but I felt they could be sorted out.

Peter told me Dean Richards was to be Bob Dwyer's replacement. John Wells would be his number two, taking over Duncan's role coaching the forwards, and Joel would take care of the backs. Wheeler brought Richards down to the England hotel to chat to the Leicester contingent. Deano was wearing a suit and carrying a mobile phone that rang every three or four minutes. I caught his eye. He looked a bit bewildered and shell-shocked − not surprisingly, given that they had ditched a man who was, ostensibly, one of the world's best coaches for him. It wasn't a universally popular move with the fans, either. I remember a Q&A evening at Oakham School a few weeks later. It was all very jolly and light-hearted until some guy stood up and asked Peter Wheeler, 'Can you explain to the supporters why the board has sacked Bob Dwyer, a man with a proven track record who has won the World Cup with Australia, and put in his place two men with absolutely no coaching experience?' I must admit I could see his point, and I thought it was a bad move and a backwards step.

Team spirit improved fairly quickly − the in-joke was that you don't mess with Austin or else you get sacked − but results didn't. Everyone found it hard to readjust to Dean and John's new positions, including the two guys themselves. When I got back from England duty, they were still getting changed in their usual spots in the dressing room. This was wrong. We had all been mates, playing together for the past seven or eight years. Now they needed to take a step back. Things were different. We limped on and just made it into fourth place to grab a spot in Europe. Newcastle won the league, although I think Saracens were probably the best side in the championship, but we helped the northerners to win the title by beating Sarries away and drawing to them at home while losing twice to Newcastle.

In hindsight, though, as the following season would prove, replacing Bob was the right thing to do. Apart from all the personality clashes, Dwyer was not as good a coach as everyone had thought he would be. He brought nothing dramatically new to the team, and Dean and John went on to do a pretty phenomenal job. It isn't as though they had spent time being groomed with the second team or at a smaller club; they were pitched straight in and led Leicester to a period of unparalleled success. Along with many of the fans and some of my team-mates, I probably underestimated Dean. It's an easy mistake to make. I remember watching him play for Leicester, this big, lumbering bear of a bloke. On the face of it, he didn't look particularly sharp, but he is actually a very shrewd operator indeed and there is a lot more to him than meets the eye. Wellsy was not a guy I was that close to. In the amateur days, he lived in Newark with his young family and had rarely gone out for a beer with us. He turned up for training or the game and then he was gone, and of all the guys I played with he was the one I knew least. He was a quiet, if blunt, Yorkshireman. As a forward, I was worried as to how he would continue Duncan's work, but from the off he did a good, thoughtful job of coaching us, which pleasantly surprised me and assuaged some of our fears.

CHAPTER SIX

WILD CARD WOODY

Leicester was not the only place where changes were afoot. England had a new coach, too. While we had been away with the Lions, Jack had taken the squad to Argentina. They won one and lost one – a decent result when increasing numbers of his better players, such as Mike Catt and Ollie Redman, were being called over to South Africa to replace injured guys – and he finished his time in charge with a one-off match in Australia. As soon as the Lions tour ended, the England contingent headed from Jo'burg to Sydney. I missed the game, having flown home for groin surgery, but the boys lost 25–6 in what was a match too far for most of them that summer. Jack had done pretty well – a Grand Slam in 1995 and a close call in 1997 – but I think the demands of his high-level business career were proving too hard to reconcile with his coaching role for the national side. When we reported for England training at the start of the new season, he had gone and a new coach had been installed: Clive Woodward.

Looking back, Clive was a real wild-card choice for the post. At the time of his appointment, he was Bath backs coach and Andy Robinson's assistant at the Rec. Apart from a successful spell at London Irish, he was pretty much an unknown quantity. Knowing him now, it is easy to see why he was chosen. He is a real 'big picture' man and an excellent communicator, and he would have impressed the Twickenham interviewers with his innovative thinking, his ambition and vision for where England should be and how they could get there.

Right from the off, Clive was not afraid to take risks. He employed John Mitchell, the former All Black tourist and Sale player, as his forwards coach. In some ways, this was a surprising move. Mitch was a Kiwi and also a young guy with little coaching experience, but Woodward's coaching appointments have generally been sound and Johnny Mitch was no exception. I remember going down to train with the new regime for the first time and finding the whole thing quite exciting. Mitch was nervous – the job was a big step up for him and he wasn't sure how we would take being coached by a New Zealander – and Clive was buzzing with new ideas and purpose. First and foremost, he recognised immediately that a first-class team needs first-class backup. In time, he would revolutionise the coaching and medical setup, bringing in high-quality staff to support the players. He would move the team to a new hotel, Pennyhill Park, where we were given everything we needed – in terms of facilities – to train together. At first, we laughed at some of his innovations. He recruited the TV show *Changing Rooms* to revamp our changing rooms at Twickenham, for example. Before, they had been fairly drab, with unfinished breeze-block walls. Clive had them painted and had action shots and mottos hung around the place. Each player had his own wooden cubicle and a brass name plaque above his bench. Our number ones – the blazer-and-tie kit we wear for post-match functions – weren't that smart. The jackets didn't really fit too well and the ties were nylon, so Clive had Hackett provide us with properly tailored blazers with the traditional silver-wire RFU badge and silk ties. It might seem almost irrelevant – as I say, we laughed at this kind of thing at the start – but after a while we came to expect it. The changing rooms are a bit more inspirational than they were and we can take pride in wearing our number ones.

In playing terms, it was almost an experimental time as virtually every week he made changes to the way we trained and to the way in which we were trying to play. Above all, he wanted to get away from the old image many people still had of England – that of a slightly boring, staid team who relied on big forwards to win games. In fact, this was an inaccurate view of our play, as we had already started moving away from that style under Jack, but Clive used to call himself the Crazy Professor and he wasn't far off. In those early days, he didn't want us to play with a game plan – he didn't even want the words 'game plan' mentioned. Instead, he wanted us to go out and play everything as we saw it, to give it a go, which is what he had been like as a player. He thought you could come up with moves on the field that were so radically different, so stunningly innovative, that the opposition wouldn't know how to handle them. In reality, it's all about executing your standard moves as well as possible, and he recognised this, but he made a lot of changes to the squad, bold selections that, although perhaps a little flawed, probably reflected his desire to stamp his own mark on the new England.

The first four games he had in charge were Australia, New Zealand, South Africa and New Zealand again in four consecutive weeks. To call that a difficult run would be an understatement and, as pre-Christmas programmes go, it made our previous few years' fixtures against the likes of Canada, Romania and Italy look pretty lightweight. It was fairly daunting. After all, not even the southern-hemisphere teams put such a heavy workload on their players. To stand any chance at all of competing in that kind of environment, you need to select your most experienced players. Clive's first England XV, however, contained debutantes – Will Green and Andy Long – in the key positions of tight-head and hooker, ahead of the stronger scrummagers, Darren Garforth and Mark Regan. Playing a top side like Australia, you would never want guys making their debuts in the front row. Back then, before our domestic league really developed, the step up to international level was much greater than it is now and including new guys was almost suicidal. The Aussies took us on up front and had us in all sorts of trouble right from the start. It was too soon for Andy. He was very young and, though he would go on to become a very good player, he was slightly out of his depth at that point. He was hauled off after the first forty minutes, with Richard Cockerill coming on to replace him, and has played only once for England since. Will was also a little exposed at tight-head, though he, too, has come back from that early disappointment to show his worth as an excellent front rower, established in the England pecking order, who would, I think, certainly do a good job for the side if selected again. Their inclusion demonstrated the slight naivety that was something of a Clive trademark in his early days; something I think he would admit to now and something he has since virtually eradicated from his make-up.

There were some other slightly eccentric decisions, too. For instance, Tim Rodber was dropped for Tony Diprose which, with due respect to Tony, a fine back-rower and a top bloke, was probably not the right move. However, Clive made some perceptive selections, too. Will Greenwood came in at centre to win his first cap after a good Lions tour. Matt Perry was soon established at full-back and, after a period with Richard Hill playing open-side, Neil Back was finally given the lengthy run in the No. 7 shirt that his ability and work-rate demanded. The Hill-Back-Dallaglio back row is now recognised as one of the best world rugby has seen and Clive must take some of the credit for establishing that partnership.

It was not a vintage Wallaby side but we lost the try count 2–0, with Gregan and Tune scoring for them, and did well to hang on for a 15–15 draw thanks to Mike Catt's boot. The next side we faced were definitely of the highest standing, though. The All Blacks, Jonah Lomu and all, were the top dogs in world rugby at that time, with a number of genuine New Zealand greats – the Brooke brothers, Ian Jones, Jeff Wilson, Olo Brown and Craig Dowd – in their side. We were to play them twice and the first game, at Old Trafford, went true to form as they exposed us a little to score three tries, though we came back to score one of our own in the second half. Despite the 25–8 scoreline, though, we had surprised ourselves with how well we had competed. I think they had become an even bigger test in our minds than they actually were, and we went on our infamous 'lap of honour' to thank the northern fans for turning out to support us. I had slapped Justin Marshall, the All Black scrum-half and captain, during the match and as a result I was suspended for the next game, against the World Champion Springboks. A number of their leading World Cup lights had left to play in the UK and those of us who had been on the Lions tour knew they could be beaten. However, they were still a very strong team, on what would become a record-equalling run of Test victories, and while we scored first, they overpowered us to win 29–11 at Twickenham.

That left us with the All Blacks once again. No one thought we would get close to them, but we had a dream start, David Rees squeezing in, in the corner, and losing a couple of teeth in the process, and Lawrence Dallaglio and Richard Hill going over, too. Unfortunately, we then fell into the trap of thinking they were bound to come back, and if you think that's what they'll do, then they'll do it. Walter Little and Andrew Mehrtens both scored, in what was a very quick, tough Test match. By the end we had pretty much fought ourselves to a standstill to finish 26–26.

They had not played particularly well, considering how they could play, and we caught them on the hop, but a high-scoring draw and three tries to two against the All Blacks felt pretty good. Looking back, we weren't a good enough team to beat those sides at that stage. We might have defeated the Aussies if we had had a really good day, but the New Zealanders and the South Africans were a level above us.

It had been a pretty tough baptism for Clive: four games, two heavy losses and a couple of draws. If that wasn't enough, our first game in the 1998 Five Nations was France. In Paris. Despite the fact that this was obviously going to be a very hard game, I think we were feeling a little blasé; we had just drawn with the All Blacks and we probably thought we were better than we were. The French have a nasty habit of making you pay for this sort of complacency and they dominated the game to win 24–17, the scoreline not really reflecting how far behind we had been. They had a very strong pack and did a lot of damage to us up front. Darren Garforth, who had been brought back in for Will Green after the Australia game, was subsequently dropped, something I felt responsible for, given that I had been scrummaging behind him. Rugby is a team game and a collective effort, nowhere more so than in the forwards, and Daz had paid the price for the whole pack's failure to compete.

So the situation Clive now found himself in was an uncomfortable one: five games in charge, three defeats and no wins. There was some consolation in the fact that we had played the best four teams in the world, but essentially it wasn't good enough. As we faced Wales at Twickenham there was a lot of pressure on the team to do well – and we certainly felt it. I don't know whether that contributed to our slow start, but the Welsh were certainly pretty uninhibited. They roared into an early lead, with two tries from Allan Bateman in the first twenty-five minutes, but then the match seemed to go crazy as we ran in try after try. David Rees got two tries and Austin Healey, Will Greenwood, Kyran Bracken, Lawrence Dallaglio, Neil Back and Matt Dawson all scored, too. It finished 60–26 in our favour, an astonishing scoreline then and one that would raise eyebrows even now. It was the start of a period of a year or two when attacks were getting on top of defences – in the Super-12, sides had almost run up basketball scores – though defence would rule the roost again by the time the 1999 Rugby World Cup came around. Phil Larder, our defence coach and one of the many specialists Clive had brought in to work with us, was pretty unhappy at the result. He would rather we had won 21–3 than conceded 26 points and won by thirty-odd.

We beat Scotland in our next game. This was the first of the championship's Sunday games, which made it a bit unenjoyable. If possible, the boys like to go out and have a beer or two after a match, especially if we have won, but we had to travel back to England to join up with our clubs the next morning. We finished with a game against Ireland, Cockers running in from the 22 to leave us with a Triple Crown and the knowledge that, slowly, we were gelling into a good side. If only we could have beaten France in the first game we would have notched up a Grand Slam in our first year under Clive. Luckily, we didn't know how far away that Slam was!

Looming at the end of the season was a four-Test summer tour to South Africa, New Zealand – where England would play twice – and Australia. It was a crazy schedule and definitely a tour too far. Most of the senior England squad had been in South Africa with the Lions until mid-July the previous summer and, with a World Cup coming the following year, we desperately needed some rest. A lot of us were carrying knocks. I needed to have my groin surgery repeated, for instance. Richard Hill was suffering with a back injury and Lawrence Dallaglio had shoulder problems. Maybe we could have coped with a Test, even perhaps two, in New Zealand. We could have flown down there, played the All Blacks, come home and still had time for our surgery, rehabilitation and so on. But four matches was mad. The last game was scheduled for 4 July and we were expected back at our clubs for pre-season games by early August. In the event, most of the first-choice players didn't tour, which upset some people. The attitude sometimes seems to be, 'They're professionals. They can play Test matches week in, week out,' but that is, of course, nonsense.

We sent a seriously under-strength squad, with Matt Dawson having the unenviable job of leading the party. Some of the players weren't quite good enough to play international rugby at that point, and certainly not against the likes of John Eales and Tim Horan, Jeff Wilson and Jonah Lomu, Joost van der Westhuizen and Mark Andrews. Later, it became known as the Tour of Hell. It was certainly murder for the guys, as they conceded 198 points and scored only 32 of their own. Against Australia in the first game in Brisbane, they were annihilated 76–0. They lost both Tests in New Zealand by a combined score of 104–32 and were nilled by the Springboks, going down 18–0 in the final match in Cape Town. The low point was that Australia game. The boys conceded eleven tries in what remains England's worst-ever Test defeat. I hope it stays that way. The ARU's chief executive, John O'Neill, summed the whole thing up by saying, 'They sent a squad with twenty uncapped players and they've been beaten 76–0. It's a sweet and sour taste. You win 76–0 and you don't celebrate. If ever there was a message to the English RFU, this is it. This is not what international rugby is about. It's not a contest. Those poor players, as determined and proud as they are, are not Test players.'

No concessions were made, certainly in the Australian media, to the youth and inexperience of the touring party. As far as everyone was concerned, this was England and they were expected to put up a reasonable fight. Instead, the team rapidly became a laughing stock. They did improve as the tour progressed, though, and some of the guys eventually established themselves as good internationals. Players like Phil Vickery, Danny Grewcock and Austin Healey have obviously gone on to have very good international careers. Jonny Wilkinson emerged from the carnage, as did, eventually, Josh Lewsey, who played in the centre and at fly-half on the tour, but others have never really recovered from the nightmare as their international careers were almost strangled at birth. I felt for them all as I watched on TV. It was not the players' faults. Whoever thought up the schedule needed shooting. It was crazy and it was embarrassing and humiliating for the guys and for English rugby. I remember Richard Cockerill talking about the whole experience before we played the Aussies at Twickenham later that year. It was the most embarrassing time of his rugby life, he said.

As that autumn approached, we were to play a further four matches. The first two, against the Netherlands and Italy, were qualification games for the 1999 Rugby World Cup. They were to be played at Huddersfield FC's McAlpine Stadium in a move designed to take the England team to fans in the north of the country. I could understand the thinking behind it, but while on paper these were important games, they didn't fire the public's imagination. Lawrence was injured for the Holland game, so I was named England captain for the first time. It is a massive honour, but as I've already said, becoming captain was never something I craved. I was much more concerned with getting through the game against the part-time Dutchmen without serious injuries, something we managed as, fairly predictably, we ran out 110–0 winners, with both Neil Back and Jerry Guscott scoring four tries each.

It all felt pretty pointless and the same could be said for the match against the Italians the following week. Before the match kicked off we were told that we had, in fact, already qualified for the World Cup and that we were now only playing for the right to play at Twickenham in our group. This was slightly ridiculous, because it was obvious that, whatever happened, England would be playing at Twickenham. The IRB wouldn't take the risk of not filling the place for their showpiece tournament and that meant having us there. To an extent, then, we were going through the motions. While you are always 'up' for any Test match, a late November Sunday in Huddersfield in a pretty meaningless match against lesser opposition – though to be fair, this was one of Italy's stronger teams – is never likely to produce a particularly fiery performance.

That attitude almost cost us the game, though, as the Azurri put on a great show, fighting hard for the ball and really making us work for our eventual 23–15 win. Dan Luger, who had made his debut against Holland, scored early on, but they came back strongly, and Alessandro Troncon was denied a legitimate try when he burrowed under to touch down, as the referee was unsighted. By the time the ref got into position, Richard Cockerill had whipped the ball away and the ref couldn't give it. The Italians were only a point behind as the final whistle approached. Will Greenwood sealed it with a chip-and-chase for a well-taken score, but many observers felt we hadn't deserved the win. The feeling in the England camp was fairly flat, too. We had played dreadfully and it was one of the few times that we have received a genuine dressing-down from the management. To an extent, as captain, I probably carried the can. We had been slow and pretty unimaginative and I think Clive felt, wrongly but perhaps not surprisingly, that was a reflection of how I liked to play.

He was certainly glad to see Lawrence back in the saddle for the next game, a much tougher encounter with the Wallabies. It was no classic, though it was never going to be a feast of tries — our defence was getting stronger and theirs was perhaps the best in the world at that time. We scored the only one after Austin Healey made a break and Jerry got on the end of it to touch down. We were leading as the game edged towards the close, but John Eales, who was kicking their penalties on the day, stepped up to put one over for a final scoreline of 12–11. We came off thinking it was a game we could, and perhaps should, have won — an unusual feeling for us after matches against Australia at that time.

As we entered December, South Africa were our final visitors. They had won seventeen consecutive matches and were going for the world record of eighteen. They were a very good side, playing a fairly 'un-South African' brand of running rugby, and they had certainly been a cut above when they beat us the previous year. The game didn't start too well for us, as we lost Tony Underwood to injury after seven or eight minutes and conceded a try to Pieter Rossouw after ten minutes, when Bobby Skinstad, their new back-row superstar, made a dynamic break. But we bounced back quickly, Mike Catt hoisting a kick to the corner and Dan Luger offloading skilfully to Jerry Guscott to score and make it 7–7 with the conversion. We camped down in their half for much of the game and a couple of kickable penalties made it 13–7 to us. We spent the last ten minutes mauling them to maintain the pressure and keep them away from our line. At one point, they almost got over with a length-of-the-field breakaway, but Danny Luger got back to stop them. Right at the death, we had a defensive scrum just outside our 22. We only needed to win our ball to be sure of the result, and their only chance of getting the score they needed lay in turning us over. They put on an almighty shove and Darren Garforth, who was later given our man of the match award, slipped when the pressure came on and fell face down in the mud. I went down behind him and the Springbok pack ran over the top of us like a steamroller over a pair of cartoon mice and we peeled ourselves off the grass feeling about an inch thick. The referee re-set the scrummage and we survived the next engagement.

We had secured our first big win under Clive. We had had something of a torrid time against southern-hemisphere sides since he had come on board and we were all pleased for him and the rest of the management. We had worked incredibly hard on our defence, in particular, and, after the Tour of Hell and the tough four-match series of the previous autumn, our defeat of the Tri-Nations champions was a great reward. Since then, victories over South Africa at Twickenham have become fairly commonplace, almost to the point of some observers taking them for granted. Sometimes I think people forget that it is only four or five years ago that this was a very impressive win for us.

If 1998 had been a hard year, 1999 was going to be harder still. The last Five Nations – Italy would join to make it Six the following year – was to be followed by a game against

Australia Down Under, a trio of autumn warm-ups and then the main event itself, the 1999 Rugby World Cup. We started well against Scotland at Twickenham, dominating the first twenty minutes to lead 14–0. But they came back at us very well and, as we made errors, they grew in confidence. We were a tough team to break down, but Alan Tait scored twice, Gregor Townsend ran 60yds for a try of his own and, by the end, we were almost hanging on for the 24–21 result. A nineteen-year-old Jonny Wilkinson, playing as centre along-side Jerry Guscott, was probably the pick of our backs. He certainly made the win for us, kicking three conversions and a penalty, with Kenny Logan missing three for them.

A shaky start, then, and as we headed for Dublin many critics were tipping the Irish for the title. They had started to emerge as a real force and their pack, in particular, were very highly rated. In the event, although it was a hard-fought victory, we were fairly comfortable winners at 27–15. Matt Perry and Tim Rodber each scored a try and, once again, Jonny proved nerveless with the boot, putting over four penal-ties and a conversion, as well as some massive hits in the midfield. One tackle, to smash back a rampaging Keith Wood, brought gasps from the crowd and certainly would have made the Irish players think twice about running at him. Ironically, given his relatively slight stature, some of us had doubted he'd be able to handle the physical challenge of playing in the centre. Jonny was clearly a very talented young guy and people were already sitting up and taking notice.

France had beaten us well in Paris the year before and were looking for a fifth consecutive victory over England, but our defence held firm. They scored only at the death and by that time we had put 21 points on them through Jonny's kicking. It was a typical English performance of that period. Occasionally, as against Wales, we cut loose, but if we won, more often it tended to be by keeping other sides out, playing for territory and maintaining possession through the forwards. We were a better defensive side than we were an attacking force, which perhaps frustrated Clive a little. He wanted us to thrill the crowds with all-out 'total rugby', but we weren't really ready for that.

A Grand Slam beckoned and, if you read the papers, we were nailed on for it. With the finishing touches still being put to Cardiff's Millennium Stadium, Wales were playing their 'home' games at Wembley that year. The place was full of red shirts and, for the last ever Five Nations game, the organisers had gone to town, with Max Boyce, Tom Jones and the Stereophonics playing to the crowd. We had suffered a few injuries, with ex-rugby league player Barrie-Jon Mather and Steve Hanley in at centre and right wing respectively for Jerry Guscott and David Rees, but we started well. Dan Luger burst away early to score, Richard Hill and Hanley followed him with quick tries, and we should have been cruising by half-time. But whenever they got within 30 or 40yds of our line we seemed to be penalised, usually for technical infringements or offsides that were marginal at best, like guys being pinged for offside when they had just come up very quickly in the defensive line. It was all very frustrating. With Neil Jenkins in the Welsh side, every time the whistle went it was three points to Jenks and he kept them in a game I never felt they looked like winning.

We turned round 25–18 ahead, but a couple of minutes

after the restart they got their Kiwi full-back Shane Howarth over in the corner and the conversion meant the game was tied. Jonny kicked a couple of penalties to give us a 31–25 lead, but after a first half in which we had been scoring tries all over the place, we couldn't get the touchdown we needed to take us away from them. The turning point people always talk about was Lawrence's decision to pass up another kickable penalty to go for the corner. We failed to score from the resulting line-out, when three points, very possible from where the penalty was awarded, would have taken us nine points — more than a converted try — clear.

There were plenty of other turning points though. A few minutes after the line-out, Tim Rodber put in a shuddering tackle on Colin Charvis from which we were awarded a penalty. Again, it was in a very kickable position. However, it was reversed after the touch judge told the referee that Tim had used his shoulder. Technically, he was right — Rodber hadn't wrapped Charvis up — but I felt this was a harsh call. From a player's point-of-view, it was just a great tackle — if it had happened to me I certainly wouldn't have been looking for a penalty. There is a famous JPR moment, after all, where he shoulder-barged a guy into touch in the corner to save a Welsh Grand Slam. Everyone always talks about what a great tackle that was. No one ever says, 'Actually, that should have been a penalty try.' So another potential three points went begging. From the penalty, they kicked to touch and called a short-ened line-out. They won possession, Scotty Gibbs charged through, a couple of guys missed him and he was over the line. That made it 31–30 to us. It was Jenks to win it with the conversion. I know where I'd have put my house and he didn't disappoint the ecstatic Welsh supporters. Over it went and we had lost by the single point.

I was absolutely sickened. It was a terrible, horrible feeling. To be three tries to nil up at half-time and not win was absolutely devastating and we felt, essentially, that we had thrown away a Grand Slam. I had to go for a drugs test afterwards and I remember sitting up in the testing area with Scott Gibbs and Scott Quinnell, listening to their fans singing and celebrating outside, and thinking there was no worse place to be. The two Scotts were fine. They knew we were feeling down and didn't want to rub it in, though I'm sure they got stuck in to the celebrations once they were back in their changing room, and rightly so.

I honestly don't feel we were beaten by a better side. It wasn't as if Wales had been battering at our line all game; they had been kept in it with lots of very technical, 'picky' penalties which were inside Neil's range. But we couldn't hold the referee – or Lawrence – responsible for the defeat. The game didn't turn on the penalties or that one decision of Lol's. Other players had let Howarth in and missed the tackles on Gibbsy. In fact, we had all made mistakes, so we all shouldered the blame. I drove home the next morning, vowing to delete that whole day from my life – I knew if I didn't it would prey on my mind – and I pretty much haven't thought about it again until now.

At least things were looking up at the club. Although the mood had improved after Bob left, Dean and John had not worked any immediate miracles since taking over and the start of the 1998–99 season had brought no real signs of improvement. We went away to a training camp in France, losing a pre-season match against Bourgoin, and then beat lowly Rotherham 5–0 in the rain at Sheffield one Sunday. The Welsh comedian Max Boyce was at Leicester shortly afterwards for a function and he thought that was a hilarious result for this great English club.

First up in the league we played Quins, who had signed Zinzan Brooke. No one would have been piling into the bookies on our behalf, but we just clicked. We had real pace on the wings with Nnamdi Ezulike and Leon Lloyd, and we had Joel Stransky at No. 10 and Austin Healey at No. 9, behind probably the best pack in the league. We put forty-odd points on Quins and carried on in that style, scoring heavily and hardly losing a game. We went down to Bedford, where Rory Underwood was now playing. We knew Rory liked to show people the outside when he was defending. We also knew Nnamdi had incredible pace. We told him what would happen and suggested he take it. Sure enough, early on we got the ball out wide, Rory showed Nnamdi the outside, Nnamdi took it and skinned him. He was lightning quick on the hard, early season grounds.

Some of the success was down to bringing on Bob's signings and Fritz van Heerden and Martin Corry were at the start of what would turn out to be great seasons for them. However, Dean and John also brought on young lads like Leon, Lewis Moody and Paul Gustard in the back row, and Derek Jelley in the front row, as well as introducing some good players of their own. The ex-Wallaby and ACT centre Pat Howard was a key signing, as was Tim Stimpson, who came down from Newcastle to replace Mike Horak at fullback. Dave Lougheed, a big, tough Canadian winger, came over and played in place of Ezulike when the ground got slower. He stopped Inga Tuigamala in his tracks when we faced Newcastle and scored the following week against Gloucester, suddenly giving us another back three option: a more physical, big-hitting back than we were used to.

Our team spirit was excellent and we were able to go up to Newcastle to win the league away from home. We had Matt Poole's stag do planned at Whitley Bay that weekend. Quite rightly, Dean had told us to cancel it, reminding us that we were playing for the title and he didn't want us distracted. 'Yes, you're right, Dean,' we said, but went on planning it in secret. The whole team stayed over in Newcastle that Sunday night. Some of the boys got up in the morning and went home, but the 'Whitley Bay 13' headed off to the coast for a legendary Bank Holiday Monday celebration of the club's third title – the first of the new era.

It was a great year for us, particularly after all the upheaval of the previous twelve months. Martin Corry, our player of the season, Fritz vàn Heerden and Darren Garforth had stood out, but we had played with heart and flair right across the team. In a long season – the league expanded to fourteen teams and there were twenty-six matches that year, although English clubs didn't play in Europe due to a TV wrangle – we were very strong defensively. Phil Larder, England's defensive coach, had joined the club and his work paid real dividends, with teams finding it very hard to break us down. On the downside, Joel Stransky had been forced to retire through a knee injury. This was a big blow, as Joel was obviously a very good player, with more pace than you thought. He had a habit of dummying his way through to score the killer blow under the posts and had formed a good partnership with Austin Healey at scrum-half. Neil Back had been his usual consistent self – if you look at the history of the league, no one touches him for games played and consistent excellence. The only guys who come close are Jason Leonard, Darren Garforth, Graham Rowntree and myself, and none of us have the same individual impact on matches as Backy does. He has been playing at the highest level for fourteen years now and shows no real signs of slowing down. Tim Stimpson proved a great signing, too. He is leaving Leicester at the end of 2003 to join the French club, Perpignan, and this is a shame, but maybe it will help him revive his international career. Tim has the lot – pace, strength, athleticism – and could yet return to the England squad.

With the 1999 World Cup now very much on our horizon, the England squad headed to the Couran Cove resort on picturesque South Stradbroke Island, a fifteen-minute boat ride off Queensland's Gold Coast, for our summer training camp. It had been sold to us as a few weeks of 'active recovery'; guys would spend time working on fitness, but the workload would be relatively light and it would be a chance to relax and spend time together as a squad. However, it turned out to be anything but relaxing, as we were 'beasted' for virtually the whole time out there. The 7a.m. gym sessions were followed by jungle runs and more weights work. It was exhausting. Most nights I fell asleep on my sofa in front of the TV at around 8.30p.m., waking up and crawling into bed by about 10p.m. There was precious little time for R&R and when the chance presented itself, I got it horribly wrong.

One day we were offered a choice between golf and a

deep-sea fishing trip. I don't really play golf. I don't really fish either, but the thought of a pleasant afternoon bobbing up and down on the ocean, sitting in the sun and reeling in the odd mangrove jack or stingray, sounded appealing. The 5a.m. start seemed a small price to pay, but by mid-morning we were miles out to sea, caught in a heavy swell and chucking up everywhere. I have never felt so ill. Our team doctor, Terry Crystal, had consumed virtually the entire squad's supply of sea-sickness pills to absolutely no avail – it was dribbling out of his nose and he was almost in tears. I had a good laugh at him, but then I stood up. By the time I was upright I had to grab his bag to throw up into it myself. I've never known anything like it. It was extraordinary. The place was like a ghost ship – deathly quiet, with guys lying around trying to get comfortable. Hilly was outside on deck, in the pouring rain, on his back with his jacket over his head and Backy had gone into the foetal position on the floor. Clive and Phil Larder were, bizarrely, utterly unaffected, but they were the only ones. I have never been so happy to get on to dry land. Guys literally kissed the ground like the Pope arriving at an airport.

Before we came back we had a couple of games. The first, against Queensland, ended 39–14 in our favour, but the second was a much tougher affair, the Centenary Test against the Wallabies. I would lead the team, with Lawrence losing the captaincy during the summer over claims that appeared in the *News of the World*. He was also missing from the starting line-up as he worked to sort out his private life, Martin Corry playing at No. 8. It was a huge match and we started well, with Matt Perry scoring after twenty-five minutes and our pack dominating most of the first forty, but the Wallabies exposed us out wide to score two tries in each half. The last one, by David Wilson, should have been disallowed when he fumbled the ball, and although we came back with a second by Pezza at the end to make it 22–15, that score probably flattered us a little. We weren't too disappointed, I guess. We had competed against them fairly well after a long season and the tough pre-season camp in Couran Cove, and the result was obviously much better than the previous year's 76–0 shocker.

The build-up to the World Cup tournament was like nothing I have experienced before or since. Back in England, we continued with our training camp, spending the whole of the summer and early autumn together, working hard on our fitness and skills. We were probably stronger and fitter than we have ever been, but we felt a massive weight of expectation on all of our shoulders. Clive had always insisted he be judged on the World Cup, which put a lot of pressure on him and us. Matters weren't helped by the draw for the competition. We were sharing our pool with New Zealand and whoever won the game between us was likely to progress relatively unhindered to the knock-out stages. However, the tournament setup – five pools of four – meant best losers in each group had to play off against each other to qualify for the quarter-finals. This was crazy, because it handed a massive advantage to the pool winners.

In retrospect, our warm-up games were not ideal. We faced two 'Premiership All Stars' sides, scratch teams made up of club players who didn't really offer us any serious opposition. We won 92–17 and 67–14, at Twickenham and Anfield, before taking on two 'proper' sides: the USA and Canada. While Canada, very strong and aggressive in the forwards, are never easy to play against, they were hardly ideal preparation for the All Blacks. We were fairly poor, but beat them 36–11, with Lawrence coming back into the side three days after being fined £15,000 for 'bringing the game into disrepute' following a ten-week investigation into the newspaper allegations against him. Earlier, we had beaten the Eagles 106–8 in a pretty meaningless game. With a month still to go before the tournament began, we spent time working on team-building exercises with the Royal Marines. It was all good stuff – they put us through our paces, simulating ship fires, emergency beach landings and so on, for us to deal with – but behind all the fun and games, I think the World Cup was becoming too big in our minds.

We weren't favourites for the tournament. We weren't even near-favourites. A semi-final spot would have been a fair result, but because we had beaten the Boks in the autumn, the press were building us up, and instead of enjoying what we were doing and giving it our best shot, we slowly got sucked in. We beat Italy 67–7 in our opening game and then turned our attention to the All Blacks. We probably had the better of the possession and territory in the first ten or fifteen minutes, but they scored first, Jonah Lomu bashing through our defence, allowing Tana Umaga to run to the line and offload to Jeff Wilson to get over in the corner. Phil de Glanville got one back for us in the second half, pouncing on a loose ball that bounced back from the posts after a kick ahead. We were maybe in the ascendant at that point, but the key moment was another Lomu score, the kind of try only he can produce, with tacklers flying every-where on his run in. That took the wind out of our sails and as we tried to force the pace to come back, Byron Kelleher got over again to make it 30–16. We had battled hard – you couldn't question the guys' effort or commitment – but it wasn't enough.

Our World Cup chances died that day. Although we beat Tonga comfortably by 101–10 in our final pool game, we now faced a play-off match against Fiji just five days after-wards, with the quarter-final, against South Africa, only four days further on. It was an impossible schedule. We defeated the Fijians 45–24, but were picking up injuries along the way and had no time to rehab them properly and no time for general rest. Jerry Guscott scored a brace against Tonga, but had ended his international career that day, and Matt Dawson also hobbled off. Austin Healey, Matt Perry and Dan Luger all picked up knocks against Fiji.

That game had been pretty intense – although the score-line was comfortable, we were almost hanging on by the end – and had come on a Wednesday. On the Thursday, we had to travel to Paris and that left two days to recover and prepare for the Springboks. In contrast, their pool had been fairly simple. They had beaten Scotland first up and that was, effec-tively, their group stage over with, as Spain and Uruguay weren't going to trouble them. I spoke to Nick Mallett, then their coach, some time later and he said that once they had beaten the Scots they spent the next three weeks preparing for us. Their squad players had all had a good run out and they were mentally and physically fresh, whereas guys like myself and Lawrence had started every game and we were all knackered.

I think that showed in the match. The first half was fairly cagey, with both sides kicking a lot of ball, but once they nosed ahead we had nothing left and, although we fought as hard as we could, we just weren't able to come back at them.

Clive had controversially selected Paul Grayson ahead of Jonny Wilkinson, by now our first-choice fly-half. Perhaps Jonny had struggled a bit against the All Blacks – though we all had to an extent – and I guess Clive probably decided to go for experience in picking Grays. It was a big decision for Clive, and it might have been the wrong one, but it's always easy to pick a team in hindsight. At the time, Jonny was a very young lad and Paul was a vastly experienced player who was never going to let us down, so Woody just made the judgment call.

The big fly-half news, though, was about the guy wearing green. Jannie de Beer applied the killer blows to our World Cup with a world record five, sweetly struck drop-goals soaring over our heads, each three points knocking a little more of the stuffing out of us. It feels, now, like a bad dream, and it was a genuinely surreal experience, similar, in its own way, to our World Cup exit at the hands of New Zealand in 1995. Once again, we were rendered impotent on the pitch. Later, de Beer said he was touched by God that day and it certainly seemed like someone up there was against us. His kicks were going over from miles out and we just couldn't get pressure on him to try to affect his accuracy. The Springboks were making good yards through our midfield, gaining momentum and putting us on the back foot. That meant that when the ball was spun back to Jannie he was able to take his time in lining up the kicks. We needed to make bigger tackles and slow their ball down, giving us time to line up quick guys to get out towards him — as Australia did the following week, having studied our defeat and learned from it.

The final score, 44–21, was pretty shattering and fairly emphatic. There were no two ways about it: we were out of the World Cup and on the way home the next morning. It took me a long time to get over the disappointment, mentally. We had put so much effort into our preparations, and had been together for so long, that it was a hell of a shock when, suddenly, it was all over. I went from feeling part of the year's biggest sporting event, surrounded by the squad, the media and the fans in London and Paris, to training back in Leicester on a wet Tuesday morning, doing one-on-one defence drills with Peter Short, a huge lump of a lad who had just turned up at the club and naturally wanted to prove himself by smashing a few 'superstars' to pieces. I was pretty down for quite a while.

We were never really good enough to win the tournament. Australia, New Zealand, France and South Africa were all better teams. With a bit of luck, maybe we could have progressed further. If a few things had gone our way against the All Blacks, we would have faced Scotland in the quarters at Murrayfield. I would fancy us to have won that, and once you're in the semis anything can happen. A few people remembered Clive's bold request that he be judged on the World Cup, and there were calls for his head in the media. The RFU don't get everything right by any means, but they made the right decision in sticking by Woody. The disappointment of the World Cup and his first few matches in charge aside, he was already making some much-needed changes to the England setup. Before long, they would start to bear fruit.

CHAPTER SEVEN

MOVING ON

The World Cup was undeniably a failure from England's point of view. We should have done better than reaching the quarter-final. However, it did mark an important turning point for us. The tournament became too heavy, too big in our minds. We were talking about it from five or six months out. Any mistake you made in training seemed to be greeted with a phrase beginning with, 'If this was the World Cup final . . .' The pressure on us became so great that we were unable to enjoy ourselves and relax, and that had an effect on our rugby. To their credit, Clive and the management learned from that and they have tended to back off a little since, creating a new England team in the process.

As we headed into the early part of 2000, I had an Achilles tendon injury. It was caused by the action of the tendon rubbing on my heel bone. The bone had responded by growing and the resultant spur was irritating the tendon. It is the kind of niggly injury that players often have, particularly line-out jumpers, but during the build-up to the World Cup and the tournament itself I hadn't had time to get it properly treated. It got worse as the weeks dragged on and I finally succumbed at the turn of the year. At the time, it was very frustrating. Surgery was an option, though in the end it would be relieved by physiotherapy: hours of painful deep-calf massage and stretching.

I was out of action for the first three games of that year's Six Nations and watched from the sidelines as Matt Dawson led a reinvigorated England to victories over Ireland, France and then Wales. Mike Tindall, with one try, and Ben Cohen, with a brace, announced themselves on the international scene in that first match against the Irish, the whole team playing some really good attacking rugby to win 50–18.

The toughest game of that period – France away – was won without either side scoring a try, but with an immense defensive effort by England. Jonny Wilkinson, in particular, made several crunching tackles, including a spectacular hit on Emile Ntamack which smashed the big winger to the ground and is still replayed on rugby shows several years on. Right at the end, with Simon Shaw and Austin Healey both in the bin, the guys forced back a wave of French attacks and held on to win 15–9. The boys beat Wales 46–12, scoring five tries, the pick of them a rampaging run by Lawrence Dallaglio that saw him cross the line with what looked like half the Welsh team clinging to his back.

It was not a comfortable time to be out injured and there was some sniping in the media, pointing out how well the side was playing without me. A few columnists wanted to know why we had not performed like this in the World Cup. The answer was kind of obvious: we had been facing New Zealand and South Africa then, and they were a little better. The defensive, dogged performance against *Les Bleus*, hard-fought and won with Jonny's boot and not by beating teams with width, showed the difference between playing the really good teams and playing the lesser sides.

I came back from my Achilles injury and played one club game before England were due to face Italy. Clive phoned me and told me that, despite the fact that I was fit, he was going to stick with the same team, including the second row of Simon Shaw and Garath Archer. These guys had been playing well, so this seemed fair enough. I told him I understood and I was genuinely not upset. Of course, I wanted to be involved in the team and I wanted to be playing. But when you have an injury, particularly one like I had had, which is niggly and hard to pin down and treat, what you want more than anything else is just to be fit. Most of the time I wasn't thinking about playing rugby at all – the real frustration was in not being able to run properly.

I went over with the A guys to play Italy's second team at L'Áquila, an hour from Rome, on the Friday. I just needed to get some game time, but the match was pretty meaning-less – they put out a very young side and it wasn't as strong as a Premiership fixture. Back in Rome, England duly cleaned up the senior Italian side to make it four wins out of four. It was England's first visit there, but I have to confess I didn't actually watch the game. Kay had come over and we spent a great weekend enjoying the sights of this brilliant city. I think Rome will become the highlight of the Six Nations calendar for England fans, particularly given that we seem to play there in the warm spring.

That left a Grand Slam decider, against Scotland, who had lost their previous four games, at Murrayfield. Once again, Clive called and explained that there was no place in the team for me. Again, I could live with that. It seemed fair enough

on the incumbent players, I had no divine right to selection
– though in hindsight it was perhaps a little strange that I
didn't even make the bench – and it meant I could concentrate on making the tour to South Africa that summer.

However, I was upset and annoyed to read a few more of
those little digs in the media. One suggested 'the word from
inside the camp' was that Johnson wouldn't make the team as
captain or player, but who knows whether that was genuine
or not? Journalists can make things up and then hide behind
the anonymity of an imaginary 'source'. I would be disappointed if it had emanated from the England setup, though.
If you're going to say something like that, say it on record. I
also remember Clive making a comment to the effect of,
'Martin Johnson needs to play some big games to get back
into the squad.' I didn't need that – I was already feeling down
after being injured for so long – but it was blindingly obvious
anyway that I had a job on to win back my place. England
had won four games on the trot with displays of style and
real guts, and everyone was buzzing about them after a poor
World Cup. If you're injured and the team looks as though
it's about to win a Grand Slam, it doesn't take a rocket scien-
tist to work out the situation. Winning teams rarely get
changed. In his earlier days, Clive had a habit of speaking
before he thought things through properly. In this instance,
I imagine he was trying to motivate me, but maybe he should
have credited me with a bit more intelligence.

I remember watching the game on TV at home. We started
well, with the Scots conceding penalties and Matt Dawson
taking a few quick tap-and-gos to keep them on the back
foot. Although they took the lead with a Duncan Hodge

penalty after a scoreless first quarter, Lawrence scored immediately afterwards from a close-range scrum and things looked
really good, with England apparently in a position to take
control. But it started to rain in the second half and the
harder it came down the more Scotland came back into it,
playing the conditions much better, while England became a
bit ragged. They suffered from one or two bad refereeing decisions. Garath Archer, in particular, was wrongly penalised
several times, with the TV commentators talking nonsense
about his 'indiscipline'. But, essentially, the boys were guilty
of trying to play too much rugby, too close to their own line,
on a day when they should have concentrated on kicking or
driving into the opposition half and pressurising them. They
hoisted a couple of up-and-unders and Scotland got nowhere
near the wet ball in the downpour. That was the way to play
but, for some reason, they didn't repeat the tactic and they
paid the price as the Scottish side ran out eventual winners
by 19 points to 13.

I am not the best of watchers. I had been elated for the
guys when they won in Paris, because I knew how big a win
it was. I had been tense at the start of the Welsh and Irish
games at Twickenham, where I was working in Leicester's hospitality marquee, but that had passed once it was clear England
were going to win. It's hard to describe how I felt as the final
whistle went in that Scotland game. Numb. Incredulous.
Unbelieving. To see it happen again, after Wales the year
before, was unreal. I felt for Matt, as captain, because I already
knew the grief the team were going to get. They would have
been feeling awful and the last thing you need at times like
that is recriminations and inquests. They were still Six Nations

champions, but that had a hollow feel to it. In his disappointment, Matt even forgot to collect the trophy from Princess
Anne, later apologising for his faux pas. I'm not sure I would
have wanted to collect it, either.

Of course, the same people who had earlier written me
off in the press now suggested Clive had made a massive
tactical mistake in not playing me; that it couldn't have
happened with Johnson on the field. That was all nonsense.
It's very easy to see from the sidelines what's going wrong;
it's much harder to fix it on the field. The bottom line was
Scotland outplayed England in that second half and deserved
their win.

If the international season had ended on a sour note,
Leicester's was, in many ways, a triumph. We had suffered
more than any other club in losing front-line players to the
World Cup. Our pack, in particular, was affected. The entire
first-choice front row was gone. Fritz van Heerden, away with
the Springboks, and I were missing from the second row. Neil
Back and Martin Corry, two starting back-rowers, were also
on international duty. In the back line, Austin Healey and
Will Greenwood, two of our most creative and dangerous
guys, had joined up with England, too. It was obviously crucial
for the younger and less-experienced guys left behind to hold
the fort, with Pat Howard and one or two older heads in
charge. On a rare break from England camp, we watched them
play Northampton at Franklin's Gardens. It made ominous
viewing as they were well beaten by a Saints side which was
less affected by the World Cup, but was still missing the likes
of Dawson, Grayson, Rodber and Pat Lam.

Some people started suggesting that it was wrong to

continue the English league schedule with so many senior players away. Instead, they were calling for the Premiership to start once the tournament was over. I felt this was wrong, because the existing timing gave the younger guys a run in the team. Ben Kay was a case in point. Signed, essentially, as cover for myself and Fritz, he rapidly proved what a good player he was and by the end of that season was pressuring Fritz for his place. Without getting the exposure to Premiership rugby he received by replacing internationals, it might have taken him longer to come through. Lewis Moody, Louis Deacon and Adam Balding were others who started to emerge that autumn.

Things gradually improved – we watched them beat London Irish away from home with a last-minute Stimpson penalty – and by the time we had got back from the World Cup, earlier than we would have liked, Leicester were still very much in touch. It was a seesaw start to the campaign, though. We were knocked out of the European Cup around Christmas time and were hammered at Saracens, too, playing poorly and looking a shadow of our normal selves. Our cause wasn't helped by injuries. Darren Garforth, a talisman for the team, damaged his neck and was out for a while. I had my Achilles problem, too. It was fairly painful, but I played on for some time, certainly beyond when I should have done. After we lost to Glasgow in the European Cup, Dean rightly made the decision for me – I needed to rest it until it was right. As well as affecting my Six Nations chances, it led to me missing two months of club rugby, with my eventual comeback delayed by a further, frustrating fortnight after I was concussed in training.

By the time I did return, we were back flying high. Light had started to appear at the end of the tunnel after Christmas, when we beat Bath at the Rec on Boxing Day, with Geordan scoring a try after coming on for Ezulike, and that was followed by a good win over Quins at home. From then on we didn't lose a league game all year. With two matches left, we had Bristol away and Bath at home and we needed to win one of them. Bristol was a spicy affair – they were a tough, aggressive team, with guys like Dean Ryan and Garath Archer in their ranks. Bob Dwyer, now installed down there, would obviously have loved them to turn us over, too, but we came through to win and became the first team to retain the Premiership title. It felt fantastic. We had been in a little bit of trouble with injuries earlier in the season and to come through as we had spoke volumes for the character of the squad. Importantly, the emergence of those younger players during the World Cup was to provide us with depth for the next few seasons. Personally, I felt good – finally a positive note after all the negatives of my injury and England's two big defeats.

That match had an amusing postscript. Neil Back, obviously concerned about the furious rate at which his hair was (and is) falling out, had secretly signed up to have some treatment at a specialist London hair clinic. In return for that and, presumably, some wedge, Backy would be endorsing their services. Everything went well until his hair started to come loose during the Bristol game, and unfortunately it didn't survive contact with the Shōgun forwards. By the final whistle it was flapping around like a Bobby Charlton comb-over. Photographs of the Tigers celebrating the title show one forlorn, little bloke, grim-faced and with a hat jammed down on his head, not exactly joining in the fun.

That left Bath at Welford Road, the final match of a long season. There was technically nothing riding on the fixture, but both sides badly wanted to win. Although we had taken the title, they had had a good late season run to finish second. There was a lot of chat in the media about how Bath were the best team in the division and how we played boring, one-dimensional rugby. We were very keen to ram these words back down the critics' throats and we did it in style, putting 40 points on them after the game opened up in the second half. Darren Garforth returned in that match, coming on as a sub. He was completely yampy and fired up, desperate for action. Dorian West, who was out with injury himself, always remembers coming on to the pitch with some water for the lads when we scored a try just after Garf had joined the fray. He was confronted by Garforth, thundering back towards our half, with a crazed look on his face and shouting, 'I'm back! I'm back!'

'Daz,' said Westy. 'Want some water, mate?'

'I'm back!' yelled Garf, right in his face, and knocked him to the ground with a forearm smash.

We received the Zurich trophy in front of our fans at the end of the game. Afterwards, the whole crowd flocked on to the pitch to join us, shaking our hands, patting our backs and grabbing autographs. It was one of those great, spontaneous moments, a fantastic scene that would not be repeated in any other sport. Can you imagine Manchester United supporters streaming on to the Old Trafford turf to mingle with Roy Keane and Co.? We were there for an hour and a half, chatting and signing away, and I remember thinking that club rugby couldn't get much better.

That summer, England were due to go to South Africa for a two-Test tour, complete with three midweek games. Six years earlier, we had won three and lost five on a similar visit. Six or seven months after Jannie de Beer had kicked us out of the 1999 World Cup, this would be a good opportunity to see how far we had progressed in relation to the Springboks. Garath Archer was unavailable, which left a position in the second row open and I got the nod. When Matt Dawson had to pull out of the tour party with injury, that took away the difficult decision for Clive as to who to make captain. In the event, I led the team out there, but I would have been more than happy to go under Matt, or anyone else. I just wanted to get back into the side.

This sort of tour can turn into the kind of trip that players would rather miss. The guys had had no real rest for a long time. There had been the pre-World Cup camp, then the competition itself, then the domestic season and the Six Nations. That's a lot of rugby, and this could have tipped people over the edge, but I think the management realised this. Previously, I think they'd felt that a big game coming up meant lots of hard work when, actually, that may be the moment to taper off. This time, there would be no 'beasting' of the players, no attempt to 'set the tone' by over-training, no doing stuff for the sake of it. They kept it to a minimum and also lessened the workload by basing us in one hotel in Johannesburg, a really plush place on Jan Smuts Avenue, which occupies the Mayfair position on the South African Monopoly board.

It was a very wealthy area, but everyone lived behind high security fences and we were given a briefing on arrival, warning us not to stray from the hotel compound. It had originally been built as apartments, with the reception at the bottom of a hill, and the players all had individual rooms up a long, winding road. It can't have come cheap – the rooms were full of nice little touches, such as TVs which magically rose out of nowhere at the touch of a button – but Clive was very keen for us to have the best possible facilities and he was prepared to spend the money to ensure we did. His thinking was that if you aspire to be the best – which surely all teams do – you need to surround yourself with excellence in everything you do. If that meant keeping us in Johannesburg, rather than travelling all over to places like Potchefstroom, Pretoria, Kimberley and Bloemfontein, where we would play some of our matches, so be it. That was welcomed by the team. Previously, on old-style tours, we would have gone everywhere en masse. That's great for public relations, because the whole South African rugby public gets to see a bit more of you, you see more of the country, and so on. However, with five games in five locations, what it actually means is five half-days taken up with travelling and on a short tour two-and-a-half days' travel is both tiring and a long time out of your working schedule. We took a bit of flak for our supposedly 'insular' attitude, but you have to do what's best for you if you want to win Test and midweek matches in a place like that.

The press and public out there tend to beat the drum for the Springboks pretty loudly, though they soon turn on them if things aren't going well, and nowhere more so than in small-town South Africa. Potchefstroom, the setting for our first midweek game, against Western Transvaal Leopards, had a tight little stadium and going there was like a return to old-school touring. The big England machine rolls in and comes up against the whole town, not just the fifteen guys on the pitch. Everyone is a rugby fanatic, everyone wants to see you and everyone wants to see you get beaten. At one stage, a fan ran on to the pitch and we watched in some amazement as the police set a dog on him and then stood back and watched as it set to work. The boys came through despite the hostile atmosphere, winning 52–22 and setting a good tone for the tour.

The first Test was at Loftus Versfeld in Pretoria. The match was something of a step into the unknown. We had beaten them in 1998, but they had kicked us out of the World Cup, so recent honours were fairly even. The odds were tipped their way by the location; at a place like Loftus, full of Afrikaner rugby fanatics, there is no hiding place. We were hit beforehand by the late withdrawal of Jonny Wilkinson, with a nasty stomach bug, and Austin Healey stepped in for him at very short notice, on the morning of the game. Fair play to Austin, that was a big ask. He hadn't played a lot at fly-half, probably wouldn't have practised too much in the position, either, and this was a pretty daunting place to find out how good you were. His attitude was spot-on. A lot of players would have been nervous as hell, but he is either a very good actor or genuinely was the calmest, most confident guy imaginable in the changing room beforehand. He sat there without, seemingly, a care in the world, wearing his favourite pre-match T-shirt. I think at that stage it was his 'Little Tinker' shirt. More recently, he has had one with the fairly obvious slogan 'Lucky

T-shirt' written on it. He played pretty well – in the circumstances, fantastically.

The game was fairly even, with Danny Luger picking and
going for a try and the South Africans keeping the board
ticking over themselves. In Jonny's absence, Tim Stimpson had
come on to the wing to kick goals and replace Austin. We
had got ourselves into a good field position and the ball was
kicked through for Stimmo to chase. He raced ahead of Andre
Vos and as the ball bounced high over the line he looked to
have got his hand on it and appeared to have just got it down,
with Vos tackling him in the process. My view at the time
was that it was a try – I think that to this day – but it went
to the video referee. There were only a couple of possible
interpretations, I felt: either Stimmo had got the ball, had
been tackled and had grounded it (try) or Vos had tackled
Tim before he had the ball (penalty try). You always feel,
though, that decisions are hard to come by when you're away.
I looked across at the referee and said, 'We're not going to
get given this. Let's just carry on with the game.' The decision came back a few moments later: knock-on, scrum to
South Africa. A tough one to take, but there's nothing you
can do.

With around ten minutes to go, I had to come off as I
was feeling sick and dehydrated and had stomach cramps.
Lawrence played in the second row for the final few minutes
and I watched as the Boks potted a penalty to win it 18–13.
It was pretty disappointing. I'm sure that, if the Stimpson try
had been allowed, we would have gone on to win the game.
We had certainly put ourselves in a position where we could
have done so. Given what had happened in Paris a few months

previously, though, it was still a good performance. Julian White had made his debut. Pretoria against the Boks is a hell of a place to play your first Test at tight-head, but Whitey had come through brilliantly, anchoring the scrum so well that, at one stage, we had wheeled them slightly, driven them back and gone right over them. He was talking to me during the game as though we were walking down the road on a Sunday morning, very laid back, which was pretty impressive, too.

The next day, the coaches said they wouldn't see us until Wednesday. This was quite surprising and a welcome change. The Test team went out together on the Sunday night, had a few beers and were late coming back — something that's pretty much unheard of. I don't think the occasional spontaneous night out during Test week is a bad thing, as long as guys don't go mad. Players get a bit paranoid about tiredness and alcohol affecting their performance when the benefit of relaxing and spending time together might well outweigh that. We did nothing at all on the Monday and, although we did organise some training ourselves on the Tuesday for an hour and a quarter, it felt very relaxed. The guys won the second midweek game at Kimberley against Griqualand West. They trailed 16–10 after half-time, but came back with 45 unanswered points, impressing the locals who commented that this was the best midweek side to tour South Africa in a long time. It was a good team, too, with the likes of Will Greenwood, Joe Worsley and Graham Rowntree in its ranks.

The rest of us worked lightly on the following three days, flying up to Bloemfontein for the second Test on the

Friday afternoon. By the time the game came around we were feeling refreshed and ready. We were looking forward to the challenge. We had enjoyed the physicality of the previous week and we certainly felt we could win. The first twenty minutes were really quick. The game was whizzing along, everyone just reacting to what was going on. As it developed, though, we started to exert some control, with Jonny kicking his penalties and dropping a goal while a sin-binning had us down to fourteen men. Right at the death there was another controversial video referee moment: we were leading 27–15 but they put pressure on us and a ruck developed right on our line. With people lying everywhere, Joost van der Westhuizen stuck his hand into the dark mass of bodies and claimed a try. You couldn't see the ball and in my opinion there was absolutely no way it could be given. Once again, it went to the video referee. Austin said to the ref on the pitch, 'Look mate, you might as well kick off because he's going to give it.' I said: 'No, he won't, Oz.' And then he did. How anyone could award that try was beyond me and I felt it brought the whole video replay system into farce.

They converted and were back in the match at 27–22 but we just knew we were going to win. As injury time ticked away, I was knocked out of the line-out by one of the Boks. The referee awarded us a penalty and there was that lovely feeling that all we needed to do was put the ball dead and the game was ours. Five metres from the touchline, Jonny swings his left boot and it is all over. It was the start of our great run against South Africa and, indeed, the rest of the southern-hemisphere sides, and up to the start of the Rugby

World Cup 2003, we didn't lose to any of them, home or away. We had deserved our win, too. Over the two Tests we had been the better team – I had felt we had been unlucky in the first – and to beat them in South Africa felt fantastic and was a brilliant way to end the tour.

We flew back to Johannesburg that night, with the then team doctor, Terry Crystal, leading the sing-song from the front of the plane. El Tel was an enthusiastic, if terrible, crooner 'in the club style'. His favourite song was 'Delilah'. As the years went by he remembered fewer of the words and hardly any of the tune, but he was always good value. There was a nervous moment when the pilot came on the intercom telling us we might have to fly back to Bloemfontein because the weather in Jo'burg was so bad. I thought he was having a laugh until I saw the fog around the airport as we came in to land. He pulled up sharply to abort the first attempt and flew round again. I'm not normally a nervous flyer, but on this occasion I did have a few qualms. I was just starting to think maybe I could live with a night in Bloemfontein when he got it down.

The midweekers still had to play, so the rest of us had two or three days enjoying ourselves. I remember they were all training away while we were messing around playing footy on the next pitch, which was probably rubbing it in a bit. They won that last game, against Gauteng Falcons. It was another really feisty encounter, with Daz Garforth coming off with a nasty eye injury after being punched, and by the time they got back to the hotel they were straining at the leash to come out with us. That Wednesday night was the biggest of the lot. We had adopted a bar in the centre of Johannesburg and a hard core of us were left in there until the very early hours – as we staggered out, blinking in the daylight, to return to the hotel, we passed people who were walking to work. A minibus with sliding doors picked us up and when we arrived back the driver slid the door open and two or three semi-conscious bodies just fell straight on to the pavement.

We managed to get ourselves inside and located the dining room, where breakfast was being served. Clive had called a post-tour press conference to debrief all the journalists and the contrast couldn't have been greater. There he was, bright-eyed and bushy-tailed, clean shaven and dapper in his slacks and pullover. And there we were, in varying states of disarray and looking as though we had been dragged through numerous hedges backwards, forwards and sideways. Garforth was smoking a large cigar and Graham Rowntree had ordered a light, crisp Chardonnay to go with our bacon and eggs. We were all lolling about swigging white wine as Clive walked by. He barely glanced at us and can't have taken in what he saw because, without batting an eyelid, he said approvingly, 'You lads are up early this morning.'

The tour was exactly what we had needed to get ourselves back on track. It was unusual in recent England history, in that we played five games, but it worked well in development terms. Will Greenwood came back into contention and would go on to establish himself as a great Test centre; Steve Borthwick came through to add depth to our second row; and Julian White made a sensational debut. We lost just one game and had a great time together. Few, if any, of us had enjoyed the World Cup and the Six Nations Grand Slam loss had been a real downer. This time, coaches had been very in tune with the players' moods and we had the feeling, as a squad, that they were looking after us. A last trip out, hungover and waving my credit card, to buy the mandatory diamond for Kay and we caught the plane home.

CHAPTER EIGHT

LONG HAUL

The 2000–01 season was going to be a hell of a long haul. It started on 14 August and for those of us going on the Lions tour to Australia wouldn't finish until 14 July, exactly eleven months later. At Leicester, we were trying to win a historic third championship and were also determined to do better in Europe. With England, we faced a big autumn: Australia and South Africa were coming over, sandwiching Argentina in an intense three-Test, two-week period. Officially, all three were friendlies. Yeah, right. International rugby is never friendly. This was going to be full on and, in the case of the Wallaby and Springbok Tests, bigger than any Six Nations match outside a Grand Slam decider. Everyone – press, public and players – was very up for it.

The first game, against the Wallabies, was the major one. They were world champions, they rarely came to the UK and everyone wanted to see how we would go against them. Tickets were apparently changing hands at £1000 a pair on the black market and media interest was enormous. We met up at our Pennyhill Park base on the Monday. The week followed our usual pre-international pattern. In the morning we talk about the game ahead and what we can expect from the opposition. We train in the afternoon and twice more on the Tuesday and the Wednesday, working on defence, attack, scrummaging, line-outs, re-starts, the breakdown. We also have a full-scale team run, looking at phase play out of defence and on attack, playing off set piece attack, set piece defence and so on. It's pretty tiring stuff and we always look forward to Wednesday nights, our team meal out at a local restaurant – usually a Chinese or an Italian, away from the gaze of the nutritionists – ahead of Thursday, our day off. Friday morning we meet up again for a light run-through and Friday afternoon is spent relaxing, ahead of the match.

The last two or three years may have changed things a little, but at this point the critics were claiming, with some justification despite our win in South Africa the previous summer, that England could beat the big teams on our day, but couldn't do it consistently. Everyone was watching closely. Although we were at home, the Wallabies were the world benchmark at that point and they had beaten us fairly frequently. They were probably favourites. It was going to be a massive game and we all felt tremendous pressure. A win would help to show that the Springbok match had not been a fluke. A loss would be a big setback.

We took some time to settle, perhaps shading the set piece and winning, statistically, the battles for possession and territory. But, as we had tended to do against the Big Three over the years, we were failing to make best use of this. They changed their tactics in the second half, playing directly, with a lot of pick-and-go from the forwards, and rapidly scored, Matt Burke touching down from a Joe Roff pass after Austin had missed a tackle on Roff. One mistake and we were punished. You could feel the crowd drop a notch, but the players didn't let their heads go down and the turning point came when Clive threw on Iain Balshaw. He was twenty-one and fairly unknown, but he would obviously go on to experience one of rugby's great rollercoaster rides – beating defences everywhere in the coming Six Nations, then suffering a slump in form on that Lions tour to Australia, before coming back into contention ahead of the 2003 Rugby World Cup. At this point, you could see the Wallabies were tired. They were doing anything they could to waste time towards the end – going down with convenient attacks of cramp and messing about behind their 22 after the ball went dead. It was irritating, but I didn't blame them. All teams do it when it suits them. You walk slower to the re-start, you take your time getting to line-outs and scrums. There's no law saying you have to run. In contrast, Balshaw, very much on the up, was fresh, bubbling with confidence and raring to go. If we could get the ball to him, I knew he could do some damage with his pace. He managed to open them up two or three times, but the crucial moment came deep in injury time. With the Wallabies in front, he saw some space and chipped ahead. I was stuck at the bottom of a ruck when his boot connected with the ball. With the astute reading of a game for which I have become renowned, I sized things up in a flash. 'Oh no, Balsh,' I groaned. 'Why have you kicked it? It's all over.' If the ball went dead I was sure the whistle would sound. Then Dan Luger raced through the Aussie defenders and touched down.

It went to the video referee. The score would be 20–19 to us if the call went our way and as he was making up his mind I walked over to the match ref, André Watson, to check how long was left. If Jonny converted, the Aussies could still grab a draw with a penalty. He told me the game was all over whatever the decision. I couldn't be bothered to look at the big screen as they replayed the incident again and again – I was too tired – but the roar from the crowd let me know which way the ref had gone. As Jonny was lining up his kick, I headed for the rest of the boys. It had been a fast, physical game and they all looked absolutely shot to bits. 'Right, lads,' I said. 'André says three minutes left whatever happens.' Their shoulders sagged. Three more minutes must have sounded like hell to them. Dallaglio and Dawson started jabbering at me, 'You what? You must be joking?' Sadly, my smirk let them off the hook. It had been another fairly controversial video decision, one on which you would be disappointed to lose a match, but maybe it was a bit of payback for the Stimmo 'try' we had been denied a few months before.

As the boys celebrated, having a laugh and stretching while they rehydrated or got some food into themselves, I put on my tracksuit and headed outside for one-to-one TV and radio interviews and then the press conference. By the time I got back to the changing room it was empty, with everyone showered, dressed and gone. That is one of the downsides of being the captain – it can feel a little lonely and anti-climactic, with no one else there to share the moment. After Six Nations games, there is a dinner at the Park Lane Hilton, a few beers and, if we're in the mood, maybe even a bit of a sing-song on the bus on the way. In the autumn, though, there is no dinner, so after a brief post-match function, we headed back to Pennyhill, where I fetched fish and chips all round – a little treat for us in victory.

We should have been able to bask in it for a few days.

Argentina awaited us the following Saturday and, while they are no mugs, particularly up front, and they play with a lot of passion, it was a game we would be expected to win. Unfortunately, we didn't have time to savour the victory over Australia. Behind the scenes, we had been involved in a long-running dispute with the RFU about match fees and our individual image rights. Having originally suggested cutting our match fee completely and only paying us if we won, they now wanted to reduce our guaranteed pay and build in a bigger win bonus element. The waters were muddied by another suggestion: that we sign our intellectual property rights away, allowing them to use our names and faces in advertising and sponsorship. The Union had signed contracts with its sponsors which entitled them to player appearances, merchandise signed by the players and the use of our images, but it didn't actually have the right to deliver those benefits. This was becoming an important issue, about which we had previously been a little naïve. My face had been used on billboards by Nike in the nineties. At the time, I had just thought, 'Great! Look, I'm in a Nike ad!' I never stopped to think that they were in fact using me to endorse and sell their product and that, strange as it may sound with a face like mine, I had a value.

As a squad, we were not happy with either suggestion. The whole issue of paying players in the first place is, in some ways, a tricky subject. Lots of people say things like, 'I'd walk over broken glass to represent my country' and, 'I'd play for England for nothing.' I understand these sentiments, but I think people forget that many of us, including me, *have* played for England for nothing. We virtually *have* walked over broken glass, too. Playing rugby at the highest level, amateur or professional, involves major sacrifice: endless hours with weights in the gym and mindless, gruelling training sessions that push guys to the point of collapse; months away from our families; sticking to rigid diets. (OK, maybe I don't *always* stick to the diet, but most of the boys are virtually religious about it.) At twenty-one, I hardly had two coppers to rub together, but I wasn't thinking about furthering my career. I was in the gym every spare minute I had trying to get strong and fit to play rugby. The fact is we would go through all the pain and the stress for nothing again if we had to. We would do so gladly because we want to play for England, because we know it is an honour and because we recognise that we are very privileged to have been chosen to do it. But if you want us to do it for nothing, don't charge £50 a ticket at Test matches, don't demand millions in TV revenue and don't look for massive sponsorship deals using us. Just cover your costs and stage the games.

The game is now a professional, multi-million-pound industry and players need to be treated fairly.

We were happy with part of our match fees being linked to winning, but it was about balance and we felt the greater proportion should be guaranteed. If it was intended as some sort of motivational tool, it was downright insulting. If we gave away our image rights as requested, the RFU could license our images to advertisers and sponsors however they liked. We could end up being used to promote almost anything, with no say in the matter and no payment. I don't think anyone would have seriously expected us to accept this without discussion.

After months of talking, the commercial dispute was rumbling on and the match fee issue had boiled down to something like £150 a player. We wanted it guaranteed, the RFU wanted it as part of the win bonus. The RFU chief executive, Francis Baron, refused to budge, saying it wasn't about the money, it was about the principle. We felt the same way and I think we had a good case. The Aussie game itself made our argument. That had turned on one moment and a video ref's decision. It could easily have gone the other way. We would still have put in exactly the same effort on the training field and the pitch. The RFU's income wasn't changed, in the short term at least, by whether we won or lost. Why should ours be?

It's not as though we were on soccer-style incomes. A few of us *were* paid six-figure sums, but a lot of the squad were on ordinary money – some of the players back then were taking home basic club salaries as low as £10,000 – for risking a broken nose or worse every time they turned up for work. Just like anyone else, they had mortgages to cover and families to support. Unlike most other people, though, they could lose their jobs at any moment. Rugby is a fragile career – you can score the winning try in a World Cup final and be injured the next day and never play again. Would the RFU pay your bills then? Of course, the top men at the Union were handsomely rewarded. I remember walking out of negotiations one morning and seeing a player's car parked next to Francis Baron's. One drove a second-hand Ford Mondeo, the other an Aston Martin with a personalised number plate. Guess who had the Aston?

It was clear that Baron was happy to let things run their

course. As long as we kept playing, the RFU had no worries. We had to do something to bring matters to a head and we had to do it immediately. Prevarication until after the matches just handed the initiative, and the bargaining power, back to the RFU. We had two options: one was to strike, something we didn't want to do and which, at that point, we had absolutely no intention of ever doing. The other was to refuse to get involved in commercial – that is, non-rugby – activities. That meant no merchandise signings, no attending the traditional pre-match sponsors' dinner and turning our sponsored clothing inside out. This was not something we agreed to lightly. A lot of us had very good relations with the sponsors, personally and commercially, and our gripe was certainly not with them. This was just the least aggressive option we could take.

Lawrence Dallaglio, Matt Dawson and myself, who comprised the players' representatives, laid out the issues for the squad ahead of the Australia fixture and they agreed with this course of action. As soon as we told the RFU, it caused uproar. Clive, naturally and rightly worried about the effect all this might have on our focus for the match, hastily called a meeting. He asked us to delay our action, saying he didn't want any messing around in Test week. If we went ahead, he said, he couldn't select any of us for England. If we postponed it, he would get the RFU president, Budge Rogers, and other senior RFU figures involved to sort everything out the following week. We called another meeting and the players agreed to the delay.

Unfortunately, when we met Rogers the following Monday, we found it made no difference. Things were now becoming very serious. The commercial withdrawal was off the agenda.

First action for the British Lions, against Taranaki. I'd been called up as a late replacement after Wade Dooley had had to return to England following a personal tragedy.

Battling for the ball with the All Blacks during the 1993 Test series. Peter Winterbottom looks on.

Martin Bayfield and I lose out in the line-out during the third Test in Auckland. The Lions lost that match 30–13 and the series by 2–1.

Four years later the Lions were back in action, this time in South Africa. There had been lots of questions as to whether the Lions format would still work in the professional era, but when you can train in the shadow of Table Mountain who would want to give it up?

While I was delighted to be chosen as Lions captain in 1997 – one of the greatest honours any rugby player could ever have – I have never been entirely happy with the PR side of the job. Here I am with our mascot, but the smile doesn't come easily.

Walking off the pitch with Lawrence Dallaglio after we'd been beaten by Northern Transvaal. Forwards coach Jim Telfer did a superb job in picking us up after that game, when the tour could have gone badly off the rails.

We bounced straight back from our previous disappointments with a victory over Natal Sharks, billed as the unofficial fourth Test. We were back on track.

After our 16–25 defeat of the Springboks in the first Test at Cape Town, you can see the exhaustion in my face and in Lawrence's. He was a huge support to me throughout that tour, and I hope he feels I gave him the same support when he was subsequently chosen as England captain.

Neither the scoreboard nor I can catch up with Jerry Guscott after he dropped the goal that gave us a 15–18 victory in the second Test and so secured the series victory over South Africa.

Trying my hand as a stand-in scrum-half. I think I'd better stick to what I know best.

The Springboks may have won the third Test comfortably but the Lions had won the series and it was time to celebrate. Only winning the World Cup could be better than this.

As you can imagine, at 6ft 6in and over 18 stone I've got perfect rhythm for joining a Samba band. This was part of the team-building exercises we went through ahead of the 2001 Lions tour to Australia.

After scoring 31 tries in our two previous games on the tour, the Queensland coach Mark McBain had labelled us boring. We were delighted to beat his side 8–42 in a match that turned out to be quite violent. Here I compare shirt material with Nick Stiles and Glen Panaho.

Ronan O'Gara leaves the field having been repeatedly punched by Duncan McRae of the New South Wales Waratahs. Ironic, given that the Aussie press had made so much of our supposedly violent streak.

Jason Robinson sidesteps Steve Larkham and Nathan Grey on the way to a brilliant try at the beginning of the first Test. The former rugby league player had already begun to answer his critics who said he wouldn't make it in union.

On the charge during our 13–29 victory in the first Test.

DAVID ROGERS/GETTY IMAGES

Coach Graham Henry (centre), Andy Robinson and I have plenty to discuss after that first Test victory, following murmurs of discontent with how the tour was progressing. Unfortunately, an article by Matt Dawson had merely added fuel to the fire.

NICK WILSON/GETTY IMAGES

In the first half of the second Test we were dominant, but the world champions came back to square the series and eventually went on to win 2–1. It was a shame I couldn't end my Lions career on a high.

It would put Clive in a position where he couldn't select us. A strike, unthinkable the week before, now seemed the only option. I held a meeting in my room at Pennyhill Park. I was very careful not to influence the other players, very careful to tell each of them to make up their own minds and not be swayed by others. I told them it was possible that if we walked out we might be walking out on our international careers. I had played fifty-odd games for England, more than I had ever thought I would. If it all ended there and then I had had a good innings. Some of these young guys were just starting out. 'My ego is not attached to this at all,' I said. 'If you guys want to take the RFU deal, take the deal. Don't go with the flow.' It's very easy in meetings for some people to take a back seat and let others decide. This was too important for that.

As we chewed over the implications, paper aeroplanes started floating around. No matter how grave the situation – and this was as grave as it gets without people being hurt – rugby players find it hard to be serious. There were moments of unintentional levity. Mark 'Ronnie' Regan has a reputation – perhaps undeserved – for coming out with classic lines. He didn't disappoint on this occasion. He listened carefully to me running through all the implications. Then he cocked his head on one side. 'Here,' he said. 'If we go on strike, how we looking for getting paid Saturday?' Then we held a secret ballot. The result was almost unanimous, with just one or two abstentions, both from senior players. We would strike.

Going to tell the RFU that we were refusing to play Argentina that weekend was traumatic. We were all very nervous and conscious that we were taking a big step into the unknown. We didn't know what the hell was going to happen. They might pick a whole new team. They might just drop me, Lawrence and Matt, as the perceived ringleaders. I like to think no one else would have played for England under either of those circumstances, but you never know. Whatever, we had to do it. Pretty much as soon as we told them, the place erupted. Clive was very upset and Andy Robinson looked shell-shocked. Robbo is a tremendously passionate guy whose own international career had not been as long as maybe it could have been. He would have paid to play and he kept saying, 'I can't get my head around this. I don't understand it.'

I hardly slept at all that night, thinking about what we had done and what might happen the next day.

On the Tuesday morning we were asked to leave the hotel and quickly exchanged home phone numbers in case the Union asked Cellnet to turn off our mobiles – which seems pretty paranoid, looking back. Clive called some of the players, checking that they hadn't been railroaded by Lawrence, Matt and myself and asking them to play. A few of the younger guys were very upset and I really felt for them. They had more to lose than the older guys like myself, but it's a tribute to them that they were brave and stood firm in the face of all the pressure. The RFU called a press conference and got their side of the story across first. We drew up our own statement and I went out to read it in the car park of the hotel, against the wishes of my agent, Tim Buttimore. He was worried I would get a bad press, but I was way past caring about that. The team had commercial agents, CSS, but I didn't want to hide behind them. Afterwards, the Leicester contingent headed to the leisure club at Wentworth golf course, phones going mad, trying to work out where we stood. Peter Wheeler and Dean Richards came down from Leicester and met us, and Peter started trying to put together a compromise.

That night, the whole team went to the Cafe Royal for a fundraising evening for BBC reporter and former England full-back Alastair Hignell, who had just been diagnosed with multiple sclerosis. Kay had come down for the dinner, but she spent most of it sitting next to my empty seat as I kept ducking in and out to listen to the various proposals that Peter Wheeler was coming up with. I also spoke to Damian Hopley from the professional rugby players' union, the PRA, but he was out of the country and unable to do much except offer his advice. There were TV cameras outside and the place was full of press men, there to support Alastair, and they all wanted to talk. At one stage, I escaped into a staff toilet right at the top of the building, just to get away from people and make a couple of calls. The upshot of all this was another sleepless night and an arrangement to meet again at the RFU the following morning.

The Cook Cup, which we had won against Australia the week before, was sitting proudly on the boardroom table. You couldn't help but see the irony. We beat the Wallabies and then they put us through this garbage for a few quid. They had obviously decided they had to move their position slightly. We finally managed to reach a settlement somewhere between the two positions and we agreed to play the game. I was conscious that the strain on the players and myself was immense. We certainly needed the whole thing sorted, but, in hindsight, I wish we had insisted on starting afresh and had drawn up a whole new agreement between the players and the

Union, instead of fudging around the one we had and our two competing positions.

Even then, they couldn't resist having a little pop. We agreed to disagree and established, also, that there would be no recriminations or backbiting. We knew rugby was being hurt by this, and we weren't proud of the fact. At the subsequent press conference, however, they said, effectively, that the problems had come about because the players hadn't understood the issues involved. Now they had been explained to us, everything was OK. This was just not the case. They were trying to make us look like fools, and it was untrue, patronising and unnecessary. I wasn't planning to apologise for anything, or say I wouldn't do it again – what had happened had happened – but I wasn't going to get into a slanging match with the RFU, either.

I was pleased that their tactics received a sceptical response from the rugby writers. Some of the early press coverage, mainly from non-rugby journalists, had been disappointing, though. Some sections of the media, not really taking the trouble to understand the issues, had piled into us in a big way, accusing us of being greedy and trotting out those old 'I'd play for nothing' pieces. Some of them also suggested that Matt and Lawrence and I had coerced the other players into taking action. This was ridiculous. Firstly, we just wouldn't do it. Secondly, we couldn't do it – these are not the kind of guys you can coerce into anything. Thirdly, why should we do it? We were arguing about a few hundred quid. Lawrence could earn thousands of pounds making personal appearances, and Matt and myself were probably in the same boat. It was much more important to the younger players financially than it was to us: a quiet life would have suited us much more.

The crazy thing is the strike need never have happened. I have to say I think Francis Baron's negotiating stance was a major issue. Someone approvingly told us Francis was a 'tough' guy who liked to play 'hardball'. He certainly appeared unwilling to compromise and you have to ask why. Look at the situation. You have a multi-million-pound business: rugby. Your key assets, the players – replaceable maybe as individuals, but not as a squad if you want to be successful – are not under contract to you to do anything. Not to play, not to do any of the commercial activity you want them to. Those players are prepared to sign up to all of that and you're holding out over a relatively small amount of money. If Francis had come to us and said, 'Look guys, I've been thinking. You've beaten the Springboks away. You nearly won a Grand Slam. You've beaten the Aussies. Things are on the up. You deserve this cash,' we would have signed up there and then for less than we were actually worth, just to get the whole saga over with. Even after we reached our supposed deal, the RFU prevaricated, chopping and changing minor details, until the spring, when the Premiership clubs got together and signed up all their players themselves. The clubs went back to the RFU holding all the aces and demanding financial support from the RFU, which now pays them millions of pounds each year. Some negotiating strategy.

After the dust had settled that week, we still had two Test matches to play. Sadly, the Argentina game was pretty poor. It seemed as though it had rained all winter and the pitch was like a bog. Both sides made a lot of handling errors as we ran out 19–0 winners, Ben Cohen – back in the side after the death of his father – scoring for us.

If we could beat the Springboks the following weekend we would have beaten southern-hemisphere opposition three games on the trot – four, if you counted the Pumas. The Boks were more familiar to us than the Wallabies, though they were trying to move away from their traditional, pack-dominated game to a more free-flowing style. They still had some great forwards, though, with the likes of Corné Krigé, André Venter and Mark Andrews, one of the great second rows, in their side. It was a physical game, with both Richard Hill and Neil Back leaving the field at points to have gaping head wounds stitched up, and it was played at a hell of a pace. They defended well, but after half an hour or so Will Greenwood broke through the line and stepped round the full-back to score. Despite Braam van Straaten touching down for them, we eventually won 25–17. There were no over-the-top celebrations in the changing room, though, which was good. It reflected the fact that we were starting to believe in ourselves. Before, beating South Africa would have been a huge thing. Now we knew we could do it and that it wasn't a one-off.

Back at Welford Road, the season was ticking along well. We were looking odds-on to retain our league title and were going well in Europe, beating Pau 20–3 away – never easy – and getting through the group stages to set up a quarter-final clash with Swansea, which we went on to win fairly comfortably. We were dumped out of the semi-final of the Tetley's Bitter Cup by Harlequins, which was disappointing, but at least that gave us breathing space to concentrate on the two bigger competitions.

As the Six Nations approached, England were, once again, firm favourites for the Grand Slam. As I always say, in many ways you would rather be underdogs. The Celts and the French love beating the English and the chance to do it against the odds seems to really stir them up. It was fair enough, though. We had beaten the Boks and the Aussies and played well in the previous year's championship. We were playing a slightly un-English style of rugby, too – a fast-flowing, dynamic, running game that looked likely to produce big scores against some of the weaker nations.

Our first game, at the Millennium Stadium, was my first match since completing a thirty-five-day ban for kneeing Duncan McRae in a tough league encounter with Saracens. It was also the first Wales versus England game at the huge new ground in the centre of Cardiff. We were all looking forward to it. There was talk of a potential upset victory for the home team and of the demoralising effect the Welsh crowd's singing might have on us. Clive laughed this off, saying, 'If they rely on the stadium and the songs they've already lost.' He was spot on.

Some of the guys have trouble sleeping before big games, and will even take pills to get themselves off. I am a good sleeper and, despite a little nervousness at the prospect of playing after a long break, this was no different. For a 2.30p.m. kick-off I like to be up and about at around 9.30a.m., giving me five hours to shake off the sleepiness and get some food inside me. You need to eat properly on match days, because you'll run out of energy on an empty stomach. I usually have three or four Weetabix, some fruit, a yoghurt and a plate of scrambled egg, which is full of protein. I don't have sausage or bacon, because it's too heavy and greasy on a game day, and I'm pretty careful what I eat in the run-up to a match, too. I like a rare-cooked steak, but I would never eat it within three days of a match because of the way it sits in your stomach. I will usually have a brunch at about 11.30a.m. – some grilled chicken with the skin removed and some pasta and a carbohydrate drink. I have to force myself to get it down, even if I'm not hungry, and sometimes it comes back up. The nerves and adrenalin really get going for me before Test matches and other big games and might make me sick. Occasionally, this has even happened on the pitch.

We felt the Welsh lacked fitness and defensive organisation and Clive had picked a back line for sheer speed, Iain Balshaw coming in for Matt Perry. Although still young, Matt was England's most-capped full-back. He was defensively very brave, had a great kicking game and was a solid attacking force, too. Balshaw had more gas, though, and Matt's career as a first-choice England player stalled from that point, though he went on to play in the Lions Test team in Australia later that year. I feel for Pezza. He's a top lad, who was one of Clive's first successful picks as coach, and he never let England down, contributing in a major way to the foundation of the current side. He has suffered with injuries in recent years and has had to watch first Balshaw, then Jason Robinson and currently Josh Lewsey wear the No. 15 jersey. Those injury problems are behind him now, though, and it would be no surprise to see Matt back in the squad in the future.

Walking out on to that Millennium Stadium pitch was a truly memorable experience, with red shirts everywhere and a deafening rendition of their anthem. As 'Land Of Our Fathers' echoed round the imposing structure, Nobby West turned to me with a tear in his eye. 'I wish this was our anthem!' he said. I nearly backhanded the little ginger, Wrexham-born hamster. The Welsh guys were fired up by it and came at us hard, but we had been right about their defence and made a number of telling breaks. Will Greenwood got a hat trick and Matt Dawson grabbed a brace, and although Rob Howley scored one try and made another for Scott Quinnell, we won comfortably, 44–15.

Italy then made their first trip to Twickenham since joining the competition. A lot was made of their relative weakness as a side and whether we could motivate ourselves for the game. I am always motivated when I pull on an England shirt and, anyway, the Azurri are no mugs. They scrummage very well, are always pumped up and they tackle big. As if to prove me right, we were 7–0 down after three minutes and 20–17 down after half an hour. That was something of a shock, but it proved to be almost their high-water mark as we pulled ourselves together and finished 80–23 winners. Jason Robinson made his England debut and I remember actually feeling sorry for the opposition. Tired, getting thumped, scorched by the lethal pace of guys such as Balshaw, Cohen and – naturally – Johnson, you don't need someone like Jase darting around all over the pitch. Although he didn't score a try, on another day he could have had three, as he always seemed to be the next in line as our later tries were run in. His signing from rugby league club, Wigan, brokered by Clive, was inspirational. It's strange to think that, back then, his selection so early after his move was viewed as something of a risk, but with a combination of hard work and his natural rugby ability he transformed himself into a great union player very quickly.

When it came to our match against Scotland, it was all about revenge for 2000 – if you read the papers, that is. I guess it was on our minds, though. Twickenham was dry and firm, in contrast to that Murrayfield bog, and our quick backs did a lot of damage. Balshaw crossed twice and you could sense the Scots wilting when Jason Robinson was brought on with twenty-five minutes to go. The final score, 43–3, was a Calcutta Cup record, but there was certainly no crowing at the post-match dinner. We knew a lot of the Scots guys, from the Lions or the club circuit, and there were some good blokes in their side. We would never rub a victory in, anyway, because we've all been well beaten in our time and it isn't a great feeling.

Our game against Ireland in Dublin was postponed as an epidemic of foot-and-mouth disease had broken out in England, but I never really understood or accepted the reasoning behind the rescheduling. OK, it stopped a few thousand English rugby fans from travelling over to Ireland, and I suppose that may have reduced the risk of the disease spreading there, but the Irish soccer team was still playing and thousands of businessmen and tourists were flying in and out every week. In fact, I would imagine that most of the fans who had booked to fly out for our game went anyway, just for a boozy weekend. After all, they had paid for their flights and hotels. Bizarre, really.

We went ahead with the game against France, though. We all have tremendous respect for French sides – most of us have been on the wrong end of big scores against them for club or country at one time or another – and you do fear their indefinable and undeniable flair. Few sides can turn a game around like the French. Look at their semi-final defeat of the All Blacks in the 1999 Rugby World Cup, when they looked dead and buried and then came back with twenty-six unanswered points against one of the world's best teams. We had played so well up to that point in the tournament, though, that the media and fans seemed to assume a big England win was a foregone conclusion. I don't know whether this affected the players, but we were certainly over-confident in the first half, turning over possession with careless mistakes and allowing them in for two high-speed scores. We were down 16–13 at half-time, a bit shell-shocked and pleased to be trailing by only three points. I told the boys we needed to play more directly, play in their half and keep hold of the ball. Then we would get chances to use our quick men. However, my words had no effect and it continued like a game of sevens after the break. It was one of the most exhausting matches I have been involved in, but we finally got the upper hand when Richard Hill ran 30m to the line and Iain Balshaw followed that with another good try. Phil Greening, Mike Catt and replacement Matt Perry all added to the score, while we held the French to a solitary three points in the second half. We ended 48–19 winners.

We had been in such a rich vein of form that I am convinced we would have won that postponed fixture in Dublin. As it was, things had changed slightly when we finally got over there. Iain Balshaw had lost his confidence on the Lions tour, key players such as Lawrence Dallaglio and Phil Vickery were missing with injury and we came up against an Ireland side relishing its position as underdogs and roared on by a big crowd. I was injured, too, and watched from the stands as the boys made break after break, only to be stopped each time by handling errors or Irish tackling. We leaked a soft try, Keith Wood bursting around the back of a line-out to score, and could never get our noses in front. Again, it's hard to describe the emotions. If I had been unbelieving when we had lost at Murrayfield, what was I now? England losing three consecutive Grand Slam deciders, in the last game of the season, to different teams? You couldn't have written the script. I came down from the stands to support the guys, although if they'd won I would have stayed put, letting them enjoy the moment they had earned. We were presented with the Six Nations championship trophy, but once again taking it felt horrible. In the background the Irish fans were going crazy as their players lapped the pitch. Ours was a quiet changing room. There were no tears, nobody wrecked the joint, they were just a massively disappointed group of lads who felt they had let themselves and each other down.

Leicester's season, though, had finished much better. With two matches still to go, we blew away a weakened Newcastle Falcons 51–7. All we needed was Bath to beat Wasps, our nearest championship challengers, in a match later the same day. We sat in a room at the clubhouse, praying for a Bath victory – a strange feeling – and cursing them when Wasps took what seemed like a winning lead. But Mike Catt scored late on to give them the win, our fans, hanging on after the Falcons game in the hope of celebrating the title, going mad in the main bars below. For us, it felt a bit weird. In the two previous years the title had come after tough matches. Winning like this, almost mathematically, was anti-climactic and it took a little time to sink in. We all went out on the town that night, having a team meal with our wives and girlfriends and then drinking the small hours away.

We went on to win the Zurich Championship — a controversial knockout competition brought in once the season had started — by beating Bath in the final at Twickenham. While the way the extra tournament was introduced was wrong, I am in favour of a rugby league-style decider. We had won the championship this season with two games to spare. Where was the drama and the excitement in that? Would you pay to go and see the remaining matches? Sport is a branch of the entertainment business and anything that maintains the sense of theatre has got to be a good thing. I still think the concept needs tinkering with, however. As things stand, there will always be arguments about the real winner. The 2002–03 league was won by Gloucester, but Wasps beat them in the subsequent knockout at Twickenham. A few Gloucester men might have moaned about this — although they voted for the system, a classic case of beware what you wish for — because they had been so strong in the league and Wasps had finished behind them. To me, it was clear Wasps were the champions, because everyone knew the score before the season started. I would advocate a complete overhaul of the Premiership system to create two leagues of seven teams. Each team would play the others within its own division home and away and it would play those in the other division home or away, alternating from season to season. At the end, then, there would be no outright champions, negating the Gloucester argument, and you would create a play-off formula to finish with a dramatic grand final at Twickenham.

Leicester's mammoth season was not quite over, though. Having completed a domestic double, the biggest club prize of all was within our grasp – we had a European Cup final, against Stade Français, at the old Parc des Princes in Paris. I was struggling and in pain with a stiff neck, injured in our semi-final against Gloucester, but everyone had knocks and niggles. All our walking wounded would make it on to the pitch. We based ourselves at a hotel next to the Palace of Versailles and trained lightly in the run-up, even taking time to wander round the palace and mingle with the thousands of Leicester fans who had travelled over. We knew Stade would be very tough to beat, especially in their home city. They were packed with quality players and French sides are always stronger at home, so it was going to be a massive game.

It being such a grand occasion, the club had produced some new kit, with 'Heineken Cup 2001' stitched into the fabric, and they wanted us to wear that. We, however, wanted to wear the same shirts we had worn all season – we had been winning in them, after all. The compromise we reached was to pose for team photos in the sunshine in the new kit before putting our knackered old jerseys back on for the match. It was a nervy changing room when the referee called us out and a heavy atmosphere once we got on to the pitch. The Stade players walked over and started squaring up to us. Our players went to meet them and the atmosphere got very charged, to the point where I thought it might all kick off before the game even started. If one guy had cracked and punched someone all hell would have broken loose.

The game itself was clean, though. It was a cagey first half, both sides kicking for territory. Diego Dominguez, their fly-half, was a real worry, because every time we erred he punished us with some perfect place-kicking. They were ahead at half-time, but we had defended very well, keeping their big runners at bay. We certainly felt we were well in contention and that if we got a score early on we could take control. Mind you, I didn't expect it to come just forty-eight seconds after the restart, when Pat Howard chipped through, Geordan Murphy kicked it on and Leon Lloyd beat the defenders to score. Bang! We were right back in the game. It was a big confidence boost. I was binned for slapping one of their players, but the guys conceded just three points in the ten minutes, which was a brilliant effort. Backy scored from close range once I got back on, but Dominguez was keeping them in it and they nudged ahead as the game neared the end. Then a great break and a superb pass by Austin Healey put Leon Lloyd in again to give us a 32–30 lead. We needed the conversion, though – we couldn't risk them winning a penalty or finding space for a drop-goal in the remaining minutes. Stimpson kicked brilliantly from the touchline and the sight of that ball sailing between the posts will go down as one of the all-time great moments in Leicester history. They made a last-gasp break at the death, but we snuffed it out. We were European Champions.

It had been a frenetic, explosive, end-to-end match and a great advertisement for European rugby. I was exhausted and exhilarated all at once. The whole squad, even the guys who were not on the bench, ran straight on to the pitch with Dean and John to celebrate with us. We saluted our fantastic supporters, hoisting the cup on a lap round the pitch, before heading for the changing room to soak everything up. To win the European Cup in Paris was the biggest and best day of my club career, and, in its way, was as good as any I have had in the game. Could we do it again?

CHAPTER NINE

SLIP-SLIDING

We didn't have long to wait to get the Ireland defeat out of our systems. Within three weeks, we would face the Wallabies at Twickenham. A number of senior players were missing, myself included, with my broken hand failing to mend in time for me to come back. Lawrence was out, too, and Matt Dawson failed a fitness test on a hamstring he had damaged in the Grand Slam defeat. I felt for Matt. He had led the side in Dublin and had come in for some unfair stick from the press afterwards. I'm sure he would have wanted to prove a few points against the World and Tri-Nations Champions. As it was, Neil Back led the side out, a proud moment for him, I'm sure. It was not the most experienced England team ever to take the field. Jason Robinson was at full-back, a position he'd only occupied since earlier that year, following his switch from league. Iain Balshaw, who had lost a little form on the Lions tour, had looked slightly hesitant against the Irish and he was left out of the party altogether. Ben Kay, a debutant in the summer against Canada, started in the second row. Joe Worsley had made his debut two years before and was still improving as a player. He came in at No. 8, with Martin Corry also injured. Charlie Hodgson, the creative Sale fly-half, Steve Borthwick and Lewis Moody helped to make up a relatively young bench. The Australians, on the other hand, were at pretty much full strength. The year before we had beaten a weaker Wallaby side and this had taken some of the gloss off the victory, according to some critics. That argument wouldn't hold water if the boys could turn the 2001 tourists over.

They had a great first half, the forwards pushing the Australians back and forcing them to give away penalties that Jonny Wilkinson duly converted into points. Three place kicks and a couple of dropped goals sent England in 15–0 up at the break. But the Wallabies came back strongly in the second half, turning down an easy penalty kick to go instead for the line-out, from which they won possession and spun the ball wide for Matt Burke to score. He converted his try and then exchanged penalties with Jonny and, when Phil Waugh touched down to make it 21–15 to England, they looked like they might force their way back into contention. However, the guys hung on well to win and retain the Cook Cup.

The following week provided a stark contrast. As the Wallabies departed, they were replaced by the Romanians, but it was a total mismatch, ending 134–0. Charlie Hodgson made his debut and helped himself to a record haul of 44 points, while Jason Robinson beat almost every player on the pitch on his way to one of the best tries Twickenham has ever witnessed. There was a lot of discussion after the match about the value of games like this. It is certainly very difficult for sides like Romania to compete nowadays. In fact, it's not that long ago that they were more deserving of a Six Nations place than Italy – very few teams won in Bucharest in the eighties and they had come within seven points of England in a 22–15 encounter in 1985. They were even potential World Cup semi-finalists in the early part of that decade. Why? Because back then, in the amateur era, they were virtually professional, drawn from their armed forces and part of the Communist Bloc programme that placed a lot of emphasis on sporting success. A number of their better players died in the Ceausescu revolution and as the country and its military collapsed, rugby went with it. It's very hard to see how they can ever get back to where they were. The RFU agreed to play them to give them exposure and a chance to test themselves against a good side, but it can't have done much for their game back home. Most of their better players play abroad, as happens with Romanian soccer stars, and that is probably the way forward. Their club game won't be great to watch if all the half-decent players are in France, but they may at least put together a competitive national team. If they manage that, interest in the game will pick up and the player base will evolve.

I was back the following weekend for the visit of South Africa and this turned into a surprisingly comfortable victory – and allowed us to become the first European nation to record five successive wins against southern-hemisphere teams. The Boks made a lot of mistakes and Jonny made them pay, kicking seven out of nine penalties. A Mike Catt drop-goal and a late breakaway try by Danny Luger, who intercepted and ran the length of the field for his seventeenth international try, gave us a 29–9 victory. I'd only played one club game since breaking my hand, so it was nice to come back and get through a physical Test match. It was our third consecutive win against them, a run that would continue, and it was starting to be less of a big deal to beat these sides, certainly at home.

Our Six Nations campaign is probably best remembered, unfortunately, as another 'nearly' year. We beat Scotland convincingly, 29–3 at Murrayfield, with Steve Thompson making his debut, Jason Robinson running in two early tries and Ben Cohen and Mike Tindall also grabbing one each. We destroyed Ireland at Twickenham, winning 45–11 and, in the process, going to the top of the Zurich World Rankings as, on paper, the number one side in the sport. France had made heavy weather of defeating Wales the same day, but they were also unbeaten and our visit to Paris looked very much like being an early Grand Slam decider.

I was able to take part, controversially in some eyes, because Leicester had chosen to appeal my twenty-one-day suspension for punching Robbie Russell in a club game against Saracens, leaving me free to play until the appeal was heard. If you listened to the press you would have thought some shady RFU conspiracy was afoot, but that was all garbage and the Tigers were just playing by the rules. You might also have assumed that my presence in the side meant we were guaranteed to win, a lot being made of the fact that I had been missing from the infamous defeats against Scotland and Ireland. Again, garbage. One man very rarely, if ever, wins or loses a match for you.

Defensively, the French were very strong and the result was that the first forty minutes were mainly played in our half. Our own defence, however, was a different story. The French broke through repeatedly, allowing both Gerald Merceron and Imanol Harinordoquy to score – both tries being converted to make it 14–0. Effectively, the game was won and lost in the first twenty minutes. Henry Paul came on to make his union debut and Jason Robinson scored just before half-time to give us a glimpse of a result. We scored a penalty after the break and if we had managed to cross their line shortly afterwards we might have come back, but when Merceron knocked another three points over it was as good as dead. Ben Cohen got in for a score right at the end, but the French got the result they deserved, winning 20–15. The scoreline flattered us, making it look closer than it really was. Their pack, particularly the back row, had been outstanding, with Serge Betsen probably man-of-the-match. We were horribly disappointed and the response was predictable. We were labelled bottlers and chokers once again, but, in fact, all we'd done is lose a game to a side which had played much better on the day and which had earned the Grand Slam they went on to claim. At least the guys won England's first Triple Crown since 1998, by beating Wales 50–10 at the Millennium Stadium in the next match, Backy maintaining his perfect record as captain and Tim Stimpson making a try-scoring reappearance on the international stage. I sat out that game, suspended, and was not brought back into the starting line-up for the final match against Italy.

Although in some ways this could be seen as a meaningless game, I was still disappointed to be left on the bench, even though the guys had played well against the Welsh. Clive had backed me through my suspension and had been keen to play me against France. Afterwards, though, he suggested I hadn't played all that well. I hadn't been at my best, but I hadn't been the worst player on the pitch and I found this frustrating. I sat on a pretty experienced bench at the Stadio Flaminio. When Woody threw on myself, Lawrence Dallaglio, Matt Dawson and Jason Leonard – 252 caps in total – with a quarter of the match to go, you almost felt for the Italians, who had been game but not quite good enough. Despite losing just one game all season it would be looked upon as a disappointment. Sure, we'd beaten our two southern-hemisphere visitors, but people only seem to remember the games we lose and the loss in Paris meant the chance of another Grand Slam had gone. You sensed that people's patience was wearing thin. If we had won the previous three Slams, I guess it wouldn't have hurt quite so much – but we hadn't.

At Leicester, we were chasing a fourth consecutive Premiership title and also looking to become the first club to retain the European Cup. Pat Howard had finally returned to Australia, hoping to reclaim his place in the ACT Brumbies side and, maybe, challenge for more international honours. Crossing in mid-air, the ACT centre Rod Kafer had joined us in his place and another big name, Josh Kronfeld, had come north, too. Many people thought Josh's signing was a strange one. With Neil Back and Lewis Moody, my brother Will Johnson, Paul Gustard, Adam Balding and Martin Corry all around, we were not short of quality in the back row. Given that Josh was the All Blacks' most-capped openside flanker, Back and Moody, in particular, might have raised their eyebrows. In fact, Neil was consulted beforehand about the recruitment and was more than happy with it. He recognised that having a player of Kronfeld's quality around would help take pressure off him. It also brought the best out in Lewis. Some guys would have let their heads drop. Backy and Josh were not going to be easy obstacles to overcome for a young guy who wanted to make the No. 7 shirt his own. Fortunately for Lewis, a pre-season injury to Josh gave him his chance and if ever a player made a breakthrough in a short space of time it was Moody. His early-season form was spectacular and he was soon drafted into the England squad for what is already turning into a very good international career. Rod was another squat, powerful guy, not too pacey, but with good hands and a similar style of play to Pat, and he would help coach the backs. They were looking like an exciting unit, with Austin, Leon Lloyd, the pacey winger Steve Booth, Tim Stimpson and young centre Ollie Smith all game-breakers and try-scorers.

Despite that, the season didn't start well and we lost on the opening day to Newcastle. Dean had been talking about giving the Lions players a rest, but with Wasps up next he sat myself, Martin Corry, Neil Back and Austin Healey on the bench. It was close for sixty minutes or so, but just as we started to get on top, he brought on the experienced players and we ended up running away with it. The same thing happened at Gloucester the following week and I enjoyed those twenty-minute run-outs in the autumn sun. We carried on pretty much unhindered and by Christmas people were starting to say a fourth league title was a foregone conclusion. We never took that view, although that was how it turned out. It was certainly a fantastic achievement, but I was left with a strange feeling. Again, we went a lot of points clear early on and people just seemed to expect us to win. If we hadn't won it would have been a bigger shock, but winning it for the fourth time is different to winning it for the first, and maybe that relative lack of excitement was the start of the troubles we experienced the following year.

In the European Cup, Llanelli jolted us in the group stages, getting to within three points of us in a 12–9 clash. They surprised us with how good a team they were. A mate who had seen the game said afterwards it was strange watching us having to dig deep at home, because we usually had it in the bag with fifteen minutes to go. That was a real wake-up call. We beat Calvisano away, but I missed our trip to Perpignan with my broken hand. Cozza was injured, too, so we took the opportunity of a weekend off to go into town and have a beer or two. As we caught a cab into Leicester, we heard that the boys were losing, but as we got to the bar the news came through that they had turned the tide. That meant drinks all round and we were persuaded to take all the wives and girlfriends to a nightclub, where Lewis Moody's girlfriend, Annie, destroyed me in a speed-drinking contest. Perpignan's visit to Welford Road started with the visitors scoring a try in the first minute and ended with us putting 50 points on them in one of the best displays of club rugby I have seen. With just Calvisano at home and Llanelli away to come, we had virtually qualified for the quarter-finals. The Italians came and went without troubling us too much, but we came heavily unstuck at Stradey Park. They needed to win to qualify and came at us very hard, outplaying us like we hadn't been outplayed in a long, long time. It was tryless, but they deserved their 24–12 win and it was a fairly humbling experience.

We had won five and lost just one, normally enough to guarantee a home quarter-final, but lots of teams had been very successful, winning six out of six, and we were relieved to find we had squeaked it. We beat Leinster at home in the quarter and then found we had come up against Llanelli again in the semis. I was worried and anxious about that match. They had played well against us in the line-out and scrum in both games, and, with powerful runners like Scotty Quinnell, Martin Madden and Chris Wyatt, they had broken past our defence, which we pride ourselves on. Also, Stephen Jones, their fly-half, was a metronomic penalty kicker who could punish you from pretty much anywhere inside your half. However, we had one advantage, because it was to be a 'home' tie, with the match played in England, and not too far away at Nottingham Forest's City Ground. We knew we would have plenty of support, though the Scarlets brought thousands of their own fans, too, creating a full house and a fantastic atmosphere.

At their ground in the group stage defeat, they had attacked us continually, running the ball at us from everywhere – close in, out wide, with pace and power. That Sunday afternoon, they were a lot quieter. We managed to bottle Quinnell and Madden up – Madden and I clashed heads as he charged at me full on, both ending up face down on the turf. I got up rapidly, determined to beat him to my feet, although I was still a little bit woozy and staggered a couple of paces before coming to my senses. We played some decent, committed rugby and once the initial moments were over I always felt we were going to win. At half-time, Lewis Moody got an amusing bollocking from John Wells. Lewis is a very good chaser of kick-offs. Wellsy had told him to split off to the far side of the field from the rest of the forwards so that, if he was unmarked, we could switch our restarts to him, allowing him a good chance of winning the ball over one of the Welsh backs. As it happened, Llanelli had spotted what we were doing and marked him, so none of the kicks had been sent Lewis's way. John, meanwhile, had obviously forgotten his instruction and wanted to know why Lewis was not competing at the re-start. 'Lewis,' he was saying, 'Where are you . . . I'm not seeing you?' 'John, I'm over on the other . . .' 'No excuses – where are you?' 'But John, you told me to . . .' 'F***ing hell, Lewis, you should be there.' Fair or not, it certainly inspired Lewis and after the break he caught an astonishing re-start with a huge leap that Michael Jordan would have been proud of, almost killing the player he landed on in the process.

We had spotted that their defence was staying very wide and thought we might profit from a pick-and-go. Sure enough, Harry Ellis, our young scrum-half, scampered over from about twenty yards, straight through the middle of a ruck, but we could never quite get clear of them. For all the pressure we placed on them, I don't think we were ever awarded a penalty in their half and that was very unusual. In fact, it was very strange indeed. Close to the end, we did eventually win a penalty – just inside our own half and quite a way out on the right-hand side. I was heading over to Rod Kafer to discuss what line-out move we should go for when we kicked it into touch, when I saw Stimmo pointing to the posts. Nothing I could do – the ref had already signalled. It was a very difficult kick and it was a brave call by Stimmo. It was one of those – pot it and you're a hero, miss it and you're the villain. He managed to get it over, pinballing it between the posts and the bar, to give us the game, 13–12. It had been a terribly close match that could have gone either way. I felt for Scott

Quinnell – he is a good guy who had put his heart and soul into it and just come up short. In fact, I felt for all of them. Llanelli is a great club with some passionate fans and it must have been gutting to lose like that, particularly after they'd lost in similar circumstances to Northampton a couple of seasons before.

In the history of European Cups only Brive have made two finals on the trot. It is a tough call to do it once. Defending the title, with everyone desperate to beat you, while you are trying to compete domestically as well, is incredibly hard. We had done it from a difficult group containing an excellent Llanelli side and a very competitive Perpignan, who would, the following year, make the final themselves. That was achievement enough in itself, but we wanted desperately to win our second. The Millennium Stadium is one of the world's great sporting venues and Munster, our opponents, have some of rugby's most noisy, colourful fans. Bursting at the seams with thousands of Leicester's green-clad fans and even more red jerseys from the Irish province, it was an awesome place, with a tremendous atmosphere, on the day of the final.

Munster were going to be a tough side to beat. The majority of their side were internationals and, like the other Irish teams, the structure of their season meant they were able to concentrate on Europe. Unlike English sides, they don't have any club games interfering with the business end of the European Cup campaign, which means they can work towards peaking at the right moment. That said, Munster – and I am not being patronising here – had done brilliantly well to get to Cardiff. They had beaten Stade Français in the quarter-final and Castres in the semi, both matches away from home. To win against sides like that in front of their home crowds is a big ask and to beat two on the bounce takes some doing. I had watched them against Stade and they had won that game on sheer guts and determination. I'm not saying they were not skilful and talented, because they were, but that had been one of the most characterful performances I had seen. We had a lot of respect for them. They had the Ireland half-backs, Stringer and O'Gara, the Lions centre, Rob Henderson, and a good back row, with guys like David Wallace and Jim Williams in their squad. However, we thought we would be able to pressurise their line-out. Mick Galwey was one of their talismans, but he was no line-out specialist and that left a lot of demands on Paul O'Connell. Ultimately, our edge in that area, and the pressure we were able to exert on them, could have been the difference in the game. It was a tense affair, which Munster led 6–5 at the break, Geordan Murphy providing our points. Austin Healey broke away in the second half for the crucial try, which Stimmo converted, giving us an eventual 15–9 win.

If the Stade win had been pure jubilation, the Munster victory was as much about relief as joy. You could almost feel the weight lift off your shoulders. We had wanted so desperately to keep the title and had battled so hard, particularly against Llanelli, that a loss would have been disastrous. You might expect that people would allow us and our fans our moment of glory. We had become probably the most successful club side in the world. Four domestic titles and now consecutive European crowns proved the argument. Unfortunately, many critics seem to have it in for the Tigers and what should have been a great day was marred, to an extent, by the almost hysterical over-reaction to a relatively minor incident.

Close to the end, Munster had applied good pressure to us and had won a scrummage a few metres out from our line. As we engaged, Peter Stringer bent to feed the ball in and suddenly it shot out of his hand into the scrum. Dorian West hooked it back, we won the ball against the head and were able to clear. My immediate thought was that our young scrum-half, Harry Ellis, had kicked the ball out of Stringer's hand. This is clearly illegal, but it's something you occasionally see happen in matches. My honest response? 'Bloody hell, Hazza – fair play, you cheeky little b*****d!' Harry was only a young lad, nineteen or so at the time, and I was shocked at his nerve. It was only after the game that I learned Backy was the guilty party. Many people saw this as a key moment in the game. To me, it was nothing like that important – for reasons I will explain – but from the media reaction afterwards you would have thought Neil had stabbed Stringer.

Firstly, if this had happened in the first ten minutes of the game it would have seemed far less important. Munster had had the entire match to score a try and hadn't. Why would they suddenly have done it now? I think we would have kept them out, because we defended very well throughout the game, Oz making one of his classic cover tackles to deny them in one of their few seriously dangerous moves.

Secondly, things that genuinely could have affected the result had happened to us earlier, but no one said a word about that. Early on, Munster had had a short line-out five or six yards out from their line. I was waiting at the back for the overthrow. We got pressure on them, they missed the ball, it came to me and I scored. It was a fair try and there was nothing wrong with it at all, but the referee then ordered the line-out to be retaken six inches away from where it had first been thrown. Bizarre. The only explanation I could come up with was that maybe he thought we had additional men in the line, but we hadn't. We were legal and so were the five points. Munster also kicked the ball straight into touch from a position a good yard or more outside their 22. The linesman gave it in, so our line-out was thirty or forty yards further back than it should have been. We won the line-out, Graham Rowntree was penalised for a fairly dubious technical offence and they scored three points from the resultant kick. No way they could have kicked that goal from where the line-out — and therefore Rowntree's 'offence' — should have happened. People talk about Backy's handiwork as though the game hinged on it, but I have just run through eight, and possibly ten, actual points that the other side gained thanks to decisions by the officials.

Thirdly, was it any worse than any of the thousands of technical offences committed by players in the course of a season? No. It was more blatant than if he had used his hands in a ruck, for instance, but no more or less a 'cheating' thing to do. Various Munster players had dabbled at the breakdown during the game — illegally winning the ball for their team — but no one said a word about that, either. Somehow, that is seen as 'just the sort of thing flankers do'. If they get caught, they get penalised — it's as simple as that. We thought Peter Clohessy's scrummaging was illegal right through the eighty minutes, but who was penalised for the resultant problems? We were.

Finally, was it 'setting a bad example to children'? I guess the answer to that is 'yes'. In an ideal world, no one would cheat and everyone would play the game absolutely by the rules, but that is unrealistic. Rugby is, by its nature, a game played close to the edge of its laws and part of the skill, part of the fun, almost, lies in getting away with things. If Leicester or England players never, ever infringed they would be in losing teams, because everyone else would be doing it. That's sad, perhaps, but nonetheless true, whatever the po-faced newspaper columnists might say. Rugby is a game of swings and roundabouts and all professional players know it. That's why we heard little in the way of complaint from the Munster guys themselves or even from their fans. I walked back to see my mum at her hotel after the match – she wasn't well at that point but she had made the trip to Wales – and I was expecting a bit of grief, but the supporters were all fine. Mick Galwey was interviewed after the game and basically said that we had scored two tries to their none and that we had deserved to win. Someone else admitted that if a Munster player had done it to us they would have made him mayor.

The whole controversy over the 'Hand of Back' was extraordinary. People said Neil should have been sent to the sin-bin or even shown the red card. Eh? You don't get binned for one incident of handling the ball in the scrum. Neil had been kicked in the back ten minutes before the incident happened, but I didn't read or hear anything about that. Which is worse? When Brive were all over me illegally at the line-out in the 1997 European Cup final, where were all the why-oh-why merchants then? Nowhere. 'Didn't Brive do well,' was the consensus. In the 1994 Cup final, Dave Hilton used his hand to nick the ball out of the back of our ruck and they scored a try. Press comment on that? Zero. I am not complaining about Clohessy's scrummaging or Brive's shenanigans, though. That is why you have officials. Let's just have a bit of consistency and fairness in the reporting. Basically, Backy had weighed up what was going on and made a mug of Peter Stringer like the crafty old pro he was. Stringer was not happy, obviously, but it's one of those things. Move on.

Looking back, that spring was the high point for Leicester. By our own high standards, we tailed off badly the following season, perhaps losing some of our work ethic – it's very hard to keep the drive, determination and hunger there year after year, especially when everyone else's is growing. A few behind-the-scenes issues developed, with some backbiting and players questioning how others were training. People started looking over their shoulder and the team spirit dipped. I don't think it has quite recovered yet, either. Our consistency disappeared. We lost away at Leeds on the opening day of the 2002–03 season, but put 50 points on Newcastle and beat Quins at home. Our match at Sale perhaps summed things up. They scored, we came back, scored ourselves and were pressurising them. Austin chipped over the defence, hoping to scoot through and regather. Instead, the ball took a right-angled bounce into the arms of their lock, Chris Jones, who burst through the pack and ran it home from 45yds. On another occasion we would have been able to overcome that, but we just couldn't come back. The Bristol game that season was another I am sure we would have won in previous years: Julian White was sent off after five minutes, we got into a winning position, but lost when we conceded a try to Phil Christophers at a crucial time. We had made a speciality of nicking close games and, suddenly, we were losing them.

Earlier, our strength in depth and fitness had told in the months after Christmas – we were in better shape than the other sides and that showed in the results. By 2002–03, teams were catching us. They were better coached – guys like Warren Gatland at Wasps, Jim Malinder at Sale and Wayne Smith at Northampton had brought a lot of new ideas and professionalism to those clubs – fitter and with better personnel. The whole league was becoming more competitive. Where we had found it relatively easy to score tries, defences were becoming much more organised and we found it tougher to run up big scores. If you're leaking tries yourselves – and we started to – that spells disaster. Maybe we had started ageing a little. Our pack has certainly had plenty of older heads in recent years, with the likes of Rowntree, Cockerill, West, Garforth, both Johnsons and Back in the mix. There's certainly a lot to be said for the experience this brings, but eventually guys in their twenties will beat guys in their thirties. Our success had been built on sound finances and a strong squad base from the amateur days. As those guys aged and retired, things started to even out. Our impressive home record went, to Northampton, and, by the time of the Rugby World Cup 2003, we had suffered the ignominy of losing five matches on the trot for the first time in our league history.

Will any other side achieve what we did? They'll have to be very lucky and very hard-working. Injuries can, of course, wreck the best-prepared, best-coached side's season. We had been fortunate in the past, but this had started to come into play as our collective form dipped lower and lower. In 1999–2000, for instance, the only long-term injuries had been to Daz Garforth and myself. We were obviously important players, but the other boys coped well. In the 2003 season, we had a much larger number of key guys out and we struggled. Lewis Moody, who had become a vital member of the team with his pace and dynamism, hardly played. Austin missed a lot of rugby with injury. Backy was out for periods, Rod was out at the start of the year.

The salary cap works against anyone putting together a run like ours, too. Take Andy Goode, for example. In the early years of our successful run, Andy had been a young lad with a lot of potential. He was happy to be at the club, getting games whenever the first-choice fly-half was missing, but by the end, he needed to move on. He had become a first choice Premiership-standard fly-half and he rightly wanted the starts and the income that went with that. It was his livelihood, after all. With the salary cap, we couldn't afford to keep Andy and Austin Healey, so Andy left. This is something all successful clubs will face in the future, I believe. Wasps won the championship in 2003. Immediately, their team becomes desirable. Fraser Waters was previously, perhaps, seen as a mid-range sort of player, but after having a great season in the Wasps centres he might end up being offered a top contract somewhere else. The natural loyalty of rugby players used to make it harder to sign players from other clubs. We had tried to recruit Bryan Redpath from Sale, but that was like trying to lure someone from Manchester City to Manchester United. In football, they would leap at the chance to move, but there is a camaraderie and an honesty in rugby which makes it hard. Bryan turned us down – and fair play to him. In the future, though, as the old amateur players retire and it becomes much more about lads who have known nothing else and who need to squeeze everything they can out of their rugby, I can see this happening more and more. Given the salary restraints, it's very important to recruit wisely. We lost some important guys and maybe didn't replace them all that well. Franck Tournaire, the France prop, came in to take over from Garforth and surprisingly struggled to adapt to the Premiership. Rod Kafer, for all his undoubted qualities, perhaps wasn't the attacking force Pat Howard had been in his second season.

In the end, lots of little things added up to create the big picture. People were pleased to see us fail, and I wasn't surprised. From a neutral point of view, it's obviously good to see someone else win the championship. It hurts, but that's life. As I write this, the boys are battling to turn round the 2003–04 season. It's not over yet and it would be foolish to write us off, but it's going to be a tough job.

CHAPTER TEN

FANTASTIC HIGHS, DREADFUL LOWS

On the pitch, the 2002–03 season promised to be England's toughest ever, with home and away matches against the best sides in the world and another tilt at the Six Nations Grand Slam – something we felt we absolutely had to win this year. Off the pitch, my personal life would go through highs and lows like I had never experienced before.

The 2001–02 season had seemed to stretch on forever. Those of us who had been on the 2001 Lions tour of Australia had had almost no time off between arriving back from Down Under and being pitched into the next domestic season. Internationally, we had had a good autumn, but we had missed out on yet another Grand Slam, losing to France in Paris, and while I would not say this was down purely to tiredness, that was certainly a factor. England's international season ended with a quick trip to Argentina for a one-off Test against the Pumas. They are not among the true giants of world rugby, but Buenos Aires is a tough place to go and play, as France recently found when they lost twice in a two-Test series. The Argentinians scrummage extremely hard, have some sharp half-backs and an improving back line. Their home crowd is always very pumped up and hostile, too.

I have never played there – I was not around to be selected in 1990 and was on tour with the Lions in South Africa in 1997 – so I would have loved to go on the trip. Had it been the week after the European Cup final, I imagine I would have been in the party. However, it took place several weeks later and in order to play I would have had to stay in shape for that period, when really I and many of the other senior players needed some rest. Mindful of this, Clive selected a team full of youngsters, with Phil Vickery, the captain, and Ben Kay just about the only first-choice players in the group. Against the odds, they turned the Argentinians over, winning 26–18 and perhaps did not get the credit they deserved.

It was a cracking finish to our international season and I heard the score on my way to the gym on my holiday in Portugal, where I was starting my pre-season training. It was fantastic to be able to begin the work in June rather than to be playing still, as I had been the previous year. You need that period of rest and then some time building up your strength and fitness in the gym if you are to be at your best when the season starts again. People assume you must 'get fit' playing rugby, but really you are just trying to maintain fitness and strength, a process made difficult by the knocks and niggles you pick up in matches.

The autumn of 2002 promised our biggest international series since 1997, when we had played the All Blacks twice and Australia and South Africa once each. This time we would play one Test against each of the big boys. The All Blacks were first up. We had not played each other since our defeat to them in the 1999 World Cup and the infrequency of our meetings, coupled with the undoubted mystique of the All Blacks, meant this was the most eagerly anticipated match of the three for the rugby public. The anticipation was perhaps slightly dampened by their coaches' decision, with the World Cup a year away, to rest many leading names – guys like Chris Jack, Ritchie McCaw, Reuben Thorne, Justin Marshall and Scott Robertson – and give debuts to some of their younger players. But there are no weak New Zealand sides and we expected a very testing encounter.

Off the pitch, I had some exciting news, too. Kay, my wife, was pregnant with our first child. The baby would be my parents' first grandchild. Normally, this would have been a fantastic and joyous time, but our happiness was tinged with terrible sadness. My mum had been diagnosed with cancer the previous spring and I did not expect her to live to see the birth.

Mum had been a tremendously fit woman, with massive stamina and an addiction, almost, to running. When I had started to get more serious about playing sport as a teenager, she and I would often go out training together. Some days we would run up and down the hills outside Market Harborough. Other times we would do what would now be called speed endurance training or interval work: a 200-metre sprint, a rest, then another 200m and so on. It was second nature to people involved in athletics – running for endurance, speed and fitness, training hard to get a return – and is similar to some of the work modern rugby players now undertake but in those days it was unheard of in the sport. People thought a few four-mile runs would get you fit; it does, of course, but not for the stop-start nature of rugby. My own endurance is obviously inherited but also probably partly the result of those afternoons with my mum. They stood me in good stead later in life; with England and Leicester, I do well at the running drills among the front five.

With her fitness, then, it had been a big shock when she was taken seriously ill in the late nineties. She had developed a rapid heartbeat – it would leap above 200 beats a minute while she was running, rather than her normal training level of around 150bpm. The doctor referred her to a specialist who immediately admitted her to hospital for an operation. It was intended to be exploratory, but the surgeon was clearly not happy with what he found because he fitted her with a pacemaker while she was under the anaesthetic. This immediately put a stop to any competitive athletics. Although she was in her fifties, she had still been running most mornings and nights and competing, too, and this was devastating for her. Running was her life and she found it hugely frustrating when she could no longer take part. Looking back, she was never quite herself again after that. Physically, she was certainly weaker and it also aged her; she went from being a young middle-aged woman to seeming quite a bit older over the next few years.

In early 2002, she was feeling off-colour and suffering from nondescript aches and pains that her doctor was unable to pin down. Again, she was referred to a specialist and, once again, she was admitted to hospital. She hated that, being ill and confined to her bed, especially in a ward. Years before she had had an Achilles tendon operation and it never really healed properly afterwards. Mum blamed the surgeon, but he said she had started running again too quickly on it and that sounded just like her – desperate to get up and be active. They ran all sorts of tests on her and initially ruled out cancer, saying they thought she had pancreatitis, an inflammation of the pancreas. However, after ten days the diagnosis came through: she had pancreatic cancer.

This form of the disease often takes a while to identify. With the pancreas being located deep within the body, it tends to present itself as a very general pain and in most cases by the time it is found it is too late to operate. Mum was no different. I got on to the internet to find out about the illness. I was numb and very upset for her as I read of horrendous survival rates – two to three months after diagnosis seemed to be fairly good, and six months was unusual. If she had been as fit and strong as she had once been maybe she would have had a chance, but I think I knew, deep down, she would be too weak and that she was going to die.

It was, obviously, a dreadful time for her and for the family. We tried to stay as positive as possible. In the summer, Dad, Andrew, Will and I took her on a last family holiday to North Devon, where we had holidayed when I was younger. We stayed in a rented cottage for the week, really enjoying ourselves. One day we all went walking on the sand dunes, with the wind whipping up the sea below. Mum was shuffling by now, rather than walking properly, and her hands had gone purple with the effort, but she was really brave and she managed a couple of miles before we had to call it a day.

Most of the specialists and nurses tried to be as upbeat as possible, though one of her local doctors, perhaps trying to prepare us for the worst, advised her against having chemotherapy. He said it was not worth it, which was not a nice thing to hear. She ignored him and went ahead with the treatment, hoping to give herself the best possible chance, but by early October we knew it was just a matter of time. She had aged dramatically and looked very unwell. Towards the middle of the month the doctor told us it was a question of days. I cried a few times in private, but tried to stay strong for my mum. I didn't want to upset her.

She had been spending time at the LOROS Hospice in Leicester, but right at the end she came home to Harborough, where she wanted to be. She was in a lot of pain – you could see it in her face – but the Macmillan nurses and the local health visitors came over regularly to keep her dosed up on pain-killing drugs. They were fantastic and we very much appreciated their help. She had a procedure which involved injecting alcohol into her spine to block off certain nerves. Fortunately that helped take a lot of the pain away and she was as comfortable as possible.

She died in the evening, on Sunday 20 October, timing it pretty well because the whole family was there with her. In the end, it was a relief. The final few days were pretty horrible and I didn't want her to go on suffering any longer. It would have been dreadful for my dad and for her, so we were grateful. Her funeral at Kettering Crematorium was very well attended, which was nice. It was a non-religious service, with 'Annie's Song' by John Denver playing at the end. We all spoke. I remembered the happy times and Will and Andrew did the same, all trying to stay deadpan to avoid really breaking down. We were all welling up. 'Chuck my ashes on the flowers so I can do some good,' she used to say, but we decided to take her up to the North York Dales, a place she had loved and not far from where she had lived as a girl. Again, I had a bit of a cry, with Kay by my side. Bye, Mum. I miss her like mad.

Within a couple of weeks of her funeral, I was back at Twickenham with England for the first of those autumn internationals, against New Zealand. Mum was on my mind as I ran out and as I sang the national anthem. There was never a question of not playing – that was the last thing she would have wanted. My brother Will had played for Leicester the day before she died and I had been on the bench. It was just a shame she could not be there to witness the year that was about to unfold. She would have loved our successes.

Clive had made a couple of interesting selections. Neil Back was left on the bench, which is always a tough thing for a selector to do, but Clive wanted to find room for Lewis Moody, who had proved his worth against Argentina. Richard Hill is very hard to leave out and Lawrence Dallaglio was back from injury, so Backy was the unlucky one. He wasn't very happy, but he took it as well as you can. It happens to us all – I had been left on the bench against Italy at the end of the previous season – and Neil got on with training hard in the week before the game. James Simpson-Daniel made his debut on the wing, where he would be up against Jonah Lomu. He had famously scored against Jonah, in the England versus Barbarians fixture a few months earlier, with an outrageous dummy switch to beat Percy Montgomery and a 40m sprint that left Lomu in his wake. The press were salivating at the possibility of 'Sinbad' skinning the big man again. Unfortunately, it did not happen.

The match started poorly for us, with Jonah touching down in the corner after he got on the end of a movement which stretched right across the field. I was disappointed that they scored; they were close to our line and with little space to work in I felt we should have been able to cut them off. They had carried out a move where the ball had been passed behind a player's back and we had been caught out. In the English Premiership, this was seen as obstruction or 'blocking' and was always penalised. It was therefore not something we had worked on defending. However, the South African referee, Jonathan Kaplan, let it go. You can't blame the All Blacks – that's the way they play in the southern hemisphere – but it raised all the old questions about consistency between north and south. Clive brought up the incident at a press conference, demonstrating what had happened using video. Amazingly, by the time we returned to our clubs the tactic was commonplace. I welcomed this about-turn, because I think it gives attackers more opportunity to break defensive lines. Northern-hemisphere referees seem to look for things to ban, while their southern-hemisphere counterparts are more liable to let things go, an approach I prefer because it leads to a more exciting game.

We managed to apply some pressure and Jonny kicked penalties to keep us in the game, but after we managed to turn over their ball and counter-attack they intercepted a pass, got it out to Doug Howlett and he managed to outrun Jason Robinson to the line. Now we were two tries down. It's not a position we find ourselves in too often and it was highly annoying, especially given that we pride ourselves on our defence. We managed to pull a try back through Lewis Moody after Steve Thompson made some yards with a bullocking run, but it was not a happy changing room at half-time.

I thought we looked rusty and hesitant; guys were getting a bit 'steppy', trying to go round the All Blacks. I wanted us to run powerfully at them. I said, 'Thommo is the only guy who is running hard at them and one of his runs has resulted in a try. If in doubt, let's go forward aggressively and commit defenders.' My thinking was that if we took them on, the chances to power through tackles or offload in the tackle would come, and after the restart, things improved. Wilko chipped over the defence and re-gathered to score, Ben Cohen smashed through and outstripped Howlett to the line: 31–14, with the conversion. We ought to have accelerated from there, but the game was far from over. Marty Holah, their stand-in openside flanker, was causing us problems at the breakdown. He seemed to have an uncanny knack of popping on to his feet and turning over ball, and we were penalised harshly a couple of times as we tried to stop him. They came back at us, Lomu scoring the kind of try only he can, boshing Mike Tindall out of the way, and their replacement scrum-half Danny Lee also scored. Andrew Mehrtens, on as a sub, converted to make it 31–28 with ten minutes to go. Fourteen unanswered points. At the death, they got down to our corner and thank God Benny Kay, on for Danny Grewcock, managed to steal their line-out ball on our line and that kept the game safe for us.

It was strange coming in after the match. On the one hand we had beaten the All Blacks for the first time in nine years. This was important, because an away win for them would have been a big psychological blow. But on the other hand, we had let a good lead slip away and conceded four tries at home against a team with a number of guys making their debuts. At times we had played OK, but at others we had made sloppy mistakes and this was frustrating, though not too surprising, as most of us had not played a Test match since April, against Italy, and they were coming fresh from the Tri-Nations. That was some excuse, but there was no one jumping up and down with joy and we had to remind ourselves that there are generations of English rugby players, even whole countries – Ireland and Scotland, for instance – who have never beaten the New Zealanders.

We had scarcely had time to recover our breath, though, before the Wallabies arrived. It was a similar game in many ways. We started OK, with Jonny kicking a few goals, and we grabbed the first try, Simpson-Daniel offloading to Ben Cohen to score. They got back into it, kicking a few points, but at 16–6 up in first-half injury time we looked good. Then Jonny slipped in the defensive line on our line and Elton Flatley nipped through to touch down, meaning we turned round 16–13 up. The previous week, the beginning of the second half had been our time, but now this was reversed as the Wallabies had a dream start. Larkham got the ball out to Sailor; this time Ben Cohen slipped and Sailor added the five points. A short while later we had an attacking ruck in their 22, an Aussie hand knocked the ball out of the side of the ruck and Flatley surprised everyone with his pace to outstrip our defence and run it in from 75yds. So now, instead of being comfortable, we were comfortably behind at 28–16. We gathered under the posts after Flatley scored his second. We recognised that we had started to be a little too restrained, too conscious of getting into trouble with the referee. They were putting a lot of pressure on us at rucks and mauls, situations where we had definitely won the ball but where they would send a guy in late to disrupt and challenge. Much of it was borderline, like the incident at the ruck preceding Flatley's score. Down a lot of points, with nothing to lose, we agreed to be more direct, more assertive in our approach, and it started to pay dividends.

When you are ahead, subconsciously you start to become protective of your lead, and they fell into that pattern. We made progress up the field, continuing to kick our goals. Although we were still behind on the scoreboard we were starting to get on top. We were the fitter team: you could see them looking at the clock, blowing hard, hands on knees, a little slow to the scrums, line-outs and in the defensive line. That boosted us and, when Sinbad dummied to send Ben Cohen in under the posts on a beautifully timed and angled run, Jonny converted and we were suddenly ahead 32–31. The crowd, exhilarated by our comeback, were starting to make a lot of noise. They had started with high hopes of an England win, but there had been a lull after the Aussies had gone so far ahead – I had sensed then the crowd thought there was no way back for us. Now we were trying to defend our slender lead, playing for territory, keeping them out of drop-goal or penalty range. I remember being pretty irritated when James Simpson-Daniel cut in off his wing, was tackled and lost the ball. 'Bloody hell,' I'm thinking. 'We're in the seventh or eighth minute of injury time and we turn the ball over and give them a chance to counter attack!' But fortunately our defence was strong and we kept them out to win.

Afterwards, we got the feeling that the ref had lost track of time; apparently the fourth official was trying to tell him the game was over, but the radio was out of action. That would have been a hell of a way to lose a game: four or five minutes into injury time that shouldn't have existed. It had been a really draining game because it had lasted so long, had been so tense and had been played at such pace. I was very dehydrated, losing about seven or eight pounds over the ninety or so minutes. You try to avoid this because it affects your performance, and you'll often see guys drinking from water bottles when they get a chance during a match, but when you are holding on to one point you don't have time. I suffered a little with diarrhoea and nausea and felt weak that night. It was compounded by problems with a recovery drink – a thick protein and carbohydrate shake – I took after the game. You're supposed to get yourself back to near full hydration before drinking one of these, but that hadn't been properly impressed on me. The compound actually absorbs fluid from the body, so the result was that it sat like a rock in my gut for about twenty-four hours afterwards.

How did we feel about the match? Better. We were particularly pleased to have come back from well behind, something many observers had wondered whether we could do. And we had beaten Australia and New Zealand on consecutive weekends for the first time ever. However, it was not all good news. We were scoring points, but we had conceded seven tries in two games at Twickenham, which was disappointing, unusual and a little worrying. Phil Larder, our defence coach, is not the kind of guy to panic – or show he is panicking – but he must have been worried. If you give away four tries you are unlikely to win. If you concede more than one you'll have to work very hard. Even our comeback felt a bit like the silver lining to a cloud – we should never have let them back into the game once we had that 10-point lead. People said it was good that we had won despite not playing well, but this was to misunderstand the game. We had not played as well as we could because we were playing two very strong teams and they defend and attack strongly, pressurising you into mistakes. You are not going to put 50 points on the All Blacks or the Wallabies. The classic case of this was when we defeated Ireland and Wales heavily in the Six Nations after we were knocked out of the 1999 World Cup. People said, 'Why didn't you play like that against New Zealand and South Africa in the World Cup?' The answer is pretty obvious – the teams we were playing were far better.

The weeks leading up to the Test matches had been very intense, with a lot of training and very little down time. The senior players, including myself, met the coaches on the Saturday night after the Australia game and said we wanted a more relaxed approach ahead of the Springbok match. We were all worried about certain areas of our game, like defence, but we did not necessarily think more training was necessarily better. With the guys' faces showing clearly that the enjoyment level was dropping off, we suggested a lighter week, both mentally and physically. The coaches listened and on the Monday of the next week we all went out in Kingston for a few beers together. This was not something we would normally have dreamed of doing, but it was an excellent way for the squad to relax together.

The week before, South Africa had been beaten 21–6 by

Scotland, their first loss to the Scots since 1969. That meant two things: firstly, that the pressure was on us to win and to win well and, secondly, that the Springboks were likely to come out fighting. They hail from a proud rugby nation and have a fanatical and unforgiving public back home expecting nothing less than world domination. When the South Africans are backed into a corner, as they have been in the Super-12s, where their teams have not always been that successful, they have been known to get physical and have occasionally crossed the line into illegality. Consequently, in the build-up to the game we had discussed the likelihood that it might get feisty and we knew we would have to look after ourselves.

As for their line-up, they had a lot of new boys we knew very little about. The old names we were used to facing – guys like Bobby Skinstad, André Vos, André Venter, Percy Montgomery, Ruben Kreuger and Mark Andrews – were either out with injury or playing overseas. Corné Krigé, the skipper, was still around, but this was a fairly new Springbok outfit, containing a number of guys who had not even played in the Tri-Nations.

Our suspicion that they would be emotional about the Scotland defeat was proved correct because, as they ran out at Twickenham, several of them hung around on the halfway line, squaring up to us and shouting things in Afrikaans as we made our way on to the field. The lock, Jannes Labuschagne, was one of them and he singled me out for a few stares and threats. Obviously, I couldn't understand what he was saying, but perhaps it was, 'I'm gonna get sent off after twenty minutes! Got that, you muppet?'

I remember thinking that this was going to be interesting

and it was nasty from the start. The first time Jason Robinson got the ball he was punched, Jonny came in for a bit of treatment and one or two other fists went flying in. The thing that really irritated me was when the referee, Paddy O'Brien, called me and Krigé together. 'Listen, guys,' he said. 'Both teams have got to calm down. The next guy to cross the line is off.' I said, 'Mate, we haven't done anything.' Within minutes, though, Labuschagne had blatantly followed through on Wilkinson. It was not the worst incident of the day – if he had done it in the first minute of a game he might not even have been carded – but in the circumstances, the referee was absolutely right to send him off.

It was clear to me what was happening and what the Boks were trying to do. Paddy needed to take control of the game quickly, but he never really managed to, which was disappointing, especially for one of the world's best referees. The game wore on in much the same vein, with, in particular, Butch James and Robbie Fleck getting stuck in. I guess it's possible Paddy and his touch judges just didn't see much of it. I certainly didn't. People said to me afterwards, 'You were so restrained.' The fact is I didn't see the worst of the violence until later, when the video arrived. The stuff that was directed at me was very petty – little slaps and punches that I hardly felt – but the knee-drops, the real kicking and the straight-arm tackles, in vivid Technicolor, were something else. Backy got his cheekbone smashed, Jason Robinson had his eardrum perforated with a kick to the head and Jonny Wilkinson was hit very late and it damaged his shoulder. If I had seen what was going on I would have had to act. If it happens to you as an individual once, you live with it, but if you see it happening across the field repeatedly it is different. I would have spoken to the referee and if he didn't take action I would have led my team from the field. The only other choice would have been to start retaliating physically.

The consensus of opinion, post-match, seemed to be that the red card ruined the game; with fourteen men on the field the Boks had no chance of winning. My response is that Leicester went on to lose to Bristol at the end of the 2002–03 season when Bristol were down to fourteen men for seventy-five minutes, so it can be done. Like a soccer team that's down to ten men, Bristol pulled together and got through it. And where do you draw the line? You can't not send someone off in case it spoils the game. Other people suggested it possibly made the violence worse, because the South Africans knew they couldn't win. Maybe so, but, again, you can't allow blatant thuggery to continue just in case dealing with it winds up the thugs. If they have to go down to thirteen men, if the game has to descend to farce, so be it.

We tried as best we could to keep some structure on the play – they had some dangerous runners – and I felt that the more the game broke down and became an unstructured mess the more chance they had to come back at us. We didn't want that, we wanted to turn the screw, and as the game wore on we managed to do so. It ended 53–3, with us pushing them over their own line from a five-metre scrum. I knew they wouldn't like that. As I walked back to our half, I asked the ref, 'How long left?' He replied, 'A couple of minutes.' I said, 'I think you should blow the whistle now.' I couldn't see any point in continuing and I was afraid of how they would react to going down fifty points for the first time in a Test match, particularly against a northern-hemisphere team. Corné Krigé was almost in tears, his eyes welling up, as he came off. Clearly, he was upset, embarrassed even, at what had happened. I said, 'Mate, we've all been there.' I have played in teams that have been heavily beaten, we all have, and I certainly didn't gloat. He didn't respond.

No one likes to be stuffed, especially when you're representing your country, but I found some of his comments at the post-match reception surprising. Krige said, 'You really twisted the knife when we were down to fourteen men. This is not Perth. We'll see you in Perth.' If you've been beaten 53–3, whether you're a man short or not, there's only one thing to say, and that's 'Well done.' You take it on the chin. What did he want? Of course we twisted the knife. Should we have gone easy on them? The Springboks asking for mercy? That would have been insulting, surely? And as for the Perth remark – a reference to our 2003 World Cup pool stages meeting, scheduled for a year later – no one in the England setup thought for a moment that this encounter had any bearing on that match.

The general mood in their camp was unrepentant and defiant. Rudolf Straeuli, their coach, was certainly in that mode. He defended his guys and came out with one of rugby's all-time classic lines: 'It takes two teams to tango and we didn't concuss our own player.' Look at the videotape, Rudolf. Actually, you did.

The crazy thing is, who got banned from that South African team? Nobody. Those Springboks came to Twickenham and were lucky to finish the game with fourteen men after one of the worst displays of illegal tactics in living memory.

Guys were throwing stiff-arm tackles, punching, knee-dropping. Matt Dawson was knocked out when he was head-butted. And they got away with it. The South African Union said they would handle it internally and the IRB acquiesced in this. End result: cop-out. If these were England players I'm sure they would have been banned – and rightly so. I had been suspended the year before for a single punch on Robbie Russell. It seemed to be a very clear case of double standards. And look where it led: a few months later they got stuck into the Wallabies in the so-called 'Battle of Brisbane', after which Robbie Kempson was suspended for four weeks and Bakkies Botha for eight, for foul play.

As I write this we are just about to leave for Australia and the Rugby World Cup. We face South Africa in that group game in Perth. Will they try the same tactics again? Who knows, but I certainly hope not. Rugby doesn't need that kind of advertisement, especially on the world stage with billions of people watching. After the Twickenham game, three guys missed club rugby for a month or so. If it happens in a World Cup match, their tournaments will be over and our chances severely damaged.

I have no problem with South Africans. From a rugby point of view, they are one of the great nations, perhaps the greatest. Their Test record is awesome, particularly at home, and they go on producing great players; big, tough guys with a combination of aggressive physicality and pace that is hard to beat. They are currently in something of a trough, but that's hardly surprising when you consider the quality of the players who have recently left: André Vos is at Quins, Percy Montgomery was at Newport, Brendan Venter was at London Irish and

Mark Andrews at Newcastle. England would not be competitive if they lost players like these. Off the field, South Africans have a reputation for being aggressive and rude people, but I'm not sure this is fair. Most of the rugby players and followers are Afrikaners, so there is immediately a language barrier. Afrikaans is a harsh, Germanic-sounding language and when they speak English that accent and guttural way of talking can give the wrong impression, so the way they talk, rather than what they say, can sound belligerent. The guys I have met, though, have been fine. Fritz van Heerden, the former Springbok lock, joined Leicester in the nineties. I was expecting some hardcore Afrikaner, but he was the nicest bloke you could ever meet: quiet, humble and great company. Joel Stransky was another South African whom I obviously got to know well at Leicester and he, too, was a top bloke.

That Twickenham encounter, though, did leave a sour taste in the mouth. Rugby is, by nature, a physical game. The Boks put in some massive legal hits – I took three or four huge tackles myself – and that is fair enough. Football has changed its rules and the way it is refereed after guys like Pele in the sixties and Marco van Basten in the eighties were kicked out of matches. It is very difficult to do that in rugby, because you can legally hit and hurt someone, so the very fact of an injury proves nothing. You have to prove it was done illegally.

So, as they jetted off and we sat down to count our bruises, we could at least reflect on a successful autumn. We had beaten all of the big three, one after the other, and no team had ever done that before. On 9 November, as we faced New Zealand, we would obviously have taken the wins, but we did feel, certainly against New Zealand and Australia, that we could have played better. Against the Springboks, the match will always be remembered for the thuggery rather than the rugby, but the record books show we put fifty points on them and that proves how far English rugby had come in ten years.

As we entered 2003, the Six Nations beckoned. On the day of the tournament launch in January, though, Kay called me. She had been diagnosed with pre-eclampsia. This is a potentially serious condition that can prevent the placenta from getting enough blood. If that happens, the baby gets less oxygen and nourishment, which can lead, in turn, to low birth weight and other problems. In extreme cases, the condition develops into full eclampsia, which can kill both mother and child. It was not entirely unexpected. Kay's mother had had pre-eclampsia while she was pregnant with Kay and her twin sister Denise and had ended up staying in hospital for a couple of months. Eventually she had been induced prematurely – that being the last resort in dealing with the problem. Kay told me she was going into hospital to be checked out and this was the start of a series of regular visits. The doctors monitor the mother's blood pressure and check for the presence of protein in the urine, two of the main tell-tale signs that the pre-eclampsia is worsening. It was to be a worrying time – you obviously would rather a pregnancy proceeded without any trouble at all – but I always felt that the consultant and his team had everything under control.

Back to the rugby and our record of missing out on Grand Slams was horrendous – three times in four years we had lost the final match of the series, each of them games that, arguably, we should have won, after good wins over the other sides in the tournament. This time out we would first meet France at

Twickenham, a fixture scheduling which prompted lots of hand-wringing from the media. There were really only two teams in the Six Nations, so the argument went, and having them meet first up was, effectively, to ruin the tournament decider. Clearly the whole thing was now going to be an anti-climax, clearly they should have engineered England versus France as the last game, blah, blah, blah, ad nauseam. It was mildly irritating and insulting to the other teams involved, I felt, but we would see. We had been beaten in Paris the year before, with their back row playing well and putting a lot of pressure on Jonny. It had finished two tries all, but we had been unable to reel them in after they got away early on. This time out they were missing a couple of key players – Pieter de Villiers was banned and Tony Marsh had been diagnosed with cancer. There were names missing from our line-up, too. Mike Tindall was recovering from injury, James Simpson-Daniel, who many observers would have pencilled in on the wing, had come down with glandular fever, and Phil Vickery and Trevor Woodman were out, with Julian White and Jason Leonard – in his hundredth Test – their replacements. Whitey, who had served a suspension during the autumn for being sent off against Leicester, had a bad knee injury and did really well to play in the game. He was later given the team's internal man-of-the-match award for playing against one of the best scrummages in international rugby with that dodgy knee. In fact, he didn't play again for some months, which speaks volumes.

Earlier, the French side's new young No. 8, Imanol Harinordoquy, had provided the journos with some copy by laying into the English. He said he had played in England in a junior international and had been insulted and abused. He hated us, apparently, and all he wanted to do was stuff us. 'As long as we beat England, I don't mind if we lose every other match in the Six Nations,' he said. It was almost childish and none of the guys could really work out what had motivated him. I have been to France and been gouged, spat at and had coins thrown at me. I do not hate the entire French nation as a result and as for not caring about losing every other game: yeah, right.

His nonsense was overshadowed, though, by the dreadful and untimely death of young Nick Duncombe, which cast an awful shadow over the whole sport. Nick, a highly promising twenty-one-year-old scrum-half, had broken into the squad the year before and looked to have a glittering future ahead of him. On holiday in Lanzarote, though, he had been taken ill with suspected meningitis on the Thursday evening before the match and died the following day. Mark Evans, the chief executive of Nick's club, Harlequins, came to our hotel at Bagshot to break the news to his Quins team-mates Dan Luger, Will Greenwood and Jason Leonard. Dave Reddin, our fitness coach, told the rest of us as we were eating our supper. To call it a shock would be a massive understatement. It was hard to take in. Nick was a likeable young man who fitted into the squad well and his death was an enormous tragedy. Dan Luger, in particular, had been extremely close to him and there was major concern over whether he would be able to play the following day, but he somehow got through a very emotional eighty minutes.

Even without Nick's death, we would have felt a lot of pressure. If we had lost to France after beating the big three it would have been a big, big blow and our Six Nations would have ended along with, possibly, a few careers. They had played well in the autumn and defeat was certainly a risk. Clive, rightly, sought to face this head-on, saying openly that anything other than a Grand Slam would be viewed as a failure. One loss was not going to be good enough this year.

Charlie Hodgson came in to play for Mike Tindall, to help take some of the pressure off Jonny. It was tough for Charlie. He is a very good fly-half but he doesn't play centre too often and he had bigger, stronger runners to deal with than he would normally encounter. We had the best of it early on, enabling Jonny to kick us ahead, but then Hodgson had a clearance kick charged down and Olivier Magne scored to bring them back into the game. At half-time it was wide-open. Jason Robinson scored in the second half and we should have opened up that gap but, with nothing to lose, they came back strong and scored a pair of tries to get to within eight points of us. We held on, but Will Greenwood summed the performance up when he said that the second half had been the worst England performance he had been a part of. It was a strange feeling, because we had now beaten the other four of the top five teams in the world in consecutive games, albeit at home, and yet we still felt we had not really clicked. I guess that was a positive thing.

Next up we travelled to Cardiff. Wales had lost to Italy and suddenly everyone was talking about us beating them by fifty or sixty points. We had scored heavily against them in recent years, but this was never going to be that sort of game. They were almost in damage-limitation mode, defending aggressively and giving away penalties if necessary to prevent try-scoring opportunities. They also targeted our scrummage. Vickery and White were missing with injury, as was Jason Leonard, who had pulled his hamstring the week before. Robbie Morris, a twenty-one-year-old tight-head, came in at No. 3. He is a big, strong lump and, with more experience, will be a really good player. The opposition will always try to target a front-row debutant, as Wales did, but Robbie did a great job in the circumstances. We tried to play a little wide on them when we should probably have been more direct, and I don't think our back line quite worked with Charlie wearing No. 12. Perhaps the most telling moment from their point of view was a good break by Mark Taylor, which ended with him brought down almost on our line. He had men outside him and, if he had passed, they would probably have scored. I don't think they would have won the match, but it would certainly have lifted them and may have made it closer. We scored through Greenwood and Joe Worsley and, in the end, after a dogged performance, we ran out 26–9 winners.

A lot of people felt this was a disappointment for England and a moral victory for Wales. We were fairly pleased with the result, however. We had gone to Cardiff in a no-win situation, with a new tight-head and had suffered injuries to key players during the game. We had kept the Welsh try-less and had won by seventeen points – a feat a generation of English players would love to have achieved. It had been a full-blooded match and I went into the home changing rooms afterwards to thank them and to let Jonathan Humphreys, their captain, know I would not be at the post-match dinner. With Kay's pre-eclampsia still a worry, I was allowed to go home straight away. Wilko was not too happy, though, because it meant he had to give my speech, but there you go.

My car was parked underneath the stadium and it flitted through my mind that I could be in for a bit of trouble driving out of Cardiff. My team-mates and I are not exactly popular in Wales. In 2001, our bus had driven through the city after the match on our way to the reception. One Welsh fan actually ran up and head-butted the coach. He turned away, head streaming with blood and a big, silly grin of triumph on his face. The same day, our wing mirror clipped another Welshman and knocked him unconscious. The bus had to wait for the police and ambulance to arrive, with an ever-growing crowd of home fans, pint pots in hand, gathering around the bus, shouting and making traditional gestures at us. I remember thinking, 'Yeah, this is pretty good-natured at the moment, but if one of those guys lobs his pint at us they're all going to do it and then we won't be laughing. Things could get interesting . . .' This time, it had been a late kick-off, so everyone had been in the pubs for hours, but even though I didn't fancy a pint of lager through my windscreen, I was actually pretty disappointed when I received zero abuse. I even drove round the city again, shouting, 'Oi, come on, let's have it!' but there was still nothing. (Not really, Kay.)

I was absolutely starving, having rehydrated but not eaten after the match, so my plan was to call in at a service station on the motorway and grab a bite – specifically, a bite of Kentucky Fried Chicken. I don't often get the opportunity to eat fast food, and I really had a craving for The Colonel, but there were no services on the M50, the services on the M5 were closed, and by the M42 I was getting desperate. I was almost drooling at the thought of that blend of eleven secret herbs and spices, so I thought I'd drive down the Stratford Road into Shirley. I reckoned there was bound to be a KFC there, probably a drive-through, but there wasn't a sign of that big, beardy grin anywhere. By 11p.m. I was in the centre of Solihull, with the window down, accosting random passers-by: 'Oi, mate, do you know if there's a Kentucky Fried about?' A very helpful couple pointed me in the right direction and off I screeched until the beautiful sight of Colonel Sanders' mug hove into view. I parked up, ran in, still dressed in my England tracksuit, and ordered a bucket of chicken (about six pieces when I could have eaten twelve), two bags of fries and, because I am an athlete, a diet Coke. As I waited for my order, I could see the lads in the back poking their heads round the corner and pointing, presumably wondering what I was doing in my kit, in their restaurant in Birmingham, six hours after a Test match in Cardiff. It was a bit surreal, but that was the Wales game out of the way.

By now, Kay had reached the point where the doctors had decided to induce her. She was thirty-eight weeks pregnant, the baby was not going to grow any more and delaying matters was only going to increase the risks to both of them. The plan was to take her in on the Monday morning, the day after the Italy match. Clive gave me the week off to spend at home and he played Danny Grewcock and Ben Kay in the second row. It meant I couldn't play in every game of the Grand Slam effort, which was mildly disappointing. However, I had a slight Achilles tweak and, given that throughout the club season I played every match apart from one, where I sat on the bench and didn't come on, the rest probably did me good. We arranged a family Sunday lunch. My dad and Kay's mum, who had flown over from New Zealand to be with her, were there, along with my older brother and his girlfriend, and with twenty minutes of the England game to go, Kay's waters broke. No matter how well prepared you think you are – and we had her overnight bags packed ready for the next morning – it is a fairly dramatic moment. Panic stations set in and I raced round the house trying to collect things, while Kay's mum and a friend who had recently had a baby made sure she was OK. Off we raced to the Leicester Royal Infirmary, leaving two big joints of beef in the oven and a couple of empty seats at our dining-room table. When we got to the hospital she was already a few centimetres dilated, which suggested things were happening quite quickly. Normally, I am told, you expect the whole process to be much slower with your first. They took Kay upstairs to the delivery suite, where they hooked her up to various monitors and made sure she was comfortable. Then ... nothing much. Everything slowed down and it changed into a waiting game. After a while I nipped downstairs to see George Chuter, the Leicester hooker whose wife had had a baby in the early hours of that morning. Then I popped off to TJs to get a burger. Well, I had missed my lunch, hadn't I?

When I got back the delivery suite was a lot busier. The registrar came in and had a look, then the consultant, then various other specialists, midwives and nurses. No one was really telling me anything, but I gathered from their comments that the baby's head was partially engaged and under a little stress. I didn't worry unduly because everyone seemed very calm and I just assumed this was the normal number of people to have around you. This being our first child, I didn't realise that it is often just you, the mum and the midwife. Eventually, though, even I got the feeling that everything was not going to be as smooth as I had hoped it would be. They mentioned the stress again and said that the baby's heartbeat was shooting up and down as a result. I was uneasy but not panicking; there was still that sense that these were extremely professional people who knew what they were doing and had everything under control. After some deliberation, they told Kay she had another hour of trying to give birth naturally. After that passed uneventfully, the consultant came in. He said we could give it another hour but that he thought it unlikely the baby would be delivered normally at this stage. We asked him what he would want for his own wife and he said he would suggest she have a Caesarian section. We made up our minds instantly.

Kay had already had an epidural, so they whipped her into the theatre and prepped her while I struggled into some green sterile clothing. The midwife had thoughtfully located the biggest pair of trousers and top she could find, but they had no size thirteen shoe covers so I slipped my feet into a pair of hats and slid in. Other players say they were in floods of tears when their child was born, but I was so nervous about Kay having an unplanned op that I didn't really have time to get emotional. They sliced her open and removed the baby – my daughter, Molly – and, after giving us a quick glimpse, rushed her off straight away to check her over. I was left with this image of a tiny alien, because poor Moll was a shiny grey colour, with these big eyes and a pointy little head from having been engaged for so long. However, soon they brought her back, told us everything was fine and gave her to Kay. The nice thing is that Molly was born at 11.40p.m. on my birthday – 9 March – and was the best present I have ever had or could ever have hoped for.

Kay was so exhausted, even the next day, that I had to jump straight in with the bathing and nappy changing – this tiny, wrinkly little creature, all 5lb 13oz of her fitting into one of my mitts. It was fantastic. My dad, Kay's mum and my brothers were there but, again, my thoughts obviously turned to my mum. I wish so much that she had been able to see Molly, a feeling that has grown as Molly has. Now, at six months of age, she is the last thing I think about before I go to sleep at night and the first thing I think about when I wake up in the morning.

Down in London, the boys had beaten Italy in a match probably most notable for Josh Lewsey's selection at full-back and the injury to Charlie Hodgson. Josh had showed he had the power and the pace to fit right in as an attacking international full-back. For Charlie, our second choice No. 10, it had seemed the perfect opportunity for him to get some Test match game time under his belt ahead of the Rugby World Cup later that year. However, within minutes he caught his studs in the turf, damaged his knee and was out for months. This was a desperately cruel blow for Charlie. He had developed into an outstanding young player and I really felt for him. The first twenty minutes or so showed England playing fantastic, mistake-free rugby, but as the game wore on into the second half, the performance level dipped slightly as Italy retained the ball, frustrated our line-out and kept the score down to a respectable 40–5.

Meanwhile, Ireland had beaten France the same weekend. They, too, were on course for a Grand Slam and would play Wales. We faced Scotland. Again, we started well and they had two guys sin-binned. The first was for a dangerous tackle, which was fair enough. The second, when Simon Taylor was carded for taking Jason Robinson out without the ball, was a little harsh I felt. He arrived so early that it was clearly genuinely mis-timed. Penalty, yes. Sin-bin, no. The Scots played quite well when they were two men down, defending with intensity and working hard for each other. Then we went down to fourteen, with Jason Robinson binned, and the game lost a little of its shape. It was fairly close until Matt Dawson tap-tackled Bryan Redpath as he went to clear and Ben Cohen leapt on the loose ball to score. After that, Jason got home for a pair of tries and the game finished 40–9. Ireland, meanwhile, had beaten Wales with a late O'Gara drop-goal to set up the final match as the fourth away Grand Slam decider for England in five years.

To that point, the opening twenty minutes against Italy apart, you would probably describe our performances as workmanlike as our team chopped and changed a great deal. For a Grand Slam team, we probably hold the record for the greatest number of different players. For instance, three guys – Robbie Morris, Jason Leonard and Julian White – had featured at tight-head. To beat the Irish in Dublin, we would need to play with precision, pace and passion, cutting out mistakes and putting away our chances. At this point, Clive was quick to re-emphasise the importance of the Grand Slam. It would have been very easy for him to come out and say that the Slam was not the major prize, that it was all about the World Cup and that this was just another game, but to his credit, he didn't do that. He was again very clear, both publicly and privately. This was a must-win game. You couldn't have written the script of what had happened to the England team over the previous four years. There was no way we could allow the same thing to happen in 2003.

Ireland were a good side, too. Brian O'Driscoll needs little introduction, Stringer and Humphreys or O'Gara were playing well at half-back and they had quality players like Victor Costello and Geordan Murphy elsewhere on the park. Of all the teams we have played in Grand Slam deciders, I think this was probably the best one.

I have always enjoyed playing at Lansdowne Road. It is one of the smaller stadiums – small, personal, quaint if that isn't patronising, and with a vociferous and partisan crowd. I have never lost there, either. We were pretty relaxed in the run-up, flying over on the Thursday and staying at the fantastic Four Seasons Hotel in Dublin. We had Friday off. I spent the day chilling out, watching a movie and grabbing a massage. I needed the rest after what had already been a long season. That night, the A team played Ireland A at Donnybrook, a stone's throw from the hotel. You could hear the PA system and the roar of the crowd as the Irish lads won. We were all sitting round relaxing over our supper as Andy Robinson came in from the match. He had one of his feisty heads on: 'Yeah, we lost. They kicked everything, chased everything. The fans sang 'Fields of Athenry'. Grrr!' We call him the Growler, because he can be a little bit terse when he is in a bad mood. 'Anyway. Enjoy the rest of your night off.' And off he stalked, having successfully wound everyone up. Thanks, Robbo . . . quite amusing, really.

Next day, a lovely warm, spring morning, we trained down at Old Belvedere, one of the Dublin clubs. Woody had made a big thing about this simply being a stretch and nothing more: when you use other people's facilities you don't know how good they are and you don't know who might be watching you. So most of the work had been done before we left England and we just enjoyed the sunshine and went through a few light moves. Looking around the guys I could see they were enjoying themselves, were feeling confident and were looking forward to the match. The pressure, the 'fear' of failure was there – we all knew that if we lost we might as well not bother coming home – but it was not overwhelming. We knew we had a good side and we were strong right through the team.

By that evening, the whole of Dublin was buzzing about the game. Our hotel was full of supporters, most of them Irish, most of them making comments and having little digs at us. Next morning, as we walked through the foyer to get on to the team bus to take us to the ground, there were several hundred fans milling around. Guys were coming right up to us and shouting, 'Come on Ireland!' in our faces or flicking V signs. I started to get my hatred going quite strongly.

Yes, the hatred. I remember Will Carling talking about how, after Scotland had beaten England in 1990, he and the other players had turned the Scottish dislike of England and the English to their own advantage, using it to fuel the aggression and power that would win Grand Slams in 1991 and 1992. Will said, 'When we play these guys at rugby they hate us and they make no bones about it. Look at the Scotland team openly supporting Australia in the 1991 World Cup final. But if we tell them we hate them they're shocked. Somehow, that isn't in the rules. The English are the hated, not the haters. I just tell them, "You hate me, so I'll hate you and let's leave it at that."' I follow the same path. Everyone hates the English, everyone likes to see us lose and in Dublin that day everyone around the world would have been rooting for the Irish. My response is 'F*** you all. We are going to beat you and we don't give a f***.'

That attitude, essential to my game, continued when I got to the ground. I went out to toss up with Brian O'Driscoll. I was jokey and relaxed with 'Drico' – I always try to take the initiative early on by seeming not to have a care in the world – but in reality the tension was there. That half-hour or so immediately before a game is always a very pressured period and that was magnified in Dublin, with all the Grand Slam history. I am not at my most approachable at this point. Ridiculously little things wind me up. We will be at Twickenham and as the team are leaving the changing room some guy from the TV will be standing there saying, 'This way, please guys.' Really? I thought we would go the other way and play in the car park. Afterwards, when all the tension is released you can laugh at yourself and it all sounds so petty. On this occasion, it was some blazer from the Irish union. As I walked back in from the toss, he thrust an England shirt in front of me and asked for my signature. I would have done it for him after the game without a problem, win or lose, but not then, thirty minutes from kick-off in such a huge game. No player would. I just brushed him off.

With the hatred now fairly bubbling in my veins, I led the guys out for the anthems a few minutes later. We lined up on the right-hand side as we walked out, in front of the red carpet. In the background, the crowd were giving us plenty of banter and grief, and then the Ireland team tentatively started walking behind us. I had no idea what was going on. The only thing I could think was that maybe they were going down to gee up the crowd. I was fine with that if they wanted to do it. Then some guy with a walkie-talkie and a tie on walked up to me. 'Johnno,' he said. 'You've gotta move the fellas. You're standing in the wrong place.' Ah, a jobsworth. I have a deep-rooted dislike of petty officials. A lot of people mistakenly think that major rugby matches are put on for guys to play in and for people to come and watch. That is not the case. They are actually organised for the benefit of people in blazers and, sometimes, even in stewards' uniforms. I said, 'What? We're not moving.' A bit petty, maybe, but why should we? We had run out and stood towards the end we would be defending. I was in a somewhat petulant mood. The crowd, who had obviously worked out what was going on, started booing and whistling.

It had become a stand-off and Backy was in my ear going, 'No, Johnno, you can't concede on this. Don't concede . . . don't concede.' Thanks, mate. The first guy's boss came out and he told us to move. Again, I refused. There was a bit of a pause and a moment of uncertainty. What would happen next? Nothing. They gave up. The Irish lads stood to the side, their president came out to meet the teams and it was all over. Later on, after the game, with the experts all claiming I had struck an 'important psychological blow', some Irish bloke collared me and said, with a knowing smile and a finger wag, 'Johnno, you know you always line up on the other side.' Eh?

I had not played there since 1999 and I had absolutely no idea where we were supposed to line up. There is, apparently, some four-page document somewhere outlining the etiquette for visiting teams on matchdays. I had never seen it and if I had I wouldn't have read it. It was an honest mistake and I'll know next time, though I will have retired by then.

We waited for the Irish to go through their two songs – their national anthem and then 'Ireland's Call'. I am not a big fan of this. What next? Three songs and a dance? Australia are the same. They play their lovely anthem, 'Advance, Australia Fair', and then they launch into 'Waltzing Matilda'. How about 'Tie Me Kangaroo Down, Sport' as a finale? As we took our positions for the kick-off, the Irish crowd started singing 'Fields of Athenry' and I could feel the hairs on the back of my neck standing up. I love the challenge that a big crowd and a hard team present. One thing was for sure, though: we would not be taking a single backward step.

Then we were off. They started well, with Humphries dropping a goal after four minutes, but we responded with a try, Matt Dawson turning their ball over for Lawrence Dallaglio to score after we pressurised their scrum. We managed to repel intense Irish pressure before half-time, Jonny Wilkinson putting in a massive hit on Kevin Maggs. He also dropped two right-footed goals, the second bang on the whistle. It meant we went in 13–6 ahead at half-time, with the breeze at our backs for the final forty.

The game was in the balance after the restart and had they scored it might have changed the outcome. A few mistakes crept into our play and we seemed unable to kill the game off, but once Mike Tindall touched down, and with Paul

Grayson on as a blood replacement for Wilko, the match was ours at 20–6. Will Greenwood darted over for his first try and then intercepted Geordan Murphy to score another and really silence the crowd. Danny Luger put the final nail in their coffin right at the death. The last five minutes, knowing we had won and just wanting to hear the whistle, seemed to last forever. The Irish boys kept going right to the end, counter-attacking and trying to score, but we held them out. People said the scoreline, 42–6, did not reflect the game. Maybe so, but perhaps when we've lost Grand Slam deciders the scoreline hasn't mirrored the play.

In the changing room, at last, there was jubilation and a feeling of release. I looked around at the guys and was more pleased for them than for myself. I was happy for Clive Woodward, as a loss would have dumped a lot of pressure on him. I was happy for Robbo, as he would probably have been hospitalised. A few of us met up with our families briefly in a marquee and then we had to race off to the presentation dinner. It was being held at the Berkeley Court Hotel. This was only a hundred yards or so away, but I thought that if we walked up there we would be mobbed, so I told the lads to get on the team bus. Off we drove, up a totally empty street, looking for all the world like big-timers who were determined to arrive in style. Should have walked, Johnno.

The Irish public, to a man and woman, were extremely gracious. Everyone who spoke to me congratulated me and said we had deserved the win. The committee men? Well, the key issue for them was that this should have been a black-tie event and everyone was in blazers. It was a formal occasion and this needed to be looked at very closely in future and

. . . blah, blah, drift away into the ether, thinking about sticking pins into your eyes.

We didn't really talk about the game with the Irish players; the chat was mainly about where we could get a good beer in town that night. We ended up in a club and sank a few pints between us. It isn't often we get the chance to sit back, take stock and enjoy the moment with each other. It felt good. We had finally laid our Grand Slam ghost and we had done it in style, playing our best game of the season.

We arrived home on the Monday and the boys were so tired that if you had flagged down our bus on the way back from Heathrow and climbed aboard not knowing the score you would have thought we had lost. Everyone was slumped against windows, dozing or staring into space, completely drained.

That was 30 March and, incredibly, we played on for two more months. Leicester's club season finished on 31 May with a massive game against Saracens to qualify for Europe, which is important from both a prestige and a financial point of view. It was played at midday in thirty-plus degrees and it went into extra-time. I have never been so exhausted. As I came off the pitch, someone tried to grab me for an interview, but I could barely speak. I needed to sit down before I fell down.

We would be playing the All Blacks, away in New Zealand, in two weeks' time, in part one of the final and biggest hurdle of our international season – back-to-back Tests away in New Zealand and Australia, with a match against the Maoris thrown in. I shot home, had a night with Kay and Molly and then packed my bags ready for departure. We flew on the Monday morning, looking forward to the flight just so we could have a kip. I did a few TV interviews at a wet, blustery Auckland airport – an unwelcome change from June back home – waiting for the transfer to Wellington. Once we arrived there early on the Wednesday morning the guys playing the Maoris the following Monday had to acclimatise immediately and start getting ready for that game. The rest of us were given Wednesday off before hitting the gym on the Thursday and Friday.

It was a long build-up. Whatever town you are stuck in it can get a little samey. Luckily, the Leicester prop Perry Freshwater is from Wellington and he was back for the close season. Bursting with pride about his home town, he took the Leicester contingent under his wing. One night we went to his house for a barbecue while we watched Geordan play for Ireland against the Wallabies. Another night we went go-karting, and he also took us out into the bush with a pal of his. But the main business, of course, was the rugby and the non-Test team did us proud with a great win over the Maoris at New Plymouth.

Many of them were due to head off to the USA for a series of games over there and some of those who would stay behind with the main party knew they were not going to make the Test side for the matches against the All Blacks or Australia. It was a wet, blustery night and, under those circumstances, there are some players who might use that as an excuse not to give their all. Instead, our guys played with a huge amount of commitment and purpose, overpowering the Maoris 23–9. It was a massive boost for the Test team and an equal disappointment for the New Zealand union, press and rugby public, all of whom would have been very keen for our team to lose and to be made to look bad in the process. There were the usual comments about England playing 'boring' rugby, but when it's blowing a gale and sheeting with rain you keep it simple, look after the pill and play very directly. We adapted better than they did, simple as that. Their coach, Matt Te Pou, had been closer to the action than any of the somewhat one-eyed writers and fans. He said, 'In the time I've had the New Zealand Maori side, that is probably the strongest team that I've been up against, definitely the most ruthless.'

For the main event, at the so-called 'Cake Tin' Stadium – a low, round ground, right on the coast – we picked the same team for the first Test as we had for the Grand Slam decider against Ireland. In the days beforehand, we had all been itching for the game to begin. Training, time off, it all blended into one, with Saturday night seeming to take forever to arrive. When it finally came, there was little talking and no faffing around in the changing room – we just rocked up and got on with it.

We started poorly, allowing them to make breaks and being pinged for offences at the ruck – we were probably lucky to avoid having players binned in the first half. As ever, Jonny kept us in touch with his boot, including one magnificent kick from the right-hand touchline. His opposite number, Carlos Spencer, was missing kicks which helped and we went in at 6–6.

The second half started better. I felt we were getting into the game more and starting to play. Disaster loomed, however, when first Neil Back and then Lawrence Dallaglio were yellow-carded for infringements at the breakdown. We were down to thirteen men and the All Blacks had a penalty close to our posts. They made the sensible decision to go for the scrum and push us over, rather than simply kicking three points. Simple maths, really: eight against six, the eight should win. We could not rope any of the backs in to help because that would have left us exposed out wide. With the crowd screaming, at first in delight and then in disbelief, we kept them out with a fantastic effort from the front row. Graham Rowntree, particularly, had worked incredibly hard to keep them from manoeuvring the scrum into such a position that their No. 8 could pick and go. Graham was penalised for his efforts, they took a quick tap and we prevented them from scoring again, the video ref awarding us a penalty in the process.

Their moment was gone. A lot of people have asked me what that scrummage meant psychologically. I guess it must have affected them – 'if we can't push these guys about when they're missing two men, we're in trouble' – and probably boosted us, though that's not the kind of thing you're thinking at the time. More than anything, it shows how much Lawrence Dallaglio and Neil Back push.

With the ball in our hands, we concentrated on doing the simple things well – keeping possession, gaining territory, quick, uncomplicated line-outs. We started going forward, playing some good rugby and actually claimed three points of our own through a Jonny drop-goal. I think we had an overlap at the time, so we might even have scored a try, but he took the right decision; with thirteen men on the field, you take your opportunities when they arise. Suddenly, we were back up to fifteen men again. Howlett scored later from a kick ahead, but we were in front and we stayed there. As the game approached its end we became slightly protective and they became a little more adventurous, but I never thought we were going to concede a try and it finished 15–13. For the first time in thirty years, we had beaten the All Blacks in New Zealand. Once again, though, we were not going overboard about our performance. It had been very stop-start and we had not played much rugby or stretched their defence a great deal. I said to Reuben Thorne at the end, 'Cheers mate, bit of an ugly game, that.' But who cares? We had won.

A few of my mates from Taupo came down for the Test and afterwards I enjoyed renewing old acquaintances over a couple of beers in the hotel. Overall, they were reasonably complimentary about our performances and even the New Zealand press accorded us a little grudging respect among all the tongue-in-cheek mickey-taking. 'White orcs on steroids', was one. Other comments were, 'There's ugly ... and there's Martin Johnson' and 'England have the ugliest forwards in the world ... any kids who watched that won't sleep for weeks.'

When we arrived in Australia, New Zealand commentators were being asked for their thoughts on how we had played. One of them was at pains to tell the Aussies how boring we were. 'I was over there in the UK in 1983 and in 1993 [when they lost],' he said. 'They play boring rugby and they win by kicking penalties.' We just shrugged our shoulders and laughed. Yes, we kick penalties, but if Jonny Wilkinson was a Kiwi do you think they would leave him out of their side? If you lose on penalties, you still lose. Anyway, we like to think our game has moved on a little in the last five years or so. It suits us for them to see us as we were.

It took two or three days to get over the Wellington match

and feel like playing a Test again. England had never beaten the Wallabies in Australia, which gave the build-up a little extra spice, but the history, back further than about 1997, was irrelevant, because most of us were not there before that and most of them were not either. We were pretty whacked after a very long season, but we refused to admit to it. Our team motto was: 'Don't let Mr Tired in. Keep him off the couch.' If you keep saying you're knackered you'll feel it. We trained when we had to and tried to rest when we could. On our day off, a few of the guys fancied a round of golf, which always worries the coaches, because it involves walking further than you ought to on your day off. My view was very much that the guys needed a rest and if golf was their preferred way of forgetting rugby after eleven months of playing, let them play golf. It would do them the world of good.

I strolled into Melbourne one day and immediately realised why I avoid city-centre shopping – identikit stores, hustle and bustle everywhere. We get to travel the world, but very rarely get to see much more than our hotels, the training pitches and rugby stadiums. I am told Melbourne is a very attractive city and I would have liked to have seen more of it, but I did not have the energy. A few English fans were knocking around so I signed some autographs and headed back to the hotel. Wednesday night we all went out for our weekly team meal. Usually, we go for Chinese. Let off the dietary leash, the boys love nothing more than crispy duck, but a word of advice: don't bother ordering crispy duck in Australia. The duck is not crispy and the pancakes are of the Shrove Tuesday variety. Disappointment all round.

The game was to be played indoors in the Telstra Dome

– the renamed Colonial Stadium. I can see both sides of the indoor/outdoor argument. One side says rugby is an outdoor game, played in all weathers, and to take the conditions out of the equation somehow devalues it. The other side says TV companies and spectators pay a lot of money to watch professional rugby and they expect a quality game, played at pace with high-skill levels. This is much easier to achieve in the dry, without wind.

Whether the roof was responsible or not, it was certainly a quick game, exploding from kick-off, with the ball pinging everywhere. We had picked Trevor Woodman and Phil Vickery to create a very mobile front row and, with Steve Thompson, they were soon getting their hands on the ball and making bullocking runs upfield. The Aussies were breaking from their own third, but we were first to draw blood, through Will Greenwood and then, with great hands, through Mike Tindall. We had a good lead at half-time and the danger was in thinking, 'What do we do next?' The answer was, 'Keep playing the same way,' but for the first twenty minutes of the second half we were lethargic and errors crept into our game, allowing them a foothold. I was starting to worry a bit and then – bang! – Ben Cohen blasted through the middle to score and take us out of reach. They managed to pull one back through Wendell Sailor, which was disappointing as we would have loved to have nilled them for tries. However, a 25–14 score-line looked pretty good.

A lot of people will remember the game for two things. One was Josh Lewsey's crunching tackle on Mat Rogers. They had had a bit of off-the-ball handbags a few moments before and Josh saw his chance to smash Rogers as he took a pass.

He hit him in the stomach and almost cut him in half. Rogers was lying on the pitch injured for about four minutes, which, in retrospect, was irritating. If a player is badly hurt, it's fine to take as long as is necessary to get him right. If he is just winded, as Rogers was, get him off the pitch and sort him out on the sidelines. The second was our 40m maul, all the way from halfway to the verge of the Australian line. We managed to create momentum and didn't lose it until the smallest man on the pitch, George Gregan of all people, dived in to stop us 2m out. Very satisfying, but disappointing that we didn't finish it off with five points for what would have been a great forwards' try.

Finally, on 21 June, our international season was over. Ten matches played, ten won, including two massive games won away from 'Fortress Twickenham'. Those victories alone were a great achievement, especially coming at the end of a very hard, long season, and that was testament to the fitness and commitment of the boys. The question on everyone's lips was: 'What does it all mean for the World Cup?' By the time you read this, you will know. As far as we were concerned, a couple of defeats wouldn't stop them being world-class teams with some of the most talented players out there in their ranks. All we could do was give it our all.

CHAPTER ELEVEN

BRITISH LION

There are few greater honours in rugby than to be selected to play for the British and Irish Lions. There is a special mystique about the Lions; a magic I have loved since I was a small boy. Players from four countries, enemies under other circumstances, coming together to take on the world's best on the other side of the planet is a unique tradition in sport. The fact that they only ever play thousands of miles away, in rugby's traditional southern hemisphere strongholds, has always added to that incredible aura, particularly in the days before the matches were carried live on UK TV and thousands of British and Irish supporters would travel round the world to follow the tours.

I loved to read books and sections in autobiographies about the famous tours of 1971 and 1974, when, for once, the northern hemisphere reigned supreme; when English, Irish, Scots and Welsh legends fought epic battles against the huge Springboks or the seemingly invincible All Blacks. My earliest memories are from 1980, when Bill Beaumont, the first Englishman to captain the Lions in many years, led the squad to South Africa. But at just ten years of age, I was too young fully to appreciate the excitement and drama of a Lions tour. I don't think it was covered on TV, so I can remember little more than one or two scores and the 3–1 Test outcome.

It was a different story in 1983, when the Irish hooker Ciaran Fitzgerald led the party to New Zealand. By now I was thirteen, the biggest sports anorak in Leicestershire and a very keen follower of rugby. I would sit glued to the telly on Saturday mornings as the games were broadcast from the other side of the world. The Lions went down 4–0 to an outstanding All Blacks side – a big disappointment, obviously, but it didn't dampen my enthusiasm or stop me dreaming, just like every other rugby-playing lad of my age, that one day I would pull on that Lions jersey. In 1989, when the Lions visited Australia under Finlay Calder, I was playing in New Zealand. I missed the first Test, which the Lions lost, but managed to catch the second and third, when they came back to win amid claims of on-pitch violence and thuggery.

By 1993, and the tour to New Zealand, I was on the fringes of the England squad. However, I felt that, realistically, I had no serious chance of making the trip. Pre-professionalism, the club structure throughout the British Isles was not particularly competitive or well organised. How could you select someone for a Lions tour on the basis of a game between Melrose and Hawick? Irish rugby was no stronger and the English scene was fairly weak, too. We had one or two decent sides in Bath and Quins, with Leicester and Wasps just about competitive, but that was it. Only Welsh club rugby was played to any real standard of intensity, but the great days of their game were over. There was no European Cup, no big provincial games and no English Premiership. So, with no other way of judging ability or potential, the Lions selectors almost always chose guys who had played plenty of Test rugby in the Five Nations. It was not unheard of for uncapped guys to be picked – Derek Quinnell had gone in 1971 – but it was the exception, rather than the rule.

I had played just one international – against France in that year's Five Nations, after the giant Wade Dooley had been injured. After a reasonable game, I had gone back to the England B team ranks to play some pretty meaningless fixtures against Italy and Spain, and a better one with Ireland B. Not surprisingly, then, there was no seat on the plane for me, but I had at least managed to get myself on to the radar, being named a non-travelling replacement. Selection for the four second-row spots was fairly straightforward: Wade Dooley and Martin Bayfield went from England and the Scotland locks Andy Reed and Damian Cronin joined them after the Scots forwards put up a good fight in a losing Five Nations cause against England. In fact, the entire Scottish front five – Cronin and Reed plus Paul Burnell, Kenny Milne and Peter Wright – went, alongside the England pack minus Jeff Probyn. Cronin had come from obscurity to play for Bath and from there had made it into the Scotland team. Andy Reed was a guy I knew. He was originally from Cornwall, had played for Bath and alongside my Leicester colleague, Matt Poole, for England Under-19s the year before me, somehow becoming Scottish and going north of the border later on.

I did not feel any resentment or bitterness – those guys had played much more international rugby than I, though having played with Bayfield for the Midlands for the past couple of years and being of the same generation as Andy Reed I knew I was not a million miles away. Anyway, there were plenty of good second rows who did not even have reserve cards. Gareth Llewellyn of Wales was one and I was very surprised that the Irishman Neil Francis – a great player and a tremendous athlete – was not in the tour party and, in fact, never played for the Lions. The players selected are not always the best available. One of the weaknesses of the Lions system is that, with players from four countries all available, a certain amount of 'horse trading' takes place to ensure each nation gets represented. For instance, Jeff Probyn, an exceptional tight-head, lost out as large numbers of England players were included, whereas the Irish second row Mick Galwey was included as a back row ahead of specialists from other countries.

So, while the Lions headed south, I went to Canada with a young England squad, led by John Olver and containing guys like Tim Rodber, Victor Ubogu, Graham Rowntree, Neil Back, Kyran Bracken and Matt Dawson, for a two-Test series. The Canadians were a strong, aggressive and talented bunch who had given the All Blacks a tough game in the quarter-final of the 1991 Rugby World Cup. We lost the first Test but won the second, which was a really good result in the circumstances.

After that second match we were having a 'court' session – a long-standing rugby tour tradition involving 'fining' players with alcohol for amusing and spurious offences – in Ontario when we got the news that Wade Dooley's father had died. Wade was flying home from the Lions tour and I was being called down to New Zealand. Tremendously excited, I was thoroughly stitched up in the session, with the 'judge', Chris Oti, fining me heavily for leaving the England tour early. After a few 'fines' I started giving the judge some grief, with the result that I was fined again, and it all turned into a horrible vicious circle. Fairly smashed, I caught my flight home, but I don't recall much of it.

Having flown into Heathrow, I drove north, went in to work at the Midland Bank (now HSBC) and said, 'Er, you know I've been on tour with England? Would it be possible for me to have another four or five weeks off for the Lions tour?' Amazingly, they said yes.

I went home to my mum's, washed my smalls and dashed back down to Twickenham, where I picked up my kit (it was as though all my Christmases had come at once, with loads of free stash knocking about, including the last of the Lions DJs for black-tie events, which I have never used to this day), and then it was on to Heathrow. There I met up with Vince Cunningham from Ireland. He was going out to replace Scott Hastings, who had smashed his cheekbone. I had spent the last 36 hours covering thousands of miles while either drunk, hungover or buzzing about the trip and, totally knackered, I slept all the way to Singapore. That probably surprised Vince – he was obviously thrilled about going on tour and must have thought I was the most chilled-out bloke in rugby.

We arrived in Christchurch before the main tour party, who had been down in Southland playing the midweek game ahead of the first Test. Next day we were straight into it, hitting tackle bags in a training session with Dick Best. I knew the Leicester contingent, obviously, and I had a nodding acquaintance with the English guys from my brief time in the national setup, training out in Lanzarote, or from playing against them in the league. I hardly knew any of the Welsh, Irish or Scots boys at all, though, and consequently I felt a little out of place. This was way ahead of anything I had been involved in before. Canada had been a tough tour on the pitch, but it had taken place in a non-rugby country, so there had been no off-field pressure. Here I was in New Zealand, training with the likes of Brian Moore and Peter Winterbottom – a guy who, as an eleven-year-old, I had watched making his England debut. I kept my head down, tried to work hard and endeavoured to win the respect of my team-mates.

I sat in the stands and watched the first Test, which the guys lost through a Grant Fox kick towards the end. The start of the tour had gone fairly well – they had come back from way behind to beat the Maoris, for instance – but the wheels were starting to come off at this point. The Lions had been stuffed by Otago and some members of the party were starting to find it hard. New Zealand is probably the toughest place to tour and this was the last of the old school, amateur trips: thirteen games and a squad of just thirty. This meant some players, like the hookers for instance, were involved in every game – they either played or they sat on the bench as cover. Every game was hard, played against high-quality opposition. It being the Kiwi winter, the pitches were often wet, muddy and soft – quite unlike the firm, fast tracks of South Africa or Australia – which took a lot out of you physically. Off the pitch, there was no respite. Certainly in those days, New Zealand was a relatively undeveloped country. Travelling took forever and we waited at airports or drove for hours from one little town to the next, stopping in pretty uninspiring, motel-type accommodation. Occasionally you had to laugh: we stayed in a tiny provincial hotel in New Plymouth that had a big sign over the door proudly proclaiming itself to be the 'Home of the Seafood Smorgasbord'. Bit of a bold statement, that.

We were, of course, surrounded by Kiwis. They are all obsessed about rugby and the Lions tour, the first there for a decade, was absolutely huge. The New Zealand public liked nothing better than to buttonhole the players for a chat but, after weeks of it, with the best will in the world it started to get a bit heavy. Most players are happy to talk to supporters, but you do need your space from time to time. I knew the Kiwi way, so it was less of a culture shock for me, but some of the boys found it very irritating. I remember one guy coming up to Martin Bayfield after a match, as Bayf was trying to relax with a beer.

'Mate, can I talk to you about rugby?' he asked, fairly bluntly.

'No,' said Bayf, more bluntly still.

The guy blinked and shook his head. Perhaps Martin had not understood? 'No, mate, I really want to talk to you about rugby!'

'No,' said Bayf very finally, in an 'if-you-carry-on-I-will-kill-you' sort of voice.

When you are winning you can put up with anything, but when you start to lose matches this kind of thing can grind you down. Some players fight their way through it, but others let it get to them and, two-thirds of the way through the tour, some members of the midweek team were starting to lose heart. The day after the first Test we travelled up to play Taranaki. I had faced them for King Country a year or two earlier – we had beaten them in one of our bigger performances – and now

I made my Lions debut on their ground. It was a typical, difficult midweek game. There was a big, partisan crowd and the
Taranaki lads were very pumped up. We were poor in the first
half, but Ben Clarke came off the bench and played brilliantly
to help us win 49–25 in the end. It was the sort of game that,
as the tour wound towards its close, the Lions second string
would lose.

I had played reasonably well, but I was surprised to be
selected for the weekend's big game, a clash with Auckland at
Eden Park on the Saturday. This was like another Test match.
A lot of the All Blacks played for Auckland and they were
the strongest provincial side in the world at that point, having
beaten all the international sides who had toured there,
including the 1983 Lions. When I had arrived, Dean Richards
had taken me aside and said, 'You've got a chance to get into
the Test side here.' I hadn't taken him seriously, assuming it
was just a bit of a pep talk to get me going, but there was a
feeling that the front five lacked a bit of toughness, particularly since Wade's departure, and maybe they thought I would
add a bit of resolve.

We started well, but Auckland wore us down and as the
game progressed we suffered a few injuries and made a few
mistakes to lose out 23–18. It was my first really big game
for the Lions and I felt I played OK against Robin Brooke,
whom I regarded as the world's best front-jumping second
row. I hoped the other lads felt the same, although in my
heart of hearts I still was not sure I was good enough to be
playing in this company. Obviously, I hoped I might be in
contention for a second Test spot, but at the same time I felt
awkward as no one seemed to know whether Wade Dooley

would be rejoining the squad after his father's funeral or what would happen to me if he did. His return would certainly have been a popular move with the other players. Wade had had a great career with England and many of his long-time team-mates, like Brian Moore, Dean Richards, Peter Winterbottom and Mike Teague, were out there. He was planning to retire from the game after the series. Nothing against me but the other players wanted him to be allowed back. I am sure Wade wanted to return and it clearly would have been the right and fitting thing to happen. Unfortunately, this was still the amateur era, with all its ridiculous, silly rules.

When the decision was announced that Dooley couldn't rejoin the tour 'because it would set a precedent', the players, particularly the England contingent, were disgusted. Looking back, it was shocking. Wade was respected around the world. After the 1989 Lions lost the first Test, coach Ian McGeechan knew he needed to change things around and Dooley was one of those brought in – in his case, at the expense of Bob Norster, the fantastic Welsh lock. Dooley was apparently told, 'You're in because you're big,' but he went on to play a huge part in the series win and the Aussies were close to being in awe of him by the end. This was no way for a guy of his stature to finish his career and I am surprised, in hindsight, that the squad didn't do something about it, even to the extent of refusing to play on.

After the Auckland game we played Hawkes Bay, a province to the east of where I had been in King Country. A few of my mates from Taupo came down to watch us lose, Norm Hewitt making some bullocking charges as part of a team which just wanted to win more than the Lions did. A lot of our guys were looking forward to going home by now. Then it was the second Test. It was do or die. If we lost that game, the series was lost and the tour would have turned into an absolute disaster.

Brian Moore and Jason Leonard were brought into the front row, Scott Gibbs came in for Will Carling to partner Jerry Guscott in the centre and I was named with Martin Bayfield in the second row. That was a fantastic feeling. Ten years earlier, as I watched the 1983 games, I had dreamed of playing in a Test match for the Lions, but had never thought it would happen. My selection was a bit of a slap in the face for Cronin and Reed. Damian Cronin was a little off with me, but he was obviously disappointed to have been passed over, probably feeling a little like a spare part, so I don't blame him. I thought Andy Reed was pretty hard done by, though. He had played well in that first Test, forcing the All Blacks to drop Ian Jones, one of the best second rows of his or any era, for the second Test after Andy had been all over him in the line-out. He was an underestimated player and we always struggled with him when Bath played Leicester.

I remember getting to the stadium and feeling very nervous. I had one Test match under my belt and I felt like I was heading into the unknown. Athletic Park in Wellington was a dilapidated old stadium, but a great Test match venue with lots of character and atmosphere. Simply by virtue of the country's distance from anywhere else, games in New Zealand are usually attended by home fans only, but on this occasion there were a fair few away supporters there and they got right behind us from the kick-off. It was a fast and furious game. Early on, Gavin Hastings made a mess of a high ball and they scored a try, but we came back at them. Bayf had a really good game in the line-out and Ben Clarke, probably the star of the tour, put in a man of the match performance.

Dean Richards was his usual self. One Kiwi had written to a local paper saying Deano was a disgrace; that his boots were dirty when he ran on to the field, his socks were round his ankles, his shirt was flapping. They were right, he was a disgrace, but what a player. He weighed around twenty stone at this point and was tremendously hard to combat in the ruck and maul situation. He was so big and strong, and so good at what he did, that he could suck people into the tight, controlling the ball and making space for Ben Clarke and others to shine out wide. People often ask whether Deano could still play today if he were young enough. Of course he could. He would be a focal point for the team, holding the ball up and generally making a nuisance of himself. When England beat South Africa in the first Test in 1994 at Loftus Versfeld, the reports were all about how well Tim Rodber and Ben Clarke and Rob Andrew had played, but it was Deano who had, almost single-handedly, won the ball and created the space for those guys to operate in.

Dewi Morris played brilliantly well. At one point he took a boot on the knee and was down on the ground, his leg twitching with the pain. I thought he was finished, but within seconds he was up, shooting round the front of the next line-out like a man possessed. Dewi is a tremendous bloke with a big, big heart – just the sort of player you need on a tough Lions tour.

And there were other stars that day, too. Jase Leonard at tight-head, Irishman Nick Popplewell and Peter Winterbottom all had great games. Brian Moore was in his element. Halfway through the match, a Kiwi fan threw a can of beer at him. Mooreo picked up the can, opened it, took a big swig and saluted the supporter before chucking the can off the pitch and running off to rejoin the fray. At the next scrum, Jason Leonard said all he could smell was Brian's beery breath.

At half-time there was controversy. Remember, this is in the days when the teams huddled on the pitch rather than heading off to the changing rooms. It was also in the days before tactical substitutions. Sean Fitzpatrick, the All Black skipper, was handed a note. He read it, looked at Mark Cooksley and looked away. A few moments later, Cooksley went off with an 'injury' and Ian Jones was on to replace him. What went on there? I'm not sure, but it certainly improved their line-out in the second half.

The key moment of the game came when Fitzpatrick lost the ball in contact. It was quickly transferred to Rory Underwood on the wing and he out-sprinted the cover to score in the corner. They tried to come back, but we held them off to record a memorable victory by 20–7. That was a brilliant moment. Any win against the All Blacks on their own patch is a big win, but the Lions had not won there since 1977 and, in context of the tour, this was a huge result. We had a chance to win the series and those demoralising midweek losses would all be forgotten.

We came back down to earth midweek, though, when we came up against Waikato. This was a tremendously strong provincial side, with the likes of Warren Gatland and John Mitchell in their ranks – hard men with great ability, who were second-string All Blacks and therefore had something to prove. Our guys, nursing injuries, knackered, dreaming of the plane home, were there to be shot down and Waikato obliged, steaming into us like it was their biggest game of the season, which it was. As the youngest forward, I was put on the bench for that match and it made unpleasant watching as we lost 38–10. Afterwards, a few members of the beaten team were in the toilets. An elderly English Lions fan came up to one of the Scottish guys and said, 'I don't really think you gave your all today.' As the player started to get into an argument with the bloke, Mike Teague turned round from a nearby urinal and said, in his West Country accent, 'My money's on the old man.'

The All Blacks changed their team a little for the third Test and their crowd, stung by the defeat and by the masses of Lions fans appearing in their own back yard, was suddenly right behind them. The match was played with huge intensity. After fifteen or so minutes we were 10–0 up, but they got back into it with tries before half-time. I am a little hazy on the details. A fight erupted at a breakdown and Martin Bayfield took a huge, haymaking swing at one of their guys, missed and smacked me instead. Had it been an opposition punch I would either have ducked it or seen it coming and been able to deflect some of the force. As it was, it came, not surprisingly, out of the blue. It was the latest in a number of concussions I had received and, although I played on, much of the rest of the game is a blur. I remember having to ask Bayf what our line-out calls meant, a sure sign I was in trouble, and hazily coming round towards the end of the match with the All Blacks about to win the game 30–13 and, with it, the series.

It was a disappointed dressing room afterwards. We had had our chances but it had not happened. It had been Peter Winterbottom's last game – he retired immediately afterwards – and would be the final time in a Lions shirt for many others.

It is hard to put your finger on exactly why we lost the series. The All Blacks were an outstanding rugby team who were always going to be very difficult to beat away from home, but we could have done it, maybe with a slightly different squad.

Choosing players for a Lions tour is always going to be a difficult job. In those days, there was a much smaller pool to choose from – I was given a reserve spot after one Test match, which says something about the lack of strength in depth – and the heavy bias towards selecting guys who had shown well in the Five Nations, coupled with the natural inclination to be 'fair' and include enough representatives from all four nations, mitigated against producing the strongest thirty. The thinking was that X had done well against Y on a given championship day. Maybe, but the England team had won two Grand Slams and had possibly lost some of its hunger, while the Irish and Welsh, both of whom beat England that year, were playing at home in front of ferociously partisan crowds and performed like men possessed. Of course that emotion produces outstanding individual performances, but you should not select Lions teams on those kind of results. When you go to a place like New Zealand, where every team you are up against is desperate to beat you and good enough to do so, you need men who can perform well away from home, not in front of their own crowd, because all your matches are going to be away. You look for character; for guys who are going to keep fighting when things are not going well, when they have niggling injuries, when they are not going to get into the Test team.

That is another issue in itself. Pick guys who are used to playing Tests for their countries and not all of them are happy to sit on the sidelines and play midweek. Once the tour got bogged down, a few of those second-string guys lost heart and lost interest. Some of the youngsters who had toured Canada with England that summer, players like Neil Back, Graham Rowntree and Tim Rodber, would have been better bets because they would have been happy just to be there and would never have let their heads go down. Don't get me wrong – I had a lot of time for plenty of the non-English tourists. I always felt Gavin Hastings was a cracking player – a big, aggressive full-back who would punch holes in the opposition, something England lacked in that era – and a good bloke too. Nick Popplewell and Scott Gibbs also announced themselves as world-class players and Ieuan Evans confirmed his own status.

From a personal point-of-view, I would have to say the tour was a success. I had played reasonably well in the two Tests, considering I was lucky to be there at all. In fact, I was lucky to get my first England cap earlier that year, without which I would not have been made a reserve. I was lucky that Wade had to leave the tour – though I felt very sorry for him and his family, obviously. And I was also lucky that when I arrived some of the other guys were not playing too well, which meant I got a look-in.

Four years later, things were a little different.

The 1996–97 season was massive for two reasons. It was

the first season of professional rugby in Britain and it would end with a Lions tour to South Africa, the first for seventeen years. Will Carling had resigned as England captain, to be replaced by Phil de Glanville. We were almost a new team, with many of the players who had been at the forefront of English rugby over the previous five to ten years having retired. In their place a new side was developing. Graham Rowntree at loose-head, Mark Regan at hooker and Jason Leonard on the tight-head. Simon Shaw had joined me in the second row. In the back row, Dean Richards was gone and Ben Clarke's decision to join Richmond in the second division had stalled his Test career. Tim Rodber, Lawrence Dallaglio, Richard Hill and Neil Back were either there or thereabouts. Andy Gomarsall and Paul Grayson were the half-backs – Jerry Guscott's great career was coming to its end – with de Glanville and Will Carling the starting centres. Tony Underwood and Jon Sleightholme were our wingers, with Tim Stimpson coming in at full-back.

England played autumn games against the New Zealand Barbarians, Italy and Argentina – not a massive pre-Christmas calendar. We played reasonably well against a Kiwi team containing many of their Test stars, were lucky to beat Argentina and defeated an inexperienced Italy.

Our Five Nations results were more solid. We beat Scotland at home, put a lot of points on Ireland in Dublin, with Austin Healey making his debut and coming on to play very well as we ripped the Irish to pieces. We lost to France, a game we blew, and beat the Welsh well. The disappointment against Les Bleus aside, we had played well and ended up not far from being a Grand Slam-winning side.

As the season wore on, the talk turned towards the forth-coming Lions tour. Much of it was very negative. The South Africans were world champions. They were a powerful, skilful and established team who were playing very well. Most people seemed to assume the tour would end in a thrashing for the Lions and humiliation for northern-hemisphere rugby. Many critics were speculating as to whether the Lions had had their day. Was it possible, in the new professional era, to band together a group of players from four countries and take them on lengthy and expensive tours halfway around the world? Would the faster, more exciting domestic and international game, played by men with more time to train and practise, so captivate supporters that the Lions concept would seem anachronistic? By the end of the summer, after the huge sporting and commercial success of the tour, those doubts would be gone forever.

The other area of speculation surrounded the captaincy of the party. There was not really an obvious candidate. Often, the post had been filled by the guy who had led the most successful Five Nations side: Ciaran Fitzgerald was in charge in 1983, after a good Irish campaign, when Peter Wheeler and Colin Deans were probably better hookers; Billy Beaumont, a Grand Slam winner with England, was captain in 1980; Phil Bennett had done the job in 1977 after another glorious Welsh spring.

In 1997, Phil de Glanville had led England well, but in fairness he was perhaps not the best centre in the British Isles and it was clear he might struggle to hold down a place in the Lions squad. What were the other options? Will Carling was playing well again, and had great leadership experience,

Battling it out in the line-out during my debut for England, against France at Twickenham, where we won 16–15.

Taking on Wales during our 1995 Grand Slam season. As ever, Dean Richards is in support.

Andrew Mehrtens goes in for a tackle on me during our semi-final in the 1995 Rugby World Cup. However, the damage had already been done by Jonah Lomu who trampled through and over our defence at the beginning of the game.

Setting off on a run during my first game as England captain, standing in for Lawrence Dallaglio. We beat the Netherlands 110–0 in this Rugby World Cup qualifying game held in Huddersfield in November 1998.

Getting to my feet after scoring against Italy in November 1996. My first try had come in my 25th game for England and I'm clearly not sure how to celebrate.

More than 20 games later and the way is clear for a second try, this time against the USA in August 1999. Lawrence Dallaglio is there in support in case I get lost on the way.

Part of the fun of touring. While in Australia during the summer of 1999
I demonstrate the surfing skills I picked up over many years in Leicester.

Tackled by David Wilson during our unsuccessful attempt to land our first ever victory
over Australia Down Under. I had been appointed captain of the side after Lawrence
had fallen foul of the tabloids.

With the indestructible Jason Leonard and Danny Grewcock. The forwards may be working well together here, but we did not perform up to expectations in the quarter-finals of the World Cup against South Africa at the Stade de France in Paris in October 1999. Clive Woodward had asked to be judged on our performance in the World Cup, and we fell short.

Our game against South Africa in the autumn of 2002 may have ended 53–3 in our favour, but most of the attention was on the violence perpetrated by the Springboks during the game.

Another year, another Grand Slam decider. For the first time in the Six Nations of 2003, we finally put together a great performance to beat Ireland 6–42. It was a very important victory and set us up for our challenge for the World Cup later on in the year.

Celebrating our success at Lansdowne Road with Jonny Wilkinson, whose goal-kicking is always so reliable.

Our 15–13 victory over the All Blacks in June 2003 was based on sheer determination never to give in and some incredible defence, especially when we were reduced to thirteen men and protecting our goal-line.

A week later and I was flying through the air as we attempted to achieve back-to-back victories Down Under over New Zealand and Australia.

Holding the Cook Cup after beating Australia for the first time Down Under. Raising this cup now would prove nothing when the serious business began in the autumn.

Offloading the ball during our vital Pool game against South Africa in the Rugby World Cup.

The World Cup quarter-final against Wales was a very tense affair, and it was only in the second half that we really began to exert any control before eventually winning 28–17.

but the feeling was that he could never be made Lions captain. Unfairly, Will was seen as personifying the supposed 'arrogance' of English rugby and would not have been a popular choice with the other nations or their fans. Ieuan Evans, Rob Wainwright and Keith Wood were possibilities and could have done the job well, as could Jason Leonard. Then, to my surprise, in the March my name started being bandied around.

After we played Ireland in Dublin, I was accosted at the evening function by my agent, Tim Buttimore. After trying, and failing, to impress a couple of young women – 'That big bloke Johnson works for me!' he kept assuring them – he moved on to the Lions. 'Mate, you're going to be the captain,' he kept saying. I was sceptical. Obviously, the skipper had to be someone who would make the Test team and I seemed to have a good chance of that, but I had relatively little leadership experience and none at international level.

I was in a hotel in Gloucester a few weeks later when I got a phone call from the BBC journalist, Ian Robertson. 'You probably already know this, Martin,' he said, 'but congratulations on being made captain of the Lions.' I had mixed emotions as I put the phone down. Elation, obviously, assuming Robertson was right, but irritation, too, because I did not want to hear the news like that. I tried to put it to the back of my mind until a day or two later, when I got a call from Fran Cotton confirming Ian's call. Later, he made his now-famous comment that they had gone for me because they wanted someone big to knock on the Springbok dressing-room door and intimidate them. I think there was a little kidology going on here. I am sure the South African players would not have been bothered by how tall the Lions captain was, but they certainly bit, saying things like, 'Well, we've got Kobus Wiese. We'll send him to knock on your door.'

The tour party was announced live on TV, with a camera crew sent up to Leicester to get our contingent's views. The club was strongly represented – myself, Neil Back, Graham Rowntree, Austin Healey, Eric Miller and Will Greenwood were all named in the squad – which was excellent for the Tigers and showed the boldness that was to be the hallmark of the 1997 selection. Will Greenwood had not played Test rugby at that point, Austin Healey was only on the international fringes and Backy had been largely, and wrongly, ignored by successive England coaches. All were great players, but it took a brave management to name them in the group.

Eyebrows were raised in some sections of the media and elsewhere at my appointment. I was viewed – am still viewed in some quarters – as a bit of a Midlands Neanderthal: grumpy, unfriendly and monosyllabic. How would I handle the most important part of the job – the after-dinner speaking? I knew at the time that this was ridiculous but, looking back, it seems utterly bizarre. I might not be the most polished performer out there, and I probably won't go on to host gameshows when I retire, but I thought I could manage 'Ladies and gentlemen, Mr President, thank you very much.' Anyway, who gave a stuff? It was what happened on the pitch that mattered, surely? Some writer asked the Leicester coach Bob Dwyer his view. His reply summed it all up: 'Who cares?'

The other concerns were over my lack of experience – I had not led England – and my supposed indiscipline. I had been involved in two incidents that season which had ended in tries being disallowed. Against Argentina, I had been lumbering towards a ruck and had obstructed one of the opposition as we got the ball away. Later, at the old Cardiff Arms Park – and I try not to think about this one too much, because it upsets me – a touch judge had wrongly penalised me for what he presumably thought was an attempted punch. I had to stand there watching this idiot flagging as poor old Tim Stimpson blasted 50m up the pitch to score a brilliant try in the corner, knowing it would not count. This same touch judge had flagged earlier in the game after Scott Quinnell had clipped me round the ear, only inexplicably to put his flag down after the ref blew up to end the phase. I had roundly abused the bloke. Rightly or wrongly, the penalties stood and enabled the press to raise those questions over my 'discipline'.

I was not involved in selection. It was bold and highly imaginative and produced a good blend of youth and experience. Alongside the Leicester youngsters were some other brave picks. John Bentley, who had played for England but had then gone to play rugby league and was now back at Newcastle, was one. Scott Gibbs, Allan Bateman, Alan Tait, Dai Young, Scott Quinnell – all guys who had recently come back from rugby league – were also included, as professionalism changed everything.

The Springbok press and public didn't give us a chance of winning the series. The South Africans, particularly as they emerged from the apartheid years, were an insular nation, wrapped up with their struggles against the All Blacks, the provincial game and the Currie Cup. They had very little concept of what northern-hemisphere rugby was like. I remember watching a rugby show, hosted by Naas Botha. It featured the Leicester versus Sale Pilkington Cup final. We had won the match 9–6, two tired teams slugging it out at the end of a forty-match season on a wet pitch in the wind and the rain. It was not a great spectacle and not a great advertisement for our game, but they obviously thought that was British rugby and that the Lions would try to play that way – kicking everything, driving, rolling mauls, no flair. We were not rated as a team and, to an extent, that was fair enough, because what did we have to show for ourselves? I don't think a British team had beaten a southern-hemisphere side since England's 1995 World Cup quarter-final victory over the Australians, and that seemed a long, long time ago.

Our own press and public were not much more confident. South Africa were world champions, after all, and we had all been weaned on a diet of southern-hemisphere supremacy. However, we had an excellent management and coaching set-up and a very good side. No tour party containing the likes of Jason Leonard, Jerry Guscott, Lawrence Dallaglio, Rob Howley, Neil Jenkins, Ieuan Evans, Rob Wainwright, Gregor Townsend and Keith Wood is going to be a pushover and the league returnees added a great deal. With union having just turned professional, the rest of us were really just amateurs with money. They knew a lot more about what it was really like to train hard and play for your living.

Against many people's expectations, the tour started really well, with good wins over Eastern Province, Border, Western Province and Mpumalanga (the former South East Transvaal) shutting up a few of the Afrikaners. Our scrummage was bearing up reasonably well, though we struggled a little in the Western Province game, with Paul Wallace emerging, surprisingly, as a strong tight-head. More importantly, our backs, long derided by the south, were punching big holes and scoring tries. In the fifth game of the tour, though, we went down 35–30 to Northern Transvaal at Loftus Versfeld. The game had featured a large number of our expected starting XV and the result would have lifted the morale of the Boks a fortnight away from the first Test. It could have had the opposite effect on us, but for Jim Telfer.

Ian McGeechan and Jim were a superb combination. Talk softly but carry a big stick, the saying goes. McGeechan was an exceptional coach, a guy with tremendous vision and tactical awareness, always trying new things and happy to give his players responsibility. Telfer, the forwards' coach, was his big stick. Forwards always need someone to make them work. A lot of forward play is just graft and there are days when, whoever you are, you do not feel like it. Guys will make excuses and slacken off in training if they can. Telfer, already legendary for beasting his Scotland players and the 1983 Lions, instinctively knew if you were not pulling your weight and came down on you like a ton of bricks. We were used to Jack Rowell, all acid-tongued, sarcastic asides. Jim did not bother wasting time with sarcasm; he just told you straight. The 1993 Lions had lacked a Telfer-like character, someone who would really have cracked the whip. Instead, we had Dick Best. Best is widely regarded as an abrasive, aggressive type but he is all 'front'. When Jim spoke there was no bulls**t. What Jim said, went. If he said 'get lower in the scrummage,' you got lower in the scrummage. 'Let's believe here, boys,' he would say. 'I'm saying "get lower" for a reason.' Some guys will make a pre-match speech and fail to find the right words, or hit the right note. Jim hit it every time.

After that Northern Transvaal defeat, Jim grabbed us by the scruff of the neck in what turned out, possibly, to be the tour's pivotal moment. He gave us all a big dressing down, followed by a beast of a session for the pack selected to play Gauteng, formerly Transvaal, in the next match. This was highly unusual, given the fact that the match was only forty-eight hours away. He had the eight form up and then hit the scrummage machine over and over again. It was a pneumatic device, designed to come back at you hard – and you had to hold it steady. Three or four of these on the trot produced an effect very similar to doing heavy squat lifts with weights. Your legs fill up with lactic acid and your muscles turn to jelly. Knowing the pain and trouble the guys were now in, Jim would bark out an instruction to break up, run 10m and start mauling. Mauling is itself very hard work, like wrestling, and it gets you gasping for air like nothing else. Then he would have everyone racing back to the scrum machine. It was exceptionally draining, hard work and by the end of the session, Paul Wallace was picking up one of his team-mates and dragging him around. It made grown men cry. It was the hardest session I have ever known, one which is still talked about among the players who were there, but it paid off, setting the tone for the rest of the tour. Don't sit around feeling sorry for yourselves, was Jim's message. Pick yourselves up and fight.

It was not work hard for the sake of hard work; it all had a purpose. Jim knew the tour was at make-or-break point: if we lost that Gauteng game it would have been very hard to lift ourselves and go on to compete in the Test matches. Two bad losses on the trot could have sent us into a tailspin. As it was, we won in a tough, Test match-style encounter, with

John Bentley scoring one of the great Lions tries, a long, curving run beating almost their entire team on his way to the line. After the match, the whole squad gathered together in the changing room, fired up by the result and its manner. The show was back on the road.

The weekend before the first international we beat Natal 42–12. It was billed as 'the unofficial fourth Test', but the home team rested a lot of their Springboks, guys like Mark Andrews, Henry Honiball, Gary Teichmann and André Joubert. It was after that win that the home press and public started to sit up and take notice of us. Midweek, the guys went to play South Africa A at Wellington near Cape Town. That was the first time we saw the mass of Lions fans who had flown in. It was like a home game for our boys and they overwhelmed the Boks, winning 51–22 and laying down a challenge to the senior side.

I got the feeling that the Springboks thought they were going to win that first Test. Maybe that was not surprising. They were world champions, were on their way to becoming one of the great all-time teams with seventeen consecutive wins around the corner, and they were at home. However, their complacency cost them dearly as we managed to beat them 25–16. Matt Dawson, in for the desperately unlucky Rob Howley who had been forced out with a shoulder injury, scored one of our tries with an outrageous dummy, and Alan Tait the other, with Neil Jenkins' five penalties keeping the Boks at bay. The decision to rest the Test players in the Natal game had probably tipped the game in our favour. It meant not only that we had had it easier against Natal, with the momentum and the extra psychological lift that a good victory gave us, but also that quite a few of their key players went into the first Test just a little 'undercooked'. No matter how hard you train, the pace and intensity of a game is a notch higher and they were just a bit lacking in match fitness. They came out after half-time with a big, all-out push, but when that did not work they had nothing left and for the last twenty minutes they were blowing hard.

I remember a great little moment in the changing rooms afterwards. Obviously, everyone was delighted with the win. We had played well in every area, including the scrum, where, after being rocked back badly at the first engagement, we had gained parity and even started to impose ourselves towards the end. I am sitting there trying to think sensibly: we mustn't let the success go to our heads, we need to stay calm and focused on the next Test, let's not celebrate until we win the next Test, and so on. Scotty Gibbs, standing somewhere behind me, seemed to be thinking along the same lines. 'No way are we going to lie down against these boys next week, Johnno,' he was saying. 'No way.' I turned round. There was Scotty, standing in his pants with a fag in one hand and a can of beer in the other. I had to grin. 'At least you're *saying* the right thing, Gibbsy!' I thought. He meant it, though.

On the bus back to the hotel later, he stood up and addressed the team: 'Right guys, we're all going training with the midweek boys tomorrow morning!' I thought that was a brilliant call and I wished I had thought of it. Fantastic for team spirit. Next morning, everyone was there, bright and early. We had all had a beer or two the previous night. Most of us had been sensible enough, but one or two had gone on and were a little the worse for wear. John Bentley took it upon himself to stand up at the team meeting before we trained. 'You've won f*** all, yet!' he started shouting. 'You've won f*** all! You shouldn't be out on the piss. You should be grafting! You've won f*** all yet!' Bentos, of course, was one of the worst offenders, having rolled back to the hotel at around 4a.m. after a serious boozing session. It was hard not to laugh.

Later that day we were due to fly to Durban to prepare for the second Test. We had packed earlier and sent our gear off to the airport ahead of the flight. All we had kept was our training gear and travel clothes. First thing Johnson does as the coach arrives back at the hotel from the training ground? He steps off the bus and straight into a large pile of dog mess. The muck was forced deep into the tread of the only pair of trainers I had with me. I obviously couldn't get on to the plane with that all over my feet, which is why a mate of mine was treated to the sight of me on my knees in my bathroom, scrubbing the trainers with the only brush I had with me – my toothbrush. Not what you expect to be doing the morning after you play in a historic Lions victory over the Springboks. The glamour of international rugby, eh? Obviously, I gave the toothbrush a good wash before I used it again.

That Free State midweek game was the best of the tour and, as Fran Cotton later suggested, perhaps the best performance ever by a Lions side. It was a breathtaking eighty minutes, John Bentley scoring a hat-trick and Stimpson, Jenkins, Bateman and Tony Underwood adding one apiece as we won 52–30. The Test players watched that game, gathered around a TV in our hotel in Durban, in awe. Once again, Gibbsy found the right words. 'Oh,' he said. 'I wish I could have played in that match.' We all did. Those boys had drawn the short straw: fly from Durban to Bloemfontein, play at altitude against a tough South African provincial side, fly back. Not a nice task, especially knowing that selection for that match meant you were probably not going to feature in the second Test a few days later. That performance showed those guys had skill aplenty to go with their character, spirit, self-respect and guts.

Durban is a great town on the Indian ocean, warm, with a relaxed feel to it. Despite the beautiful surroundings, though, our build-up was troubled. We lost Ieuan Evans in a training accident during the week and Will Greenwood was out of the tour after a horrific concussion in the Free State match. He had landed heavily on his head and needed to be resuscitated by James Robson, the tour doctor, in a frantic few minutes in the medical room.

We knew the Springboks would come back strongly in the second Test. They had been heavily criticised by their media and the public for losing to a team they had been expected to beat. We were right. They had three game plans and all of them were to come at us hard. It was rocky out there for the first few minutes. Early on there was a break for a penalty and Lawrence Dallaglio and I looked across at each other, both raising our eyebrows. We certainly knew we were in a match as the Boks threw everything they had at us.

Luckily, they seemed to get on the wrong side of Didier Mené, the referee. On several occasions, he warned them, only for them to repeat the offence a minute later. He got very exasperated with them and starting penalising them repeatedly, and every time that happened within kicking range, Jenks was there to pot it. That kept us in the game, despite the fact that they were scoring tries, through van der Westhuizen, Joubert and Montgomery. Jenks' inclusion, out of position at full-back, was another good selection move by Geech and Jim. He was not the best attacking No. 15 in the party – Nick Beal or Tim Stimpson would have filled that role better – but his accuracy with the boot was phenomenal. The Springboks, on the other hand, had chosen to line up without a recognised goal kicker and that cost them a lot of points as kick after kick sailed wide.

The defining moment came at 15–15. A ruck formed after a tackle and we pretty much gave it up for dead. If you watch the video, you'll see that we are all hanging back – all apart from Neil Back, who got in there and nicked the ball in the way he does. The ball found its way to Keith Wood, who shoed it up the touchline. It was recycled back to Jerry Guscott, unmarked in midfield. He looked up, swung his right boot and dropped it over to make it 18–15 to us. The next five minutes were among the most tense of my life as we defended against wave after wave of South African attacks. At one point they kicked through, only for Austin Healey to race back and clean up, allowing him to claim, to this day, that he saved the series for the Lions or even, on his larger days, that he won the series.

Our defence was excellent, strange as that sounds in a game where they scored three tries, and we managed to hold them out. That final whistle was a marvellous moment. Guys were hugging each other, screaming and laughing. The feeling of elation was remarkable. They had scored three tries to nil. Fifteen of our points came from Jenks' boot. Some said it was a moral victory for them, but that's rubbish. Every penalty they gave away stopped us from attacking – and who knows whether we would have crossed from any of those positions? Tries are nice, but all that matters is the numbers on the board. And they say we won.

The pressure was now off. We still had a Test left, but the series was won so everyone had a big night on the Saturday. Backy and a few of the other guys ended up taking their duvets and a few crates of beer down to the beach, only to wake up the next morning and find the beer, and the duvets, had been stolen in the night. On the Sunday, we all left Durban to head up-country on a Fran Cotton-inspired bit of luxury R&R. He had booked the whole party into a resort up near the Vaal river, where we could all chill out between the second and third Tests. Great, we thought, as we headed there, but it was absolutely dreadful. The high Vaal, bitterly cold in winter, is no kind of tourist destination and it was totally empty. The sunshine of the south coast, with its great bars and restaurants and thousands of Lions fans, was a distant memory. The midweekers played their final match, against Northern Free State, the 'Purple People Eaters'. It was the only game on the whole tour that no one really wanted to play. It all seemed a bit pointless, the pitch was like yellow concrete and these guys were huge – their scrum-half was 6ft 4in tall. They really wanted to leather the Lions with lots of cheap shots going in, but the Lions shrugged them off to win with a basketball scoreline of 67–39.

And so to the third and final Test. Mentally, it was very hard for us to pick ourselves up for that game. I went out to warm up and all the nerves and anxiety I had experienced before the previous two matches had vanished. I remember thinking to myself, 'Ellis Park, Johannesburg, Lions versus South Africa, third Test, and I'm not the most nervous man in the world. This is very strange indeed!' On the other hand, they were fuelled by adrenalin, playing for pride and really needing a victory. We played some good rugby and, having slipped behind, battled our way back to the point where, if we had been hungry and desperate for the result, we might have got into contention to win. But, as the cliché has it, they wanted it more than we did, winning 35–16.

Knackered, elated, not quite believing we had done it, we trooped off the field. As the boys went to the changing room for a beer or two together, I headed for the medical room. I had been suffering for some months with a long-standing groin injury. I could play with it – indeed, it was better on the hard grounds of South Africa – but it needed attention. I was due to have an operation within a day or two of arriving back home but, somewhat optimistically, I had informed my surgeon, Gerry Gilmour, that it had been feeling OK and that I did not think it would need surgery. He was out in South Africa visiting his son and arranged to examine me in the medical room at Ellis Park at the end of the match. Tired, sweaty and a bit emotional, I suffered the indignity of having Gilmour lift up my scrotum and prod the area behind it with his little finger, while I screamed like a small child, excruciating pain on prodding being the classic symptom of this condition. I guess it was something of a surprise to the three or four wide-eyed Lions fans, in the medical room having various cuts and bruises attended to, to see me having my testicles manhandled. It was all terribly amusing for Jerry Guscott, of course, who lay there howling with laughter at my embarrassment as he held the arm he had broken during the match. I was very tempted to break the other one for him.

It had been a hell of a tough tour, with a number of players suffering injuries, but also a phenomenally successful one. All the talk about the Lions being finished as a concept in the professional era vanished almost overnight. Instead, they were rightly acclaimed as being one of the world's greatest sporting traditions.

So what were the key factors in our win? Well, firstly, Fran, Geech and Jim were a great management team. A few of the players thought Fran, our front man, was 'grandstanding' and enjoying the limelight as he stood in front of the cameras on an almost daily basis. They were forgetting the weight he was taking off our shoulders. The pressure from the South African fans and media was huge. The Lions don't tour there very often and they were still talking animatedly about the famous 1974 trip, with Willie John McBride's infamous 'ninety-nine' call. Fran had the personality and character to take some of that attention away from the squad.

Geech and Jim simply knew rugby inside out. First off, they had got the selection of the squad spot-on, not shirking the chance to pick young guys, players out of favour in their home countries or league returnees. They had a game plan, too. They wanted forwards who could handle and run with the ball – guys like Neil Back and Tom Smith, who would be quicker and more attacking than the huge Springbok pack. They wanted us all to think on our feet. Geech's catchphrase for the tour was, 'Be in the right place at the right time.' And they covered all the bases. It was the first time I had ever been part of a team that actually worked on its defence, where the coaches had ideas on how to stop the opposition in broken field play, on how to line up across the field, or on how to deal with key Springbok players. For instance, Henry Honiball, the South African fly-half, was a potentially devastating runner, who was also able to put others in space with accurate passing both inside and outside. Geech had all of us, but particularly the midfield and the back row, very alert to Honiball's threat. As soon as he had the ball, someone would be there to take him. If he stepped, someone would be there for the step. Others would be watching the guys he could pass to. Everyone else would look to cover in case a tackle was missed. It's very basic by today's standards, but back then it was eye-opening and it worked.

They were never satisfied and there was no conservative, safety-first approach. After you win a game, most coaches stick with a winning team. Jim and Ian would want to change things, looking for improvements. I remember a meeting to discuss selection for the Free State game. By then, we had won every match bar one, including the first Test, and were playing some of the best rugby ever seen by a northern-hemisphere side. I was surprised at how critical Geech and Jim were of the boys. As they ran through the list of errors and mistakes from the Test, Geech, almost to himself, asked, 'How did we ever win it?' They were right to be critical, though, and the way they even agonised over the line-up for the final match showed their impressive determination and drive. A lot of coaches would have settled for 2–1.

To be fair, they also had the advantages brought by the new professional era. They could afford to take a thirty-five-man party, following the trend that had been set recently by the All Blacks. It was an important departure from the old way, which involved taking a thirty-strong party: two teams, one playing at the weekend and one midweek, with each covering the other's bench. They moved away from the traditional system of playing one day and travelling the next. Often, the non-playing guys did not travel with the match-day squad, allowing them more time to train or for recovery. We also stayed in the best hotels in South Africa and had the best training facilities. When we did travel, our bags were collected from our hotel reception by support staff and we would find them waiting for us at the next hotel. When you got off the plane at the destination, the tour bus was there on the tarmac, waiting to whisk us away. There was no lugging cases around or standing waiting by the carousel and little things like that – things we now take for granted – were revolutionary at the time and they made all the difference. It gave the guys less to worry about and also projected professionalism, setting a tone for everything we did.

Most of all, though, I guess we won because of the players. The selectors had given us a squad packed full of character. It's wrong to single out individuals, but allow me to cite the example of Jason Leonard and Graham Rowntree. They had boarded the plane as the first-choice props but ended up playing midweek instead. However, they never, ever, let their heads go down.

The league guys were another factor. Those guys were tough and physical, even in the backs. Forwards love to see their backs getting stuck in and taking it to the opposition, bouncing bodies off them and smashing through tackles. With England at that time, we had some very good wings and centres – Will Carling, who I have always felt was under-rated, Jerry Guscott, the Underwoods – but they were not used for penetration. It always seemed to be down to the pack to bash the ball up and hand those guys the tries on a plate. That Lions side was different. Guys like Scott Gibbs, John Bentley, Alan Tait and Allan Bateman were aggressive, mean players and they got us going forward, destroying the myth that southern-hemisphere backs were bigger, stronger and more damaging than ours. Gibbsy's famous, rhino-like charge through the twenty-stone prop Ollie le Roux in the Natal game was almost a pivotal moment in the whole tour. People were goggle-eyed when they saw it: a centre has just run over one of the biggest Springbok forwards of all time, leaving him face down, dazed and confused, in the turf. Bloody hell, game on!

The day we played Border, Alan Tait was sitting on the bench. He had not featured at that point and I remember thinking he probably would not get much of a go on the tour. Then they brought him on as a replacement and he immediately started rampaging around, bouncing people off him. I pretty quickly revised my opinion, thinking 'I like that! That's good!' He's not a big guy, Taity, but he's a hard man with a physicality and an attitude of mind that few are blessed with. John Bentley was another aggressive winger. With England, the forwards did most of the talking, on and off the pitch. The backs were generally quiet and reserved. Not Bentley. He had chat to burn. On the phone home to his wife, he was crowing: 'Eh luv, you won't believe, I mean *you will not believe*, how famous I am over 'ere!' On the pitch, he was just as full of himself. First chance he got, he'd be pointing at his opposite number shouting, 'I'm going to f***ing terrorise you, you've had it today, mate!' in this broad Yorkshire accent. Famously, he got right under the skin of the Springbok winger James Small – himself a little firebrand – and he was the same with us in training, always trying to cream people in tackling practice. It was the behaviour of nutcase forwards, not backs, but I loved it all. These were the kind of guys we needed on tour.

We built a tremendous camaraderie. No one expected us to win, but far from caving in, our midweek team never lost a game and they destroyed a few South African reputations along the way. Afterwards, they claimed they were the best Lions team out there and they had a point. We may have won the two Tests but they were narrow victories. Their games were high-scoring, featured some astonishing rugby and made a major, and probably vital, contribution to the series win.

That tour was a happy coincidence of factors. It came at a moment in time that will never be repeated. It was just after professionalism, when being paid to be on a Lions tour to South Africa was, in itself, a wonderful thing. Guys who thought they would never play rugby union again had been welcomed back into the fold from league. For the first time, thousands of fans from back home had come out to support us. We were flying business class and staying at the best hotels. We were in a wonderful, rugby-mad country, playing tough games against hard teams – and beating them. Everyone believed in the coaching team and we had some great characters, full of life, full of fight and pride, team players who would not let their heads go down. We had beaten the World Champions. Now all we had to do was do it again in 2001.

CHAPTER TWELVE

LIONS DOWN UNDER

Before we left for South Africa in 1997, many people had questioned the relevance of the tour in the professional era. Most people thought we would lose and the prevailing wisdom seemed to be that there was no place in modern rugby for this outdated concept. The final whistle in Durban, sounded in front of thousands of jubilant travelling fans, answered that fairly emphatically. The sporting and commercial success of the tour confirmed that the eternal magic of the Lions was stronger than ever. Ahead, four years away, was Australia and many people's thoughts turned there almost immediately.

I never took for granted that I would be going on my third tour, particularly since I had spent much of 2000 perhaps not exactly in the international wilderness, but in somewhere that felt not too far from it. I had missed most of that year's Six Nations with an Achilles tendon injury and failed even to make the bench for the last game or two after recovering. However, I reclaimed my place in the side for the summer tour of South Africa and went on to lead England as we won in the autumn internationals and in the 2001 Six Nations. By the time the squad was announced, I was hopeful of selection.

As it was, I was named as captain. The phone rang at home

as I sat at a table in my conservatory filling in my census form. It was Donal Lenihan, the tour manager. 'Hello Martin,' he said. 'I'd like to offer you the captaincy of the Lions.' 'Thank you very much, Donal,' I replied. 'I'd love to accept.' And that was pretty much it. I went back to my census form. Kay didn't even look up. Eventually she murmured, 'Who was that?'

If that all sounds a bit blasé, the fact is I had mixed feelings. I had known that, if selected for the touring party, I was one of the favourites for the post and I had seriously considered declining if the offer came my way. This might seem hard for people to understand. Guys say things to me like, 'I'd give my right arm to lead the Lions.' I can understand what they're saying. I was obviously aware that it was a massive honour to be asked to captain the Lions again. On the other hand, though, having led the Lions before, and now skippering England, I had a very good idea of what lay in wait. Behind the glamour of a Lions tour lies lots of hard work and pressure. It's a major sacrifice, at least of your time and your body, and the captaincy obviously demands even more of you.

People also make a lot of the fact that I was the first man to captain the Lions twice. That never entered my head. If I had allowed myself to think about the enormity of leading the Lions it would have blown my mind; I'm no Willie-John, no rugby legend. I'm just an ordinary bloke from Market Harborough. Of course, when you meet Willie-John you realise he is just an ordinary bloke, too. Maybe in years to come I'll start to appreciate what I have achieved in my career, but while you're still playing, you don't have time. A guy called Mike

Singletary, who played in an awesome Chicago Bears team, was asked how he remembered his Superbowl win. He said he probably hadn't enjoyed it as much as he should have, because as soon as one win was out of the way, or one season ended, they were looking forward to the next. I can see what he meant, because you probably don't get the chance to sit down and take it all in until your career is over.

The other thing people always ask when they talk to me about the Lions captaincy is how I celebrated. The simple answer is I didn't, either in 1997 or 2001. My main concern, having accepted the job, was to do the job well. Until you can say you have done that, there is nothing to celebrate: there is no honour in doing the job badly.

Before we flew, we all spent a week together in bonding sessions and training at Tylney Hall, a magnificent hotel outside London. It is never going to be easy to bring together thirty-seven men from four different countries and mould them into a team, but you have to try. We spent hours in team-building exercises – playing tambourines and beating drums together, all making fools of ourselves and joining in to break down barriers. Some of what we did was quite deep – talking about our private hopes and fears in front of guys we hardly knew. Martyn Williams, the Welsh flanker, told us about the death of his brother and Matt Dawson talked about the break-up of a relationship. It was quite moving and I think it helped us grow closer.

We trained hard, too, at the Army's physical education centre in nearby Aldershot. It was very draining, especially after our long, tough season, and there were voices raised in protest, but it was important, because as well as building team spirit, we needed to create understanding on the pitch. Defence, for instance, was a key area. England, through the former rugby league coach Phil Larder, had built up a formidable defence over the past two or three seasons and Phil had been recruited to instil the same patterns and organisation in the Lions. It isn't rocket science, but it does take time and concentration.

And then, almost before we knew it, we were arriving in Australia. Within a few hours of landing, we were back into the hard training and, once again, there were complaints from some of the players. I didn't agree with them, though I was concerned about the type of work we were doing. Graham Henry, the coach, wanted us to play in a very structured way, with detailed plans for multiple phases of play. With most professional teams, the first three phases are almost programmed. Everyone knows what they should do off first phase, from the scrum, the line-out or the kick-off. You try to influence the subsequent play in a certain way, with each of you taking up pre-determined positions. After that, the play will become more instinctive with, generally, your fly-half and scrum-half directing matters as you look to attack. However, it is important that the direction of those attacks is spot on. Defences are now so organised that if guys get isolated you will lose the ball. Graham was hoping to guard against this by trying to orchestrate the fifth, sixth, seventh phases of our attacks. Individual players were instructed which rucks they would go into and which rucks they would not. A lot of us, myself included, were not used to our play being so pre-ordained and we were finding it difficult, both to carry so complex a game plan in our heads and also to execute it.

Ultimately, this approach did not work, as proved by the fact that we produced our best rugby after we decided, as players, to play it as we saw it.

It was in one of those early training sessions that we lost the first member of the party, Phil Greening damaging his knee in tackling practice. It put him out of the tour and set the tone for what was to come as we suffered a serious attrition rate.

Ahead of our first game, against Western Australia, Graham gave a little pep talk. He ended it by saying, 'These people down here in the southern hemisphere doubt your skills. I know. I'm one of them.' One or two of the guys were slightly irritated by it, but what he meant was not that he shared this view, but simply that he was aware of the prevailing feeling in those parts. Looking back, this was just one of several incidents where Graham was either misinterpreted by the guys or where he himself misread the situation and what he needed to say and do. Sometimes it was minor stuff – like many Kiwis, his humour was extremely dry, to the point where it was lost on many of the players. I am married to a New Zealander – he reminded me of my father-in-law – so I understand them, but few of the boys really 'got' his jokes. Other times it was a bit deeper. I think Graham was very aware that he was the first foreigner to lead the Lions. As a result, he made a big deal about how he knew the history of the Lions, how he had watched them play in the sixties and seventies and was aware of their traditions and culture. I don't think he needed to go into all this. Not everyone is an anorak like me and most of the lads didn't know or even much care about the distant history of the Lions anyway. All he needed to do was show us that he passionately wanted us to win.

I would always prefer a British coach but, to an extent, his nationality was irrelevant. John Mitchell had coached England against New Zealand. If it came to a war between the two countries, he would obviously have fought for New Zealand, but this was rugby and there was no doubt where his loyalties lay – his eyes and veins were popping out as he exhorted us to win. John understood that it was, ultimately, about a team of guys pulling together, and this was the same. It was not about the British Isles. After all, we have been fighting each other since the dawn of time; the Scots and Welsh will always dislike the English; the Ulstermen may not see eye to eye with the southern Irish; and so on. It is not even about playing for your family and friends. It is about playing for the other guys in the team and the squad, and reducing it to this level, instead of focusing on the bigger, more dramatic picture, would probably have been a better bet.

The match was significant in that, in a short lead-up period, it offered guys a chance to play themselves into the reckoning and we ran out winners 116–10. However, the result was cast into shadow by our second and third injuries. Before the game Mike Catt had tweaked his calf. Mike had been struggling to make the tour with a back spasm and I wondered whether the leg injury had come as a result of him favouring his back. Simon Taylor, the impressive young Scots No. 8, was also finished, having damaged his knee after coming on as a replacement during the second half.

Next up, the Queensland President's XV offered stronger opposition, featuring around ten players with Super-12 experience. In the first half, they really made our midweek team work and passes went astray, tackles were half-missed and balls were repeatedly dropped. Although we scored two tries to lead 10–6 at the break, we had blown a number of other opportunities and come close to conceding a score ourselves on several occasions. It was frustrating watching in the stands. The Aussies have a talent for barracking and one guy in particular was sledging Jason Robinson, as he had a quietish first half. This fellow kept yelling at him, 'Go back to rugby league! Go back to rugby league!' In the second half, the team relaxed, cut out the silly errors and stepped things up a gear. And we absolutely smashed them, racking up a further 73 points in the process. The stand-out man was the little bloke from Hunslet in Leeds and, in a pretty staggering performance, Jason became the first Lion ever to score five tries on his debut. After the fifth, all you could hear was a chorus of British Lions players shouting, 'Go back to rugby league ...'

Next stop was Brisbane and the Queensland Reds, my 2001 Lions debut. The flight south was frustrating. Instead of chartering our own planes, we were usually on scheduled flights and we often ended up in economy class. Many of us were 6ft 6in or taller, and 18+ stone, and cramming our legs into the smaller space you get at the back of the plane not long after two or three hours of strenuous training makes you stiff. We couldn't stretch out and relax, as we should have, and Scott Quinnell, who had suffered a knock to one of his knees, was in particular pain. I do not need star treatment. When I fly as a private individual, I go economy, but when you are on tour with the British and Irish Lions, playing and training like we were, you need to keep yourself in the best possible shape. If that means chartering plans with plenty of business-class seats, we should have chartered. A lot of the English guys were starting to resent this sort of thing. In 1997, the tour had been so much bigger and better than anything we had been involved in before and we all felt great about being there. By 2001, the England team were used to Clive Woodward and his insistence on absolutely everything being spot on. We had moved to a level of expectation which proved to be beyond what the Lions management gave us.

With the serious action not far away, the Aussie media were starting to get stuck into us. I was surprised at how one-eyed and one-sided they were – they were certainly far more nationalistic than our own press corps. Their attack was two-pronged: they were starting to rake over the ashes of the 1989 Lions tour Down Under, which had been marked by some pretty rough play by the Brits, and they were also accusing us of being dull to watch. A headline in *The Australian* read, 'McBain labels Lions boring' and quoted the Queensland coach, Mark McBain, attacking our style of play. In particular, he seemed to think we played too forward-oriented a game. 'The rolling maul . . . it's just not a spectacle, is it?' he had apparently said.

I found that a bit odd, given that we had scored thirty-one tries in two outings at that point, twenty of them by our backs and a number of the forwards' scores coming not from mauls but from loose play. I hoped, too, that we would be able to make him eat his words in the upcoming match and we did just that, running out 42–8 winners. Jonny Wilkinson, also playing his first game of the tour, had slotted in fantastically well for a fly-half who had not played in weeks, missing his first kick at goal but potting the next seven. Rob Howley and Brian O'Driscoll had shown their flair and skill and Rob Henderson and Martin Corry, the latter recently arrived from North America as a replacement for Taylor, were both outstanding.

Afterwards, one or two influential figures in the Australian game ratcheted up the media pressure, building up their allegations that we were boring and violent. First the violence: Eddie Jones, ACT Brumbies and Australia A coach, and heir apparent to Rod Macqueen with the senior Wallaby side, accused us of illegal play. He moaned, 'There were a number of off-the-ball incidents against Queensland that were disappointing. I hope the officials at Gosford [the venue for the Australia A match that would follow on the Tuesday] keep a strict eye on this and take the appropriate action.' I thought this was a bit unnecessary. It had been hard and niggly, but that's what it's all about. There were incidents on both sides, although Queensland had been by far the more culpable. They seemed to have targeted Rob Howley, in particular, and he had to leave the field after being knee-dropped. As Rob later put it, 'They started it and we stood up to it . . . toe to toe.' It was only when they found they could not beat us up that they started trying to beat us.

Now for the 'boring' claim. Here the moaning was led by Mark McBain, the Reds coach, who said, 'They looked to throw it wide, to use their speed, and if that doesn't work I wonder if they have a Plan B.' This was a laughable statement. It was McBain, after all, who had earlier complained that our only attacking weapon was the driving maul. After a good win it was nice to enjoy the feeling and I wasn't going to let a war of words spoil that.

Three games, three wins. Things looked good and I felt our midweek team would continue the trend against Australia A. Pre-match, Graham Henry was clear about the challenge ahead. 'This will be the toughest game we play outside the Test matches,' he said. 'We've got to play out of our skins. At Tylney Hall we talked about the courage and the heart of the Lions and words like commitment and hunger and ruthlessness. We need to put some meaning into those words tonight.'

It was the right sentiment, but it somehow failed to hit home with the boys. Backed by a sizeable and vociferous contingent of home fans in the 20,000 crowd, the Wallaby second string came at the Lions aggressively from the start, looking slick, organised and committed. Our boys struggled to make inroads in their tight defence, while themselves making a lot of errors – dropped balls, wild passes and even guys running into one another. It was a poor and seemingly unmotivated display and the home crowd piled in as the game wore on. Before half-time, we lost Catt, who pulled up as he chased a kick-through and hobbled off clutching his damaged calf. That was the end of his tour. We finished the first forty minutes 15–6 down, which was better than it could have been and not impossible to come back from.

Inside, a furious Henry laid it on the line to his team, focusing on the need for them to show some pride. 'We're flat as bloody pancakes,' he said. 'You guys have got a responsibility here which goes back a hundred years.' The non-playing members of the squad lined up outside the changing rooms and clapped the lads back on to the pitch for the second forty, hoping to get their heads up. At first, it seemed to have worked, the team playing with more fire and determination and looking likely to get straight back into the game. Unfortunately, the killer score came at the other end, with the centre Scott Staniforth running on to Graeme Bond's pass. Manny Edmonds was out-kicking a struggling Neil Jenkins and we were always going to find it hard to come back from that point. Things looked a little better after Jenks was taken off for Matt Dawson, who took over from Austin Healey at scrum-half, allowing Austin to go to 10. We scored three times in the final quarter of the game through Taylor, Perry and Robinson, and Matt, kicking in place of Neil, missed a penalty almost on full-time, which would have given us an undeserved draw. We had outscored Australia A by three tries to one, but had been well-beaten and were flattered by the 28–25 scoreline.

We took some heart from our fitness, the way we had come back towards the end and the decent individual performances of guys like Robinson, Healey, Cohen and Dawson. Will Greenwood had been outstanding. His defence was great and he had taken the ball up very hard and created openings. He is not normally a workhorse, Will, but his attitude was great and he was taking the extra load all in his stride. It had been his third start in the four games so far and he was also due to play on the Saturday, against Bob Dwyer's New South Wales Waratahs.

That, though, was the only gloss we could put on things. We had been outplayed by an Aussie second-string side who had been hungrier, better organised and more skilful than our side.

Graham Henry did not mince words with the press. 'Our line-out was unacceptable and we lacked basic sharpness,' he said. 'This is a reality check for us to show us where our base-line has to be set. This will tell us what the tour is all about. If we can learn resolve from it, then maybe it will benefit us in the long term.' Asked how the squad had taken the reverse, he replied, 'The dressing shed was a morgue. This could be a defining moment. Better to strike reality now than in the first Test.'

That was fair enough, but his next comments were a little surprising: 'We might have to concentrate more on the Tests than on the other guys.' This caused uproar in the press and did not help morale in the camp, which was in danger of fracturing. A few players clearly felt that they had already been written out of the Test plans – though no one had been at that stage – and their heads were starting to drop. A division had started to develop. It was not quite a them-and-us situation yet, but some players definitely felt other guys were being favoured over them. Here, apparently, was evidence right from the horse's mouth. I had some sympathy with Graham's view. We needed to focus on winning those Test matches. I just wish he had not said it in public, rubbing the midweek guys' noses in it. We needed to be a thirty-seven-man squad, not two diverging camps.

Training ahead of the Waratahs brought more injury headaches when Dan Luger was knocked out of the tour with a fractured cheekbone after a clash of heads with Neil Back. This was seriously bad news as Dan was our Test left wing and an experienced guy we knew we could rely on to damage the Wallabies.

Match day dawned with more jibes at us, this time from Wallaby coach, Rod Macqueen, and the Waratahs' Bob Dwyer.

They accused us of illegality in the scrum, line-out and at the breakdown. I wonder how they felt after four seconds, when Tom Bowman was binned for elbowing Danny Grewcock in the face at kick-off? It went on to become an infamous game, best remembered for Duncan McRae's amazing assault on Ronan O'Gara. McRae pinned O'Gara to the turf and smashed him several times in the face without reply, leaving the young Irishman with blood streaming down his face from a deep gash under his left eye. It was a disgraceful incident that had looked virtually unprovoked, though McRae later claimed O'Gara had struck first. Referee Scott Young had no alternative but to send off the Australian. A few minutes later, a brawl broke out between the packs, leading to four players – Lions Phil Vickery and Danny Grewcock and Waratahs' front-rowers, Brendan Cannon and Cameron Blades – being sin-binned. Ten minutes of completely unstructured rugby ensued, with Young unsure as to whether he could allow opposed scrummaging. Eventually, it was allowed with a farcical merry-go-round of substitutions, but we took control eventually and eased ahead to finish 41–24 winners.

I was pretty down afterwards – angry about the O'Gara incident and irritated that we had let the Waratahs get that close to us on the scoresheet. Mostly, though, it was our injury jinx that worried me. Will Greenwood had gone off with what turned out to be a serious ankle injury, Neil Back had injured a rib and would miss the first Test and Lawrence Dallaglio, needing a big game to confirm his fitness, was out of contention after taking a knock on his knee. The Wales hooker Robin McBryde was also going home after suffering a nasty blow to his thigh.

The split in the camp between the perceived midweekers and the Test team widened on the Monday, ahead of the next fixture, against the exotically named bunch of part-timers, the New South Wales Country Cockatoos. Normally, we trained in split sessions, one for the Saturday side and the other a team run to prepare the Tuesday boys for their game the next day. Now that went by the wayside. First we all watched videos of Australia in action. Then the midweekers were told they would have to play as the Wallabies to try out the Test twenty-two's defence. These were guys already upset by Henry's remarks about concentrating on the Test team in the wake of the defeat against Australia A. This latest snub really upset them, and understandably so. They needed to prepare mentally and tactically for their own game and they were not going to be able to do it. Some felt this meant they didn't count and were just there as cannon fodder. It all widened the sense of a divide. Again, I could see where the management were coming from. The Cockatoos were a side we should deal with almost in our sleep and the Test matches were what the tour was about, but, again, it was not handled with the necessary sensitivity.

The day went from bad to worse when Anton Toia, our ARU-supplied liaison officer, had a heart attack and died in the sea after a fishing trip with some of the boys. He was a lovely guy, Anton, and his death put our problems into perspective while reinforcing the feeling that, somehow, the tour was ill-fated.

We went on to beat the Cockatoos 46–3 in a flat match the next day. The atmosphere in the changing room afterwards was shocking. Scott Gibbs, a Lions talisman and one of the South Africa tour's most enthusiastic members, had played in the match after joining us as a replacement. Tyrone Howe and Gordon Bulloch had made their first Lions starts, David Wallace had come on from the bench to make his first appearance in a Lions shirt and Nobby West had been on the bench, also a Lion for the first time. The place ought to have been jumping with excitement and adrenalin, but with Anton's death and the plummeting morale of the midweek guys, it was subdued, miserable even. It was the second week on the trot, after Australia A, that these guys had failed to get any buzz out of their game.

For the rest of us, the first Test loomed. The night before the match, the team meeting was alive with nerves and pressure. I have never known so anxious a bunch of guys. I think it was due to a combination of factors. Australia were World Champions and formidable opponents. Thousands of people had spent a lot of money travelling halfway around the world to watch us. The media presence and interest was huge. And the situation in the camp was affecting everyone. The whole thing felt enormous.

We channelled those feelings into a good warm-up in our team area, deep in the bowels of the Gabba stands. Guys ran around, hitting tackle pads and shouting, with the noise bouncing off the walls, and it gave us all a lift and a feeling of togetherness. Graham and Robbo had a few last-minute words and I gave the lads a final pep talk.

The game could hardly have started better. We won a line-out on the halfway line in the third minute. Danny Grewcock caught it and gave quick ball off the top to Rob Howley. Rob passed to Jonny, who missed out Hendo to find

O'Driscoll. He was brought down by Nathan Grey 35m out, but managed to throw the ball back out of the tackle. Howley scooped the ball up brilliantly off his feet, and formed the ruck as he was tackled by George Smith. Scott Quinnell picked up and popped it short to Wilko, who handed it on to Matt Perry. Pezza, with soft and very quick hands in the face of an onrushing defender, passed the ball to Jason Robinson, steaming up outside him. Jase was still a few yards outside their 22 and the full-back, Chris Latham, thinking he had him covered, showed him the outside. Big mistake: Robinson's awesome step and explosive pace took him straight past a diving Latham to the line.

The whole move had taken just eighteen seconds and with two minutes and forty-four seconds on the clock we were five points up. The Lions supporters in the crowd were going wild as Robinson ran round behind the posts, punching the air and screaming, before disappearing under a heap of red shirts. It was a dream start, just what we had wanted, and gave us the belief that we could penetrate what was then the world's best defence. The match carried on at the same furious pace, the ball pinging from one end to the other in seconds. Our second try came off a scrum in the thirty-fourth minute. We went right and Rob Howley fed Brian O'Driscoll, who stepped through the Wallaby blindside defence. Robinson had come across to make the extra man and he passed on to Daf James, who scored in the corner, Latham again missing his man and Jonny converting. It was especially pleasing because this was a set move. We had felt we could exploit Owen Finegan's lack of pace and it had worked beautifully. Half-time rushed up on us and the score was still close: 12–3.

In the changing room, the nerves had gone and we felt good, but the Wallabies do not panic and we knew we had to keep the heat on – something we did straight after the re-start. Danny took the restart kick and we drove it up 10m. It was spun down the back line to O'Driscoll, who lost it. Richard Hill dived on the loose ball and flicked it to Iain Balshaw, on for the injured Matt Perry. He made five metres and set up a second maul before the ball was smuggled back to O'Driscoll, still inside our own half. He set off on an amazing run, stepping Nathan Grey and shrugging off a tackle by Jeremy Paul. Still 30m out, Brian had Matt Burke – on for the substituted Latham – ahead of him. He feinted right, but went round the diving full-back to the left, sprinting on to touch down between the posts as Joe Roff dived on him. Forty seconds of the half gone. It was one of the best tries ever scored in a Lions shirt, in any shirt. Jonny knocked over the conversion to the unfamiliar strains of 'Bread Of Heaven' and the score was 19–3.

Still, we couldn't relax. In the fiftieth minute, we kicked for touch after winning a penalty. Martin Corry took the line-out ball and Rob Henderson beat tackles from Larkham, Burke and Roff before finally being dropped 5m out by John Eales. The ruck formed, Howley gave it short to Balshaw, but he was held up. A second ruck, and Scotty Quinnell picked up and drove, taking Burke and Toutai Kefu over with him. Four tries to nil, Jonny converts to make it 29–3. Scarcely more than half the game gone, and we are in dreamland.

They came back to score two consolation tries, but we held on to win 29–13. I actually felt the pressure lift off me as the final whistle sounded. With all that had been going on behind the scenes, it had been perhaps the worst and hardest week I have ever had in rugby, and to get that victory was priceless. I hoped, above all, that it would bring us back together. Sitting there in the changing room, basking in the warmth of a win, everyone together, relaxing and joking, is the best time you get as a player. I said to the guys, 'This is what it's all about, winning these games . . . everyone's a part of this.' I was trying to get the whole squad feeling good about it. Whether things had gone too far I don't know. I think everyone was in good spirits – obviously the guys who played the match were euphoric – but it's difficult to judge how people really feel.

After a few minutes basking in the win, I had to leave to go to the press conference. The press only wanted to talk about one thing: a newspaper column, written by Matt Dawson, criticising the way the tour was going, had appeared back home on the morning of the Test. He had accused the management of treating the players like children and of forcing 'mindless' training upon us. We were 'spending too much time on set-pieces and not enough on reacting to what's in front of us . . . everyone is too bogged down by calls'. He also claimed some of the younger players had decided to 'leave the tour'. The journalists all wanted to know whether he would be sent home.

Matt was obviously down, not least because he was losing out to Rob Howley in the battle for the No. 9 shirt. Mainly, though, the column was his way of showing he was unhappy with the way the tour was going. To an extent, the response was overblown and down to problems in interpretation. Take the word 'mindless'. People thought that meant the coaches did not know what they were doing. In fact, it is just a word we use to describe very strenuous work. Guys will say, 'Bloody hell, that session was mindless.' It was still a criticism – he felt we were working too hard – but it was not as aggressive a remark as some people felt. And I agreed with some of his points. Graham Henry's desire to play a structured game meant we *were* spending too much time worrying where we were supposed to be at a given moment and not enough on reacting to the game as it developed.

However, despite all that, it was still a crazy thing to write and I was amazed that a player of Matt's experience allowed it to be published, under his name, when he did. It is one thing to make criticisms – however valid they may be – in a book or interview after the tour has ended. It is another thing altogether to publish them just before you are about to play the first Test of a British and Irish Lions series against the World Champions.

I told the journos I didn't want him sent home, though. Ultimately, I said, I didn't care what he had written. Words were irrelevant. His attitude, within the squad at training every day, was what mattered, because that demonstrated his commitment and his desire for the tour to be a success. He was a valuable and talented member of the party and I wanted him staying right where he was. Later that night, I chatted privately with Daws. He was upset and embarrassed about what had happened and obviously concerned as to what the consequences might be. At worst, of course, there was that possibility of an early flight back to the UK. I said, 'Mate, if they send you home we are all going home.' I meant that. As a friend and team-mate, my loyalty to him was unquestionable.

If he had been playing or training badly I would have been the first to let him go if he had wanted to. Graham and Donal, both of whom had copped personal criticism in the piece, were angry, but they decided to let him remain on tour, big enough to let bygones be bygones. Instead, he was forced to sit in front of everyone like a naughty schoolboy and say sorry, desperately trying to avoid catching anyone's eye as we pulled faces at him and giggled. I felt the punishment was probably a little too lenient: I would have preferred a public thrashing, with his little naked buttocks being whacked through the streets of Brisbane.

Midweek, we faced the Super-12 champions, ACT Brumbies. Admittedly, they were without some key players – Joe Roff, Andrew Walker, Stephen Larkham, Owen Finegan, George Smith, George Gregan and David Giffin – but they had been to New Zealand for a couple of warm-up games and, with guys like Jim Williams, Graeme Bond and the newly returned Pat Howard in their side, they still had a strong line-up. Dai Young, the skipper, made the point to the boys beforehand that the ACT players still had a chance to wear a Wallaby shirt in that series and they would give us a real game.

Despite his speed, they started poorly, conceding three tries and trailing 19–3 in almost no time. They defended poorly, their line-out failed to function and whenever they did get into a position to put pressure on the Brumbies they made silly mistakes and turned over ball. The Lions' only first-half try was Austin Healey's interception of a Pat Howard pass. He anticipated where Paddy was going to throw it – maybe it helped having played alongside him so much – and jogged home under the posts.

At half-time Graham tore into the players. 'What's this shirt mean? What you talked about before the game, is that all bulls**t? Where's the f***ing honesty? It's 22–10 out there. We can do these b*******s if everybody gets right up there and on their toes and does the business. And you can look at yourself in the mirror after the game and say I gave one hundred per cent . . . I'll tell you what, a lot of you couldn't do that right now. It's a huge honour to wear that shirt, but a hell of a big responsibility, and we're not taking on the responsibility.'

It did the trick. Things were turned round in the second half. David Wallace scored early on and penalties were exchanged, Matt Dawson missing some but potting others to get us closer to their total. We started knocking them back, but despite our pressure they were holding us out, with a five-point lead. Eighty minutes came and went, and injury time stretched on. Then the hooter went, signalling the end: if the ball went dead the game was lost. The boys were desperately fighting their way closer to the ACT line while fighting to retain possession. I could not sit down. The match had gone from a non-starter to one of the tour's most thrilling and I just had that feeling that we were going to do something, that we were going to score.

Eventually, in the eighty-ninth minute, Darren Morris took the ball forward, attracted a couple of defenders and managed to flick a pass out the back. The ball went wide to Austin – he had played a great game, full of heart – and he stepped inside two players to score. In an ironic climax, Matt Dawson, villain of the recent past, became our hero by converting the try. He had not been kicking well and the bench had earlier sent on an instruction to switch to Ronan O'Gara. But Ronan apparently said to Matt, 'No Daws, you keep going at it and keep your head up', which was a top thing to do. I remember thinking, 'He's going to redeem himself here,' and, sure enough, it sailed straight through the posts. It was a great sight and it was great, too, to see Matt being hugged and back-slapped by the other players as they came off. It really had been an unbelievable comeback after the way they looked in the first half and it gave those players – some of whom might never wear a Lions shirt again – a great buzz. In the changing room, Matt was very emotional, close to tears and very choked up. Henry came in, beaming. 'Absolutely superb performance, guys,' he said. 'Magnificent guts and character. You can look at yourselves in the mirror and feel bloody proud.'

It set us up well for the second Test, in Melbourne. Graham Henry was very pumped up before the match, telling us, 'They are apprehensive. They are concerned. They are brittle. They are starting to fall apart. We have got to continue that process.' Donal Lenihan laid out the opportunity for us, 'The Lions are 125 years old and in all that time, only once have they achieved back-to-back Test series wins, in 1971 and 1974.' It was in our hands to be the second Lions side to do so.

We started the match pretty much as we had left off, breaking apart the much-vaunted Wallaby defence almost at will. We could have scored very early had Daf James spotted Jason Robinson outside him as he was tackled close to their line. As it was he didn't, knocking on as he was brought down. That set the tone for our performance. We went ahead through a Neil Back try from a catch-and-drive, but as the halfway stage approached we led narrowly, 11–3. Then, on thirty-seven minutes, Nathan Grey put in a disgraceful tackle on Richard Hill, hitting him with a flying elbow as he went by. It should have been a yellow-card offence at the very least. Corry replaced Hill while he went off for treatment, but when he tried to come back on he was clearly concussed. Concussion is distinctly odd. You only appreciate what has happened when you come round from it and you realise you have lost the last twenty minutes. You get a sort of déjà vu feeling, with all your short-term memory gone, as had happened to me in my first game for England. In the old days guys could go on with concussion, and often did, because there was far less to remember in terms of moves, calls and so on. Now, that is not an option and in fact Hilly's tour was over.

Amazingly, Grey was not sin-binned for his actions. Even more incredibly, the match referee later refused to hold a hearing into the incident. I thought that was disgusting and, frankly, amazing, especially after all the garbage we had taken before and throughout the tour about our supposed dirty play and intimidatory tactics. Right at the end of the half, Matt Burke kicked a penalty to bring them up to 11–6 and we went off, wondering why we were not much further ahead. We had clearly been the more threatening side and had enjoyed most of the possession. I felt that if we played the same way in the second half the match, and the series, were ours.

And we were great – for the first thirty seconds. We won the kick-off and drove the ball back at them, making a lot of yards. Then Jonny Wilkinson took the ball up the blind side and tried to throw a pass over the top of their defender. Joe Roff intercepted to score in the corner and the downhill slide began. It was a turning point in the match, because it lifted them and knocked us back, but it was not *the* turning point. If we had replied quickly it would not have mattered. And once again, we started well. We kicked off, won the ball and drove it up. Unfortunately, I turned over possession, losing the ball in contact and knocking it on, and from that play we gave away a penalty which Burke kicked. The half was only four or five minutes old and it had started badly. Roff scored again after they turned our scrum ball over, the conversion was kicked and the score was suddenly 21–11, with two tries, a conversion and a penalty conceded in ten minutes.

We tried hard to fight our way back into contention, but kept making silly individual errors, turning the ball over and giving away penalties – all of which added to the Wallabies' momentum. The game ended 35–14, a record defeat for the Lions against Australia. Worse news was that Rob Howley was injured. We should have flown Kyran Bracken out as cover, and he could have spent all week learning our moves, but it never happened, maybe for financial reasons, which, if it were the case, would be hard to take. And when Austin Healey, our scrum-half cover behind Matt Dawson, went down with a back spasm just before the final Test we found ourselves in difficulty.

In the end, the Scotland No. 9 Andy Nicol, leading a supporters' tour party, was drafted in. He was nervous as hell – and in his position who wouldn't have been? Not having played in weeks and now on the bench for the deciding match in a Lions series? He would have done a fine job, I am sure, if he had been required. In the end, he wasn't and has a unique record in Lions history. He came out on the 1993 tour to cover for injury and again sat on the bench, getting three minutes against Taranaki before leaving the tour party once the guy he had replaced recovered. Technically, then, he has been on two Lions tours and played 180 seconds of rugby. He was certainly good enough in his prime to have started for the Lions, but was unlucky in that his best years, when he was injury-free, didn't coincide with tours. Still, he is a Lion and no one can take that away from him.

On the morning of the third Test, we had another diary issue to deal with. This time it was Austin Healey. A piece published under his name in the *Guardian* back home was headed, 'And For Our Finale . . . Stuffing The Arrogant Aussies.' In a column ghost-written by Eddie Butler, Austin was quoted as describing Justin Harrison as 'a plod', 'a plank' and 'an ape' and attacking the 'Aussie male' in general. A fuming Graham Henry described it as 'a ready-made team-talk for Rod MacQueen'. Unlike Dawson's piece, we knew a little about this before the match and the management had to contend with a few media questions, but I was all but oblivious to it until I logged on to planetrugby.com to have a browse through their pages. There it was. 'Oz,' I said. 'What have you written now?' He replied, 'Not a lot, really.'

And that was the general attitude throughout the squad, I would say. We certainly weren't worrying about whether it might motivate the Wallabies – teams like that don't need motivating. The outside world, of course, didn't see it that way and two or three months later, bizarrely, I would find myself on a disciplinary panel in Dublin sitting in judgment on Healey, a friend and a team-mate who I had gone on holiday with immediately after the tour. I could have withdrawn, but felt that would have been to dodge my responsibilities, although it was something of a waste of time to be doing it in September. We dished out a fine for bringing the game into disrepute – and that was that. However, I couldn't help spinning back to the second Test and Nathan Grey's illegal challenge on Richard Hill. Did that not bring the game into disrepute? It's a strange world when words mean more than flying elbows.

That third Test, played in Sydney's magnificent Stadium Australia, was another fast-paced affair. We swapped penalties early on and were soon 9–3 behind, but I felt good and thought that we were well in the game. Twenty minutes into the half, Jason Robinson showed once again that he is one of the world's great finishers. Henderson made a good break, the ball went through the hands of Wood and Smith and out to Jase, who raced over. Jonny converted, to give us a 10–9 lead. Missed tackles on Kefu and Finegan enabled Daniel Herbert to respond, with Burke converting. Going in at half-time with the score at 16–13, the feeling in the changing room was that this was a very finely balanced game and that we stood every chance of winning.

The second half started very well, with Jonny diving over, the conversion making it 20–16. We should have gone on from there to kill the game off. Instead, we suffered from a moment of madness from Colin Charvis. In our half and with no support, Colin took a quick line-out to himself and suddenly realised he had nowhere to go. With Australian attackers bearing down on him he tried to hoof it clear, but his kick was horrible and the Wallabies built a position from which Herbert scored his second. Burke converted to make the score 23–20. Herbert was sin-binned for a high tackle on O'Driscoll, but we failed to add to our score while he was off. A Jonny Wilkinson penalty made it level with twenty minutes to go, but two more penalties gave the Aussies a 29–23 lead.

We needed a converted try to win. We kept pressing and pressing, creating two golden opportunities right at the death. Two minutes to go and we won an attacking line-out around 5m out. If we took our own ball we had a chance to drive them over or win a penalty try if they pulled down the maul, as they had been doing throughout the series. I called the throw to me and got up OK, but Justin Harrison came up in front of me and got both hands on the ball to nick it. Looking at the video later, the throw may have been slightly low, but Justin, who was going very well, might have beaten me even if the ball had been perfectly positioned.

The ball was cleared, but we brought it right back at them. Time was ebbing away and there was that desperate, desperate feeling of straining and struggling to get that score with the clock ticking relentlessly in the background. The hooter went and it came down to whether we could get over their line before the ball went dead. We were in their 22 and they couldn't afford to infringe, because the referee can't end the game on a defensive penalty. The ball was recycled and recycled and suddenly it moved out towards their left corner, reaching Matt Perry. A charging Iain Balshaw was coming up on his right shoulder at full pace. If the ball went to his hands he was in . . . but Pezza's pass went slightly behind Balsh, he lost momentum and the ball was turned over. Walker ran it into touch and the game was over.

In some matches – thankfully not too many – you are well

beaten and you know it. The 1995 World Cup semi-final against New Zealand, where Lomu went on the rampage, was one such encounter. You don't give up, but you know it's lost long before the whistle goes. This time we could have won the match, and with it the series, right up until the last moment. The deflation was sudden and horrible. All that we had worked for, all our dreams, all gone in a matter of seconds. I was close to tears – for the guys who had worked so hard, for the supporters who had spent so much time and money following us and who, to an extent, we had let down. It was my last time in a Lions shirt, a dreadful memory that will live with me forever.

So what went wrong? There were problems in all areas – players, coaching staff and, I have to admit, with my captaincy. A big issue, though, was the selection of our squad, which was conservative, pretty unimaginative and motivated by outside factors. Underlying it all was the choice of Graham Henry, in charge of Wales, as coach to the Lions. I am sure Graham knew that, after the tour was over, he would have to come back and face his Welsh squad in the dressing room at Cardiff. It would have been very tough for him to work with and motivate those guys if he had chosen only three or four of them for the Lions a month or two previously. Because he knew them so well, he may have been keener to select them. This issue often arises with the selection of a Lions squad.

Some of his picks were perfectly justified: Scotty Quinnell, Rob Howley, Dafydd James and Mark Taylor were all in on merit and gave their all from the moment they joined the party. Colin Charvis was a gifted, athletic back-rower and his selection was reasonable at first sight, though less so as things turned out. But Dai Young, a great guy and a tremendous servant to the game, had seen his best years. Julian White, the young English tight-head, was a stronger scrummager and would have been my choice instead of Dai. Neil Jenkins is one of rugby's great characters, an absolutely top bloke, brave and committed on the pitch and a good laugh off it, but poor old Jenks, a major factor in our 1997 series win, was hobbling about before he even got on the plane. It was clear he would play almost no part in the series and, much as I like and respect him, he should have been left at home for the Scottish stand-off, Gregor Townsend. Robin McBryde and Martyn Williams were not at that time, I felt, the best available players in their positions. Dorian West or Gordon Bulloch were better all-round hookers than Robin, and Budge Pountney or David Wallace were better opensides than Martyn, though he was another good guy and has now come through as one of the best Welsh forwards. The inclusion of Mike Catt and Lawrence Dallaglio were worthwhile gambles bearing in mind what each can bring to a team, but they failed to pay off when Catty and Lol broke down with injury.

Allied to this, we had few imaginative picks. Where Geech and Jim had gone for league returnees and exciting, uncapped players – guys who would be glad just to be there and whose enthusiasm for the cause would have lifted everyone – Graham stuck mainly with the tried, tested and experienced internationals. A player like Geordan Murphy could have made his name on that tour. I think Graham had looked at the midweek itinerary and had seen that there were only two big matches, against Australia A, which would be tough, and against an ACT Brumbies side likely to be shorn of much of its Wallaby talent. I imagine he felt that players like McBryde, Dai Young and Jenks, and possibly Charvis and Taylor, who might not challenge for Test spots, would be more than able to cope with this limited midweek schedule. It would not impact on the tour and would prevent issues arising back home in Cardiff later on. The problem arose when some of our main players dropped out through injury and we lacked some of the immediate strength in depth we needed. Additionally, unlike the 1997 midweekers, some members of the tour party became disillusioned with their failure to make the Saturday side.

I had known from the start that it was going to be tough. That limited itinerary meant we had a couple of 'softer' games, against Western Australia and the Queensland President's XV, before we played Queensland. You didn't have a lot of time to acclimatise or to prove yourself. It was obvious that a guy who had a bad game early on might never recover and that his tour could end almost before it began. That is what happened to Ben Cohen. Against Western Australia, he allowed himself to be barged into touch near their line and then missed a difficult tackle that enabled WA to score one of their two tries in the match. Ben, now unquestionably one of the world's best wingers, didn't make the next two games, was in the losing side against Australia A and never really made the impact he could have, becoming disillusioned.

Iain Balshaw had gone to Australia after an outstanding Six Nations in which he had destroyed teams with his pace. Against better defences and struggling to come to terms with Graham's system, he found himself less involved and it got to him, damaging his confidence. He started trying too hard, rather than letting things happen naturally, and it became a vicious circle. The Irish lock, Jerry Davidson, had been a star of the 1997 tour, but Jerry hadn't had a great season immediately prior to the tour and he had really been picked on history. The selectors had, wrongly in my view, decided to take five second rows. In that situation at least one of you is going to have limited opportunities to play and Jerry found himself getting squeezed out, something I think he found hard to cope with. A versatile guy like Martin Corry, able to play both back and second row, would have been a better bet, as he proved when he joined the party later.

I found Colin Charvis's attitude strange. When we asked him to jump in the line-out after the Scottish No. 8 Simon Taylor and Lawrence Dallaglio both quit the tour with injury, he didn't feel able to take it on. Later, he gave an interview complaining that he should have played a bigger part in the tour. To be fair to Colin, he didn't get an opportunity to play in any of the three big matches ahead of the first Test, with the management keen to give Lawrence and Scott Quinnell game time to prove themselves. 'I heard I hadn't been picked for the big games because I wasn't a line-out forward,' he said. 'Why not tell me to work on this a few months before the tour?' I couldn't understand this. If he had reacted positively and had a crack at it, he would have won everyone's respect. Jumping at the back of the line is, admittedly, technically quite difficult, but no one would have expected miracles.

As it was, I think he let himself down and in doing so allowed Martin Corry to overtake him in the pecking order. Compare Colin's response with Corry's, when he bowled up as a replacement from England's Canada tour, dishevelled, jet-lagged and not quite sure where he was, but immediately put his hand up to play in the next game. He played well in that match, against the Queensland President's XV, and started again on Saturday against the Queensland Reds. Again, he was outstanding and, before you knew it, he had played himself into the Test line-up.

Some guys were struggling with the workload in training even before we left England and it was an issue that would crop up repeatedly. Yes, the tour was hard work and, looking back, I think Graham's game plan meant we did spend too much time on the training field. But any successful international team needs to work hard, because modern rugby demands it, and I felt some of the players didn't really understand the level of commitment needed for success at that level. It had been heading that way in 1997, though people seemed to have forgotten what it had been like. The day after the midweekers beat South Africa A, we all went through a tough ninety minutes in the morning and in the afternoon we had another crack at it with a full contact session, with serious tackling, against each other. I guess it's like childbirth: you forget the pain over time and all that is left are the good memories. Admittedly, 2001 was tougher still, but even so I found some of the issues the guys were raising confusing. Initially, they were arguing that we spent too much time on preparation for matches. Then, after we lost to Australia A, the same people were saying that they hadn't had enough time to prepare for the game. That defeat was not about preparation time – whether too much or too little. It was about some individuals lacking the necessary commitment and determination to win a difficult midweek tour game.

I have to take some of the blame. I think I could have

done a better job of leading the party. Things had changed
since 1997. Back then, a lot of people had just been happy
to be there and keen to show the world that the northern
hemisphere could play rugby. My own attitude had changed,
too. In South Africa, I had been very aware of my position
as a young and inexperienced captain, with plenty of more
senior players under me. Four years on, having led England
and a very successful Leicester side for some years, I was more
aware of what I wanted and needed from the players. As a
result, I was probably more demanding and harder on the
guys than I had been before. When things started to go wrong,
I think I retreated into myself and expected people to get on
with it, as I would do myself. By the middle of the tour I
was pretty annoyed with some of the complaining. I felt that
things were tough for everyone, not just particular individuals, and that they needed to stop feeling sorry for themselves. I tried not to let this show, but maybe people who
didn't know me too well found it hard to come to me for
help or advice. As a result, I think a few of the guys thought
I was less interested in them, less caring about their problems
and issues than I actually was, and as the tour ended I couldn't
honestly say where I stood with a few of them. Looking back,
I wish I had done more. Maybe I could have been a bit more
sympathetic and had more chats with the boys whose heads
had gone down to see what I could do to help. If I had my
tour again I would certainly spend more time on man management, though to be truthful, I was finding it hard enough
concentrating on myself. We were into our eleventh month of
rugby and the strain was getting to us all.

Would someone like Keith Wood have been able to lift the

team in a way I couldn't? Maybe. Woody is a good guy, always very positive, more of an obvious 'people person' than me. I am sure he would have been in the reckoning for the job, possibly losing out because of fears over whether his body would last the course, given how much effort and commitment he put into his game. In 1997 I had come out of left-field and was, essentially, not Will Carling. By 2001, I had been England captain for a while and was much more associated with the England team, Twickenham, 'Swing Low' and all the other stuff that everyone else loves to hate about the English. Perhaps the fact that Woody was Irish would have helped with some of the other players, a few of whom were definitely a little anti-English in their attitudes. I honestly don't know.

Basically, a Lions tour is very, very hard work, with a few rewards along the way – for individuals, a Test spot and match victories and, for the squad, a series win. In 1997, we had lots of those little rewards: great nights out together, big wins against the provinces and the 2–1 Test scoreline. We felt it was everyone's series and when we won, we celebrated together. Everyone had played their part in the success, from Neil Jenkins, who kicked the points, to Kyran Bracken and Tony Stanger, who came out as replacements. In 2001, the tour was shorter and, for those guys who were in the side beaten by Australia A, I think they felt strongly that there would be no opportunity to put that right and get back into contention. Their tour, effectively, ended then.

I think the management could have done more, too. Graham knew there was a problem and Donal Lenihan had raised it at a team meeting ahead of the first Test, saying he couldn't believe how quickly heads had gone down. We probably should have gone on to discuss what we could do about it, but we didn't, for several reasons. Firstly, on a tour like that the management are so busy working on training, selection, game plans and tactics for matches a couple of days away, dealing with the media and everything else, that time runs out and things get missed. Secondly, Graham Henry is from New Zealand and he essentially fulfilled the cliché of the hard-nosed Kiwi rugby coach. Rugby is everything in New Zealand. They are brought up on it to a much greater extent than most British or Irish guys and I suspect Graham just didn't realise the depth of feeling among some of the players. Young lads on tour with the All Blacks wouldn't be moaning about the workload, however hard, and it would have been alien to Graham, used to the generally tougher players bred in his home country.

Looking back, it wasn't a very sociable tour, which was perhaps inevitable given that every game, bar one, was played at night, thanks to the demands of TV back home. By the time you had finished the match, spoken to the press after-wards, attended the reception and arrived back at the hotel, it was midnight. We all had to train or recover the following day. What would you do? We went straight to bed. I only went out for a drink after the Queensland game, the first I played in, and the final Test. There were players on the tour who I hardly spoke to. This was another failure on my part, I admit, but there was precious little time for chatting unless someone actually sought you out. That lack of team bonding cannot have helped the spirit in the camp. In South Africa, where the time difference is just a few hours, we often played in the afternoons, which meant we were able to go out much more as a squad. We would go to restaurants together and, on Saturday nights, most of us had a beer or two – even those who were playing midweek.

Travelling time ate into our available hours, too. In a country such as Australia, touring sides have to fly from place to place. It wasn't feasible to base ourselves in one city and have the relevant team strike out from there – the whole party has to travel. In the average week that means two travelling days taken out. With two days to play, and time required for recovery, that leaves very little time for preparation or socialising.

There is, apparently, a fabulous war memorial in Canberra, erected to the memory of the Australian servicemen who died in the two world wars. We were criticised by the press for not taking a trip to see this monument. For the record, I would love to have seen it. I am interested in military history and I am well aware of the sacrifices the Anzac troops made in both wars, but there just wasn't time. We had played the first Test in Brisbane and travelled to Canberra the following evening, Sunday. We were to play ACT Brumbies on the Tuesday. I was on the bench so I had to train on Monday morning with the midweek team. Monday afternoon I had to train with the Test team. By this point, I just needed to get some rest. Tuesday morning I again trained with the midweekers, then went back to the hotel, grabbed some lunch and started trying to focus on ACT. Post-match, I returned to the hotel around midnight, was up Wednesday morning for training, and then went off to Melbourne in the afternoon. Where was the time to visit the memorial?

Despite all the negatives, though, I am proud to have been

on the tour and proud to have led the boys. We played some great rugby in the first Test and in the first half of the second. Immediately after the final game I said that we couldn't have asked for any more from the players who finished that match in Sydney. After a long season playing many more games than the Australians, with the splits in our camp, the death of Anton and a lengthy injury list, they did fantastically well against a team whose season goal was to peak for and beat the Lions. And it turned on a few moments: Jonny's pass, intercepted by Joe Roff for a score, at the start of the second half of the second Test was one, and I have replayed that final line-out in my mind many times.

I think they had worked our calls out – there has since been talk of spying missions and other skulduggery but you can do it by listening to the match tapes, where the calls are picked up by the pitchside mikes. We initially called the code for a throw to Danny, but the Wallabies marked him immediately so I called it to me, again in code. They quickly switched to mark me, with Justin Harrison at the front of their line. I looked across at him and decided to take him on. Woody threw in and although I was above Harrison he got in front of me and nicked it. It was a gamble for them. If I had taken the ball it would have left a huge gap for us to drive through and we would almost certainly have scored. Fair enough, it paid off. Those are the moments a match and a tour can turn on.

Although we lost the series, I think we were probably a better team, and were certainly more competitive in the Tests, than the 1997 vintage. In South Africa, a lot of the luck of the draw went our way. In Australia, the rub of the green was pretty even. Look at the two squads and I think you'll agree. Phil Vickery would perhaps have just edged it over Paul Wallace at tight-head, with the rest of the front row staying the same. Jerry Davidson and me versus Danny and me in the second row? That's hard to call. Jerry was more dominant in the line-out in 1997 than Danny and I were in 2001, but the line-out had changed dramatically in those four years and was a more competitive area altogether, with the opposition much more prepared to challenge on your throw. I would probably take our half-backs from 2001 over the 1997 pairings: Rob Howley or Matt Dawson with Jonny Wilkinson outside them. Brian O'Driscoll would be in most people's World XV, though the Scott Gibbs of four years previously might have edged out Rob Henderson. Jason Robinson and Dafydd James were competitive wings and Matt Perry, a reassuringly solid presence at full-back, would probably get the nod over a Neil Jenkins relieved of his kicking duties by Jonny's presence in the side.

One thing I know for sure, though, is that I would have swapped anything, apart from a World Cup win, to have taken that series. I have played my last game in a red shirt and it was a losing game. I will not make the 2005 series. I recently heard Scott Quinnell and Rob Howley put their names in the frame, but at thirty-five I will be even slower and more decrepit than I am now.

How will the Lions fare in New Zealand? Well, a lot of the problems we faced in Australia will be multiplied for that party and they'll experience plenty of travelling, late-night kick-offs, intense media scrutiny from both home and foreign media, thousands of expectant travelling fans and a Kiwi public who will be reluctant to leave them alone. To make matters worse, there will be no easy games – no Western Australia, no Queensland President's XV and no New South Wales Country Cockatoos. In New Zealand, every team is good enough to beat you on their day and every team desperately wants to beat you.

I hope that the management are hard-headed and clear-headed in their selection. They need to find guys with character, players who will be tough and hard and who will lead the line in the midweek team when things are not too great and they are up against one of the New Zealand provincial sides in a small town out in the sticks. They need blokes who will stand up and fight with no Test match at the end of the week and no glamour.

How do you identify character? It's not easy. For a start, it's much more about what people do than what they say. Ahead of the tour we had to fill out media forms with lots of silly questions on them, including, 'What does it mean to you to be a British Lion?' I didn't take it very seriously. I think I put, 'A new set of clothes,' because that's my way. (Q: What do you do in your spare time? A: I fill in questionnaires about what I do in my spare time.) Lots of other guys wrote, 'It is the biggest honour in my life.' By the end of the tour, for some of them, those words were completely meaningless. Donal Lenihan had actually defined character himself before we left the UK: 'It's down to how they react to getting a kick in the b******ks,' he said, and he was right. It's about watching players in action. Who gets up quickest after a big hit? Who is trying to rally his team-mates as they stand under the posts waiting for another conversion to sail overhead? Who puts his body on the line? Who keeps going until the final seconds? Who busts everything to make the try-saving tackle when the game is already lost?

They will need a good coach, too. I think that, if possible, he has to be from these islands. As things stand, Clive Woodward must be favourite, though there will a natural reluctance to make the party too 'English'.

As for the structure of the tour itself, although the Lions as a concept is stronger than ever, some concessions have already been made to professionalism, with much shorter tours than previously. If we want to stand a serious chance of winning against sides like the All Blacks, maybe we need to look at further changes. Perhaps we should consider sending two squads of players over. There is no point having the Test players sitting on the bench as cover on a Tuesday night game, ahead of a two-hour flight to wherever the next international is. The All Blacks certainly won't be doing that. I remember Clive Woodward saying to me in Canberra, as we were all there preparing for the ACT game after the first Test, 'I'd have you all down in Melbourne now getting ready for the second Test. There's no need for you all to be here.' That would have split things even more, but would anyone have cared if we had won that second Test? So, a total of forty-four guys, split into two groups. The groupings wouldn't be set in stone. Those who initially found themselves in the midweek side would still have the possibility of being promoted to the senior squad if they played well, but at least they would travel knowing where they stood. I guess the Waikato fans, knowing from the start that their team was playing against an advertised Lions 'B' team, might object, but if it's all about victory you have to be prepared to be radical. There is an argument that there should be no midweek games at all – just a couple of warm-ups and then the three Tests. However, I strongly believe that Lions tours are as much about the provincial games as they are the internationals, so I would hate to see the schedule stripped that bare.

To cut down on the amount of training done once the party comes together, I would pull together eighty players for a couple of Lions camps to run through some basic ideas, so that people are starting from a base of knowledge when the final group is announced. If they get everything right, they will stand a chance against the All Blacks and their provincial teams. Here's hoping! I will be out there, for sure, but I will be watching from the safety of the stands.

CHAPTER THIRTEEN

THE ART OF CAPTAINCY

I was never really bothered about being a captain. To be honest, I would have been just as happy – happier, in some ways – if it had never happened. Some guys like all the extra attention and higher profile which go with the job. For me, whether for Leicester, England or the Lions, just playing the game and being one of the troops has always been enough. As I had no burning ambition to lead a side, I never consciously watched my own captains to try to learn from them. But without noticing it, even when you're sitting there thinking, 'This meeting's boring ... He's got nice trainers on ... I wonder what's for tea?', you are obviously absorbing things.

Dean Richards and Will Carling are the two big influences on me and I picked up important elements from each of them. As captains, as players and as men they were like chalk and cheese. Carling, a rugby modernist years ahead of his time, was fresh-faced, well-spoken and immaculately turned out. Richards, the Tigers skipper in my early years at the club, was just Deano – one of the lads, bit of a belly, socks by his ankles and false teeth. But both were outstanding players and excellent leaders in their own ways.

Dean led Leicester mainly by example. He didn't waste much time on team meetings or big speeches. His way was to roll up his sleeves and lead the rest of us into the trenches. After the match, he would be first to the back seat of the bus, playing drinking games, running the card school or fighting with the lads. He was particularly adept at To My Left, a strange little diversion that helped us pass the time on long journeys or in hotels ahead of games. Essentially, it involves punching the guy to your left – hence the name of the game – in the face. Believe me, no one wanted to be to the left of Deano, all twenty stone and ham-sized fists.

He was, essentially, utterly old school, the anti-modernist and one of the least pretentious guys you could ever meet. One of my abiding memories of him is of seeing him on TV when he was dropped to the bench for England in the 1991 World Cup. It was the final of the biggest sporting event in the world that year and there was Dean, sitting on the sidelines in his training suit, chewing sweets and wearing, of all things, a tweed flat cap. That was him all over. In the same year, as England prepared to end their Cardiff hoodoo, stretching back almost thirty years, Geoff Cooke had given his squad tapes of Welsh singing to help them prepare for the fearsome noise they would face at the Arms Park. Other players took this very seriously, going off to listen to the tapes on their Walkmans. Deano lobbed his straight into the bin.

That was the sort of no-nonsense attitude he brought to his captaincy. When I joined Leicester, rugby was just opening its eyes and ears to new ideas about training, fitness and diet. Young guys like myself, Neil Back and Graham Rowntree were very keen to explore some of these innovative theories. Around that time, pre-match warm-ups had just come into fashion. Tony Russ, our coach at Leicester, wanted the team to go out and warm up together ahead of each game. Deano would have none of it. He would turn up, run out and play. 'All you need to do to warm up,' he used to say, 'is sit on the bog, have a crap and read the match programme.'

We used to go through a last-minute routine, all huddled together in the changing room, running on the spot with knees lifted high, just before heading out on to the pitch. It was a final psyche-up for the game and helped to channel a few nerves and create a bit of togetherness. We would all be high-stepping in the middle of the room, taking it very seriously, and my eye would catch Deano's as he went through his own pastiche of it, all uncoordinated arms and lolloping legs, in a corner. I would end up almost wetting myself laughing.

He seemed to hate all training, though I think he worked fairly hard in secret. Luckily for him, as a policeman in those amateur days, he had a ready-made excuse for not turning up. We would all be ready to get started when someone would poke his head round the door. 'Dean can't make it tonight,' the guy would say. 'He's just taken a couple of prisoners.' Given the number of arrests he seemed to make, he must have been the scourge of Leicester's criminal classes. Maybe it wasn't the ideal example for a captain to set – and certainly not the kind of thing you could do in the professional era – but things were different then and the guys would have followed him anywhere.

Mostly it was because he was such a good player, one of the true greats of English, and indeed world, rugby. He was tremendously strong and that, coupled with his excellent rugby brain, made him extremely effective at competing for the ball or slowing down its release in the tight loose situations. He had a presence that could lift everyone, even older, experienced players. I remember sitting in the England team dining room one day ahead of the game against Wales in 1994. Dean had been out with a dislocated elbow, but had been cleared to rejoin the squad. In he walked and someone shouted: 'Hey . . . Warren's back!' Deano (Warren Ugly-Bastard was another of his nicknames) stopped in his tracks, grinned and pushed his belly out. He clearly hadn't been training too hard, but his return gave everyone a boost and we went on to beat the Welsh, killing off their Grand Slam hopes in the process.

If Dean was a great leader, though, Carling was perhaps the more methodical, better-prepared captain. He was the antithesis of Richards – a smooth front man, a meticulous trainer and, above all, a good-looking lad who had all his own teeth and two legs of roughly the same length. (Dean was born with one pin an inch or so shorter than the other, which explains his slightly rolling gait. It also shows how exceptional a guy he is, given his sporting achievements.) After being made England skipper in the autumn of 1988, while I was in the Colts, Will took the side, and the national captaincy, to new levels. He was, astonishingly, just 22 years of age. Geoff Cooke wanted a captain who would be in place for a long period and together they led the side into the modern era. England beat Australia in Will's first game in charge and gradually became the dominant force in European rugby, with guys like Dean, Jerry Guscott, Rob Andrew, Brian Moore and Carling himself forming the core of a team able to compete on the world stage. As youngsters, we had always been taught to revere the All Blacks. With Carling's England making the 1991 World Cup final, kids had a new set of heroes to follow and the country at last had a serious rugby team.

In that era, with just a couple of coaches behind the scenes, the captain was more influential than he is today and the results Will's England achieved speak volumes for him as a bloke. It would have been absolutely impossible for me to captain England at 22. At that age, I still had a lot of physical and mental maturing to do. Sitting in the team room ahead of my first squad session for England, I remember Mooreo striding in like he owned the place. I thought, 'Bloody hell, that's Brian Moore!' I was not in awe, exactly, but I was very much aware that I was just a young kid. All I wanted was the respect of my peers and to show I was worth my place. Anything else was going to be a bonus. At the same age, Will was a very confident young man and already an international class player.

Even so, it cannot have been easy for him. Rugby was changing from the days of guys who played purely for the enjoyment, hardly trained and enjoyed a good drink after matches. Now fitness work was becoming more important, the game was getting quicker and expectations of players were increasing as teams started trying to do things properly. Will, a man ahead of his time in terms of professionalism, was very keen to bring all of this to England. He worked very hard at his own fitness, thought a great deal about the game and asked the highest standards of himself and his players.

I got the feeling that some of the experienced hands under him were somewhat cynical about all this and that there was something of an undercurrent against Will from some members of the squad. Guys such as Richards, Moore and Jeff Probyn never really got on with him. I remember a Leicester versus Quins game, when harsh words, said quietly but with real venom, were exchanged. On another occasion, during England training, Brian Moore made some sarcastic remark and Carling rounded on him. Brian shut up and the incident was over as soon as it had begun, but it was obvious there was more needle there. Part of it may have been to do with Will's age, part of it perhaps to do with his attitude. He was never 'one of the boys'. He rarely ate out or drank with the team after matches, he did not join in the general banter – in the early days, at least – and you always felt a slight sense of separation from him, something I have tried very hard to avoid in my own captaincy.

I also think his success off the pitch irritated some people. The other fourteen guys in the side worked for a living and tried to fit their rugby in around the edges. Will was essentially full-time England captain; when he was not training or playing he was running a business addressing conferences and giving motivational speeches as 'Will Carling, captain of England'. It was making him a fairly wealthy guy and some players, I think, resented that. After all, his off-the-field career was based on the success of the whole team. Since they had all worked for that success, it perhaps seemed unfair to some that only he appeared able to cash in on it. As a young B teamer, I once got a lift to England training with one of the older players, a guy on the fringes of the squad. He said bitterly that when Will made his pre-match speeches you could see it was all about himself. He had pound signs spinning in his eyes, apparently. I took it all with a pinch of salt. Will seems to be one of those guys to whom people take a dislike without knowing him. I am often asked what I thought of him as England skipper, and it is pretty clear the questioner is looking for a negative response, but I speak as I find and I liked and respected him.

On that first appearance of mine, I had been called up late to replace Wade Dooley. Nowadays, with a wider England squad made up of around forty-five players and a strong Premiership packed with internationals from all round the world, plus a very hard European Cup competition, most newcomers to the international setup fit in fairly seamlessly. In those days, it felt like a real baptism and it was a major step up from what was a pretty poor domestic club scene to the international arena. One weekend you were playing in front of a couple of thousand people away at, say, Nottingham. The next you could be out at Twickenham in front of 70,000 against a very strong outfit from the southern hemisphere. I was understandably nervous, but this is when a good captain can come into his own.

I remember Will's words to me: 'Don't worry that you haven't been here for three days training with us. The training wouldn't have made any difference anyway. You're either going to be ready for the real thing when you get out there or you're not.' He ended by saying: 'You're a good enough player to be here and you'll be fine.' This was exactly the right thing to say to a young player. When you come into a team like that, especially as a last-minute replacement, the thing you want more than anything is acceptance from your peers. You need to feel like you belong and Will helped me relax.

I always remember those words when I chat to youngsters

coming into the modern England team now. The key thing is to reassure them that they are worth their place and that you are looking forward to playing alongside them. They will feel nervous, sure, but that's only natural and it's also a good thing, because adrenalin helps you perform. It doesn't get any better with experience, either, and may even get worse, given that you perhaps feel the responsibility and the weight of expectation a little more with experience. I tell them they are sitting there with twenty-one other guys who feel just as bad and that, across the corridor, there is another bunch in exactly the same state. I try to stress, too, that once you get out on the pitch it is just another game of rugby. If you're facing the best sides in the world you need to be up to that challenge, but in some ways international rugby is easier than the club game because the people around you are better players.

Will often used a little crafty psychology to gee us up, too. In 1994, we went to Paris to play the French. We were all apprehensive. They were a very good side and this was a huge game. Will came in from tossing up with Olivier Roumat, the French skipper. 'Bloody hell,' he said. 'That Roumat is nervous as hell. You can see it in his eyes. He looks really anxious and wound up.' Instantly, you could sense the dressing room lift. They're as tense as we are! They must be worried about us. And we went out and beat them. I thought that was an excellent ploy and it's one I have used myself. When the Lions played the first Test against the South Africans in 1997, I came back from tossing up and told the boys that Gary Teichmann had been really on edge. I completely made it up – he had looked fine – but, again, we relaxed slightly, played well and won.

Like Dean, Will did not go in for dramatic, passionate speeches ahead of games. The England dressing room has always been a pretty down-to-earth, even cynical, place and he would have been ripped to shreds. Instead, he would slide little messages under your hotel door ahead of a game. Early on, his notes to me would tell me not to underestimate my importance to the team. He had obviously thought it through and worked me out – I was a fairly shy young lad and needed just that sort of boost.

I also respected his professional approach. In that mid-nineties period, many of the other players still enjoyed a booze after a match and didn't mind training with a hangover. Nothing particularly wrong with that – they were amateurs, after all – but it obviously doesn't enhance performance, especially if it's happening a lot. Will was never a part of that. He kept himself fit and in great shape, trained hard and tried to do things properly. He thought deeply about the game and played a key role in creating our game plans.

He would have thrived in the modern-day game, both as a captain and a player. The English back line of my early career contained some excellent players, like Jerry Guscott and the Underwoods, and Will was up there with the very best of his generation. He was a very good centre. Big, quick and defensively very strong, he was outstanding in our victory over the All Blacks in 1993 and he scored some brilliant tries, but he didn't shine as brightly as he could have done. Maybe our coaching was slightly blinkered, focusing on our strong forward pack. Maybe it was because Rob Andrew, who spent most of the early to mid-nineties at 10, was a fly-half who kicked more often than he passed or because, until the emergence of

Mike Catt, we lacked a good attacking full-back to inject pace and aggression into the back line. Whatever the reason, Will and his fellow backs were under-used for many years. In the professional era, coached better and used more effectively, he could have been a genuinely great player, probably playing outside centre. The one slight criticism you could make of his play was that his hands were not that great, but on the end of passes from the likes of Wilkinson, Greenwood or Catt he would do some serious damage.

Many would argue that Will's huge profile helped rugby. He was, for want of a better phrase, 'big time'. That certainly raised awareness of the sport. In 1988, if you had asked the average man in the street who John Orwin or Mickey Harrison (Will's immediate predecessors) were, few could have told you. Within a couple of years of his appointment, that had all changed. In Julia, his first wife, he had a TV presenter partner. They were almost the mini Posh and Becks of their day. With that, and the various unfortunate twists and turns in his private life, Carling was on the front pages more often than the back. I would guess that, even now, most non-rugby fans would know him by sight.

His sacking, in May 1995, was one of the more ridiculous episodes I've witnessed in rugby. The sport was beginning the revolution that would lead to professionalism a year later. The England team was starting to strike deals with sponsors like Cellnet and Courage Bitter. Young guys like myself were happy just to get a free mobile phone and a few cases of beer out of it, but Will, Rob Andrew and Brian Moore saw the bigger picture. Increasing sums of money were being proffered and the RFU, desperately trying to keep the game amateur, were on a collision course with the squad. Against this backdrop, Will – expressing an opinion held by almost everyone who had ever had any dealings with them – gave an interview in which he called the powers-that-be at the RFU 'fifty-seven old farts'. Although the Rugby World Cup in South Africa was just a few weeks away, the old farts clearly decided this was the moment to make an example of Will and show the players who was boss. They called him in and fired him, proving, along the way, the accuracy of his description.

It was clearly absurd. A month before we had won a Grand Slam. Five years earlier, some of those disgruntled senior players in the squad might have stood by and let Will go. Now, it provided a perfect rallying point for the team and a way to seize some ground from the RFU. I was away for the weekend when the news broke, but by the time I got back down to our HQ at Marlow the whole thing was almost over. Rob Andrew had written a letter on behalf of the squad saying that no one else would take on the captaincy and demanding Will's reinstatement. The RFU climbed down after Will helped them save face with an apology and he was back almost before he had gone. Maybe it was some extremely clever reverse psychology by the powers-that-be, but I very much doubt it, although it certainly bonded the team. The other thing it did was to reinforce the view that the amateur era was on the way out.

After the 1995 World Cup, he carried on for a little longer before stepping down to concentrate on playing. I guess he had just had enough of the hassle and stress the captaincy can bring and, having been there myself, I can certainly see why he might want to go back to the ranks.

The new, professional era had arrived as a number of the older players, such as Dean Richards, Rory Underwood and Brian Moore, finished. There were few obvious candidates to replace Will. Ben Clarke had gone to second division Richmond, damaging his hopes of playing internationally. Tim Rodber, another possibility, had been out injured for a while. Jerry Guscott — known as '(I'm all right) Jack' — was seen as being too much of an individual to lead a side. One or two people talked about me as a possibility, but I felt I was very much an outsider and certainly wasn't looking for the job. There weren't too many other experienced guys to choose from and the Bath centre Phil de Glanville got the nod.

Perhaps not surprisingly, given the length of Will's tenure and the way the job's profile had risen, the captaincy turned out to be something of a poisoned chalice. Phil was a solid, intelligent guy, well-spoken and good with the media, and was liked within the team. He had the confidence, too, to stand up in front of the guys and say his piece. The only question was whether he could hold his place in the side. He had played well against the All Blacks in 1993 and played the 1994 season when Jerry was out, touring South Africa along the way. However, when both Carling and Guscott were fit Phil was probably third choice and you can't captain from the bench. I liked him as a bloke and I think he did a good job, winning most of the games in which he led the team. We played some good, attacking rugby under him and should have won a Grand Slam in 1997, but ultimately you couldn't have a truly great player like Guscott sitting on the sidelines and Phil de Glanville on the pitch. He led the team to Australia that summer, but when Clive Woodward replaced Jack Rowell as England coach at the start of the 1997–98 season, he was removed. Typically, he did not flounce off and retire, but stayed around, playing right through to the 1999 World Cup where he got stuck in and put in some good performances.

Like Geoff Cooke, Clive wanted to start his era with a captain who was going to be there for a long period. He called me and told me that the choice was between myself and Lawrence. I had led the Lions to South Africa during the summer of 1997. We had won the series and the tour had seen a number of English players, such as Richard Hill, Will Greenwood and Austin Healey, make real names for themselves. Dallaglio was another who had returned home firmly established as a world-class back-rower. His leadership qualities had also been apparent for all to see.

Ultimately, Clive went with Lawrence. I was not surprised. I felt friends and supporters of Lawrence had been pushing hard for him and, to some extent, they were pushing at an open door. I was seen as a fairly Neanderthal second row, described regularly by the press as 'dour' and 'taciturn'. (I had to look up taciturn in the dictionary; they had a point.) Lawrence, on the other hand, was a chatty, personable guy, with a high profile and lots of media interest. I also think Woody recognised that Lol was more of a risk-taker than me and felt that I would probably go for the safe options. Safety was not what Clive wanted in his early days in charge. He was trying to rid English rugby of its 'boring' tag and perhaps believed that Lawrence would be more aggressive and attacking than I might have been.

Lawrence was obviously going to be an inspirational leader, he was going to be great on TV and, most of all, he really wanted the job. While I would have been honoured to have been made captain, I was actually pleased with Clive's decision. I was shattered after the Lions tour and the long season that had preceded it. I was only just recovering from groin surgery and was entering my first full-time season as captain at Leicester. Bob Dwyer was about to be fired and we were heading into what would become an up-and-down season at the club. The last thing I needed was to lead England during the kind of ridiculous autumn international series the RFU had scheduled: two Tests against the All Blacks, plus one apiece against the Wallabies and the Springboks. The pressure, from the media and the fans, was going to be immense and the rugby was going to be incredibly hard. I wouldn't have been in the right position to do the job and was happy just to think about playing.

A lot of journalists asked me how I felt, having led the Lions successfully, not to be appointed. My response was simple: Lawrence had been a senior guy on that tour and he had backed me completely. Now I would back him one hundred per cent – not because Lawrence did it for me, but because that is what you do. I think the hacks were expecting me to sulk and stamp my feet and say I would not play, but I was there to play the game, not worry about the captaincy. Lawrence is a born leader. People gravitate towards him and are prepared to follow him. If you had a group of twenty blokes stuck in the jungle, he would become a leader of that group. He is a strong, charismatic character, who enjoys taking on responsibility and thrives on it.

Those early days under Clive were difficult, with both guys finding their feet in what was, given that horrendous four-match schedule, the toughest start possible. Lol was popular with the guys, if a little headstrong at times. If you were to make any criticism of him at all it would be that, occasionally, he was too keen to have a say, whatever the issue. I think he would recognise this himself, now. He has certainly mellowed out a lot in the last three or four years and I think he would be an outstanding England captain if he were to get the job again. It is unfortunate and unfair that his reign is probably best remembered for two things.

On the field, it is the game against Wales at Wembley in 1999. Close to the end, with a Grand Slam beckoning, we had a kickable penalty that would have taken us more than a converted score clear of the Welsh. Lawrence opted to kick for touch, win the ball at the line-out and drive over to kill the game off. Afterwards, when the catch and drive had failed and Scott Gibbs had scored in the dying seconds to win the game for Wales, he admitted, 'We should have taken the points!' But that's all classic hindsight stuff and none of us ever blamed Lawrence for that defeat. The match was lost by the whole team over eighty minutes, not through that one decision. We had been all over the Welsh and would have been well clear if we had taken the chances on offer in the second half and not been so heavily penalised.

Off the pitch, he will always be remembered for his encounter with the tabloids. There was a sense of permanence about his leadership. He was picked to go through to the 1999 World Cup and probably the 2003 one as well and, at three or four years younger than me, would surely have done so if it had not been for the *News of the World*. It was just a few weeks after that Wales game and Leicester were due at

Twickenham to play the Barbarians in their end-of-season fixture against the English champions. I woke up on the Sunday morning ahead of the game and flicked on the telly, still half asleep. It was some breakfast news show and they were talking about Lawrence Dallaglio. 'Bloody hell, what's going on?' I thought.

I flicked to Teletext and immediately got the full story. The newspaper was alleging that it had recorded him admitting to dealing drugs in his youth. It is very hard to describe how I felt. I was almost in shock. It was the most surreal thing to have happened in my rugby life. This was Lawrence Dallaglio, a guy I knew well, the England captain, on the front page of the *News of the World* . . . as a drug dealer? None of it made any sense. Later, as we met up at our hotel in Leicester prior to the journey south, Richard Cockerill arrived in his car and, with a look of astonishment on his face, just drove past with the paper pushed against his side window. I simply couldn't believe this was happening and felt very sorry for Lol. We drove down to London in our coach and played the game, but I don't remember much about it.

We were all due to head off to our pre-World Cup camp in Australia almost immediately afterwards. Lawrence had announced his resignation and gone to ground. He would miss our tour, staying behind to get on top of the allegations. I knew Clive would ring me and offer me the job. The call duly came on the Sunday night. It was a strange ten minutes. I never sought the captaincy, but it is obviously a great honour and, under normal circumstances, I would have been delighted. As it was, there was no elation, no sense of achievement. Clive and I didn't really talk about the job or rugby issues. We were both concerned for Lawrence and how he was coping and that formed the majority of the conversation. Obviously, I accepted the offer, but I hated, really hated, the way it had happened. Will Lawrence come back to lead the side again? I would like to think he will, though the circumstances of his departure may count against him. Whatever, he will always be one of the leaders of the team irrespective of who is skipper on the team sheet.

So how do I approach the job of captaining a side? I have to be myself. I don't set out to make rousing speeches, stick notes under doors or engage in too much management speak. I am a fairly straightforward bloke and that is how I captain. With England, it is a much easier job now than it was in Will Carling's day. Will had just a couple of coaches to help him and much of the workload fell on his shoulders. The RFU have given Clive Woodward the finance and the tools to take care of all aspects of training, coaching and management. That has taken a lot of the hassle and work away from the captaincy. The professionalism of young players in the modern day means there is very little to do in terms of introducing them to the international scene. It is only six years ago, but the change since 1997 and that Lions tour of South Africa has been huge. Then, the management actually printed little sheets detailing the behaviour and standards the players would be expected to keep to. That was probably a good idea at the time, but nowadays, certainly with England players, it is totally unnecessary — they know what is required of them. I have never had to have words with any squad member about their attitude. If it was poor, they wouldn't be there in the first place; they would have been weeded out earlier.

My attitude is very much that guys can do as they please as long as it doesn't impinge on what they do in training and on the pitch. As a player, when you are with the team, you must do absolutely everything you can to play well. You must be a hundred per cent focused and committed – not for yourself, but for those around you, your team-mates. The rest of the time is your own. Some guys like a couple of beers in the pub from time to time. Others might want to lock themselves in their rooms and watch rugby videos twenty-four hours a day. Half an hour after a defeat, some can be laughing in the changing room. Others, who take it more obviously to heart, may assume this means they don't care. Dorian West, my Leicester and England colleague, has a phrase: 'He's not one of us, is he mate?' My response is, 'They can't all be like us, mate – and certainly not like *you*. That would be a very boring world indeed.'

The fact is that whatever works for the individual is fine, as long as he is sensible. Trying to rule guys' lives would be impossible and insulting. Back to South Africa and I actually had grown men coming up to me the night before a midweek game and asking my permission to go to a pop concert half an hour away. My response was, 'Will it affect the way you play tomorrow? No? Then of course you can go.' That hasn't changed.

It is important, too, to have the help of other senior players. With England, it is guys like Lawrence, Phil Vickery, Neil Back, Jonny Wilkinson, Matt Dawson . . . all England captains in their own right. When I was chosen to lead the Lions against the Springboks, the management team – Fran Cotton, Jim Telfer and Ian McGeechan – were very supportive. Older members of the squad, too – guys like John Bentley, Dai Young, Alan Tait and Ieuan Evans, who I didn't know and who I had seen play as a youngster – helped me enormously, when conceivably they could have taken exception to being led by a bloke five or more years their junior. It is a mistake to think that being called 'captain' means you can do everything yourself.

I am not particularly comfortable with the extra pressure that goes with leading rugby sides. With England, particularly, there is masses of media work to undertake, particularly during the week leading up to a match and matchday itself, when the interview requests, press conferences and photocalls all reach a fever pitch. I understand why it has to be done, but I don't much enjoy it and I would prefer to take a more low-key approach. On the 1997 Lions tour, the press liaison officer was always telling me to make sure I was seen leading the team off planes when we arrived at airports, that I was first off the bus at the stadium, that I was carrying the cuddly lion mascot for the photographers. We exchanged views and he eventually left me alone. I was much happier being one of the guys and that meant getting off the bus when it was my turn.

Much of what I do involves trying to gauge the mood of the team and either calm them down or rev them up accordingly. As matchday approaches, I will speak to senior players like Neil or Lawrence and ask their view of the team's approach. Their answers will determine the tone I will take when I speak to the guys just before the game. If you're playing the All Blacks or Australia away from home, as we did in the summer of 2003, everyone is absolutely wired because they know it is do or die – if they're not on their game they are going to get destroyed. No one needs psyching-up. Instead, I try to reassure the squad, saying, 'Look around the room. You know these guys will back you up. We're good enough to win this.'

Occasionally, a different approach is needed. When we played Wales at Cardiff in the 2003 Six Nations, after having beaten them fairly comfortably in all our recent encounters, I felt the adrenalin was not there. We did not have the fear – of failure and humiliation – that gives you the edge in your preparations. We had won against France and I was worried the players thought this would be routine. As we huddled up on the Millennium Stadium turf after our warm-up, I really laid into them. 'For f***'s sake,' I ranted. 'If we're not ready we're going to get f***ing stuffed here.' It was real aggressive, psyche-up stuff, and hopefully, a wake-up call. Yes, we were favourites and Wales were not the team they had once been, but any international side can beat any other and if the opposition gets on top in a Test match, particularly away from home, the momentum can be hard to turn.

In the changing room ninety minutes before kick-off, the players will be preparing in their own ways. Jonny is very meticulous and likes to get into his match kit and get straight out on to the pitch to practise his kicking. The front five like to sit around, have a bit of a chat, read the programme, just relaxing our way into things, coping with the nerves and trying to focus. The TV people usually interview me as I walk in. Then I go out to have a look at the pitch and the conditions, before coming back in for a Deano-style warm-up with the programme and the loo. Just before we go out for the anthems we will have a huddle together in the changing room. It is a togetherness thing and you look round at your team-mates and talk about not letting each other down. It can be quite emotional, actually. A bond forms between you over the months and years together and these few moments bring it all home. Then I will remind the guys of the basics: do the simple things well, look after the 'pill', beat your opposite number's work rate.

Once the game starts, a lot of my chat is technical. I will be talking to the half-backs and guys like Dallaglio, Back and Will Greenwood. What are they seeing? Do we need to change the way we're playing? What do they think of the options we're taking? Every area of our game has a 'captain' whose responsibility is to ensure that that part of our game is functioning well and enabling us to beat the opposition. For instance, Jason Leonard is responsible for scrummaging, Ben Kay will oversee line-outs and Neil Back and Will Greenwood are in charge of defence. They are chosen for their experience and know-how in the various disciplines and they help build a picture of what is happening on the field and, if there are problems, how we can fix them.

Take scrum engagement, for instance. Our style is to form up and then hit the opposition front row hard, take them on aggressively and try to keep moving. Southern-hemisphere teams tend to prefer to press together more slowly and then try to build the pressure gradually. The referee has to come down on one side and if he sides with the other team we have to adjust our technique. Jason will quickly talk to the guys to ensure we do this smoothly.

The line-out is another area where we have to think on our feet. It might be that the opposition are defending in a way we have not seen before or didn't anticipate. Your best attacking ball is the one thrown to the back of the line-out, because you can get the ball out to the backs much more quickly. Australia have traditionally marked the back jumper and the one in the middle, but allowed you to win the ball uncontested at the front. Our line-out, therefore, will be geared accordingly, with Ben Kay calling a variety of moves designed to defeat their defence. On one or two occasions, though, they have reversed this, letting us throw to the back but contesting the front. It is up to Ben, with help from the rest of us, to change his approach, making sure the hooker and the rest of the team are with him. If they switch back, we have to adjust again. Similarly, Backy will be watching to see how the other side are attacking – out wide, say, or close to the breakdown – and marshal our defence accordingly. My role in all of this is to oversee what these other 'captains' are saying and doing and make sure it is the right approach.

There is very little ranting and raving. Against the All Blacks in New Zealand in the summer of 2003, we were reduced to thirteen men, with Backy and Lol in the sin-bin together. The Blacks had a scrum, on our line, against our six-man pack. Against the odds, we kept them out. Journalists have since asked me repeatedly what I said to the boys, as though there was some sort of Churchillian magic I could have worked. Basically, it was a case of 'bend over and push'. What else could I say? 'Right, lads, we're up against it here.' 'Really, Johnno? Thanks.' We all knew we were going to have to scrummage for our lives. The only thing I did say was to Benny Kay and that was that the two of us needed to get out quickly as soon as the scrum was over. Down two flankers, someone else was going to have to make Neil's and Lawrence's tackles and we would be needed to make the next two. I need not have wasted my breath. Ben was already there.

At half-time, my talk tends to be technical. I will speak about how the opposition is playing and whether our defence needs to do this on their scrum or maybe that on their line-out. You don't want to be blinding people with science, though. People who talk rugby tactics are often talking to make themselves sound clever. It's actually a simple game. It's about winning the battle of the work rate, winning the collisions, keeping the ball and going forward with it. If you have the go-forward, if you are hungrier and keener and are out-hustling them, it's an easy game. If it's not there you will know five minutes into the game and you need to check it as soon as possible. On the – very – rare occasions a team seems not to be putting in enough effort, I will have words with them. If the work rate is not there, you can't put any plan into practice.

There are a certain number of givens in rugby and one of them is that if you all work harder than your opposite numbers, make fewer mistakes and put in more tackles, you will almost certainly win. The only example I can remember is when Leicester played Llanelli away in the European Cup in 2002. We were being beaten because we were getting out-worked and they were playing with much more passion. I laid into the boys at half-time. We still lost but we played better in the second half, up the hill and into the wind.

I can be a petulant captain, sometimes, and there are those who criticise me for this. I do a lot of gesticulating. I talk to referees, sometimes angrily if I think their decisions are poor.

I have seen myself on tape later and thought, 'Oh God, what am I doing?' But that is just the way I am on the field. If a referee cocks up, I need to get it off my chest. Luckily, in international rugby it's so noisy you can shout and swear at them from 15yds away and they can't hear you. I have had my run-ins with the citing officials, too. Again, some would say this is a bad example for a captain to set. I would say, again, that this is just the way I am and how I play my rugby. I cannot play it laid-back. And I have never deliberately and pointlessly hurt someone on the field. Most of the incidents I have been involved in have either been accidental, retaliatory or in the course of righting the occasional wrong.

I am also criticised sometimes for a slightly defensive approach. In penalty situations, I will often hand the ball to Jonny to go for goal, with the crowd howling for the kick to the corner and the catch-and-drive or a quick tap. I do like to take the points when they are on offer, because they are hard won in professional rugby. Plenty of matches are won and lost by a point or two. However, having said that, I am often wrong and some of Leicester's best moments, scorching tries scored by the likes of Austin Healey after a quick tap-and-go, have come with Johnson screaming frantically in the background, 'No, no . . . go for the three points.'

Having exciting, talented and motivated players who can play with their heads up and take advantage of situations on the pitch as they develop makes the job of leading a side much easier. Interviewers often ask me how special a win was for me 'as captain'. I find this a little embarrassing. My answer is simple: 'It's no different from winning as a player.' As the skipper I often get the plaudits when things go well, but the fact is that I have been extremely fortunate, with Leicester, England and the Lions, to lead some fantastic guys. Anyone could captain them. They deserve the credit.

CHAPTER FOURTEEN

TERMINATOR IN SHORTS

Neanderthal. A glowering thug. The Terminator in shorts. And that's just my wife's opinion. Sometimes you have to laugh. Professional rugby is a hard game of physical confrontation and everyone who takes part knows that. We all get cut and we all get stitched up from time to time. We get stud marks down our bodies, we break bones and we lose teeth. We play rugby. That's the way it is and that's the way it was in the old amateur days, too.

The old stories of lumpy-faced forwards rolling around in the mud fighting are a part of the game's folklore. The former England and Lions lock, Martin Bayfield, now works as an after-dinner speaker, appearing at sporting functions around the country. He often tells how Dean Richards, a fellow policeman in those amateur days, whacked him in a club match. 'You can tell which copper works behind a desk,' said Deano, as Bayfield crumpled to the floor.

Another favourite tale of Bayfield's concerns the fighting that erupted in the third Lions Test against New Zealand in 1993. Aiming for one of the All Blacks, Bayf offloaded a haymaker, but missed and smacked yours truly instead, concussing me in the process. Big chuckles all round, often from the great and the good of rugby, the administrators, the committee men and the like on their fifth port of the evening. The Welsh legend Phil Bennett, another after-dinner speaker, likes to tell stories about the fearsome French pack of the seventies or Bobby Windsor's hard-man antics for Wales. Everyone knows about the Lions' 'ninety-nine' call in South Africa where, on Willie-John McBride's order, each Lion simply found the nearest Springbok and punched him.

These yarns always get a laugh, and rightly so. The game is much the richer for them. They are also regularly and fondly recounted by journalists in the national press, looking for a bit of colour to spice up their articles. When it comes to a bit of modern-day handbags, however, it is a different story altogether. The attitude becomes much more censorious, and few players have attracted censure more often than me. Somehow, unfairly I believe, I have developed a reputation for illegal physical violence on the field of play.

I am sure part of it is my size and general appearance; it doesn't help being 6ft 7in tall and 19 stone, with one big black eyebrow stuck on the top of a pretty bashed-up face. Referees tend to see you as a hulking great second row and they act accordingly. Part of it is the way I have been built up as 'Johnson the Enforcer'; the man picked to captain the Lions against South Africa purely because he was some big b*****d who would intimidate those poor little Springboks. All nonsense, frankly, but it gives the writers the angle they need to hype things up. Partly, too, it is because I *have* been involved in one or two high-profile incidents. But being involved in incidents is not the same as being a dirty, dangerous player. In a world where most players occasionally cross the line, it is about being caught and even, sometimes, about being singled out.

The two most recent episodes both involved matches between Leicester and Saracens. The first came just after the 2000 autumn international series. The England squad had briefly gone on strike before taking on Argentina, Australia and South Africa in a tough autumn schedule. As captain, I had come in for some criticism in the media and from sections of the general public over the way the dispute had unfolded. Its swift resolution, though, and three good wins against our southern-hemisphere visitors, had lightened the atmosphere. My agent, Tim Buttimore, who had been worried about the effect the strike would have on my image and commercial position, was now a little more relaxed. 'Johnno,' he told me shortly after the third Test, 'somehow, you have come out of this all right . . . Everyone loves you now.' 'Don't worry, Tim,' I said. 'I'll probably smack someone next week and they'll all hate me again.' Bit unfortunate, that.

Over the years we had had some good games with Sarries. Often they had been a bit tasty – guys like Danny Grewcock, Scott Murray and Julian White do not back down – and our encounter at Welford Road was another one out of this mould – a hard match, fractious and intense, with plenty of niggle. It was the sort of game you would get excited about watching. We were on the attack. One of our players was looking to pass to Neil Back and as he did I spotted their Australian fly-half, Duncan McRae, grabbing Backy off the ball. I hate this sort of offence – we are all guilty of it occasionally I guess, though I honestly rarely do it – because there is somehow something weak and spineless about holding people back and obstructing them. Shoe me or punch me if I am making a nuisance of myself in a ruck or a maul, but don't obstruct me. If you are caught, the least you can expect is a whack from the player you are holding.

The ref had missed it, but I caught up with McRae at the next ruck and followed him in, going in hard. I wanted him to know I had seen what he had done and I wanted him to think twice, or preferably three times, about doing it again. I charged into the ruck and my knee caught his body hard. At that pace, and with so many bodies around, you can't control which part of your body comes into contact with which part of your opponent's.

As he went down I walked over him to follow the play. The play then came back that way and I saw that he was still lying on the floor. He looked up at me and said, 'You've hurt me, you dirty dog,' which actually sounded a bit comical, like some sort of cartoon insult. I said, 'You shouldn't f***ing obstruct people, should you?' Before I knew it, though, he was being stretchered off – it later transpired I had broken his ribs – and as I saw him go I turned to Benny Kay. 'I'll get cited for that,' I said. 'Probably,' said Benny, with a thoughtful nod.

And he was right. After a flurry of unfavourable headlines, I was given twenty-one days for the knee-drop and thirty-five days for the 'stamp', along with a further week for a separate punch on Julian White – all to run concurrently. The committee discounted the sentences to reflect 'the overall nature of the game'. It had been a nasty match – we identified ten occasions where we could have cited a Saracens player, including one where Whitey had punched me – and that has to have a bearing on how you react. It took into account what it described as my good disciplinary record. I missed a couple of European matches and a domestic cup semi-final against Harlequins, but came back just in time to play for England against Wales in Cardiff.

The papers were full of conspiracy theories, suggesting the disciplinary committee had acted leniently to allow me to rejoin the national squad so I could continue to play in the Six Nations. 'How convenient' ran one headline. I didn't feel it was lenient or convenient. The recommended suspensions were twenty-one days for punching, forty-two days for stamping and twenty-eight days for use of the knee, so the ban was at the upper end of the scale. I felt five weeks out was fair, though I was actually being punished not for my actions, but for their outcome. Eight, maybe nine, times out of ten, McRae would have got up, winded and bruised, and walked away. On this occasion, he was unlucky.

He had deserved to get aggressively rucked out for what he had done. I would expect the same treatment, and if Backy had caught him, a betting man would have put money on McRae receiving the dreaded one-inch death punch – and the Fist of Back can do a lot more damage than the Knee of Johnson, believe me. However, he did not deserve broken ribs and I regretted that. I have never deliberately set out to inflict that sort of pain and damage on anyone. It is not what the game is about, particularly when a professional player's liveli-hood is at stake.

An interesting postscript to the story came later in the year when the British Lions travelled to Australia. In a warm-up game, McRae pinned Ronan O'Gara to the floor and repeat-edly punched him in the face as he lay there. It caused some nasty injuries and, as he left the field, he didn't seem to show much contrition. Suddenly, the journalists who had castigated me earlier were joking about whether I had known something about McRae that they had not.

If I felt my punishment for that knee-drop was fair, the same could certainly not be said of the second Saracens incident. This time we had travelled to them. Once again we anticipated a hard-fought match, though as it turned out it was one of the easiest games we played all season as we ran out 48–7 winners. It was Richard Hill's 200th game for Sarries and I felt really bad for him as we racked up the points. He was dead-legged halfway through and was obviously struggling. We scored yet another try and I said to him, 'Mate, why don't you get yourself off?' Typically, he hung on like the great player he is.

Early in the second half, the ball came loose. Josh Kronfeld dived on it, but the ref blew for a penalty. I picked the ball up, not knowing who had been pinged. I looked over, realised it was us and kept hold of the ball. I shouldn't have done that, though it's one of the things that all players do. As I stood there, however, Robbie Russell, Saracens' Scottish-Aussie hooker, charged into me from behind, sticking his shoulder into my back and trying to grab the ball. I turned around and he was right in my face, all aggression and grappling arms. In the heat of the moment, I lashed out. It was not intended as much of a punch – it was more of a slap. You either let a guy cannon into the back of you and take it or you draw a line in the sand and say, 'Mate, don't ever do that to me again.' Rugby is a game of physical confrontation and you cannot afford to back down, even if you want to.

A few other players got involved to separate us and we

walked away. The referee came over and pulled us both aside to give us a talking-to. As I stood there I looked down at Russell and immediately saw that he had been cut. He was bleeding quite badly and I remember thinking, 'Ah, this doesn't look too good!' Meanwhile, he was whingeing, 'I just wanted to get hold of the ball, I just wanted to get hold of the ball,' to which I replied with an expletive or two. I got the feeling, actually, that the ref was not even going to sin-bin either of us, but once we started arguing in front of him that was it. Exasperated, he gave us our marching orders.

Off I trudged. I thought very little more about it and the mood in the dressing room, post-match, was great – we had won well, away at Sarries, and we looked odds-on to retain our league title. There I thought the matter would rest – as it should have done. The RFU's own rules, after all, stated that if an incident had been dealt with by the match official, it was to be considered closed. I stayed down in London that evening, ready for the England squad pre-Six Nations meet-up the following day. As I arrived at the hotel, Clive Woodward called me. Sky Sports had gone berserk over the incident, showing dozens of replays – which, admittedly, looked worse on tape than it had felt at the time – and the Sunday papers were following it up.

Saracens boss François Pienaar, a man who should have known far better, was mouthing off all over the place. His team had just been humiliated in front of their home crowd and he had more pressing worries than one of his guys having a little cut under his eye. Pienaar, who was obviously trying to deflect attention from the performance, was no angel himself during his playing career. We had visited Vicarage Road three or four years earlier and there had been an almighty brawl in the corner of the pitch, during which the same François had thrown several huge haymakers at Leicester players. I didn't recall any action being taken over that.

Still, despite all the hoo-ha, it was nothing to get too concerned over and Woody told me he had spoken to the relevant people at the RFU and nothing would be happening, but then I hadn't thought it would – double jeopardy and all that. Things rumbled on over the next few days. The referee's judgment was called into question, with comment pieces appearing asking what you had to do to be sent off in rugby these days and suggesting he had been intimidated by me. This is a common misapprehension. In fact, far from being intimidated, I feel referees are actually keener to penalise me because it's a way for them to be seen to be stamping their authority on a match. Also, my reputation comes into play again and they think I am always up to something even when I am not. I felt sorry for the ref, actually. He was a fairly in-experienced guy, but he had had a good game. He had been on the spot and he had acted quickly and decisively.

The press also got hold of Robbie Russell and persuaded him to pose for pictures showing his damaged eye and quoted him demanding an apology and claiming it could affect his chances of appearing in the Six Nations. My initial reaction was that this was somewhat over-the-top, given that it was the sort of injury that, if it happened during a match, would be stitched up at the side of the pitch before you came back on. You've got a one-inch cut under your eye, Robbie, for God's sake. You're a grown man and a professional rugby player, not a little old lady who's been beaten up on her doorstep. And as for moaning about your place in the Scotland side – stop throwing line-out ball to me and Benny Kay and *that* might have more of a bearing on whether or not you get selected.

A year or two on, however, I have mellowed a bit. The guy was obviously angry and was probably naive, rather than simply pitiful and weak as I first thought. Look at it from his point of view. Saracens had been stuffed, he had had a poor game with his throwing and he had been sin-binned, a little unfairly. 'Want to pose for a picture, Rob?' Yeah, why not? 'Hacked off at Johnno, mate?' Too right, I am. Next thing he knows he's all over the papers bleating about his stitches and looking like that little old mugging victim. I doubt he thought ahead to how it would all be presented. In fact, Richard Hill phoned me a week or so after that stuff appeared. He said Robbie was upset with how the whole thing had been portrayed and wanted me to know that the press had exaggerated his distress. I felt sorry for Hilly, having to make the call. 'Look mate,' I said. 'It's all right, don't worry.' It was bizarre. I was being apologised to on behalf of the man to whom I was supposed to be apologising. 'No problem, let's forget it.'

I went to the England press conference on the Tuesday, where the incident was still the main topic on the media's agenda. Remember, I thought – and had been told – that, since the referee had seen the incident and dealt with it, that was the end of the matter. What I wanted to say was, 'Guys, it was one punch. Punches are thrown in every Premiership game. What's the big deal?' A pertinent case in point was that on the same day as my little fracas with Robbie Russell, the Newcastle prop Mickey Ward had thrown more than one big uppercut in a brawl during their match. He had been yellow-carded and that was the end of the matter. No hand-wringing in the press about that. Had I said this, of course, every columnist in Fleet Street would have been sharpening their pencils in mock horror: 'Rugby is a game for thugs ... the England captain says so!' They were giving me a hard enough time as it was, so wanting both to keep the peace and to play things down as much as possible, I was contrite. Too contrite, actually. You have to take responsibility for your actions, I told the press men, and what I had done was wrong. 'I'll take what's coming to me,' I added, thinking, of course, that nothing was coming to me.

How wrong I was. On the Wednesday evening, Clive came into our team meeting and handed me a sheet of paper informing me that there was to be a hearing that I needed to attend. I was pretty surprised given that I thought the whole thing was already done and dusted. I duly appeared in Bristol a few days later in front of a panel consisting of Robert Horner, the RFU's then disciplinary officer, a QC and a couple of RFU guys. I knew, as soon as they called the hearing, that they were going to ban me. They were not going to convene a panel and drag everyone down the M4, with the press camped outside, to take no action. These are people who literally live in fear of what the press headlines may be.

In my opinion, the whole thing seemed a bit of a sham. We had a lawyer, they had lawyers, and those boys can talk, plenty of it garbage. No wonder trials take so long. A month to decide whether the Major cheated on *Who Wants To Be A Millionaire*? Play the tape, listen to the coughs. Did he cheat? Of course he did. Job done in sixty minutes. I sat through several hours of long-winded chat, full of professional etiquette and niceties, trying not to think too much about what was going on in front of me because I felt that if I did I might explode and start demolishing the room. Cut through the crap, get to the point, it's the early hours of Tuesday morning in Bristol and we all know where this is going.

We pointed out that the RFU's own rule book laid down that once a referee had dealt with a matter on the pitch it was finished. Robert Horner said my case was 'exceptional'. No, it wasn't, we replied. The very existence of rules to deal with punching and subsequent punishment proved that it was not exceptional; by definition, if a law has been created it is to deal with a recognised problem.

We showed them a video of Mickey Ward's punches. Why had Mickey not been hauled up before them, too? There was no answer to this and they didn't really try to give one. The fact was that the whole thing was media-inspired. Horner, the chairman, gave the game away, despite asserting the coverage had played no part in matters. He said, 'As soon as I saw the incident and noted all the media attention on it, I decided not to read any newspaper coverage of the incident. However, the number of telephone calls I received from people expressing their disgust and horror at the incident persuaded me I needed to call a hearing.'

There were three responses to this and I wish I had made them because my legal team didn't do so and look where that got me. Firstly, Robert, the people who have phoned you obviously *have* read the papers. Secondly, can you not make your own mind up? And, thirdly, can I have your phone number so all my mates can ring you up and put my point of view?

Or ring you to ask why you are taking no action against Mickey Ward?

I doubt it would have cut any ice, though. As I say, I am sure a ban was inevitable. It all came down to how long. Three weeks was the answer. We appealed, which left me free to play in England's game against France, but got nowhere again. The guy in charge of the appeal said it was important that they 'protected the image of the game'. That was not the point of the appeal, or the original hearing, but they would brook no argument.

I considered taking matters further still. Here was a sporting governing body ignoring its own rules to make arbitrary decisions that affected my employment. There were serious legal issues involved, including certainty, equity and restraint of trade. The High Court might have taken an entirely different view of the matter. However, I ultimately felt that to take legal action against the RFU would only drag the whole affair out. It would also have set an unwelcome precedent. Better that the sport governs itself – though better still that it does so by its own rules, with logic, fairness and common sense.

I found the whole basis of the hearing and the ban frustrating. I could almost have accepted it – and certainly could have understood the RFU's point of view – if they had said to me, 'Martin, you're England captain. Because of that you can't go around punching people and because you did we are going to ban you for a week.' This was a position taken by Commodore Jeff Blackett, the Royal Navy's chief judge advocate, when he chaired the hearing into the McRae incident. He told me then, 'Your position in the game is that of an

Imanol Harinordoquy successfully takes us on during the World Cup semi-final against France.

I felt for French captain Fabien Galthié at the end of the match. He had announced he would retire after the World Cup and I'm sure he would have liked to go out with a win.

Lote Tuqiri scored early for Australia in the final. It wasn't a great start for us.

The highlight of the first half for us was this stunning try by Jason Robinson.

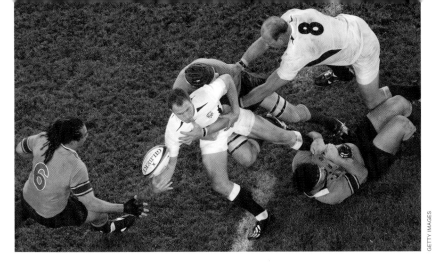

Mike Catt came on for Tindall towards the end of the final, giving us a much-needed fresh pair of legs.

Jonny's winning drop goal: the best thing I've ever seen on a rugby field.

Words can't describe how we felt when the final whistle blew.

Receiving the William Webb Ellis Cup from Australian Prime Minister John Howard.

Prince Harry came to the dressing room to congratulate us after the final. He's always very supportive of the team.

Posing in the dressing room with the trophy.

I wasn't expecting many people to show up for our arrival at Heathrow in the early hours of a freezing cold winter morning, but the scenes that greeted us were unbelievable.

8 December 2003. A surreal but enjoyable day kicked off with our victory parade in London. The size and enthusiasm of the crowd took my breath away.

We then headed to Buckingham Palace to meet the Queen and ended the day at Downing Street for a reception with Tony Blair. An amazing experience for the team.

icon and many people look up to you. But with this privileged position comes responsibility.'

I understand that, inevitably, my profile means I will be subject to closer scrutiny than other players. But does that mean I am playing to a different rule book than anyone else? And if so, maybe they could show it to me so I could have a flick through? Yes, I deserved to go to the sin-bin. I would have accepted a red card. But no other player would subsequently have been further punished in the way I was. The funny thing, by the way, is that the damage to Russell's cheek may well not even have been caused by me. A few weeks later, one of our players sidled up to me and said, 'I'm glad you smacked him, he was annoying me all game … and I gave him a few after you.' If you watch the video, you see Russell's head rocking back as he gets punched a number of times by unspecified Tigers in the ensuing melee.

I received plenty of mail in the wake of both of these incidents. Some of it described me as a disgrace to the game, an affront to humanity and a stranger to civilisation. A large proportion of letters, though, were positive. One nine-year-old lad wrote to me after the Robbie Russell affair saying, 'I loved it when you punched that Saracens bloke. It was wicked!' I think it is safe to assume he meant 'wicked' in the modern youngsters' sense rather than in the modern, hand-wringing sense. I am on the side of the nine-year-old. I was a fan before I became a player and I remember the excitement and drama when a match erupted. Rugby needs feistiness, a little extra edge. You can sense the supporters sitting forward in their seats – they know the game means something to the players. No one wants to see guys seriously hurt, but people do want to see big old units coming into contact, with pace and aggression.

I was not surprised by the press reaction, though. I have been involved in other high-profile incidents and their image of me as rugby's pantomime villain is pretty much fixed. The earliest, I guess, was in 1997. The All Blacks were playing fantastic rugby at that point and we were not given a chance as they arrived in the UK for a two-Test tour. One of the games was to be played at Manchester United's Old Trafford ground. It was the match made famous by our hooker Richard Cockerill's aggressive response to the New Zealanders' haka. As the Blacks started, Cockers inched forward until he was right in the face of his opposite number, Norm Hewitt. Hewitt, obviously just as fired up, shoved him backwards and I had to grab Cockers to prevent a fight kicking off before kick-off, so to speak.

That had set the tone for a feisty encounter and it continued throughout the match. I was not blameless. Early in the match, Justin Marshall, the AB scrum-half, had come offside to compete for the ball a couple of times. The third time, as he got the ball away, I caught him with a stiff arm – not even a proper punch – around the back of the head. He would hardly have felt it, though if the referee had seen the incident he would probably have given me a yellow card – this was before sin-bins – and that would have been an end to the matter. After all, Frank Bunce punched Neil Back square in the face right in front of the ref in the same game and he was carded. I played on, thinking nothing of it, and we eventually lost 25–8.

As the Kiwis trooped off, incidentally, we went on what

was later described as a 'lap of honour'. Josh Kronfeld, later my Leicester team-mate, has since said he and the rest of the All Blacks laughed at us as they watched. Just to set the record straight, we were not on any sort of victory parade. We were simply applauding the fans who had turned out to support us, Manchester not being a traditional hotbed of English rugby.

As we came into the changing room, someone said that John Hart, the All Blacks' coach, was very angry about both Cockerill's attitude to the haka – he had told the press, 'I thought it was totally disrespectful and I don't think it has any place on the football field'. – and my 'punch' on Justin Marshall. I was surprised he was upset at my actions. I don't recall him saying anything about Frank Bunce smacking Neil Back. I had a few words about the game in general with Robin Brooke and Ian Jones and then we all went our separate ways. Again, I thought that would be the end of the matter. That all changed the following day.

I woke to damning press headlines and a call from the RFU to say that they were going to suspend me for a game to avert the possibility of a citing by John Hart, which could have landed me with a thirty-day ban. What was more, a press release had gone out saying that, yes, I had whacked Marshall, I very much regretted it and would be making a full apology to the player. This irritated me, to say the least. Firstly, it was not a punch. Secondly, though I did regret my actions there was no way I would be apologising to anyone. These things happen in the heat of a match and as soon as the game is over they are forgotten. Was there any call for Bunce to say sorry to Backy? No, and Backy would not have wanted or expected an apology. Most players, Justin Marshall included I am sure, would not.

The 'apology' line also had the unwanted effect of extending the shelf life of the story. For days afterwards, reporters would keep asking whether I had said sorry to Marshall. I finally saw him at the reception after the second Test at Twickenham and he was not whingeing (though as we toured the southern hemisphere in the summer of 2003 he would describe what happened as a 'cheap shot'). It was ridiculous and vaguely pathetic. Jamie Joseph had stamped on Kyran Bracken's ankle in the Twickenham Test match in 1993 and I can't remember him apologising. It all smacked of double standards, which continue to this day. In England, we take this all terribly seriously. In the rest of the world, particularly in the southern hemisphere, they often seem to sweep it all under the carpet.

Danny Grewcock gets a dig or two in on Lawrence Dallaglio and the RFU ban him for it, causing him to miss our 2003 tour of New Zealand and Australia. During the Test against the All Blacks on the same tour, Ali Williams stamps on Josh Lewsey's head and the NZRFU take no action. On the 2001 Lions tour, Richard Hill was caught full in the face with a flying elbow. I didn't think it was an accident and it ended Hilly's tour with a Test and a half still to go. What was the match commissioner's view after he studied the tape? There was nothing in it and he was on the next plane out of there. The infamous game against South Africa at Twickenham in 2002 has been widely described as the most brutal and violent match in modern times, with the Springboks basically punching, kicking and stamping on England players from start to finish. What happened to the guilty men? Nothing.

Hypocrisy is not confined to those south of the equator. When my appeal over the Robbie Russell ban allowed me to play for England against France, the French made a lot of unhappy noises about my selection. Lo and behold, one of the French forwards gouged me badly towards the end of the game. Was Paris awash with protestors? Did the FFR immediately launch an enquiry and ban the guy? Not exactly. I came off the field seeing double out of my left eye and wondering at their double standards. I have been gouged before in matches against French sides and, at the end of the England versus France match in 2003, Julian White was kneed in the back of the head. Again, not a word from the FFR. No enquiry, no ban, no apology.

Clearly, I am not an angel. I straight-armed the Argentina scrum-half in a game in 1996 and could have cost us the match with my stupidity. I have been binned a few times for throwing punches and fair enough. I smacked Matt Dawson once, though one or two people might congratulate me for that! On a number of occasions, however, I am sure I have been punished because of my reputation.

Richmond were a tough league team a few years back, in the days when they numbered the Quinnells, Allan Bateman, Ben Clarke and Agustin Pichot in their ranks. We turned them over at their place one year on a cold, midweek January night. We were defensively very strong and their coach, John Kingston, later complained that we had cheated – the usual whine of the loser. The same season, we drew them in the cup and as Clarke and I tossed up he was badgering the referee, Steve Lander. 'Have you seen the video of the previous game, then?' Clarke was saying. 'Did you see all the cheating?' 'Yes, I watched it,' said Lander. This irritated me massively. We had beaten Richmond three tries to one, fair and square. This was just the usual Leicester-kill-the-ball argument, but I could imagine it affecting the refereeing.

Some twenty minutes into the game I found myself in the middle of a ruck near the touchline. I was trying to compete for the ball and slow it down, but legally – I was on my feet and onside. As Pichot went to pick it up I managed to put my foot on it and kick it out of his hands. The Richmond players in the vicinity immediately started shouting about the sin bin and Lander obliged, saying at the time that I had played the ball with my hand. Now, if I had played the ball with my hand it would also have been legal. As soon as Pichot picked the ball up, as long as I was onside – which I was, coming through the middle of the ruck – I had every right to tackle him or grab the ball. Off I went and they scored in that time to end up winning the game. Cue headlines: 'Johnson blows fuse.' Unbelievable.

At the subsequent hearing at the East India Club (on the same day, Austin Healey, up for stamping on London Irish scrum-half Kevin Putt's head, employed the brilliantly imaginative defence of, 'It was the only place I could put my foot') Lander gave a quite different explanation. Now, rather bizarrely, he said something along the lines of: 'I saw Johnson use his foot. I thought that was illegal. I've since talked to lots of other referees and they all said they thought it was illegal as well. But actually it's not illegal.' It was pathetic. I could have accepted it if he had held his hand up and said, 'Sorry, my mistake, I thought you had used your hand offside in the ruck.' It may or may not have cost us the cup tie, but I could live with it. In light of his about-turn, the disciplinary committee had little choice but to rescind the yellow card. Of course, all the newspapers immediately apologised for those 'Johnson blows fuse' headlines and published massive 'Johnson wrongly sent to bin' stories. Not. Funny, that.

It was a similar story when I was yellow-carded by David McHugh for my 'stamp' on John Leslie in our 1999 Calcutta Cup game against Scotland. We had started well, with Danny Luger and Tim Rodber both scoring, but the Scots came back at us to shorten our lead and it was turning into quite a close game. We were trying to reassert some control and had an attacking ruck. As I ran towards the play, I saw the Kiwi centre, John Leslie, lying at the back of the ruck, slowing down our ball. Tim Rodber had seen it, too, and we each had the same intention: to ruck him out. Any player lying there would have expected it just the same. Incredibly, though, as I ran in I stood on Leslie's throat with my left foot. I clearly remember thinking, 'How the hell have I done that?'

I was very lucky – as was John, obviously – because I had long studs on that day and if I had caught him with those it could have been extremely serious. I guess I must have used the flat part of the boot between the front and back studs. I looked up at David McHugh with a look of utter and quite genuine amazement, incredulity even, on my face. I said, 'I can't believe I've done that.' To his credit, he gave me a yellow card rather than a red and I wandered away, still mystified. It was only later, on watching the tape, that I realised what had happened. I always plant my left foot and go into the ruck with my right. Tim Rodber had got there fractionally before me. He had caught Leslie with his knee, causing him to roll away on to his back just as I put my left boot down – on his neck.

There is absolutely no way that I would deliberately kick a player in the head or tread on his throat. The idea is ludicrous. It was simply that, running at a ruck at 75 per cent of top speed, I just didn't have time to react to his movement. I had been cut on the scalp myself in the same match by a flying Scottish boot. It had been unintentional, clearly, so that was that. It happens all the time in training. John Leslie knew that and knew that it had been an accident. I went up to him after the match ended and said, 'Look mate, sorry about that, I didn't mean it.' He was fine. Kenny Logan was standing next to him and he looked at me in astonishment, saying, 'I'm amazed you're even bothering to apologise.' They had the professional rugby players' understanding of what had happened. Jim Telfer, the Scotland coach, accepted my story, too, and the SRU sought no further action, while putting out a statement stressing that 'the minimum recommended sentence in Scotland for a first offence for a kick or stamp to the head would normally be twenty-six weeks'.

This told its own story, but some elements of the press, of course, saw it differently. I had given a series of interviews in which I had explained that I had not acted deliberately. One of the journalists wrote this up in a very sarcastic way: 'Johnson says it was an accident . . . yeah, right! A likely story!' That made me angry. If the guy wasn't going to believe what I said, why should I bother talking to him? I wasn't going to lie.

Chris Goddard, the *Leicester Mercury*'s rugby reporter, came up to me at the club a few days later and asked me how I felt when things were getting personal. I said I didn't know they were, so he advised me to have a peek at *The Times*. Aadel Kardooni, our scrum-half at the time, had written a letter to the paper defending me against a piece in one of the nationals. Some columnist I had never met – and who had no idea about my character or personality – had really got stuck into me. The general gist was that I was a violent neanderthal. To anyone who gave a damn it might have been hurtful. I found it laughable

The media love to hype up 'foul play' but the irony is that they often miss the real nasty stuff. There are a few dirty players in the Premiership, guys who are known throughout the system, but they never seem to get picked up on by the press.

As I have said, rugby is a game of physical confrontation – if you are weak or passive you will lose – but illegal violence in matches is actually amazingly rare. Given what goes on, you would think people would lose their cool much more often than they do. There is the odd shot here and there, a bit of shoe dished out for blatant ball-killing, but it's not a lot and it's not a major problem. Anyway, there are plenty of opportunities to hurt someone legally in a match if you so wish. A big tackle – like Josh Lewsey's hit on Mat Rogers when we played Australia away in 2003 – hurts every bit as much.

I missed the real fighting era, the seventies, by a distance, though there have been a few hard men knocking around in my time, too. The All Black prop Richard Loe, whom I played against in New Zealand, was probably the toughest character I have come across; a pretty uncompromising customer. We played against his Waikato side, I saw him in action in a brawl and he was not one to cross, but by and large the modern game is so fast that there is not the time for violence. Most rucks and mauls now only have four or five players in them and the guys involved are much more concerned with gaining possession or stopping the opposition using it than dishing out punches. It wouldn't bother them anyway. The people you really fear on the pitch are the guys who can hurt you with their pace and skill, not their knuckles.

If it does happen, you tend to accept it as part of the game. If Danny Grewcock punches me in the side of the head in a match my attitude will be, 'Cheers, Grew, nice one ...' and I will get on with the game. You do not even really feel it, with the adrenalin flowing. Next week, we are on the same side internationally and I am watching his back against France, or vice versa. Neither of us are going to hold a grudge against the other for what has happened in the Premiership.

The times when you feel like doing something but don't are far more numerous than those where you act. If someone goes over the line — in this country, at least, we do not kick each other in the head, gouge guys' eyes or grab their testicles — I suppose the victim might seek retribution later. I can only think of a couple of times in my career where I have really wanted to pay someone back, both for silly little things. Alessandro Troncon, the Italian scrum-half, spat at me during a game. That was pretty disgusting and I would have liked to get hold of him. Philippe Carbonneau, another feisty little No. 9, threw a piece of turf at my head — great shot, actually — at Twickenham in 1997 as he ran back in glee after they had scored the try which took them into the lead. I thought, 'Right, you little b*****d, I'll get you back for that!'

and ran after him, muttering dark threats, until two or three of the French lads got hold of me and I realised how ridiculous I looked.

I think the main problem with the current system as it relates to on-pitch incidents and their punishment is its total lack of consistency – the thing that players want more than anything. If you throw a punch at someone, there is a range of potential outcomes. You get seen by the ref and he penalises you. You get seen by the ref and he sin-bins you. You get seen by the ref and he sends you off. You don't get seen by the ref, but it's picked up by the media or the opposition, you are cited and dealt with. You don't get seen by the ref, it's spotted by the media, but no one cites you so nothing happens. Add to that the revolutionary approach of the RFU in the Robbie Russell case: you get seen by the ref and he sin-bins you . . . *then* the RFU convenes a hearing and you are suspended. Such is the arbitrary nature of rugby's 'justice' system.

One week a player is sin-binned for 'stamping', the next week the same thing is just 'rucking out'. Austin Healey lands on Kevin Putt's head and receives, quite properly, a lengthy ban. Richard Arnold of Newcastle kicks Austin in the head at Welford Road and gets a yellow card. Some people might have thought he deserved a commendation, but that is another story.

We played Bath at home and Gareth Cooper, their Welsh scrum-half, threw a punch at me after the whistle had gone following a scuffle for the ball, right in front of the crowd. He missed me and I just swayed out of the way. Because he is only a little fellow the crowd all burst out laughing. I said to the ref, 'Is that a penalty for us then?' He just said, 'No, no, settle down you two and play on.' I said, 'Settle down? I haven't done anything, mate. He's just thrown a punch at me.' 'No, no,' he said. 'Play on.' If it had been the other way around and I had thrown the punch at Cooper you can bet your bottom dollar it would have been a penalty and possibly a yellow card. Even worse, if I had thrown a punch at Cooper that the referee hadn't seen I could, and probably would, have been cited for it and banned. Leicester have a tradition of not citing and so that was the end of the matter. People will point out that I could do a lot of damage to a guy of eleven or twelve stone, but frankly he could do a lot of damage to me. He's a strong lad and if he caught me right he could easily break my jaw. And anyway that isn't how the laws of the game are framed: backs can hit forwards. It was at least a penalty.

Similarly, we played Llanelli at Welford Road in a tight game in the European Cup. I had been sin-binned for hitting their prop Martin Madden with an open-hand slap to get him off me after he grabbed me at a ruck. In the same game, I was involved in an altercation with Stephen Jones, the fly-half, and he punched me. Amusing scenes of Johnson lying on the ground, arms spread wide, looking up at Jones. Afterwards the line the press took was that this was the new, non-retaliatory Johnson. Were you cool under pressure, Johnno? Were you thinking about yellow cards? Are you pleased with your new discipline? As far as I can remember, there was not a single call for Jones to be punished for assaulting me on the field of play and no series of why-oh-why articles questioning the state of rugby, refereeing and society in an age when guys can get away with punching on the pitch. And Jones was not banned.

The system needs changing, so that incidents are dealt with by someone who understands the game and who has an empathy for the players. The guys currently sitting in judgment over us have not the slightest idea about modern, professional rugby. Things happen on the field which have a bearing on players' reactions and unless you have the insight and understanding to appreciate the initial spark you are left with the bare videotape of an 'incident'. The amateur regulators who dish out the suspensions may be costing professional players a substantial amount of money in match fees. That is no way to run a professional game.

A full-time paid commissioner responsible for discipline, perhaps a recently retired player, should be appointed to oversee incidents. Referees should have the power to put players on report, as happens in rugby league. With almost every Premiership game now on tape, the commissioner should collate and examine all the videos at the start of the following week. His judgment could be handed down quickly, with no need to go to the trouble and expense of putting together quasi-legal panels at hearings around the country. Having one guy overseeing all decisions would certainly create consistency, as he would be able to set each incident in the context, firstly, of the match and, secondly, of his previous decisions. The certainty, when you step on to the pitch, that X will happen to you if you do Y, would be welcomed by all players. Such a commissioner would not get everything right, but it would be better than the current rather ad hoc system.

CHAPTER FIFTEEN

A LIFE MORE ORDINARY

It's the sort of question you get asked now and then: what do you do in your spare time, Johnno? I don't know whether people expect some exotic, magical off-pitch existence, but if they do I'm afraid they're disappointed. The truth is fairly dull. For starters, I don't actually have much free time. If I'm not training or playing, I'm travelling up and down motorways to England sessions, testimonial dinners or for sponsor requirements. I'm not moaning. I do very well financially out of it and, at least for part of the time, I get to mess around with a rugby ball and my mates, something I still very much enjoy, but when I get home I lead pretty much the same life I would have led if I had continued working in the bank.

I surprised myself recently by getting into koi carp. It could be an all-consuming hobby if you let it, but I think it's under control. I like music, mainly late seventies stuff, like the Jam. We played some of their stuff in the Lions changing rooms in Australia and it made a nice change from the modern dance stuff most of the boys listen to. Dorian 'Nobby' West is also a fan and just after we won the Grand Slam, the two of us formed about twenty per cent of the crowd at a gig by a tribute band called the Jamm, in Ibstock. Close your eyes and you could almost imagine it was the real thing, though I'm obviously too young to have seen the original group live, given that they split when I was twelve.

Most nights when I get home, I do pretty much what everyone else does. When I get the chance, I crash out either with a book or magazine or in front of the TV. I'm a big fan of *The Simpsons* and like to catch the double bill on Sky at 7p.m. I like documentaries, things on the Discovery Channel and the History Channel. Sports-wise, I can turn anything on if I'm in the mood and I can turn anything off if I'm not. One thing I tend not to watch is rugby. Some of the guys will go home and watch *The Rugby Club* or even play rugby-based video games, but not me, thanks. If I watch games I find myself getting all wound up and I like to relax when I get the opportunity.

I like a bit of rugby league, a game we have drawn on since turning professional, particularly in the forwards where we now get our hands on the ball much more than we did. People talk about a unified game and it is something I would quite like to see. New players and new blood, plus a genuinely national club competition, would be a great thing. I can't see it happening, though, because there's too much history and that old class-divide rubbish. I remember when Bath played Wigan in those league and union games five or more years ago, and all the Wigan fans were chanting about how much they hated the fifteen-man game. I just thought, 'Why? Why do you *hate* rugby union? It's just a game. Watch it if you want, don't if you don't.' But those attitudes are very deeply ingrained.

I read autobiographies and thrillers by the likes of Tom Clancy or John Grisham or sports books and mags. I've got a retentive mind and wide-ranging interests, and the combination has earned me the reputation of being a bit of a Statto. People seem to have this image of me sitting around poring over football programmes from the fifties or the yellowing sports pages of papers from years gone by. 'Want your tea now, Johnno?' 'Not yet, love – I'm just trying to memorise the Olympic winners of the long jump since 1900.' Not entirely fair, but I think my reputation as a sport trivia bore arose the first time I got involved with the England squad.

We had a New Year training session in Lanzarote in 1992. On the first night, someone organised a quiz that was ripped off from the *Daily Telegraph*'s end-of-year sports quiz. It was full of questions like: 'Who is the only man to have scored first-class runs and a World Cup goal?' Answer: Geoff Hurst – quite easy. There were some slightly harder ones, though, such as: 'Why did Sir Garfield Sobers never fulfil his football ambition to play in the English league?' Answer: He found it too cold to wear shorts in England. I was in a team with Will Carling and Rob Andrew. Unbeknown to them, I had already done the quiz with my dad, back home in Harborough. Not surprisingly, therefore, I kept coming up with the answers. Rob fancied himself a bit on the old trivia. I would give an answer and he would frown, shake his head and say: 'No, can't be that.' 'Trust me,' I would say. 'I'm right.' After a while, they started looking at me with a mixture of scorn and awe – like I was some kind of amazing sports anorak, horribly dull but somehow weirdly fascinating. We won by miles and a legend was born.

I guess the sport I follow most closely is American football. I read the NFL mag to keep abreast of the latest developments across the Atlantic or I'll pick up a back issue of *Sports Illustrated* to re-read one of their classic articles about the sport. I've been interested since I was a youngster, playing junior club rugby. Back in the eighties, televised sport was nowhere near the level it is at now. There was *Match of the Day* for your football, the Test cricket and a bit of rugby league. The rugby union internationals came around now and then and on Sundays there was *Ski Sunday* and *Rugby Special*. That was about it. On *Rugby Special* you could watch Rosslyn Park and Richmond running round on a muddy Athletic Ground in front of 1,500 people, but it wasn't exactly compelling. In fact, if I had grown up near there instead of near the Tigers – where there was a bit of glamour and something to aspire to – I might never have had a career in rugby. However, in about 1983, they started showing American football on Channel Four.

It was an hour-long programme, with the highlights of the best game of the previous week – possibly the best way to watch it, because there are a lot of breaks and standing around in NFL. It was just something different to watch, something much more exciting and glitzy and entertaining, much more of a show, than anything in British sport at the time. It was on around 6p.m., which led to battles with my mum, because she wanted us to come for our tea and Will and I wanted to watch the telly. I can still remember some of those matches now – like the Washington Redskins against the (then) LA Raiders, with huge blokes running around smashing into each other and long, 50-yard passes being thrown. It was full of characters and drama and seemed a million miles away from Nigel Starmer-Smith and *Rugby Special*. There, if anything untoward happened, the cameras would cut away and there would be a bit of harrumphing and 'oh-we-don't-want-to-see-that-in-the-game'. With the NFL, it was all shown, in slo-mo, and it was talked about by the commentators – and rightly so, because it's all part of the game. The Redskins had a posse of guys called the Fun Bunch. Whenever they scored they would get together in the end zone and go through this orchestrated 'high fives' routine. One day, the Dallas Cowboys took exception to this and another mass fight broke out. It was great entertainment. Would you rather see that or foot-ballers rolling around on the floor pretending they've been badly hurt in a tackle when they haven't? I think that's a far worse example to set youngsters than a couple of guys throwing a few inconsequential punches.

By the late eighties, lots of American football teams had sprung up around the country and one of the guys I played rugby with was also playing at the Leicester side, the Panthers. They were looking for youth players, so I went down and got involved. I was a county rugby player and I had been with England schools. People used to look at me and ask why I wanted to play this silly game? I think there was something of an undercurrent suggesting that British American football teams were full of 'wannabes', blokes who enjoyed strapping on the pads and running around, but who were basically wasting their time. Nothing could be further from the truth, certainly in Leicester. At that time, the Panthers were fitter, stronger, better trained and more professional than the Tigers just down the road. They trained three times a week in season, not twice, and they had masses more to learn and memorise, in terms of tactics and game plans, than their rugby counterparts.

Many of them spent a lot of their spare time lifting weights in the gym, too. Coaches were hired in from the States and guys came from places like Luton and Birmingham to get involved. Sean Payton, for example, came over from US college football to coach and play quarterback for us. Later he was offensive co-ordinator when the Giants went to the Superbowl and he now coaches the Cowboys in the NFL.

It was a good standard and it helped me with my rugby. Take defence – or defense: they were into aggressive tackling, making big hits on your opponent, whereas in rugby at that time it was all about grabbing the guy around the waist and slipping down to the ankles. I played a few games in positions like tight-end, outside linebacker and defensive end, and thoroughly enjoyed my time there. I mixed with guys from different backgrounds to the rugby crowd – a lot of them were doormen around the town, with some great stories from working the clubs – and there was none of the 'blazer-and-old-school-tie' stuff that rugby was full of. Having played the game, I obviously have a better understanding of it and I have continued to follow its fortunes. In its heyday, guys like Dan Marino and William 'The Fridge' Perry were fairly well known in the UK, but its popularity here has now declined. They started trying to show games live, or partially live, which was fine until you got a bad game and people just turned off. Also, British sport is so much better covered now, with so many more channels, that the niche has probably disappeared.

A year or two back, Tetley's, one of my sponsors, and the *Observer Sports Monthly* got together and took me over to San Francisco to spend some time with the 49ers. That was a fantastic experience and I got a taste of the buzz England rugby fans probably have when they win competitions to come to watch us training. For the 49ers, as it obviously can be for us, it was probably just another day at work. For me, it was awesome. Wanting to generate publicity for their sport in the UK, the NFL PR guys were keen to get me involved. 'Come on, Martin,' they were saying. 'Let's get you on to the field and you can do some stuff with the guys!' It was a bit embarrassing, to be honest. I put myself in the players' places. It was a boiling hot, Californian summer's day. They wanted to get off that field as soon as training was over, grab a shower and go home. The last thing they needed was some lanky English bloke they had never heard of messing them around. Still, I didn't complain when they pinned down Jeff Garcia, the starting quarter-back, to throw me some passes. I was like a schoolboy being punted to by Jonny Wilkinson.

Afterwards, I was fortunate enough to sit down in the players' cafeteria and chat with some of them. As the headquarters of US rugby was located at Berkeley University, just down the road, they knew a little about our game. They were particularly interested in the fact that we don't wear pads or helmets, though I would if these boys were facing me. They had some incredible specimens – guys of 22 stone, with forearms like my thighs, who are quick as well as immensely powerful. Those kind of athletes permeate the whole of the US system. If ever they get their act together with rugby they will be able to build a world-beating side just from the castoffs of college football. Over there, if you don't make it into the professional setup, there is really nowhere to go – there's no equivalent of our football's professional Divisions One, Two and Three, so hundreds of very good players just drift out of sport altogether. Duncan Hall, Bob Dwyer's number two at Leicester in the nineties, was in charge of the US team for a while and I asked him why he didn't tap into this source of talent. The answer was that guys who had played college games, even in front of crowds of 40,000 people, which is fairly small by their standards, were pretty unenthusiastic about playing rugby, an almost unknown sport, in front of no one. I've just started writing a column for the NFL, but I wouldn't consider myself an expert on the game. I just find it interesting, probably as much for the off-field soap opera of million-dollar deals and extravagant lifestyles that surround it as for the sport itself.

Back home in England, the rest of my time tends to be taken up with family things, particularly since the arrival of Molly. I am never happier than when I am chatting to or playing with her. In some ways, I am even glad my career is coming to an end. I missed her – and Kay – like mad when I was away on tour in the summer of 2003 and for the early part of the Rugby World Cup, and when I am finished with rugby I will have more time to spend with the two of them. With a dozen or more years of top-level rugby behind me, I just hope I can still walk to play with her when she grows up! I have said before that Molly is the last thing I think about at night and the first thing I think about in the morning, and it's true. If I'm at home, I check on her before I turn in and she will be gurgling and chattering in the room next door when I wake up. She is so utterly dependent on Kay and me that it is almost frightening. I would like more children – I am one of three and I think three is a good number. I don't care if they're boys or girls. If I had a boy I would like him to be into sport, to be healthy, but I wouldn't push him to rugby – if he wanted to play, fine. You always feel a bit for the sons of famous sportsmen, because there is something to live up to, but I'm not exactly Ian Botham and if I had a lad he would almost certainly have more pace and a better step than his old man anyway.

What will I do when I retire? I'm quite drawn to coaching. I certainly feel that it's a very important element of rugby that has moved on tremendously since the old days. Then, you had a backs coach and a forwards coach, and before that, just a coach, and before that, no coach at all. Rugby is a game of very specific skills and in the professional era that has been recognised. Now, with England, we have a defensive coach, a guy who teaches throwing-in for the hookers, vision coaches, people in charge of the forwards, fitness experts . . . you name it. Clive has been criticised for bringing in such a large team, and there is always that danger of over-training, but, on balance, it's been a good thing. Modern rugby demands masses of analysis, way too much for one or two guys on their own. Our setup has taken a lot of the pressure and grind off the players and enables us to concentrate on playing. Besides, these guys don't just coach the senior squad. They go off around the country, working with youngsters and people throughout the representative age groups. I'm not sure that I would want to get involved at that sort of level, though. I think I'd be quite happy helping out with a bunch of lads at a junior club. There's much more to rugby than the top end, after all.

CHAPTER SIXTEEN

WORLD CUP HEAVEN

It's every rugby player's dream to lift the World Cup, but no England side had come close to doing so since 1991 and the defeat in the final against Australia. The 1995 campaign had turned into a Jonah Lomu-inspired nightmare. The 1999 Cup had been Jannie de Beer's moment in the spotlight, as he drop-kicked us out of the tournament at the first of the knockout stages.

With that single final appearance, then, our Rugby World Cup record had, some felt, been one of underachievement. Many critics felt that was about to change. The Zurich Rankings, based on results in the previous twelve months, said we were the world's number one team – and had us going into the tournament as favourites. Even some Australian, South African and New Zealand commentators were confidently predicting an England win on 22 November. It was an unusual feeling.

We had had a good summer, with three weeks off, three weeks spent in training, a further week at home and then three Test matches, one against Wales and two against the French. The balance between working hard as a group and spending too much time together felt right: you need to get away with your family and friends, and it was a policy Clive would carry through to the Rugby World Cup itself, with wives, girlfriends and children allowed to join us in Australia if they wanted. With all the build-up and then the actual tournament, the players would be looking at fourteen or fifteen weeks together. You can go 'stir crazy' if you're not careful and having your other half around occasionally can provide a welcome distraction.

We knew that if we came out on top in those three summer games we stood a good chance of going on to take the world record for consecutive wins – our first World Cup fixture, against Georgia, was likely to be our eighteenth straight victory. But it wasn't even in our minds. Our mantra had long been 'a Test match is a Test match' and each is as important as any other, but these were genuine warm-ups for the main event of the year. Yes, we wanted to win them and, yes, the record would have been nice but we had to keep our eyes on the World Cup itself. That meant we did not necessarily field our strongest side for all games. That didn't matter, when a team made up of younger guys and others who were perhaps not automatic first-choice players travelled to Cardiff to play Wales. They dominated them up front and ran them ragged in the backs, quietening the home fans by running in five tries in a 9–43 win. The same team, backed up by a few first-choice players such as Mike Tindall, Ben Cohen and Josh Lewsey, then faced the French the following weekend in an exciting match in front of a full house in Marseille.

The atmosphere was immense and left me wondering why Les Bleus don't play Six Nations games there. They love their rugby in the south of France and had turned out in force to support the home team. A lot of England fans had travelled down to enjoy the weather and it couldn't have been any bigger had it been a full-on Test with something tangible hanging on the outcome. France had never been beaten at the Stade Velodrome and unfortunately that record stayed intact. They edged the match 17–16, though we could have won it with a Paul Grayson drop-goal that sailed wide in the dying seconds. It meant our chance of that record streak of wins had gone, but collectively we took a lot of positives home with us. We carried those through to the following Saturday, when a much stronger England side took on and fairly comfortably beat a weaker French XV 45–14. It had been a pretty good summer, then, if not quite a perfect one. One issue was a feeling – unusual for us, with our long season – that we were, if anything, slightly short of game time. Lawrence Dallaglio and Phil Vickery had both been injured and had not played in any of the matches, while myself and Jonny had been pulled off after about forty-five minutes of the third. But we had worked very hard and we got on the plane to Australia feeling fit, confident and looking forward to the start of the tournament.

Squad selection had been tough. A lot of guys had put their hands up and some of them were going to be disappointed. This is always the way, particularly given the tactical decisions to be made. Do you take four or five props? Do you take four locks or three and a back-rower who can play in the second row? These are tough calls and we all felt for two guys in particular. Graham Rowntree was very unlucky. He had been first choice in the Grand Slam team and also a major element of our summer tour Down Under, part of the six-man pack that kept New Zealand out in that win in Wellington. He had done nothing wrong but he still missed out as the management decided to opt for four props. Phil Vickery and Trevor Woodman were pencilled in as the starting tight-head and loose-head. Julian White travelled as Vicks' back-up and Jason Leonard, with his crucial ability to cover both sides of the front row, was the other reserve. Simon Shaw was also unfortunate. He, too, had played well in the summer but he lost out as Clive went for myself, Ben Kay and Danny Grewcock, with Martin Corry – who had, himself, played exceptionally well – as back-up. Austin Healey's utility skills always put him in the frame, but he had suffered a nasty injury in the spring and, though he had done very well to get back into contention, he missed out as Mike Catt was brought back. Catty's was a surprising selection, as he had not been named in the original party and had been out of the international picture for the previous two years, but his World Cup showings would later demonstrate that it was a sound move. Ollie Smith and James Simpson-Daniel were a couple of young lads who were there or thereabouts but missed the cut in the end. Overall, I felt Clive and his team had got the selection right; that knowledge didn't make it any easier as I chatted to guys like Rowntree and Shaw when the travelling group was announced.

We had reconnoitred our Perth training base in the summer, so we had a fairly seamless arrival in Oz, flying out on the Wednesday night and arriving on the West Coast in the early hours of Friday. That morning and the next we spent some time in the gym on a little light work, just trying to get over the jetlag, beginning our Test week preparation ahead of the Georgia game, as we would back home, on the Monday. Perth is a nice city – it's home to around 1.5 million people but it has a very laid-back, personal feel to it. We were based in the Sheraton, a mile or so outside the city centre, and although there were plenty of English and South African fans around for the big pool match, the guys were able to stroll into town for a coffee without too much bother. It's a fairly warm place, even in October, the Aussie spring, and we felt the heat on the training park. There had been a lot of talk before the tournament started about how, as one of the older teams, we might feel the heat but that didn't worry me unduly: most of our matches would be played in the relative cool of the evening to coincide with TV scheduling in Europe.

We were lucky that Georgia were our first opponents, rather than South Africa or Samoa. Lacking a little match fitness and sharpness, we needed to get a game under our belts. Although we won by 84–6, it was by no means easy: they were big, physical guys and they flew into the tackles with relish. When you haven't played for a while the contact comes as a bit of a shock and they gave us a very good workout. It took us a couple of days to get over the stiffness and soreness. We also picked up a few injuries: Danny Grewcock had broken his toe in the warm-up and Mike Tindall, Lawrence Dallaglio and Matt Dawson were all hurt during the eighty minutes. But the biggest blow was the loss of Richard Hill who had pulled up with a hamstring tear.

Hilda is a world-class flanker and a key player in our team, and his injury was to prove both frustrating and unsettling. At first, it looked fairly minor and the medical staff were confident that he would be back in action the following week. That became a familiar refrain as the tournament wore on and the hammy stubbornly refused to clear up. Clive was criticised by some pundits for giving conflicting reports about the injury, but there was no intention to deceive anyone – Hilly seemed to have good days and bad days and just as you thought it was coming right he would fail another fitness test. He eventually came back only in time for the semi-final, which shows how highly we rated him: other players might have been sent home and replaced.

The number of niggles and strains floating around after just one fixture was a little disturbing, particularly because it meant we couldn't really train properly ahead of the match against the Springboks. Dawson and Hill were both ruled out and there was more potential bad news during the week when Kyran Bracken's long-term back problem flared up again. It is something he has suffered with for a long time; his back goes into spasm and he can't move properly; at one point, a day or two out from the game, he couldn't tie his own shoelaces. We called Austin Healey, but he had tweaked his Achilles so Martyn Wood, the Wasps scrum-half, was flown out as standby in case Andy Gomarsall had to step into the starting line-up for Kyran. In the event, Kyran recovered for the game and poor old Martyn had to turn round and fly back to the UK after a few hours on Australian soil, a fate that would also befall Austin later in the tournament.

It was a strange week – Clive later said it was the most stressful and anxious seven days he had known in rugby to that point and I have to agree. There was no getting away from the events of a year before, our 53–3 defeat of South Africa at Twickenham amid a flurry of flying elbows, knees and fists. Our World Cup encounter had been looming since that match, spiced up by Corné Krigé's defiant post-match statement: 'This isn't Perth. We'll see you in Perth.' All year, I only had to be walking down the street in London and some South African would come up and say 'We'll kill you in Oz.' Now here we were and, not surprisingly, it was all the media wanted to talk about. It had been billed by some as the biggest pool game of the tournament and it was certainly the biggest of the World Cup at that point.

Additionally, and unusually in the history of encounters between England and South Africa, we went into the match as very strong favourites to win it. That just added to the enormous pressure and nervousness that the whole team was feeling. If we had lost it would have been a huge downer: we had flown out as the world's best team, on paper, and in a pretty confident mood. If we lost, it would have made our progress in the World Cup much harder. A lot of our impetus would have disappeared, our morale would have been hit and we would have been faced with a barrage of headlines along the lines of 'England Blow It Again'. Worst of all, we'd almost certainly have to play the All Blacks in the quarter-final instead of, probably, Wales.

It was a tough game, as we had known it would be. We started brightly, making forays down their wings, but they applied pressure on us and we started to give away penalties. Fortunately, their fly-half, Louis Koen, missed three kicks at goal in the first half. The score was level at 6–6 as we went in at half time. It was a calm dressing room, with no panic and no ranting and raving. We focused on the need to avoid infringing and to retain possession and returned to the pitch.

The turning point came when Lewis Moody charged down a clearance kick by Koen and Will Greenwood raced on to the rebound to score. Jonny converted and then dropped a goal fairly quickly afterwards. At that point you could feel the wind go out of their sails as they realised they were not going to win. They rallied, though, and nearly scored at the end, but by the time the final whistle went we had racked up nineteen unanswered points to take the result 25–6. The general consensus on the outside seemed to be that we had been fortunate to score the try. Rubbish. There was nothing fortunate about it; we work hard on getting pressure on kickers and Lewis had done very well to get the charge-down.

The Australian press were, predictably, unimpressed. 'Is That All You've Got?' ran one headline, over a picture of Jonny kicking another penalty. In many ways, it was a compliment: this was the Springboks we'd beaten, after all, and nineteen points was not a small margin.

The disappointment was echoed in the English press and by some fans. Essentially, it was brought about by false expectation. People thought we would run in lots of tries and win by a huge margin. But circumstances had changed since we had done that at Twickenham. The South Africans had retained only a couple of players from that earlier game and their new-look team was much more impressive. The back row was dynamic and aggressive, their line-out was functioning well and they had more pace and adventure in their back line. Their defence was also much tighter. Added to that, very rarely do top teams beat each other by huge margins in World Cups. We weren't the only ones to find it hard going, either. Australia struggled a little against Argentina and Ireland in their group, but they had come through and the Wallabies knew what we knew: it was all about winning your pool.

The Australian reaction was not surprising. Those of us who had travelled south with the Lions in 2001 were used to their biased, one-eyed nature and we had experienced it earlier in the summer, too. They call us Poms 'whingers' but they are the world leaders in the art. At one point, they wheeled out John Eales on TV to talk about our supposed 'truck and trailer' mauling style. Eales was trying to suggest that our mauls were little more than illegal obstructing tactics. But when they rolled the video he could find no evidence. 'Ooh, that's marginal,' he'd say, or 'Ooh, that looks a bit . . .' It was laughable, but the fact that it was a non-story didn't stop the Aussie press getting all hot under the collar about it. No mention, of course, was made of Australians diving into the side to pull down rolling mauls illegally.

Importantly, the match had been played in a good spirit with none of the thuggery that had marred our previous meeting. Some elements of the media did their best to dredge up controversy over one incident right at the end. Dallaglio had found himself on the floor with a hand over his face and had pushed out to get the guy off him. His fist found Thinus Delport's face and apparently cut his cheek – though Delport looked straight at the camera immediately afterwards and didn't seem to have a mark on him. Both players were adamant afterwards that it had been nothing and the South African management themselves didn't seem bothered. But the media made a lot of fuss about it. I guess it was to be expected: this was the World Cup and we were all under the microscope; the smallest thing was bound to be blown up out of all proportion.

Corné Krigé made his trademark defiant noises to the papers

afterwards. 'We know how to beat England,' he said, 'and we know how to beat New Zealand, too.' Bit surprising, under the circumstances, I thought – if you know how to beat us, Corné, why didn't you? – but that's the Boks for you: they believe they belong at the top and they won't be happy until they're back there.

All week, our try-scorer Will Greenwood had trained with the knowledge that, back home, his wife, Caro, was having serious problems with her pregnancy. They had lost their first baby, Freddie, just after his birth and now Caro was in intensive care, with doctors fighting to save their second. To be on the other side of the world, at least twenty-four hours away, must have been a nightmare for him. I had been told about the situation but most of the boys were in the dark, though they realised something was amiss as the week dragged on. Will had asked the management not to discuss it because he didn't want them worrying about anything other than the South Africans, but he obviously couldn't completely hide how he was feeling. One morning he was late down for a meeting, which is pretty much unheard of. His body language told how worried he was. For him to perform as he did, both in training and in the game itself, was incredible and a tremendous testament to his courage and character. As I write, Caro and the baby are doing fine, so the story has a happy ending. At the time, it certainly put rugby into context for the whole squad.

From the sunshine of Perth, we headed for the rain and cloud of Melbourne.

All of the pressure of the South Africa week had evaporated to be replaced by a flat feeling as we looked ahead to

Samoa. We tried to counter any complacency by telling ourselves that the islanders would be very 'up' for the game with us. They would have known that they were unlikely to qualify from a group containing us and the Springboks and, until then, had faced only Georgia and Uruguay. They had played well in those games and had won them both. They would be straining at the leash – an unnerving thought when you look at the size and physicality of some of their guys – and this would almost be their 'final'. But whatever we said to ourselves, we struggled to believe it; with the toughest game of the pool stages out of the way, it was almost as though the job had been done and all we had to do now was get the next two matches over and done with.

We were rudely awakened within the first few minutes of the kick-off.

Samoa played fantastic rugby from the off, spinning the ball very wide and running it at us from deep inside their 22. They broke a few tackles, were quickly on the board with a penalty and then scored one of the best tries of the tournament, a flowing move in which virtually every player seemed to touch the ball about five times. We were 10–0 down and it felt like we were chasing shadows as the play switched from one touchline to the other and back again, almost in the blink of an eye.

At that point, I was seriously worried: if they were going to carry on playing mistake-free rugby at that pace, we were going to struggle. For the whole of the first twenty minutes, there was only one side in it. We hardly touched the ball and when we did get our hands on it we made error after error – we lost our own line-out, we knocked on and were repeatedly penalised by the referee. In contrast to the flawless kicking of Earl Va'a, Jonny proved he was mortal by missing a couple of fairly easy shots at goal. We gradually came back into things, scoring after half an hour when Neil Back touched down as we drove over from a line-out, but we went in at half-time down 16–13. The game plan had been to keep hold of the ball and try to use our forward power to pressurise and tire them: get line-out ball and drive it at them, get scrummage ball and drive that at them, too. But we had been turned over too easily and had not really got going.

They had been tiring towards the end of the first forty minutes, with guys going down for little injury breaks, and the hope, as we sat in the changing room, was that our superior fitness would start to tell on them and help us, belatedly, to take control. To some extent, this worked: we certainly had the upper hand in the forwards and won a penalty try after they collapsed a scrum close to their line. But though they never really looked like getting over our line a second time they continued to make regular inroads into our half, we continued to give away penalties and Va'a continued to pot them. On sixty minutes they still had the lead, at 22–20, though by this point I did at least feel we would win – I was sure we could get into their half and score enough points to take us clear. When Iain Balshaw scored from a lovely Wilkinson cross kick and Phil Vickery dummied over from close range for his first international try, we knew the game was safe.

No doubt about it, though, Samoa gave us a real fright. They had had everything to gain and nothing to lose: if they tried something and it came off, great. If it didn't, and we scored a try, so what? People expected that. Freed from those shackles, they played the game of their tournament, a game the World Cup needed. Everyone other than England fans would have been rooting for the islanders, and rightly so. Everyone wants the underdogs to come through and they nearly did. Unfortunately, they couldn't repeat their feat against South Africa the following weekend. The Boks had worked them out a lot better than we had and ended comfortable winners.

Our match had been marred by a bizarre incident in the dying seconds. Mike Tindall got injured on the far side of the pitch and had gone off the field for treatment. Initially, they wouldn't let him go back on and they wouldn't let Dan Luger, warmed up to replace him, on either. The official apparently told Dave Reddin, the England fitness coach who was pitch-side for us, five times that he couldn't get Dan into the action. Frustrated by the delay, Clive eventually used the radio link to order Dave to send Luger on, irrespective of the official. At just about the same moment, Tinds rejoined the fray. For a few seconds at the end of the match, then, we had sixteen players on the field. I've since been told that that sort of thing actually happens a lot – with all the to-ing and fro-ing, it is not uncommon for teams to have an extra guy on for a moment. It would probably all have been ignored but for an incident after the final whistle involving Reddin and one of the officials, the New Zealander Steve Walsh. They had words in the tunnel, Walsh squirted water at Dave and the whole thing got blown out of proportion.

An investigation was begun, focusing mainly on the fact that we had deliberately ignored a direct instruction to keep

Luger off. A lot was made of this – the general view seemed to be that this was yet more evidence of the 'typical English arrogance' the southern hemisphere countries seem to find everywhere they look – and a hearing was called in Sydney. It seemed to drag on for days, with jibes flying around that we needed sixteen men to beat Samoa and talk of the penalties we might face. At worst, the tournament officials could dock us points and move us into second place in the group. While we thought that was unlikely, there was a feeling that people were gunning for us and would have relished an opportunity to put us in our places. In the end, common sense prevailed. We were fined £10,000, Dave received a two-match touchline ban and Walsh was suspended for one match 'for inappropriate behaviour' – pretty much unheard-of in a case involving a match official. Looking back, it feels now like a storm in a teacup but at the time it seriously affected our focus for the next match.

Luckily, that was against Uruguay. A lot of guys got their first starts, including Dorian West, Danny Grewcock, Andy Gomarsall and Martin Corry, who had only just arrived back in Australia after flying home for the birth of his first child, Eve. The dice were always heavily loaded against the South Americans. They were a team of amateurs and those sides will always struggle to live with any of the world's top teams; they can hold their own in the tight, particularly early on, but they can't compete once the ball goes wide and the fast backs start to open them up.

The tournament planners, though, had conspired to make their task harder still with an impossible schedule. They had played against – and beaten – Georgia just five days before.

Now they were asked to face England. Frankly ridiculous and quite unfair. They were very game and they worked hard, but there was no way they would come close to competing in those circumstances and we ran out 111–13 winners. There was no satisfaction in it. The Uruguayans did grab a consolation score through their tight-head prop Pablo Lemoine but we ran in seventeen of our own, Josh Lewsey scoring a record-equalling five of them. There had been criticism all tournament of demolitions of the 'minnows' by the major teams – New Zealand, Australia and France, the other eventual semi-finalists, had all run up big scores against the weaker nations – and the schedules faced by Uruguay and other sides certainly compounded the problem. Obviously, the authorities want the big teams playing at weekends because that maximises the world-wide TV audience and, therefore, the revenue. They also feel, correctly in my view, that it is important to play games during the week to keep the momentum going. That means, inevitably, some teams will end up playing midweek and at weekends, and at the weekends they will be playing the top sides. It's tough to see how this situation can be resolved but mismatches of this sort help no one.

Danny Grewcock had broken his hand in the match and was out of the competition – a nightmare for Danny, given that he had only just recovered from a broken toe – and Simon Shaw was flown out immediately as his replacement. Balshaw, after looking sharp and scoring a brace of tries, had turned his ankle and gone off on a stretcher. This was to be another frustrating injury. We needed Iain at least to sit on the bench for the quarter-final and initially thought he would be fine but the problem stubbornly refused to go away.

The other fall-out from the match was the furore surrounding the exit of Joe Worsley. Joe had rightly been yellow-carded at the end of the game for a high tackle on one of the Uruguayans. As he meandered slowly off the pitch, the sizeable England contingent in the crowd started to clap him and Worzle raised his hands and applauded them back. It was pretty thoughtless, given that his 'victim' was still lying prone on the grass behind him – we were all thinking 'Just get off the bloody pitch, Joe' – but that's just him. He certainly didn't mean anything disrespectful or unpleasant by it. Of course, the Aussies wasted no time in interpreting his actions as further evidence of that 'arrogance' and it soon became world news – they were talking about it on CNN, for goodness' sake.

We came off the field nursing our bumps and bruises and mentally starting to prepare to face the Welsh the following week. We switched on the TV at the post-match reception and watched as the All Blacks built an immediate lead. Normal service, we thought, with the score 10–28. But then the Welsh started taking them on, breaking tackles and running at them from everywhere. The TV was turned off for the speeches, but Kay sent me a text message saying Wales were ahead and we started thinking that, just maybe, it might be the Kiwis the following week after all. In the end, of course, the natural order of things reasserted itself and New Zealand went on to win 37–53.

We had spent the week of the Uruguay game on the Gold Coast. It's a popular holiday destination for the Aussie public and we, too, got a bit of a holiday feeling, getting away from rugby a bit more and spending time at the beach and just chilling out. Now we headed for Brisbane and it was very much back to serious business. The city was filling up with fans as the knock-out stages of the tournament approached. You could feel the sense of anticipation starting to build. The Welsh performance had been a major surprise – probably to themselves as much as anyone else – and had certainly seen them play their best rugby of the World Cup. It had made us sit up and take notice. Richard Hill was still not fully fit but Matt Dawson returned, being named at scrum-half in place of Kyran Bracken. Jason Robinson started at full-back after Josh Lewsey injured his hamstring in training and with Iain Balshaw also out Dan Luger came into the side on the wing. The run-up to the match was less than perfect for me. I had tweaked my calf on the Tuesday and couldn't train for the rest of the week. It was frustrating; I had thought at first it was a minor niggle which would quickly go away but it hung around up to the Sunday, though I was always confident I would be OK to play. The adrenalin rush you get during games masks the discomfort you might otherwise feel on the training pitch.

We felt that our attack would get through the Wales defence, but we knew they had a good attacking game which was capable of causing us problems too. We didn't expect the problems to be as serious as they were. They absorbed our early pressure and hit us on the counter-attack to run up a ten-point lead in the first half. We made plenty of breaks of our own but somehow weren't managing to turn them into tries. We had chosen a few wrong options, too. We passed up the opportunity to score three points from a penalty well within Jonny's range, with Ben Cohen hoisting a quick kick to the corner. It's something we look to do if we're in the right position, but on this occasion we weren't: Neil Back, one of the shorter guys in the side, was waiting underneath it but was up against a taller Welsh defender and was unable to take the catch and score. Mike Tindall, too, had punted deep into Welsh territory with only Ben Kay out on the wing and Welsh defenders around him who were able quickly to run it back at us to score one of their three tries of the match. Half time felt awful: welcome to my nightmare. Wales had tackled well but our attack had become very narrow and predictable and our play had not been great. We were 10–3 down, and we ran off to the gleeful taunts of the travelling Welsh support.

'Oi, Rodney Trotter, you're gonna win nothing!' one of them shouted at Will Greenwood. Will – who does actually bear a resemblance to the *Only Fools and Horses* actor Nicholas Lyndhurst – had to grin and put his hand up to that one.

There were not many smiles in the dressing room, though. All around I could see a lot of very tired guys. I was struggling myself. We had trained very hard in the heat all week, with two-hour sessions on Tuesday, Wednesday and Thursday and a further hour-and-a-half on the Friday. It was also very humid on the night – which saps your strength quickly – and the combination made us very leg-tired and weary which, in turn, was leading to the boys making mistakes. If we had been fresh, I would not have worried. We would be able to outlast them. As it was, I honestly wondered whether we had the energy to come back. The unthinkable seemed horribly possible: an exit in the quarter-final.

But a good piece of tactical thinking by Woody helped to rescue the situation. Clive brought Mike Tindall off for Mike Catt, gambling that Catty's fresh legs, kicking skills and ability to step in as first receiver would help take pressure off Wilko. We were also feeling a lot stronger for the few minutes' rest, and when Jason Robinson made a dazzling run through almost the entire Welsh defence to put Will Greenwood in for a converted try we were back to 10–10 in quick time. From that point I didn't think we would lose, and we scored twenty-five points to seven – with Jonny knocking over a number of penalties – to win that second half comprehensively and the match reasonably comfortably. It had been anything but the cakewalk some pundits had been expecting, though. 'Boring England,' said the Aussie media, 'they can only kick goals.' Three tries to one was presented as, somehow, a victory for Wales. This ignored two important points. First, we kicked penalties only because the Welsh infringed and it was this that helped to stop us scoring tries. Second, they were on the plane home.

We were privately critical of ourselves, though. We should have scored more than once and we shouldn't have conceded three tries. We were also extremely concerned with how tired we had been at the break, something that would lead to a change in our pre-match training ahead of the semi-final clash with France. They had beaten Ireland earlier that day and had looked fairly awesome in doing so, getting to 37–0 before easing off a little and allowing Ireland to come back into it a little towards the end. Fridiric Michalak, their twenty-year-old fly-half, had directed the play very well and looked a high-quality young player. His kicking was excellent and his distribution skills were impressive, too. People were starting to build him up as the best No. 10 in the tournament, comparing him favourably with Jonny. We never doubted Wilko. His kicking and defence were as awesome as ever, and if he had not looked at his best in attack so far that wasn't down to him. Our attacking game was a team thing. There were no numbers whenever we passed the ball and he was having to hit rucks to try to win it. Next ruck, he would be expected to be in position to receive the ball. It was too much to ask of anyone.

With New Zealand beating South Africa and Australia defeating the Scots, the four semi-finalists were known. There had been talk of the tournament's predictability and I guess these four would have been the sides people expected to make the last four. But the pool stages had thrown up some exciting matches – England vs Samoa, Ireland vs Argentina and Australia, Wales vs New Zealand, for instance. True, the Rugby World Cup is still not as unpredictable as its soccer counterpart but that's because in soccer a poorer side can occasionally – say one or two games in ten – sneak a goal and defend a lead. In rugby, the stronger, fitter and better-trained side will win close to 100 per cent of the time.

Up until the France game, we had been expected to beat teams heavily and to do so in style. Over recent years, England had broken down the old stereotype and become a free-scoring side that used its backs and often ran in three, four or even more tries. Now we had reverted to type, the experts were saying, relying on keeping the ball tight and using Jonny's boot to grind out the wins. The French, meanwhile, had snuck up on the rails almost unseen. They had put together some excellent performances and the one against Ireland, in particular, had had people drooling. Suddenly, everyone was sitting up and raving about them – I thought it was about time, because France never seem to get the respect they deserve in the southern hemisphere – and the effect was that they became the favourites for our semi-final. This took a little of the pressure off us and transferred it to them. Suddenly we were in a game which was do-or-die, win-or-lose. It wasn't 'win, but you've got to play well doing it'. One scrappy drop-goal would do it.

We had a rethink, post-Wales, about our training schedule, cutting sessions right back to forty-five minutes and holding them in the late afternoon when it was cooler. This helped us keep a sharpness and a freshness to what we were doing and the week went really well. The Thursday session, particularly, was full of pace and eagerness.

We were tense early on in the week. Jonny was really feeling the pressure, I think, with most of the spotlight falling on him. One press conference question addressed to him was: 'Have you turned the corner?' What corner? We were in the semi-final of the World Cup, for God's sake. Weird.

Behind the scenes, we knew that the French were a good side. We were very on edge over the set piece. They have long had a deserved reputation for hard, physical scrummaging, but were also now becoming known for the athleticism of their line-out. In our match in Marseille, the back-rower Imanol Harinordoquy, with a single guy lifting him, had beaten double-lifted English jumpers. He is probably the only man in the world who could do that. We worked hard on analysis as the week progressed and gradually started to feel less and less nervous. The French might have been the form team and we knew they could beat us, but we had won two of the last three games between the sides. Additionally, temperatures had started to drop and the weather forecasters began to predict rain for the weekend. We always feel we play better in the wet than the French. It shouldn't be the problem many people say it is. The ball does get greasy and slightly slippy but as long as the surface is firm you can cope with it. We just seem to cope better than they do: maybe it's a psychological thing.

Bernard Laporte, their coach, had been quoted as saying that he hated the English and that so did everyone else – so tell us something we don't know, Bernard – and that was whipped up by the press. He later claimed he had been misunderstood. Who knows, or cares? All I can say is that it always surprises me when coaches come out with this sort of thing. Their backs coach was at it too, claiming all our backs were 'running on diesel' while his were 'five star'. It was like the garbage the Aussie press had been coming out with; while it is never going to be the main factor in your motivation, it's all good stuff to use in the week leading up to a game. I think England have had it about right – the boring, safe approach of saying we fear and respect the opposition. And it's usually true because most of the teams you play are good enough to beat you so, if you've any sense, you try to avoid giving them any ammunition.

The night before our encounter, we ate our dinner watching Australia play New Zealand in the first semi. We'd been talking about the match on the bus back from training and I'd said I had a sneaky feeling the Aussies would do it. They have a habit of winning the matches that count, and this one was at home. Everyone seemed to be forgetting that, with the Kiwis apparently at 4–1 on to win the tie with the bookies back home in England. They started brilliantly and took the initiative, quickly getting 10–0 up. It could still have gone either way but the Wallaby defence held strong – Smith and Waugh were superb in the back row – despite the All Blacks creating chances. It started to dawn on us that the New Zealanders were not going to score many points and that they would have to fight for everything. When they eventually came up short that gave us a bit of a jolt: if we lost to the French we'd have the All Blacks four days later in the third and fourth place play-off game. They were the side everyone wanted to avoid and none of us would have relished the prospect of their quick backs coming at us. The other feeling was that this proved that whatever had gone before, these were just one-off games. The All Blacks had swept all before them up to that point and had been turned over by a Wallaby side that had been heavily criticised at home. Now, of course, they were heroes. Strangely, they weren't 'boring' despite the fact that all their points had come from penalties and one interception.

As we drove to Sydney's Telstra Stadium – the renamed Olympic Stadium, or Stadium Australia, where the Lions had lost the series two years earlier – the skies got greyer and greyer and the threatened rain arrived. The scene inside was absolutely incredible: a sea of white jerseys, England flags and banners. The place holds 80,000 people and the majority of them must have been English. It was better than Twickenham: when people are away at a sporting event, particularly in a place like Australia, they become more nationalistic, they wear their England shirts and they sing their hearts out. Even at the Australia vs New Zealand semi, the most noise was made by English supporters who had found their way into the crowd and drowned out the Kiwi and Wallaby fans with 'Swing Low' – getting booed and accused of being 'disrespectful' in the process. A bit rich, coming from Australians who pride themselves on being disrespectful. At our semi-final, the noise and the whole spectacle was just amazing. The travelling support for us, and the Scots, Welsh and Irish, far exceeded anything that the French produced and there were very few French fans in the crowd. It obviously helps to have big support, but on the downside it does put more pressure on you when you see all these people there and you know how much money they have spent to come out here. Someone will ask you for an autograph and say something like 'You've got to sign this … I've come all this way to support you!' That doesn't feel too far from 'You've got to win … I've come all this way to support you!' Guys are shouting 'Go on lads' and clenching their fists at you – on Monday morning. I totally understand their enthusiasm and it's a great thing, but the level of expectation does heighten your nerves.

By kick-off it was pouring down, very unusual in Sydney in mid-November. The French started well, winning a line-out not far from our line. We disrupted their throw, but Serge Betsen got his hands on the ball and did well to reach the try line. It wasn't immediately clear whether he had dropped it in the act of grounding it so the video referee was called into action. I didn't bother looking at the replays. If it's down properly it's a try, and if it's not and the video ref still gives it that would just irritate me. The try was awarded and Michalak converted from ten metres in from the touchline.

We didn't panic, though, and got on with trying to play our game. They were defending well with plenty of bodies in the centre of the field. We tried at first to go outside those bodies but they turned us over on several occasions and it became something of a duel for territory. Mike Catt's kicking ability meant he had started in the centre ahead of Mike Tindall, and he and Jonny swapped kicks with Michalak and other French players. They won the early exchanges but as the rain came down, swirling around in the wind, we started to get on top. Both Mike and Jonny were able to pin France back in their own half and once Jonny had kicked three or four penalties to take us into the lead it was very hard for them to come back at us. Our line-out was functioning pretty well and, perhaps surprisingly given that their pack was so strong, our scrummage was pushing them back on their own ball, causing Harinordoquy to knock on at the base several times and depriving him of go-forward ball for him to pick up and run with.

We turned round 12–7 ahead and produced a very strong second-half performance. It wasn't particularly pretty: we kicked a lot and put them under pressure, waiting for them to knock on or concede penalties. Then Jonny would step up and make them pay. We could see them losing heart with every three points he added. We knew we'd won it when Olivier Magne tried to kick out of his 22 and was sandwiched between myself and Lawrence. As he lay there on the deck he started gesturing at Lol and moaning at the ref rather than getting up.

They didn't score another point after Michalak's tenth-minute conversion and it finished 24–7. By then, he had been replaced by the older and more experienced Girald Merceron — it would have been a brave move, but they maybe should have made a late change and started with him once they saw the conditions — but things were too far gone and he wasn't able to make much of an impact. Michalak had proved vulnerable to pressure as we had suspected he might. From the start, his clearance kicks were going vertically or straight into touch and, the conversion apart, he missed his place kicks too. Part of our game plan, obviously, involved getting pressure onto him. You always target the half-backs but he was young and relatively inexperienced in the position, having started out as a scrum-half. He'd looked very good to that point but we just wondered how much of that was down to the easy ride he'd been given. Now we knew the answer.

I felt for their captain, Fabien Galthié, at the end, and went over to commiserate with him. At thirty-four, he had announced he would retire after the World Cup ended for them and I'm sure he would have liked to go out with a win. They had played really well earlier in the tournament but the conditions hadn't suited them on the night. Having said that, if it had been hot and humid and they had run in lots of tries, I doubt many people would have allowed that as an excuse for us.

We weren't jubilant — I later heard that the Wallabies went on a lap of honour after their win over the All Blacks, but we've got something of a history with laps of honour so we just headed for the changing room. Clive reflected this in his positive post-match press conference, telling the reporters that we hadn't come all this way to finish second, that we had won nothing yet and that we expected to win the dream final:

Australia against England. Phone calls, emails and text messages were arriving from home in their hundreds, if not thousands, which gave us some clue as to interest back there. Down Under, it was just as mad. Aussie newspapers were printing pictures of Jonny Wilkinson and instructing their readers to stick pins into him, Voodoo-style. Sydney was crawling with English supporters and planeloads more were arriving almost round-the-clock.

Most of the pundits were tipping us, but I thought it would go right down to the wire in much the same way as the third Lions Test had in 2001. The Wallabies were not going to give up without a fight and we were still waiting for things to 'click' for us. That said, I thought we would win. Seeing Australia do a lap of honour after beating the All Blacks, celebrating just reaching the final, I felt we had the psychological edge. The New Zealanders are their big enemy, and they had stuffed the Wallabies in the previous Tri-Nations. You could see the anxiety, the positive fear of being beaten, and maybe well-beaten, in the Aussie players ahead of the match. Maybe they hadn't thought they would get to the final at all and, having raised their game once, would have trouble doing it again.

Again, we had a light training week, with a day less than the Wallabies to prepare. We didn't scrummage once – unheard of in a Test week – as our front row were stiff and sore after the battle against the French. We had short sessions on Tuesday, Wednesday and Friday and that was it. You'd think, with the World Cup final just a few days away, that we'd all be nervous wrecks but I have never seen the boys so relaxed. They were full of life and energy. I guess partly it was because they were in the final and partly that they could see light at the end of a seven-week tunnel. No matter what the occasion, you want to get home after that length of time. It was strange: I caught myself thinking 'This is the World Cup final' and wondering why it felt like any other week, why I wasn't more jittery. It was only by Friday and Saturday that one or two negative thoughts started to creep in: what if I make a bad mistake, what if I give away a silly penalty, as I had against France, and it costs us the game? I tried to banish these feelings: you'll be all right, I would tell myself, you know what you're doing. Once we got out there, and once we got past all the hype, it would be just another game of rugby.

On the Friday night, we had a team meeting. We have a motivational video which the boys like to watch – big hits, tries, good moments set to music. We watched that and I said my usual few words to the squad. I kept it short. My main message was: 'Let's play our normal game. Let's not force things, try to do things we wouldn't do in any other match, and by the same token, let's do the things we would. Don't let the occasion get to you. If you start thinking "It's the Rugby World Cup final" as you receive the ball the likelihood is that you'll end up paralysed by the moment. We've got all the guts and courage we need. It's big, yes, but let's just go and play our game.'

Our usual Saturday morning line-out practice took place in a downpour which was not unwelcome; cooler, more European conditions had to help us. It's always a long wait for evening games and this was no exception. But by 5.15p.m. we were on the bus and on our way. The drive to the stadium was odd; the hour-long route from our base in Manly took us through quiet, residential areas and we didn't see too many people, unlike when we play at Six Nations grounds where there are hundreds of people spilling out of pubs. Twenty minutes out, we started to see fans but they were mostly parking their cars and getting onto buses and once we actually arrived at the complex it was quite sterile: it's such a massive area, sprawling over hundreds of acres, that you miss the mass of the fans and are driven straight to an underground bay to offload. It was totally different to arriving at, say, Cardiff for a Rugby World Cup final, where the narrow streets around the city centre stadium would be going crackers. We arrived a couple of hours ahead of kick-off. Then it was very much business as usual: we got into the dressing room, changed and started our individual warm-up routines.

Mike Tindall back in for Mike Catt was the only change to the team which had beaten France. Clive had made the right tactical choice on both occasions – Catty's kicking game would be less of a factor against the Wallabies, while Tinds' more imposing physicality would help defensively against the likes of Stirling Mortlock and would also allow us to get a go-forward on the Wallaby defence. Catty took his move to the bench very well, as had Tinds previously.

I felt for the eight guys who would play no part, either starting or on the bench. We needed those guys to be there supporting us – and to stay focused, avoiding distractions – but it must have been very tough for them not to make the match twenty-two. That said, there were plenty of guys sitting at home in England who would have loved to be in that eight.

My main concern ahead of the game was that it should

not be too hot or humid and my wish was granted: the cool and showery pattern continued.

In those few moments before we came out, I just asked the players to look round at each other, at the guys with whom they had been through so many experiences. I found it very difficult to say anything profound but it wasn't necessary. It was a World Cup final, for God's sake. As we came out for the anthems, I guessed the crowd was split 60–40 in favour of Australia, an amazing effort from our fans, who were never outsung.

Australia started the game very well. We made a couple of mistakes and one of the front row was penalised for an alleged punch. They scored early when they kicked to the corner and Lote Tuqiri got up above the smaller Jason Robinson to touch down. That wasn't great, though they missed the conversion. We got back on the attack quickly, going through plenty of phases but not making much inroad as their defence held firm. However, I started to feel their forwards were getting worn down: our attack was making progress and gaining momentum, and they started to give away penalties. The highlight of the half was a stunning try by Jason Robinson. Lawrence Dallaglio made it with a bursting run round a ruck, off-loading beautifully to Jonny who passed on to Jason. With a pair of Wallabies homing in on him, Robbo dived in, sliding across the line on the greasy surface before his momentum carried him back upright, yelling 'Come on!' and punching the ball into the air. Cue huge singing from the many thousands of England fans inside the ground.

We knew coming in how dangerous the Australian attack could be but we were keeping Sailor, Mortlock and Tuqiri pretty much in check and making a few little half-breaks ourselves. We had to watch our defence, though. Australia tend to attack right across the field, phase by phase, all the way to one touchline, and then suddenly going wide the other way and looking to get around you. As forwards, we had to concentrate hard on keeping our spacings in the defensive line spot-on, because there was always the risk of letting them in if a ten-metre gap appeared between me and, say, Phil Vickery. Anyone with pace could step inside us and we'd not be able to cover each other.

We managed to keep our penalty count down reasonably low, though we were pinged several times for alleged front-row offences. Their prop Ben Darwin had been carted off the field in a neck brace during the semi against New Zealand after a very nasty scrum collapse. He would have been paralysed – at least – if the opposite prop Kees Meuws had not heard his shout of 'neck, neck, neck' and pulled back immediately. As it is, he is expected to make a full recovery and a tragedy was averted. His replacement, Ali Baxter, had just a handful of Tests and their loose-head, Bill Young, is not the strongest of scrummagers. When you consider the difference in size, power, experience and ability between our front row and the Wallaby one, it was mystifying to me that the referee could imagine that we would be scrummaging illegally. Why would we need to? Vicks and Trevor were taking them apart as it was.

We were making a number of silly handling errors, though, and I wasn't happy with that. One of the biggest sins in rugby is to lose possession cheaply. I seem to have spent my whole career saying 'Look after the ball, hold onto the ball, cherish the ball, worship the ball, protect the ball, look after the f***ing pill!' Here, in the World Cup final of all places, it seemed continually to be dropped or knocked on. It's the only thing I could criticise our squad for: we sometimes gave the ball away too easily, with guys trying to force things and that makes it hard to win. It takes away your momentum and it gives hard-won possession to the other side. One of the knock-ons was by my second row partner Ben Kay. We'd broken through down the Wallabies' right flank and Matt Dawson was surging to the line, with Ben to his right. Two metres out Matt drew the defence and gave it to Ben – who promptly spilled the ball over the line. His are normally the safest of hands and I couldn't believe my eyes. A definite try, gone begging. He'd probably made the fatal mistake: thinking about it. 'I'm going to score a try in the Rugby World Cup final and…oops!' Credit to Ben, he didn't let it get to him. We went in 5-14 up at half time, but 5–19 or 5–21 would have felt even better and would probably have signalled the end of the game as a contest.

In a calm changing room, we talked through a few technical points: line-outs, scrummage and how to adjust our game plan for the slight breeze we'd now face. As I sucked down some fluids, I assessed how I felt: calm, strong and full of running. The rest of the boys looked in a similar way. The Wallabies had been breathing hard as they came off. How were they doing, just a few yards away? Knackered and worried, I hoped.

We started the second half very well, nicking line-outs – though we lost a few of our own, too – and smashing them back when we tried to go forward directly. We were the stronger, more physical side but every time we got pressure on them it was the same old story – a dropped ball, a needless penalty, allowing them to claw back six precious points. Jonny tried a couple of snap drop goals but they slid wide to raucous Australian booing and we stayed scoreless in the half as the minutes ticked away.

Suddenly, though, we found ourselves in the dying seconds of the game, still ahead 14–11. The Aussies had the put-in to a scrum, we got the shove on them and their tight-head, unable to cope, folded in. There is no doubt that referee Andri Watson should have awarded a penalty to us. Game over. Instead, he ordered the scrum be reset and then he penalised us. Right at the end of the match, Elton Flatley – nerveless under immense pressure – kicked the goal to level the scores and the final whistle went: extra time. If we had dwelt on the fact that they had potted three penalties in the second half to no points from us, despite our many opportunities, I think we might have had problems: had we just thrown away the World Cup? As it was, no one was dwelling on anything. We huddled together and confirmed with the coaches that it was 10 minutes each way. Myself, Daws and Wilko made a few tactical points and then Jonny wandered off to practice his kicking before the re-start. Backy was geeing up the boys: we felt we were the fitter team, he said. Now was the time to prove it. Extra time would play right into the Wallabies' hands, if you believed their press. We were old, we were past it, we were 'grumpy old men', we were 'Dad's army'.

Yeah, right. Age wasn't going to come into it: I would have backed our fitness against anybody's and the proof of the pudding was in which side had made the biggest number of substitutions. They'd used theirs and we'd made just a couple of changes at the end of the second half.

You think 10 minutes each way is a long time but it flashes by. I'm dragged down in a line-out, Jonny slots the penalty from really long range – it was never in doubt, which lifted us and must have been like a knife in the ribs to them – and before you know it the half-time whistle sounds: 14–17. One hand back on the trophy.

The second ten starts after a minute's breather and the play moves back and forth, with Mike Catt – now on for Tindall – taking the ball up extremely well. Ninety seconds to go: we are penalised for a nonsense rucking offence inside kicking range.

Flatley, massively cool again, puts it through the posts.

The score is 17–17 and we are heading for sudden death: first team to score points wins the World Cup.

I know, from speaking to people who were in the crowd, that the tension in the stands was almost unbearable. Kay had to leave because she couldn't bear to watch any more and I know how she felt. I'd have been out of there myself. The players have it easy: the best place to be at times like that is on the pitch. No time to think about anything but what is in front of you, too much concentration to let your mind wander to what ifs and maybes.

Sixty seconds to go: we decide to kick long at the re-start, try to pressure them into kicking into touch and concentrate on winning the ball. Mat Rogers takes the kick and hoofs it into touch as we had hoped. He doesn't make much ground. We throw long at the line-out, Lewis Moody, on as a sub, wins the ball at the back and it gets taken up. A ruck forms, the Wallabies all over it like a rash. They're all watching Jonny, expecting the drop-goal. Daws spots this and realises no one's on him. Bravely, he manages a sharp show-and-go to burst through. He makes us 10 or 15 metres or more straight up the field. If you're defending, you detest that kind of break – Matt's trademark – because it means the attacker is immediately behind your entire defensive line. If you're attacking, it's fantastic.

Eventually, the scrambling Australian defence nails Daws, leaving him pinned at the bottom of the ruck. Backy, a schoolboy scrum-half, gets into Matt's position and looks as though he's thinking of shipping the ball out to Wilko. Respect to Backy, but his passing is not as sharp as Dawson's. I have a momentary flash of horror – Backy spinning the ball out on the bounce or way over Wilkinson's head. I make a run, trying to catch Neil's eye and, thank God, he spots me and pops the ball up. I get nowhere and am taken to ground but it's not the distance that counts: Matt Dawson is now up and in position.

Thirty seconds to go: the ball gets squeezed back. George Gregan, acutely aware now that we've manufactured a perfect chance for Jonny, is yelling 'Field goad! Field goal!' Australian defenders, desperate to get their hands on it, can't help themselves: they keep coming offside and then retreating as Daws crouches over the ball and looks up for his fly-half.

Then it's out and Jonny swings back his wrong right foot. It's an ugly kick, they later tell me, but it's the best thing I've ever seen on a rugby field . . . a tumbling, swerving punt smashed between the posts.

We are in the lead again.

Running back, I glance at the clock on one of the big screens. Time is almost up so I know this is the last play of the game.

Twenty seconds to go: the Australians race back to re-start before we can get properly into position. They kick short. They need to recover the ball because if they don't, as long as we don't infringe and give them a penalty, the Webb Ellis Trophy is on its way to Twickenham. Someone – I don't see who, I later find out that it's Trevor Woodman, in the wrong position but safe as houses – catches the re-start and sets up the ruck. The ball comes back, Matt lets a few seconds tick away and then gets it out to Mike Catt, over the head of the crouching Will Greenwood who has knelt down to avoid getting in the way. Catty hoofs the ball into touch and it's all over.

Unbelievable.

One minute, you're thinking about winning the kick-off, keeping the ball, not making a mistake, what to do next. The next, the World Cup is over. One second it couldn't be any more exciting, the next . . . all gone.

Music starts up, a PA announcer comes on, but you're not really listening: you're looking at each other, feeling great for each other, for Woody and the rest of the coaches, for the fans, who've gone absolutely bananas. Guys are running on, going crazy, hugging each other.

The Aussies are standing round or on their knees on the floor, a few in tears; in some ways, maybe, the dejection hits you before the elation. When you've lost, you've lost and that's it: it's all over for you and you know it. When you've won something that big you just can't take it all in at first.

A few of the guys started a haphazard lap of honour – I think they got away with that one, eh? – and others ran to their families and friends in the crowd. I had to walk to the far end of the ground to do a television interview with George Gregan. George is a good guy – he's a bit chippy on the pitch but we've got on well off it when we've met after games. He congratulated me on the win and we chatted about our families for a few seconds. He was obviously pretty low. I knew how he felt: I'd been on the losing side here two years previously with the Lions, a very bad personal memory for me given that the series had been snatched away from us when I lost attacking line-out ball to Justin Harrison right at the death. That had chipped away at me ever since, and at the other England players who had been part of that tour. I don't know if that feeling will ever be fully exorcised but this was going to go a long way towards it.

I said a few words for the cameras, but really I just wanted to get back to be with the players.

We lined up behind the Wallabies as they received their losers' medals – their fans started singing 'Waltzing Matilda' and my overriding impression was of the song as a funeral dirge – and then took our places on the huge podium. The noise from the England supporters – and, to be fair, the many Aussies who had hung around – was amazing, the thousands of flashbulbs going off in the crowd dazzling, as we raised our arms. Australian Prime Minister John Howard looked like a man sucking a lemon as he placed the winners' medals around our necks. He was heavily criticised by the Aussie press and public afterwards, for that and for the speed with which he hastened along the line. To be fair to Howard, I think the

TV people had asked him to get a move on so they could get to an ad break or something. As for his facial expression, I guess he could have been a bit more dignified and 'statesman-like', with a worldwide TV audience looking on, but, frankly, it was a normal human response. I couldn't have cared less, anyway. If anything, it made me happier seeing him like that: Yes, we've beaten you, mate, and in your own back yard. You should be looking miserable.

Then it was time for me to lift the William Webb Ellis Cup. A few people have said to me, 'I'd love to have gone and lifted the cup' but that's not how I felt. It's not about the cup: that's just the icing on the cake. We've won two European Cups with Leicester and I wasn't first to lift the trophy either time. It was the same now. I just don't have a big ego thing about it: it would have made absolutely no difference to me if someone else had gone up to get the cup and, to be honest, I'd much rather the whole squad had gone up together and given it the big one as a group. But I guess that's not the way these things are done.

I can't remember what I was thinking as I picked it up: pride in the boys, pride in my country, relief that we'd finally done it. Most of all, I wished my mum had been there to see it; she would have loved it.

Then we set off, parading the cup round the stadium in front of thousands of our fans as Queen's *We Are The Champions* blared out, all of the supporters going crazy, singing, cheering, crying. It was absolutely brilliant, a quite incredible sight. The sense of release and relief must have been huge for them. As I've said, you feel the tension and pressure more as a spectator than as a player. On the pitch you are just trying to get the job done. Off it, every half-break or missed tackle, every point scored by either side, every minute ticking by just ratchets up the anxiety and we had put them through plenty of that. Now that had all gone and euphoria and elation took over. As the Oasis hit *Wonderwall* echoed round the stadium, I found my way to Wilko and put my arm round him. The guy had been under so much pressure, both external and internal. Now he was grinning from ear to ear. 'Mate,' I said. 'It's all been worth it, hasn't it?'

I don't know how long we were on the field but it was one of those extended moments which you never want to end. I could have carried on walking around all night. But when we did finally get back into the changing room – the same room where I'd sat, beaten and dejected, after that final Lions game in 2001 – it was nice to have that few minutes of private time alone with the boys. You looked around at everyone, smiles everywhere, Josh Lewsey in tears, I remember, someone repeating 'We've only gone and bloody won it!', and just felt awesome.

I thought of all the guys, how fantastic it was for us all to have done this together. Guys like Kyran Bracken, on the bench that day but a great player for England for 10 years, Mike Catt, who'd gone through so much injury heartbreak in the months before the tournament, Jason Leonard, who had lost a final to the Australians in 1991 and must have been savouring the moment more than most of us, Lawrence Dallaglio and Will Greenwood with all their personal problems, Backy, Daws, Hilly, how long most of us had been together, how much we'd been through. For once it had all worked out. Winning the Grand Slam had been good but winning the Rugby World Cup was in a whole different league. All the teams work hard but we had put a hell of a lot in and it was fantastic to see everyone getting the reward for their sacrifices. Good, too, to see people so happy. The World Cup had been very little fun to that point. We'd enjoyed beating the Springboks but the glow from that lasted a couple of days before we were back into training. Samoa, Uruguay, Wales; none of those games saw us come off with big grins on. Even the France semi-final, great result that it was, was greeted in a very businesslike way. We were happy to be there but conscious we'd won nothing. This was, naturally, different.

John Howard came into the room at some point, I think to congratulate us.

'How's tricks, John?' I said. 'The economy seems to be doing well. Wish I'd put my money in your stock market and not ours.' Maybe he thought I was being facetious – actually, I wasn't – but he had no chat on him, just blanked me with a sour face. Fine, no problem.

Prince Harry was also in there. Yes, he's privileged – he gets the best seats in the house and I don't suppose he paid for his flight out to Oz – but he also gets hassled by photographers everywhere he goes and puts up with plenty of crap along the way. I think he's a good lad, always very supportive of the team, punching the air and high-fiving his mates when we score and all that. He had come in after the semi-final against France, absolutely raving about the game whereas we were mostly fairly businesslike and thinking about the following weekend: calm yourself down, son, there's a few tired old blokes in here. Now he was really enjoying himself, and good on him.

I got myself stitched up by the medics and then…you're not really sure what to do. The usual recovery process, ice baths and carbohydrate drinks and the like, goes out of the window at a time like that. Should you be jumping up and down? Should you be hugging people? I pretty much just sat there, soaking up the atmosphere. Nobby West had the team stereo under control so we had some top music blaring out: a bit of The Jam, some Clash, some Madness.

Me and Nobby, Dave Reddin and Andy Robinson all enjoying the sounds.

Everyone else: 'What is this rubbish?'

Medals round every neck, the big gold trophy being passed around, guys taking photos and videoing each other, beers and big smiles everywhere. It was a truly awesome feeling. It couldn't have been any better and I wanted to try and remember it. Like a few of the other guys who were also edging towards the end of their careers, I had known there would be no more World Cups for me. We'd said in the week leading up to the final that we needed to enjoy this experience, to take everything in, soak it all up and remember it. Despite this, looking back now the whole thing feels unreal, like a great dream. Maybe it's because we're all so used to watching life's major events on TV; ordinary people like us are not there for 99.99% of the big things that go on, so when you are actually there it feels weird.

I've often been asked how big the post-match party was. The answer – for me at any rate – is that there wasn't really one at all. Obviously, we hadn't planned anything in advance: that would be tempting fate and you just wouldn't do it. But the other issue was the time. The game kicked off around

8p.m. and when you factor in extra-time and laps of honour and medal presentations it was probably close to 11.30p.m. before we got off the pitch. Then we had to shower, change and do our press interviews. I have no problem with the press: I just don't like talking all the time, being pestered and having to answer the same questions over and over again. So my main concern, apart from being very keen to avoid appearing smug in victory and taking the opportunity to ransack their hospitality bar for crisps, was to get it all over as quickly as possible so I could go and find Kay and my dad. Even so, we didn't climb onto the team bus until around 1.30a.m. I remember sitting there, staring out into the deserted, pitch black streets around the complex, rain streaming against the windows of the coach and wondering what was going on back home. A lot of the boys were getting text messages from the UK. My phone only holds 10 messages at once but other guys were shouting out that they'd got 50 or more coming through so we rapidly realised it was going crazy. The coach took us to the official post-match do in the centre of Sydney where our family and friends were waiting. It was probably 2a.m. by then. I had a couple of beers with Kay and my dad, chatting to a few people like my agent, Tim Buttimore of SCG, and Benny Cohen's uncle, George, a football World Cup winner with England in 1966 and a really nice man. But after a couple of hours we knocked it on the head. Kay's mum was back at their hotel looking after Molly but she was booked on an early flight back to New Zealand and we needed to get back for her. Anyway, Kay was knackered after a long day, with a fairly boozy cruise upriver to the game, and the old man had consumed a few celebratory drinks so we decided to find a cab and get back. Out into the drizzle, we headed towards the nearest taxi rank. A good plan, in theory, but there were at least 200 people waiting at that rank and no sign of any cabs. So we walked back the two or three miles – my dad, with all his weaving, probably covered nearer 20 – watching the England fans singing and messing around in the rain. A nice memory. We tumbled into bed just after 5a.m. and were up again within half an hour as Kay's mum's alarm went off. No sleep but I can't remember feeling tired. I made my way back to the team hotel in Manly for breakfast.

Sunday lunchtime I finished off the first edition of the book you're reading now – unbelievably, it would be on the shelves back home the following Thursday – and that night went to the IRB awards dinner. Clive won Coach of the Year, we were named Team of the Year and Jonny Player of the Rugby World Cup. A clean sweep but to be honest it was a pain in the neck; I would much rather have been able to go mental at a private dinner for the squad and our families than to sit through speech after speech with the great and good of rugby. On the Monday morning we all had to go to the beach to pose in our club shirts with the World Cup for a photo for Zurich, sponsors of the Premiership. The business side of professional sport never ceases.

We flew just after noon. Kay had managed to get onto the same flight – a BA jumbo renamed 'Sweet Chariot' for the occasion – which was good news: Molly had started teething since coming away and was also a little unwell, so I was able to take a little of the burden off Kay. A lot of the guys took the trophy around the plane, showing if off to the fans flying back with us. It was our first glimpse of what it meant to people close up – they were going crazy.

I looked after Molly for the first leg to Singapore, and then tried to get my head down on the way in to London. We arrived back at around 4a.m. on a miserable late November morning. The plane was surrounded by photographers, as I guess you would expect, all clamouring for the traditional photo on the steps down from the plane. More waving of the trophy and then I nipped back inside to carry little Moll, all wrapped up tight and warm, carefully down the greasy stairway. I didn't need any of it, to be honest; I'd rather have pushed her through the usual covered walkway in her buggy.

I'd idly wondered on the way back whether anyone would turn up to welcome us home. But it was in the early hours of a work day, out at Heathrow and it would be cold and wet. I reckoned on two or three hundred hardy souls.

A few airport workers and passengers from other flights were wishing us well as we came through baggage reclaim. Then, as we went through passport control, we were all pulled to one side by the police.

'Listen guys,' says one of them. 'We're going to let you through in twos and threes only. We're worried about public safety.'

'Eh? What do you mean?' says one of the players.

'It's crazy out there, absolutely crazy.'

'How many people are there?' says someone else.

'Thousands,' says the copper.

Then we started to hear noise from the arrivals lounge. Clive and Jayne Woodward went out first and you could hear the roar. I had the cup – I'd had to pose for yet more photos with it – and I didn't want to be carrying it. So I handed it to Backy and we walked through the sliding doors together.

What greeted us was one of the most astonishing sights I've ever seen. Even allowing for the fact that I was a bit spaced-out – tired, jet-lagged, feeling slightly unreal as you do after a long flight – it was mindblowing. There were, as we'd been told, thousands of people. The number alone would have been amazing. But it was more than that: it was the way they were acting.

Everywhere you looked people were roaring, screaming, crying, clenching their fists in triumph, kissing their England shirts, pogo-ing up and down, waving flags, trying to grab you. It was like a friendly riot, with people almost fighting to get closer as the police battled to keep them back. You couldn't pick out any individual faces or words in the din; you were just hit by a reverberating surge of sound and, with so many people packed into such a tight, low-ceilinged area you could actually feel it, the compression from the sound-waves breaking over you.

'Don't stop to sign any autographs,' one of the policemen said.

Like there was any chance of that. You would never have got out alive if you hadn't kept walking.

Outside, thousands more had gathered and they, too, were going absolutely mad: they were hanging off lampposts, stacked 20-deep on the pavements and spilling all over the road, screaming and waving and shouting at us from every floor of the multi-storey car parks outside the airport – really, really into it, much more than even we, as players, had been. I battled my way through to be one of the first on the coach – my brother Andrew had come down to the airport to pick Kay and Molly up so they could get home as quick as possible; he had been given a police escort in, such was the mania – and you almost feared for the guys coming after you.

'Throw Jonny to them,' someone said. 'Sacrifice him! We'll go home while they're ripping him to shreds!'

Gradually, the bus filled up with wide-eyed players and eventually we edged our way out of the airport and away from the mayhem and back to the gloomy reality of the M25 on a winter's dawn, thinking that, actually, Manly hadn't been all bad after all.

You almost half-wondered whether that had really just happened? It was fantastic, incredible and moving but somehow a bit surreal. We're all sports fans too, of course, and I'm sure I'd go mad myself if the England soccer or cricket teams won their World Cups. But when you're involved in sport yourself, when it's your job, maybe that's different from being a pure fan. We certainly hadn't been prepared for that welcome.

An hour later we were at our hotel near Bagshot, where a press conference had been arranged. What more was there to say? The first reporter to stand was a young girl.

'I'm from the Harborough Mail,' she said, looking very nervous and clutching a copy of the paper as if to prove the fact. It's my local paper and it's only a little weekly so she probably doesn't go to too many big national events.

'I just want to say that Market Harborough is really, really proud of you!'

And that was it: quite sweet really.

A few questions from the usual suspects and, not a moment too soon, I was out of there, back on the team bus and on the road back to Leicester, nice and low key. There was more media, a couple of camera crews, waiting for me at home. Surely there couldn't be any more angles? I gave a couple of interviews, told them that was their lot and closed my door on the world.

Peace and quiet, and a cup of tea on my own sofa for the first time in months.

People seem to find this desire for normality strange. Who'd want to give up being part of the England World Cup squad, particularly after you've won the thing? Staying in the best hotels, flying at the front of the plane, everyone hanging on your every word, all the adulation. Why wouldn't you want that? It sounds glamorous but it was just a lot of hard work. Living out of a suitcase for weeks on end, unable to leave your room without being hassled, all the media, all the training. Yes, there are great moments but a lot of it is sheer grind and graft. By the end of it, all you want is to slob out in front of your own telly and sleep in your own bed.

But there was precious little time for putting my feet up. Leicester's position as the most successful club in Europe had slipped away and the club was in desperate need of points. We were training on the Thursday – with every young forward desperate to knock lumps out of a world champion – and playing on the Saturday.

Six days earlier we'd paraded the World Cup around the touchline at Sydney. Now we faced a dogfight with Bath. Benny Kay started and I was on the bench. It felt very weird, sitting in the subs' changing rooms at Welford Road, but as soon as I ran out onto the pitch to warm up that all changed. Back at the club, back at work. It just felt right.

Of course, the country didn't want to let the World Cup go. The papers were full of it, crowds were up at rugby grounds across the country, young kids were clamouring to join their local club and Jonny Wilkinson was a bigger name than David Beckham. I was getting stopped in the street. Last summer, if I passed three people in the street one of them might know who I was, the second might half-recognise me and the third would just assume I was some big thug and cross the road to get away. By early December, everyone seemed to know who I was and wanted to shake my hand and have a few words. It's still happening. People can be quite emotional, too.

'Well done for winning the World Cup.'

'Thank you for putting so much pride back into England.'

'Apart from the birth of my kids, that was the best day of my life.'

'That was awesome. Brilliant.'

Often people prefaced their comments by saying 'I know you must have heard this a million times and you're probably sick of it but ...'

To which I usually reply: 'No, I'm never going to mind hearing that, thanks very much. Yes, thanks a lot. Leave me alone now. Go on, mate, on your bike. Do I have to chin you?'

Joking aside, I never will tire of hearing it and I'm hugely honoured to have been a part of something which has given people so much enjoyment and pride in their country. Nearly everyone I have spoken to since I got back says they were there in Sydney and those who really did go have got memories to treasure for the rest of their lives. It's great for rugby to get this recognition and I hope it will take the sport to a higher level. But even if people watched just that one game and got a buzz out of it, that will do for me.

Not long after we'd got back, the RFU told us we were to parade the World Cup through London. To be honest, I didn't want to go and I don't think many of the other players did. Partly, I couldn't see the point of it and felt it might turn into a damp squib, an embarrassment even. A Monday morning in December seemed bad timing: who was going skip work to come and watch a bunch of guys drive round in a bus in the cold?

Still, it had to be done. The other Leicester boys were going down in a mini-bus so Ben Kay and I arranged to get picked up a few miles from our homes at junction 20 on the MI. It was one of those winter mornings where it's just getting light and everything looks grey and dull and we found ourselves waiting in a lay-by just off the motorway. We'd been ordered to dress in our grey England suits – the nice, lightweight, thin suits, specially designed for the Australian climate. I knew it was going to be cold and I was already pretty p***ed off. My mood wasn't helped when my mobile went.

'Er … we've missed the junction.'

To which I replied: 'How can you miss a f***ing junction? It's not a surprise. You know it's there and it's signposted a mile away.'

'Er … we've just missed it.'

'Where are you?'

'We're underneath the bridge.'

So Ben and I are in our nice, thin, freezing suits with our lovely, brown, standard issue, gripless leather-soled shoes sliding all over the place as we walk across the sliproad and down the embankment to a mini-bus which is parked on the hard shoulder – dangerous at the best of times but no fun whatsoever in the half-light of a morning rush-hour – and is, clearly, driven by an idiot.

I was livid and I had a bit of a go at the driver as he pulled away, much to the amusement of the rest of the passengers. The traffic was a nightmare and we got held up by an accident near Northampton. The radio was on and they kept going on about how 'all the England team were down in London for the parade'.

No mate, we're stuck on the M1.

It's going to be crap, we don't want to be there and we're going home. But eventually we turned up at the Intercontinental hotel by Hyde Park, hardly having seen a soul as we drove into town and still feeling very cynical about the whole exercise. Who the hell was going to bother to come out and see us?

It was good to meet up with the rest of the boys, though, and after a bit of chat we found ourselves on an open-topped bus, driving along an empty Park Lane and through Marble Arch – an honour normally reserved, apparently, for royalty – to begin the drive. Still no one in sight, this is going to be embarrassing . . . until we turned onto Oxford Street.

It literally took my breath away. The pavements on either side of the road were absolutely rammed with people who started cheering and going berserk as soon as they saw the bus.

Incredible, amazing, Heathrow x 10.

As we nosed along the road I was almost speechless for a

while. And when we headed into Regent Street, which slopes away slightly, we could see further into the distance and everywhere you looked there were people in white, waving the flag of St George, holding up banners, shinning up or sliding down lampposts and street signs, waving to us from shops, hanging out of every available window, even sitting on roofs. It took us ages to get through, with people spilling onto the road itself. There was no way they could move along Regent Street so as we passed side roads you could see thousands more running along parallel streets to get to Trafalgar Square. Once we got into the square and saw the whole place just teeming with people, with more trying to get in, guys sat on top of the lions, splashing around in the fountain … to be honest, words fail me. It was just stunning. I can't find any other way of saying it.

We stood there waving randomly for ages. And then we waved some more. And some more.

Tetley's, our beer sponsor, had filled the bus with cans and we weighed into those quite heavily, which seemed like a good idea at the time but less so when we worked out there was no toilet on the bus. One or two of the guys ended up replacing the liquid in the tins.

The sun was starting to dip in the sky by the time we moved off, heading for Buckingham Palace where we were meeting the Queen. We were lined up in a semi-circle, me and Clive in the middle, and briefed on the etiquette.

'Go forward and present Her Majesty with the trophy that you have won for her,' we were told. 'She may touch it but she will not take it.'

Right-ho, chief.

Two corgis led the way like outriders, walking slowly ahead as the Queen came into the room. I was presented to her and we exchanged pleasantries but I don't think I made much of an impression on her apart from being a lot bigger and uglier than her; she was in a bit of a bad way, with a knee op due at the end of the week, and talking to me was probably about 150th on her list of things she'd like to do. Prince William was in there chatting to the boys, moaning about how Harry had been texting him from Australia after every game while he'd been hard at work at university. We stayed for half an hour or so before posing for a photo of ourselves with her Majesty. That done, we headed off again, this time to Downing Street for a reception with Tony Blair and the heads of the other parties. All very informal and not altogether unenjoyable but that ride home was beginning to look very appealing.

When I did finally make it out of there, it all felt very surreal. I'd started the day trudging down a motorway embankment to a minibus, been screamed at by 750,000 people with TV cameras beaming my face all round the world, then met the Queen and then the Prime Minister. Now I was back on my sofa having a cuppa in a sleepy little village in Leicestershire. Remarkable. Did it really happen?

And it continued in similarly mad vein for some time.

I was asked to do some pre-Christmas signings of the hardback edition of this book in London. Hundreds of people turned up, some having started queuing in the early hours, and they were buying up to 20 copies at a time. For some reason best known to themselves – perhaps delusions of my grandeur – my publishers, Headline, had hired a Rolls-Royce to ferry me around. Shoppers in Oxford Street were treated to the unedifying sight of Johnson, hotly pursued by hordes of professional autograph hunters, chucking pens and scrawled-on pieces of paper out into the slipstream as the Roller zoomed away from one store, like some kind of capitalist fat-cat dispensing largesse to the masses. All that was missing was the big cigar. We went to Canary Wharf where hundreds of people were patiently waiting in line. The publishers had me on a tight schedule and the Headline girls I was with apologised to people after a certain point, telling them that I wouldn't be able to sign their books. Not only did they ignore them and carry on waiting, they also chased me out of the complex like a lynch mob after a sheep rustler.

I had more time at other signings. In Nottingham, there were five or six hundred folks queuing. I got through them and looked up to find another five or six hundred standing in front of me. That night I managed to hang around until the last book was defaced with my semi-legible scribble – long after the shop was supposed to have closed. I started getting the yips: I was literally unable to sign my own name. Unsigned copies are probably rarer. I'd love to say the fuss was based around the book's marvellous prose but unfortunately it was pretty much all about That Game and That Cup.

I attended a lunch for Mike Catt's testimonial before Christmas and the trophy got a standing ovation when it was carried into the room. It came to Leicester on an RFU tour and guys were straining just to touch the thing. I couldn't help thinking of *The Life Of Brian*. They announced that it would be taken to the club at 5p.m. People queued right round the ground, until 3a.m. – yes, for 10 hours – just to have their picture taken with it. It wasn't just ordinary fans who were going World Cup crazy. Wealthy businessmen were bidding tens of thousands of pounds to have lunch with players – not a pretty sight, I can tell you – and Philip Green, the High Street entrepeneur, bid £500,000 for Dorian West's Sydney match shirt at an auction.

Bizarre times, really.

And against it all, the constant question I was being asked was: 'Are you going to quit?'

It wasn't uppermost in my mind but as the New Year approached the question of retirement started bubbling around. I'd even considered packing it all in 18 months before the World Cup – I'm glad I decided against that now – and, deep down, I think I had always known I was finished after the tournament. It was a feeling that had crept up on me before the Wales game and had become stronger still before each succeeding match. But I had not been morbid about it. I had used it as a positive, as a helpful motivation: if we lose, you probably won't play again. One chance, Johnno, and that's it. Of course, in the immediate aftermath of actually winning the thing, it's the furthest thought from your head. You're on such a high you want to play for ever and think you'll never lose. But in moments of realism you think about the aches and pains which aren't getting any better, about the hours on motorways to and from training and the days, literally, that you spend in airports and planes when you're touring. You are aware that you can't make a snap decision because your emotions are all over the place. You need time to think and you need to make your own mind up. Everyone has an opinion, they all mean well, but it has to be your own decision. It's a hard thing to do, turning your back on playing for England, turning away from something you were always desperate to do and a life which millions of others would love. But if the hunger isn't there any more, that's it. I'm older and I've got a family now.

I want to see Molly grow up and being part of the relentless machine of international rugby makes that very hard.

STATISTICS

Compiled by Stuart Farmer

ENGLAND CAP SUMMARY

Opponent	ST	REP	T	PTS	W	D	L
Argentina	3				3		
Australia	8				5	I	2
Canada	2				2		
Fiji	I				I		
France	13				8		5
Georgia	I				I		
Ireland	8				7		I
Italy	5	I	I	5	6		
Netherlands	I				I		
New Zealand	7				3	I	3
Romania	I				I		
South Africa	9				6		3
Scotland	9				9		
Tonga	I				I		
Uruguay		I			I		
USA	I		I	5	I		
Wales	9				8		I
Samoa	3				3		
TOTALS	82	2	2	10	67	2	15

ENGLAND CAPS

Cap	Date	Opponents	Venue	Result	Notes
I	Sat 16 Jan 93	France	Twickenham	W 16–15	
2	Sat 27 Nov 93	New Zealand	Twickenham	W 15–9	
3	Sat 5 Feb 94	Scotland	Murrayfield	W 15–14	
4	Sat 19 Feb 94	Ireland	Twickenham	L 12–13	
5	Sat 5 Mar 94	France	Parc des Princes	W 18–14	
6	Sat 19 Mar 94	Wales	Twickenham	W 15–8	
7	Sat 12 Nov 94	Romania	Twickenham	W 54–3	
8	Sat 10 Dec 94	Canada	Twickenham	W 60–19	
9	Sat 21 Jan 95	Ireland	Lansdowne Road	W 20–8	
10	Sat 4 Feb 95	France	Twickenham	W 31–10	
11	Sat 18 Feb 95	Wales	Cardiff Arms Park	W 23–9	
12	Sat 18 Mar 95	Scotland	Twickenham	W 24–12	
13	Sat 27 May 95	Argentina (RWC)	Durban	W 24–18	

Cap	Date	Opponents	Venue	Result	Notes
14	Wed 31 May 95	Italy (RWC)	Durban	W 27–20	
15	Sun 4 Jun 95	Western Samoa (RWC)	Durban	W 44–22	
16	Sun 11 Jun 95	Australia (RWCQF)	Cape Town	W 25–22	
17	Sun 18 Jun 95	New Zealand (RWCSF)	Cape Town	L 29–45	
18	Thu 22 Jun 95	France (RWCP)	Pretoria	L 9–19	
19	Sat 18 Nov 95	South Africa	Twickenham	L 14–24	
20	Sat 16 Dec 95	Western Samoa	Twickenham	W 27–9	
21	Sat 20 Jan 96	France	Parc des Princes	L 12–15	
22	Sat 3 Feb 96	Wales	Twickenham	W 21–15	
23	Sat 2 Mar 96	Scotland	Murrayfield	W 18–9	
24	Sat 16 Mar 96	Ireland	Twickenham	W 28–15	
25	Sat 23 Nov 96	Italy	Twickenham	W 54–21	Try
26	Sat 14 Dec 96	Argentina	Twickenham	W 20–18	
27	Sat 1 Feb 97	Scotland	Twickenham	W 41–13	
28	Sat 15 Feb 97	Ireland	Lansdowne Road	W 46–6	
29	Sat 1 Mar 97	France	Twickenham	L 20–23	
30	Sat 15 Mar 97	Wales	Cardiff Arms Park	W 34–13	
31	Sat 15 Nov 97	Australia	Twickenham	D 15–15	
32	Sat 22 Nov 97	New Zealand	Old Trafford	L 8–25	
33	Sat 6 Dec 97	New Zealand	Twickenham	D 26–26	
34	Sat 7 Feb 98	France	Stade de France	L 17–24	
35	Sat 21 Feb 98	Wales	Twickenham	W 60–26	Replaced
36	Sun 22 Mar 98	Scotland	Murrayfield	W 34–20	Replaced
37	Sat 4 Apr 98	Ireland	Twickenham	W 35–17	
38	Sat 14 Nov 98	Netherlands (WCQ)	Huddersfield	W 110–0	Captain
39	Sun 22 Nov 98	Italy (WCQ)	Huddersfield	W 23–15	Captain
40	Sat 28 Nov 98	Australia	Twickenham	L 11–12	
41	Sat 5 Dec 98	South Africa	Twickenham	W 13–7	
42	Sat 20 Feb 99	Scotland	Twickenham	W 24–21	Replaced
43	Sat 6 Mar 99	Ireland	Lansdowne Road	W 27–15	
44	Sat 20 Mar 99	France	Twickenham	W 21–10	
45	Sun 11 Apr 99	Wales	Wembley	L 31–32	
46	Sat 26 Jun 99	Australia	Sydney	L 15–22	Captain
47	Sat 21 Aug 99	United States	Twickenham	W 106–8	Captain. Try
48	Sat 28 Aug 99	Canada	Twickenham	W 36–11	Captain. Temp replaced
49	Sat 2 Oct 99	Italy (RWC)	Twickenham	W 67–7	Captain
50	Sat 9 Oct 99	New Zealand (RWC)	Twickenham	L 16–30	Captain
51	Fri 15 Oct 99	Tonga (RWC)	Twickenham	W 101–10	Captain. Replaced
52	Wed 20 Oct 99	Fiji (RWC)	Twickenham	W 45–24	Captain
53	Sun 24 Oct 99	South Africa (RWCQF)	Stade de France	L 21–44	Captain
54	Sat 17 Jun 00	South Africa	Pretoria	L 13–18	Captain. Replaced
55	Sat 24 Jun 00	South Africa	Bloemfontein	W 27–22	Captain
56	Sat 18 Nov 00	Australia	Twickenham	W 22–19	Captain
57	Sat 25 Nov 00	Argentina	Twickenham	W 19–0	Captain
58	Sat 2 Dec 00	South Africa	Twickenham	W 25–17	Captain
59	Sat 3 Feb 01	Wales	Millennium Stadium	W 44–15	Captain
60	Sat 17 Feb 01	Italy	Twickenham	W 80–23	Captain
61	Sat 3 Mar 01	Scotland	Twickenham	W 43–3	Captain
62	Sat 7 Apr 01	France	Twickenham	W 48–19	Captain

Cap	Date	Opponents	Venue	Result	Notes
63	Sat 24 Nov 01	South Africa	Twickenham	W 29–9	Captain. Replaced
64	Sat 2 Feb 02	Scotland	Murrayfield	W 29–3	Captain
65	Sat 16 Feb 02	Ireland	Twickenham	W 45–11	Captain. Replaced
66	Sat 2 Mar 02	France	Stade de France	L 15–20	Captain
67	Sun 7 Apr 02	Italy	Rome	W 45–9	Rep
68	Sat 9 Nov 02	New Zealand	Twickenham	W 31–28	Captain
69	Sat 16 Nov 02	Australia	Twickenham	W 32–31	Captain
70	Sat 23 Nov 02	South Africa	Twickenham	W 53–3	Captain
71	Sat 15 Feb 03	France	Twickenham	W 25–17	Captain
72	Sat 22 Feb 03	Wales	Millennium Stadium	W 26–9	Captain
73	Sat 22 Mar 03	Scotland	Twickenham	W 40–9	Captain
74	Sun 30 Mar 03	Ireland	Lansdowne Road	W 42–6	Captain
75	Sat 14 Jun 03	New Zealand	Wellington	W 15–13	Captain
76	Sat 21 Jun 03	Australia	Melbourne	W 25–14	Captain
77	Sat 6 Sep 03	France	Twickenham	W 45–14	Captain. Replaced
78	Sun 12 Oct 03	Georgia (RWC)	Perth	W 84–6	Captain
79	Sat 18 Oct 03	South Africa (RWC)	Perth	W 25–6	Captain
80	Sun 26 Oct 03	Samoa (RWC)	Melbourne	W 35–22	Captain
81	Sun 2 Nov 03	Uruguay (RWC)	Brisbane	W 111–13	Rep
82	Sun 9 Nov 03	Wales (RWCQF)	Brisbane	W 28–17	Captain
83	Sun 16 Nov 03	France (RWCSF)	Sydney	W 24–7	Captain
84	Sat 22 Nov 03	Australia (RWCF)	Sydney	W 20–17	Captain

LIONS CAPS

Cap	Date	Opponents	Venue	Result	Notes
1	Sat 26 Jun 93	New Zealand	Wellington	W 20–7	
2	Sat 3 Jul 93	New Zealand	Auckland	L 13–30	
3	Sat 21 Jun 97	South Africa	Cape Town	W 25–16	Captain
4	Sat 28 Jun 97	South Africa	Durban	W 18–15	Captain
5	Sat 5 Jul 97	South Africa	Johannesburg	L 16–35	Captain
6	Sat 30 Jun 01	Australia	Brisbane	W 29–13	Captain
7	Sat 7 Jul 01	Australia	Melbourne	L 14–35	Captain
8	Sat 14 Jul 01	Australia	Sydney	L 23–29	Captain

ENGLAND 18-GROUP

Date	Opponents	Venue	Result	Notes
Tue 7 Apr 87	Scotland	Hartlepool	D 3–3	
Sat 11 Apr 87	Wales	Ebbw Vale	L 10–15	
Sat 18 Apr 87	Ireland	Limerick	D 12–12	
Tue 21 Apr 87	France	Bedford	L 6–9	
Sat 2 Apr 88	France	La Rochelle	L 3–12	
Wed 6 Apr 88	Ireland	Cambridge	W 21–10	
Sat 9 Apr 88	Scotland	Glasgow	W 32–0	
Sat 16 Apr 88	Wales	Redruth	W 19–4	

NZ NPC APPEARANCES FOR KING COUNTRY

Date	App	T	Pts
1989	13	0	0
1990	12	0	0
TOTALS	25	0	0

NZ UNDER-21

Date	Opponents	Venue	Result	Notes
Sun 24 Jun 90	NSW Country Colts	Maitland	W 57–0	
Wed 27 Jun 90	Western Australia	Sydney	W 26–16	
Sat 30 Jun 90	Australia	Sydney	W 24–21	

ENGLAND UNDER-21

Date	Opponents	Venue	Result	Notes
Sun 1 Sep 91	Belgium	Wolverhampton	W 94–0	

ENGLAND B

Date	Opponents	Venue	Result	Notes
Sat 15 Feb 92	France	Paris	W 22–18	
Sat 7 Mar 92	Italy	Rome	W 16–10	

ENGLAND A

Date	Opponents	Venue	Result	Notes
Wed 3 Feb 93	Italy	Bath	W 59–0	
Fri 5 Mar 93	Spain	Richmond	W 66–5	Try
Fri 19 Mar 93	Ireland	Donnybrook	W 22–18	
Sat 22 May 93	British Columbia	Victoria	W 26–10	
Sat 29 May 93	Canada	Vancouver	L 12–15	
Sat 5 Jun 93	Canada	Ottawa	W 19–14	
Fri 17 Mar 00	Italy	L'Aquila	W 33–27	Captain

ENGLAND XV

Date	Opponents	Venue	Result	Notes
Sat 21 May 94	Natal	Durban	L 6–21	
Sat 28 May 94	Transvaal	Johannesburg	L 21–24	Concussed
Sat 30 Nov 96	New Zealand Barbarians	Twickenham	L 19–34	
Sat 19 Jun 99	Queensland	Brisbane	W 39–14	Captain

LIONS TOURS

Date	Opponents	Venue	Result	Notes
Wed 16 Jun 93	Taranaki	New Plymouth	W 49–25	
Sat 19 Jun 93	Auckland	Auckland	L 18–23	
Sat 31 May 97	Western Province	Cape Town	W 38–21	Captain
Sat 7 Jun 97	Northern Transvaal	Pretoria	L 30–35	Captain
Sat 14 Jun 97	Natal	Durban	W 42–12	Captain. Temp replaced
Sat 16 Jun 01	Queensland	Brisbane	W 42–8	Captain. Replaced
Sat 23 Jun 01	New South Wales	Sydney	W 41–24	Captain
Tue 3 Jul 01	ACT Brumbies	Canberra	W 30–28	Captain

BARBARIANS

Date	Opponents	Venue	Result	Notes
Mon 20 Apr 92	Swansea	St Helens	W 55–12	

MIDLANDS AGAINST TOURING TEAMS

Date	Opponents	Venue	Result	Notes
Wed 4 Nov 92	South Africa	Leicester	W 32–9	
Tue 26 Oct 93	New Zealand	Leicester	W 12–6	

TIGERS APPEARANCES

Season	All games			League			Cup			Europe			Club Honours
	App	T	Pts	App	T	Pts	App	T	Pts	App	T	Pts	
1988–89	2	0	0	1	0	0	0	0	0				
1990–91	5	0	0	0	0	0	1	0	0				
1991 tour to Canada	2	0	0										
1991–92	23	0	0	10	0	0	4	0	0				Cup winners
1992–93	21	2	10	8	0	0	5	1	5				
1993–94	22	1	5	15	0	0	5	0	0				Champions
1994–95	18	2	10	15	2	10	3	0	0				
1995–96	25	1	5	17	0	0	5	1	5				
1996–97	34+1	0	0	19+1	0	0	4	0	0	7	0	0	Cup winners
1997–98 Captain	31	2	10	21	1	5	2	0	0	8	1	5	
1998–99 Captain	28	1	5	24	1	5	2	0	0				Champions
1999–00 Captain	15	1	5	10	0	0	2	0	0	3	0	0	Champions
2000–01 Captain	27+3	3	15	16+1	2	10	2+1	0	0	6	0	0	Champions, European Champions
2001–02 Captain	19+3	2	10	12+2	2	10	0+1	0	0	7	0	0	Champions, European Champions
2002–03 Captain	29+3	0	0	19	0	0	2+1	0	0	5+1	0	0	
2003–04 Captain	17+3	1	5	10+2	0	0	0	0	0	5+1	1	5	
TOTALS	318+13	16	80	197+6	8	40	35+3	2	10	41+2	2	10	

INDEX

Dwyer, Bob 107, 111–12,
115–28, 164, 280, 307–9,
351

Eales, John 45, 84, 138, 141,
313, 404
East India Club 380
Edmonds, Manny 307
Edwards, Gareth 16
Ellis, Harry 208, 211
European Cup 115, 117, 125,
163, 197–8, 204, 209–10,
213, 360, 386
Evans Geoff 16
Evans, Ieuan 276, 279, 282,
288, 356
Evans, Mark 239
Ezulike, Nnamdi 147–8, 164

Finegan, Owen 312, 316, 322
Fitzgerald, Ciaran 263, 278
Fitzpatrick, Sean 31, 88, 273
Five Nations championship
119–20, 135, 142, 144, 264,
277
Flatley, Elton 227, 429–30
Fleck, Robbie 232
Foot, Michael 17
foot-and-mouth disease 192
the 49ers 383–4
Four Seasons Hotel, Dublin
248–9
Fowler, John 91
Fox, Grant 31, 267
Francis, Neil 265
Franklin's Gardens 100, 162

French rugby 115, 120, 136,
192–3, 202–3, 238–40, 345,
379, 415–22 passim, 425
Freshwater, Perry 255

Galthié, Fabien 422
Galwey, Mick 210, 213, 265
Garcia, Jeff 384
Garforth, Darren 90, 100–1,
108, 116, 133, 136, 142,
148–9, 163, 165, 172–3,
215–17
Gatland, Warren 215, 273
Gauteng 284–5
Geech, Ian 289, 292–3, 325
Gibbs, Scott 145–6, 271, 276,
281, 286–8, 293, 310–11,
334, 352
Gilmour, Gerry 291
Goddard, Chris 382–3
Golden Wonder Cup 13, 15
Goldsmith, Jasin 44
golf 259
Gomarsall, Andy 277, 402, 410
Goode, Andy 216
Grayson, Paul 119, 162, 252–3,
277, 399
Great Bowden 9
Gredig, Kay see Johnson, Kay
Gredig, Malcolm 34–5, 39
Gredig, Pete 37–9
Green, Philip 450
Green, Will 133, 136
Greening, Phil 191, 193, 301
Greenwood, Caro 406
Greenwood, Will 107, 111,

Match of the Day   1–2, 391
Mather, Barrie-Jon   144
Meads, Colin   30, 35, 41, 43
Meads, Glynn   30–1
Mehrtens, Andrew   135, 226
Melbourne   259
Mené, Didier   288
Merceron, Gerald   202–3, 422
Meuws, Kees   427
Michalak, Fridiric   415–16,
   420–2
Midland Bank   89, 266
Millennium Stadium, Cardiff
   189–91, 209, 357
Miller, Eric   117, 121–2, 125,
   280
Milne, Kenny   264
Mitchell, John   131, 273, 302
Mizuno   93–4
Montgomery, Percy   224, 231,
   235, 289
Moody, Lewis   147, 163,
   199–200, 204–8, 216, 224–5,
   403–4, 430
Moore, Brian   83, 87, 92, 119,
   267, 270–1, 273, 341–3, 347,
   349
Morris, Darren   317
Morris, Dewi   84, 87, 119, 272
Morris, Robbie   241, 247
Mortlock, Stirling   425–7
Moseley   98, 105, 127
Munster   209–13
Murphy, Geordan   164, 197,
   210, 248, 253, 325

Murray, Julian   20–1
Murray, Scott   365

New Plymouth   267–8
New Zealand rugby   255–6,
   267–8, 275, 331, 334–5
Newcastle   95, 97, 100, 128
News of the World   150, 353–4
Nicol, Andy   320–1
Nike   179
Norster, Bob   270
Northampton   162
Ntamack, Emile   158
Nuneaton   103–4

O'Brien, Paddy   232–3
Observer Sports Monthly   393
O'Connell, Paul   210
O'Driscoll, Brian   248, 250, 305,
   311–13, 323, 334
O'Gara, Ronan   210, 247–8,
   303, 318, 367
Ojomoh, Steve   26
'old farts' incident   348
Old Trafford   376
Olver, John   265
O'Neil, John   138
orienteering   4–5
Orwin, John   347
Oti, Chris   265
Owen, Michael   3
Owen Delaney Park, Taupo   40

Packer, Kerry   88, 96
Palmer, Tom   106
Pau   115–16, 125, 188

Williams, Ali 378
Williams, J.J. 16
Williams, J.P.R. 16, 145
Williams, Jim 210, 316
Williams, Martyn 299, 325
Wilson, David 84, 98, 151
Wilson, Jeff 134, 138, 152
Windsor, Bobby 364
Winterbottom, Peter 267,
 270–5 *passim*
Wood, Keith 143, 194, 279,
 282, 289, 322, 329–30, 333
Woodman, Trevor 238, 260,
 400, 427, 432
Woods, Martyn 402
Woodward, Clive 16, 19, 130–7,
 141–2, 144, 150, 154–6,
 157–62, 166–7, 173, 177,
 182–4, 189–91, 203–4, 219,
 224–5, 240, 243, 247, 249,
 253, 304, 336, 349–54,
 369–72, 396–402, 409, 415,
 422, 432, 439–40, 447
Worcester 104–6
World Cup rugby
 1987 competition 33

1991 competition 32, 92,
 107, 249–50, 265, 339,
 342
1995 competition 82, 282,
 324, 397
1999 competition 11, 136,
 139–40, 143, 149–57, 193,
 350, 352, 397
2003 competition 234–5,
 261, 352, 397
World Cup soccer 416
Worsley, Joe 170, 199, 241, 412
Wright, Peter 264
Wyatt, Chris 207

Yeomans, Rich 22
Young, Bill 427
Young, Dai 281, 316, 325–6,
 356
Young, Scott 303

Zurich rankings 165, 195, 202,
 397